More Praise for *Am*
A Compact History, Revised and Updated

"In endorsing the first edition of this work, I said that the authors had 'brilliantly accomplished the exceptionally difficult task of distilling the scholarly essence of their larger works into a more concentrated and accessible form without compromising the academic excellence and narrative interest of the originals.' That remains true of this revised and updated edition. While a number of helpful corrections or clarifications have been made throughout the text, the major benefit of the new edition is the additional chapter, primarily authored by Ashley Boggan D., which provides an admirably succinct and wonderfully clear-eyed account of the past two decades in the life of The United Methodist Church, extending the usefulness of a classic classroom text."

—Rex D. Matthews, Th.D., Russell E. Richey and Merle Umstead Richey Visiting Professor in Methodist and Wesleyan Studies, Candler School of Theology, Emory University, Atlanta, GA

"This valuable book is made even more useful with updates into the 21st century. It covers topics such as General Conferences struggling to deal with questions about sexuality, the response to the Covid pandemic through on-line worship, global complexity and generational shifts. This updated book is essential for understanding our unfolding history."

—Sarah Heaner Lancaster, Werner Professor of Theology, Methodist Theological School in Ohio, Delaware, OH

"The revised and updated *American Methodism: A Compact History* enhances an already invaluable resource. Alongside important updates, the volume includes a new chapter insightfully addressing the challenges and developments within Methodism from 2000 to 2022. The authors, including the excellent addition of Ashley Boggan D., General Secretary of the General Commission on Archives and History, draw deeply from the Methodist tradition as well as their extensive scholarly skill and knowledge."

—Laceye Warner, Associate Dean for Wesleyan Engagement and the Royce and Jane Reynolds Associate Professor of Evangelism and Methodist Studies, Duke Divinity School, Duke University, Durham, NC

"These leading historians have produced an up to date, condensed, yet comprehensive account of American Methodism that is indispensable for students of the United Methodist heritage. There simply is no better, usefully succinct resource for studying and understanding this historical movement. Beginning in the colonial period in North America with the likes of Otterbein, Heck, and Strawbridge, the authors take us into the twenty-first century to include recent events such as United Methodism's response to the Coronavirus pandemic, the turn to technology for communications and public worship, and the handling of contemporary debates related to biblical interpretation and human sexuality. In short, I highly recommend this timely, well-written volume for all students of American Methodism."

—Wendy J. Deichmann, Professor of History and Theology, Director of the Center for Evangelical United Brethren Heritage, United Theological Seminary, Dayton, OH

AMERICAN METHODISM

A Compact History, Revised and Updated

Ashley Boggan D.

Russell E. Richey

Kenneth E. Rowe

Jean Miller Schmidt

Nashville

AMERICAN METHODISM:
A COMPACT HISTORY, REVISED AND UPDATED

Copyright © 2010, 2012, 2022 by Abingdon Press

Library of Congress Control Number: 2022947494

ISBN: 9781791016593

MANUFACTURED IN THE UNITED STATES OF AMERICA

To Kenneth E. Rowe

*Beloved and brilliant colleague, catalyst, and co-creator,
without whom this volume and several others of ours
would never have come to be*

CONTENTS

Contents

Contents

Contents

PREFACE

METHODIST HISTORY IN A DIGITAL AGE

To keep this history compact, we presume that students and instructors have access to our *Methodist Experience in America: A History* and *Methodist Experience in America: A Sourcebook* and will make good use of the daily growing number of print and digital resources on American Methodism and on the Wesleyan movements more broadly. A number of Methodist and United Methodist universities, seminaries, and libraries are mounting materials on websites, referencing other pertinent digital resources, and working collaboratively on larger projects: General Conference journals, biographies of major figures, conference journals, older general and conference histories, and key reference items, including the two-volume *Encyclopedia of World Methodism*. General agencies, in addition to UMC General Commission on Archives and History (hereafter GCAH), are putting important resources on their websites. We encourage you to use GCAH's UM History Hub (umhistoryhub.teachable.com) to access the primary sources for the final chapter, 2000–2022. There you can download all primary sources for in-classroom or personal use.

For portraits of major Methodist figures, Google Images provides ready access. More than one hundred illustrations from the Archives and History Center of The United Methodist Church can be accessed in an online version of *200 Years of United Methodism: An Illustrated History* by John G. McEllhenney (published by Drew University and accessible through Drew and GCAH websites). The availability also on the GCAH site of a two hundred-page online version of the Kenneth E. Rowe and now Christopher J. Anderson

United Methodist Studies: Basic Bibliographies makes such inclusion unnecessary here.

USING THIS NARRATIVE WITH THE TWO *MEA* VOLUMES

This volume is closely related to, indeed, a companion to two other Abingdon Press volumes: our *Methodist Experience in America: A History* and *Methodist Experience in America: A Sourcebook* (*MEA* I and II). It can be used independently. However, we recommend ready access to the two *MEA* volumes, particularly the *Sourcebook.* The overall structure of this volume follows the periodization of both prior books and the structure and narrative flow of our *History.* For fuller treatment of events, figures, developments, controversies, and aspects of the Methodist movements, we do refer the reader to the *History, except for chapter XIII, "Polity Pushed to Schism: 2000–2022," which is not covered in the MEA.* At places we will invite attention to the more comprehensive discussion with the shorthand in-text notation (H **xx**), the H standing for *Methodist Experience in America: A History* and in place of xx the appropriate page number(s). Several extensive omissions from the *History* deserve note here. To shorten the text, we have dropped the three "Snapshots"—chapter-long treatments of Methodism at a local level—"Methodism in 1816: Baltimore," "Methodism in 1884: Wilkes-Barre, Pennsylvania," and "Methodism in 1968: Denver." Likewise from Likewise from chapter X we omitted substantially from the ten-page treatment of worship and worship architecture, 1939 to 1968. We presume that instructors, as enthralled with these in-depth treatments as we, may assign these on a library reserve basis. Instructors may also find useful the background to the two volumes provided in "Methodist Experience in America: An Introduction" in the April 2010 edition of *Methodist History.*

The *History* features more than a hundred pages of endnotes, the documentation for quotations or allusions or the authorities upon whose work we rely. Where such acknowledgment seems warranted here, we refer the reader to the note in this fashion (H **565n6**). By this shorthand, actually used below, we indicate that end note number 6 on page 565 of the *History* provides publication data for books mentioned two paragraphs below. The endnotes begin on page 565, so in-text referrals above that number invite attention to an endnote or to the index that begins on page 671. (In-text referrals to numbers below that invite attention, as noted already, to expanded treatment of the topic at hand.) Reserve library access to *MEA History* should serve the student eager to follow up on our treatment more fully or on that of our references.

The *Sourcebook* we do recommend as a purchase. We developed the two-volume *MEA* as a set, and this volume relies on and references *MEA* II, the *Sourcebook*, as does *MEA* I. The *Sourcebook* contains documents, a vast array of them organized chronologically. A header on each document specifies the date, with a following letter distinguishing multiple documents for a specific year. We refer the reader to the *Sourcebook* with the in-text shorthand of (S **xxxx** or S **xxxxa**), the **xxxx** or **xxxxa** standing for a document's date. For instance, (S **1785a**) calls the reader's attention to the first *Discipline* of The Methodist Episcopal Church, published soon after the founding Christmas Conference. Primary sources from the final chapter in this book will be made available in digitized form via gcah.org. The **bolding** of the document numbers helps distinguish them from other dates. By relying on the two *MEA* volumes (in the library or as a common purchase) for documentation, illustrations, and further treatment, we are able to contain the length and cost of this volume. For the final, additional chapter covering 2000–2022, we have used a designator of (eS **xxxx**) to indicate that this is an electronic source. These electronic sources are housed by GCAH and can be found using their online teaching platform, UM History Hub (umhistoryhub .teachable.com). The documents are provided free of charge through their course platform. A printable index for this book is also available at the site.

COMPLEMENTARY UNITED METHODIST RESOURCES

We should acknowledge that this short history presumes not only the *MEA History* and *Sourcebook* but also other United Methodist resources developed by Abingdon Press in the overall scheme for denominational instruction and formation. In particular, we have assumed prior treatment of the Wesleys, their sojourn in Georgia, and early British Methodism in Richard P.

Heitzenrater, *Wesley and the People Called Methodists* (2nd edition, 2013). We presume access also to Thomas Edward Frank, *Polity, Practice, and the Mission of The United Methodist Church* (2008); Lacey C. Warner, *The Method of Our Mission* (2014); Rex Matthews, *Timetables of History for Students of Methodism* (out of print); Theodore Runyon, *The New Creation: John Wesley's Theology Today*; and the two volumes of Thomas A. Langford, *Practical Divinity*, the second volume providing the rich theological fare that we have consequently slighted. We presume as well ready access to other standard Methodist studies items: Scott J. Jones, *United Methodist Doctrine: The Extreme Center*; Ted A. Campbell, *Methodist Doctrine: The Essentials*; Walter Klaiber and Manfred Marquardt, *Living Grace: An Outline of United Methodist Theology*; Karen B. Westerfield Tucker, *American Methodist Worship*; W. Harrison Daniel, *Historical Atlas of the Methodist Movement*; and our own *Perspectives on American Methodism* (H **565n6**).

We appreciate the support given the *MEA* project and this volume by our several institutions, their deans, their libraries, and their librarians, and by UMPH, GCAH, and GBHEM (for these and other acronyms we use, see the appended "Abbreviations").

Ashley Boggan D., General Commission on Archives and History,
   The Theological School, Drew University
Jean Miller Schmidt, Iliff School of Theology
Kenneth E. Rowe, The Theological School, Drew University
Russell E. Richey, Candler School of Theology, Emory University

INTRODUCTION
SPONTANEOUS BEGINNINGS: 1760–68

We start the narrative that yields American Methodism with "spontaneous" colonial ministries in the 1760s of Robert Strawbridge in Maryland, of William Otterbein and Martin Boehm in the Middle Colonies, and of Barbara Heck, Philip Embury, and Thomas Webb in New York. These disparate evangelical initiatives belong, we suggest, within the broad Pietist movement. One can certainly start elsewhere—with formative experiences in the Susanna and Samuel Wesley home. Or with John and Charles Wesley in Georgia in the 1730s. Or with John's Aldersgate experience. Or with George Whitefield's American tours and the First Great Awakening.

Viewing American Methodism as an expression of transatlantic Pietism honors the local context but also the waves of religious reform breaking across the Western world. In the colonies, "the First Great Awakening" points to several decades of religious ferment. For the British Isles a common designation is "the evangelical revival." On the continent, the term "Pietism" points to its Lutheran pioneers, Philipp Jakob Spener and August Hermann Francke, and to Pietism's institutionalization in Moravianism. There are, moreover, Pietist-like resonances in Roman Catholic Jansenism, Hasidic Judaism, and late Puritanism.

CONVERSIONIST RELIGION

Pietism, then, was a transatlantic, transconfessional, diffuse reform to recover the authentic (and personal) witness of the faith. Its early leaders claimed the Reformation banner and criticized religious authorities and the institutionalized Lutheranism (or Calvinism) known as Protestant Orthodoxy. (A later foil would be the Enlightenment.) Protestant Pietism shaped experimental religion around the conversion experience, understood not simply as a forensic alteration in one's status with God but as a discernible inner change. In this transformation one became a reborn Nicodemus, a re-creation in Christ, whose character and life manifested a new identity in fruits of the Spirit. Pietism resourced those reborn and those seeking rebirth in small groups (conventicles or religious societies) that encouraged members to make the Scripture normative for everyday life, that sheltered individuals and families from "the world," and that empowered them to counter its claims and demands. In and through such religious societies, little churches within the church, *collegia pietatis,* laity (male and female) gained voice and exercised leadership, a challenge and threat to public and religious conventions.

Pietism drew such leadership into active missionary endeavor at home and abroad. It extended the gospel and the invitation into Christian community to populations previously ignored. The resources that Pietism offered—new identity, community voluntarily created, a competitive missionary spirit, courage to persist despite society's disdain, outreach to the poor and marginalized, willingness to forge new alliances—proved highly functional for community-formation in the new American environment.

Wherever Pietism prospered, it challenged those who had settled for formal, notional, legal, or outward religiosity and repudiated the easy compromise that religion had made with status, wealth, power, display, and prerogative. Against such worldliness, Pietists invoked the witness of the prophets and the teaching of Jesus. Worldliness, a sin, separated individuals from God. So Pietism offered prophetic critique of established, more priestly, and unregenerate forms of Christianity and leaders so characterized (among them, the Protestant Orthodox). Instead, Pietism provided a new way of life for its adherents and motivation to tackle society's ills. It spoke of corruption, of power, of authority, of legitimacy. By identifying the corrupt—the luxury of gentility or laxness of clergy—it broke social conventions of deference and passive obedience. It did not, however, weave these elements of social critique into a program for systemic reform or a theory of new world order or a vision of the godly state or even of the church as an anticipation thereof. Such a civil or societal theology, as offered by Puritans and other Calvinists, had brought chaos to Europe. Pietists, though highly communal on a local level and creatively productive of new ecclesial institutions, would work their transformations from the bottom up rather than the top down. Renewal would start with the conversion experience rather than parliamentary act, with a conventicle rather than a reform program, with missionary outreach rather than armed insurrection.

Their conversionist approach to change has earned for Pietists labels of individualistic, moralistic, and otherworldly. And certainly by contrast to Puritanism, Pietism offered a social ethic unwedded to a theory of the state and strategies for reform. Yet some who felt Pietism's denunciation of worldliness found it radically transformative. Others experienced it as socially revolutionary. Many denounced it as tasteless. Where it prevailed, Pietism had the capacity to shape society and culture. The transmission of this culture then became a communal and preeminently family project, permitting and requiring vital roles for women as well as men. In the eighteenth and particularly in the nineteenth century, women involved themselves on behalf of revival—within families, nurturing the piety of spouse, children, and servants; in congregations, through prayer groups and Sunday schools; and outward into community, nation, and world through mission, benevolent, and reform societies. Pietism expanded the gateway into ministry and raised the expectations of laity, thereby drawing women as well as men, Blacks as well as Whites, into public witness, lay preaching, and eventually formal ministry. (For examples in early Methodism see S **1760, 1773, 1775a, 1780b, 1785a, 1785b, 1785c, 1787, 1789a, 1791b, 1791c, 1798** on class meetings, and **1800b**. For an explanation of such notations see the preface.)

COLONIAL AWAKENINGS

The collective identification of the diverse Pietist explosions that rocked the American colonies is "the First Great Awakening." This several-decade effervescence of heart religion revived discipline, revivalistic preaching, mass conversions, and new religious alignments, which successively disturbed the religious status quo in the Middle, New England, and Southern Colonies. Among the revival leaders who achieved transcolony reputations were Jonathan Edwards and George Whitefield. The latter, by his six evangelistic tours, 1738–70, gave the seaboard colonies a good exposure to Calvinistic Pietism and Calvinistic Methodism. He popularized and legitimated patterns of extemporaneous, expressive, open-air preaching. He showed the power of itinerant evangelists to stir conversions among diverse peoples and across confessional lines. He made theatrical revivalism the prototypical American religious style. He pioneered promotion, self-promotion, and use of the press for evangelistic purpose. And Whitefield gave Methodism its first American hearing (S **1768**). Though he did not organize his converts, many who found their way into the order that Wesleyanism provided had been affected by Whitefield's preaching. Some of his converts provided key leadership to early classes and societies, notably Edward Evans and James Emerson in Philadelphia. And Whitefield issued an early request of John Wesley to send itinerants.

Whitefield's role and salience as Methodism's colonial herald contrast with those of the Wesleys, John and Charles, whose efforts in Georgia (1736–37) left little in the way of continuing Methodist influence, and some considerable embarrassment. The Georgia episode evidenced more of the Wesleys' Anglo-Catholic piety than of their Pietism. Only after his return from Georgia, it should be noted, did John become involved with the Moravian-led Fetter Lane Society, undergo his Aldersgate experience, make his visit to the Moravian headquarters at Herrnhut, and form his own religious societies in the Anglican orbit. The Georgia mission, however, left its enduring and important effect in John Wesley's own development. It established for Wesley and within Methodism concern for the well-being and evangelization of Indigenous peoples and Black peoples, one that was, while sincere, also inherently colonial and White-supremacist. And it came to belong to the longer story of American Methodism through its literary placement in the Wesley saga as "the second rise of Methodism." By other routes the leaven of Pietism and the Methodist versions thereof came to the colonies.

OTTERBEIN AND BOEHM

William Otterbein (1726–1813) belonged to a family of pastor-theologians steeped in the German Reformed tradition and the Pietism of their native Herborn. Confessional, churchly, apologetic, orthodox, covenantal, and christocentric, Herborn Pietists grounded the religious life in doctrine and Scripture as read through the Heidelberg Catechism. This sixteenth-century ecumenical, pastoral, personal compilation guided Herborn Pietists to a life lived in the Spirit. It mapped the spiritual life as a pathway, ladder, or series of steps toward salvation and as followed under and directed by covenant. Herborn kept its counsel understandable, attainable, and practical, and accented the Christian's ability to live a holy life.

Like his five brothers and father, William studied at the Reformed university at Herborn, a Pietist institution. He passed ordination examinations, subscribed to the Reformed confessions, and was ordained (1749). He served for three years in Germany, demonstrating early his ability as a teacher, preacher, and pastor. By organizing Bible and prayer groups, Otterbein earned a formal reprimand from authorities for holding such "divisive" conventicles. Responding to a plea for ministers made on behalf of the Pennsylvania (Reformed) Coetus (synod), he became pastor in the important Reformed community of Lancaster in 1752. There he found himself amid the religious ferment, through which churchly and Pietist groups emerged to give stability and direction to the Dutch and German settlements in the Middle Colonies. Otterbein served in Lancaster (1752–58) and Tulpehocken, Pennsylvania (1758–60); Frederick, Maryland (1760–65); York, Pennsylvania (1765–74); and Baltimore, Maryland (1774–1813), but consistently itinerated out from his residential pastorates to preach to German communities in southeastern Pennsylvania and northern Maryland. So he exercised "episcopal-like" leadership among the Pietist Germans (H **566n5**) while continuing to play leadership roles within and remaining a member of the Coetus (till death).

In 1755 Otterbein experienced "a more perfect consciousness of salvation in Christ" (conversion experience) and redoubled his efforts to hold himself and his people to a covenanted and disciplined life through prayer and Bible groups. Otterbein's evangelical Pietist convictions radiate through the little gospel, a sermon before the Coetus, in 1760 in Germantown (S **1760**). Preaching sin and salvation, the necessity of repentance, the possibility of assurance, and the Christian way as one of "denial, inward renewal, and holiness," Otterbein made clear to hearers that his Reformed doctrine eschewed hyper-Calvinist notions of predestination and made a significant place for human volition and responsibility. Similar effort and discipline, insisted Otterbein, should inform the corporate life of the Christian community, much needed amid the moral confusion characteristic of new communities. He therefore made provision in the churches with which he worked for small prayer, Bible study groups, the *collegia pietatis*, for the catechizing and schooling of children, and for a covenant to order the entire community. An example of the latter is

"The Constitution and Ordinances of The Evangelical Reformed Church of Baltimore" (S **1785b**).

During Otterbein's ministry in York and on one of his itinerations, he attended a "great meeting" at Long's Barn (a UMC Heritage Landmark), near Neffsville in Lancaster County. The event, perhaps in 1767, a several-day ingathering, anticipatory of later camp meetings, had been common in the colonial German community since the early 1720s. The leader at this event was Martin Boehm (1725–1812), a Mennonite preacher whose evangelistic style, personal religious experience, and insistence on assurance resembled those of Otterbein. After hearing Boehm, Otterbein embraced him, announcing, *"Wir sind Bruder!"* Thus began an association that would eventuate in the United Brethren in Christ.

Boehm, a Swiss-German Mennonite, had been selected by lot as preacher in the late 1750s and made bishop in 1761 by his Lancaster County congregation. A farmer, Boehm received his training, not in the university like Otterbein but through the traditioning of the Mennonite community. Believer's baptism, opposition to oaths and violence, a life lived out of the New Testament, and personal assurance through the Spirit defined Boehm. Like Otterbein, he itinerated, responding to pleas from Mennonite communities in Pennsylvania and Virginia. His evangelistic efforts yielded "revival" among the Mennonites but also controversy. Sometime in the late 1770s a Mennonite conference excommunicated him. Among its findings were "sins" of association and of insufficient stress on the sacraments. Boehm had wandered into patterns of expansive revivalism that were unsettling to more traditional Mennonites. Boehm's example and influence drew colleagues as well as adherents. The movement gravitated into increasing contact with those of Otterbein and of early Methodism. And the further association of the communities around Otterbein and Boehm evolved into proto-denominational and denominational organization (H **7–9**).

WESLEYAN INITIATIVES

Similar "spontaneous" initiatives established small communities that identified themselves with the Wesleyan movement. The absence of any official commissioning by John Wesley makes the actual beginnings of Methodism tricky to specify, one reason for a long-standing and ongoing bragging-rights contest between New York and Baltimore Methodists concerning priority. As early as 1787, the *Discipline* found a way of finessing the question of priority and adopted the phrase "About the same Time" to date the beginnings of American Methodism around Barbara Heck and Philip Embury in New York City and Robert and Elizabeth Strawbridge in Frederick County, Maryland (H **10**).

Both the New York and the Maryland ventures date to the mid-1760s, both involved important female as well as male initiatives, both drew in Black as well as White converts, both expressed the aspiration of immigrants for the order and community construction that Pietism provided, and both involved Irish immigrants. In the former case, the community twice exiled itself, first from the Palatinate (Germany) and then from Ireland. Here, as for the Reformed and Mennonites, religious community solidified around and gave expression to ethnic identity (Irish and Irish-Palatine).

Strawbridge, a local preacher before emigrating, began preaching and established, with the help of his wife Elizabeth, a Methodist class in their home in Sam's Creek, and subsequently erected there a log meeting house. Elizabeth gained the first convert, John Evans, who became the class leader. Robert Strawbridge itinerated in Maryland, both Eastern and Western Shores, in Virginia, and into Pennsylvania. He established classes that became the nucleus of later societies in Baltimore, Georgetown, Washington, DC, and Leesburg. Preachers converted by him included Black Americans, like Jacob Toogood; notable White leaders of the Methodist movement, William Watters and Freeborn Garrettson; and many of the early local preachers, including Richard Owens, Hezekiah Bonham, Sater Stevenson, and Richard Webster.

Strawbridge, though not ordained, began to baptize as early as 1762/63 and eventually to offer the Lord's Supper, celebrating out of a sense of mission to his new flock and their needs. Strawbridge issued no plea to Wesley to send preachers, to provide for ordinations, or to spread his wing over his efforts. Indeed, initially cooperative with Wesley's early missionaries, Strawbridge resisted their efforts to bring him and his circles into conformity, thus showing something of the Irish spirit that he and others built into the foundations of Methodism.

As for Sam's Creek, spontaneous, lay-led initiatives led to the founding of what would be John Street Church. Several families of Palatine immigrants, including some who had associated with the Methodists in Ireland, settled in among the New York Lutheran community. Barbara Ruckle Heck enjoys credit for initiating New York Methodism. Finding members of her family trivializing the time by playing cards, she swept the cards into the fire and implored her cousin Philip Embury, who had been a class leader and local preacher in Ireland: "Philip, you must preach to us, or shall we all go to hell together, and God will require our blood at your hands!" He complied in his own room with five auditors, including two servants, one a Black woman named Betty. A class was formed, and with continued preaching the members outgrew Embury's room and moved to a ship's rigging loft.

Onto this small Methodist community in 1767 stumbled Captain Thomas Webb, whose impact—preaching in his scarlet regimentals with a green patch over an eye—and whose doctrine Thomas Taylor detailed in an importuning letter of 1768 to John Wesley (S **1768**). Taylor requested guidance on how to establish societies in accordance with the Wesleyan scheme, monetary assistance, and "an able, experienced preacher—one who has both gifts and graces necessary for the work." Webb had seen military service in the colonies in the Seven Years' War (French and Indian War), lost an eye, married, became barrack master at Albany, returned to England to sell his commission, underwent conversion, gravitated into the Methodist orbit, did some preaching, returned to Albany, and there began preaching and conducting meetings. In 1766 he and his wife moved to Jamaica, New York, and he began preaching there, elsewhere on Long Island, and in the city. He converted two dozen, over half of them African Americans. Where he met success, he established classes in true Wesleyan fashion. Associating with Embury, Webb encouraged the New Yorkers to buy land on John Street and build a preaching house, providing the largest donation himself (thirty pounds) and raising a comparable amount. Embury preached a dedicatory sermon in the church on October 30, 1768.

On a fundraising trip to Philadelphia, Webb encountered another small group, a legacy of Whitefield's efforts, and organized what would become St. George's. Like Otterbein, Boehm, and Strawbridge, Webb itinerated widely to preach and to organize. Frank Baker called him a "consolidator," a term that nicely captures the initiatives he undertook and the fact that he made contact with religious communities already in the process of formation. His efforts keyed Methodist beginnings at Albany and Schenectady, on Long Island, in the Philadelphia area (Chester and Bristol), in New Jersey (Trenton, Burlington, and New Mills), and in Delaware (Wilmington and New Castle). Everywhere he convinced "his fellow sinners of sin," offered "free and universal grace," taught the divinity and coeternity of Son and Spirit with the

Father, grounded hope on Christ's tasting death for everyone, insisted that sinners were justified by faith alone, but that grace could be resisted or lost, and pointed believers toward the holiness that the Spirit made possible.

Another individual operating on his own initiative and authority was Robert Williams, a Welsh local preacher who had preached effectively in northern Ireland. He offered himself for the colonies after Taylor's appeal for assistance (S **1768**). Wesley allowed him to come at his own expense and with the understanding that he would be accountable to Wesley's officially commissioned missionaries. Williams apparently intended, from the start, to publish and sell Methodist materials, an enterprise already underway when Wesley's appointees arrived. Williams had also taken charge in New York and itinerated as far south as Virginia.

SPONTANEITY AND ORDER

By these "Pietist" initiatives, the Methodist folk (Wesleyan and United Brethren), female and male, Black and White, English- and German-speaking, in new community after new community laid foundations on which the record-keeping preachers would build. The Emburys and Hecks did so more than once. They soon moved into upper New York and thence into what is now Ontario, there to participate in constituting Canadian Methodism. Such "spontaneous" beginnings exhibited, as Dee Andrews notes, "the imperatives of Wesleyan Methodism—missionary drive, cross-denominational appeal, enthusiastic preaching, and household recruitment of followers" (H **567n18**). Such efforts brought individuals into face to face, family-like communities, but families without established "heads," without formal structure, with little literature other than the Bible, with little purpose beyond themselves, connected to no larger ecclesial authorities, lacking clarity about norms, ritual, belief, and practices. These families, in short, lacked legitimacy. Letters like Taylor's requesting help and efforts like Webb's and Williams's connecting existing small beginnings began the process by which spontaneous efforts "found" the authority of Wesley and the British movement. Such communities might cry out for a leader "of wisdom, of sound faith, and a good disciplinarian" only to find themselves yielding grudgingly the family-like atmosphere that informality had afforded. Ordering of spontaneous Pietist communities would not be conflict free.

CHAPTER I
REVOLUTIONARY
METHODISM: 1769–84

Responding to pleas from the infant Methodist societies in North America (S **1768**), John Wesley sent over successive pairs of itinerants. Richard Boardman and Joseph Pilmore came in 1769 (S **1769, 1771**). Francis Asbury and Richard Wright followed in 1771, Thomas Rankin and George Shadford in 1773, and James Dempster and Martin Rodda in 1774. Preachers coming on their own included John King, Joseph Yearbry, and William Glendenning. Wesley's itinerants came to bring order to Pietist ferment.

PILMORE AND BOARDMAN

Joseph Pilmore, educated at Wesley's Kingswood School near Bristol, followed Wesley's precept and example by keeping a journal, as would Francis Asbury, Thomas Rankin, Thomas Coke, and other preachers. Landing October 22, Pilmore encountered Captain Webb, "a real Methodist," and discovered the Philadelphia society. Boardman, the senior of the two and Wesley's assistant for America, preached the next day, "on the call of Abraham to go forth into the Land of Canaan." Employing biblical self-images, Methodist itinerants imagined themselves as Abrahams or Pauls and so crafted their journals. A more accurate biblical type might have been Ezra or Nehemiah. Itinerants rebuilt walls, restored temples, and renewed covenants. Ezra-and-Nehemiah duties completed the Wesleyan system—preaching in the open air, itinerating on a planned basis, making and meeting appointments, inviting into connection all of any confession who would "flee the wrath to come," admitting the same as probationers, organizing classes, holding love feasts, maintaining the

1

society's boundaries, establishing circuits, and cultivating good relations with the churches and their clergy. Implementing the Wesleyan system meant also discerning those who could serve in leadership—steward, class leader, exhorter, local preacher—and appointing them to these key local posts.

Two weeks after arriving, Pilmore "read and explained the Rules of the Society to a vast multitude of serious people." In late November, he cooperated with Webb in acquiring a shell of a building from the "Dutch Presbyterians" (German Reformed), St. George's (a UMC Heritage Landmark). Ten days later, Pilmore laid out the "Wesleyan" order to the Philadelphia society, distilling the General Rules into eight-point guidelines for the newly acquired property (H **16**) and for "those of every Denomination who being truly convinced of sin, and the danger they are exposed to, earnestly desire to flee from the wrath to come."

In enumerating Methodist rules, insisting that "the Methodist Society was never designed to make a Separation from the Church of England or be looked upon as a Church," and referencing deeds and plan of settlement, Pilmore declared colonial uniformity with Methodist standards, connection to Wesley, submission to his ordering, and prohibition against (irregular) celebration of the sacraments by unordained preachers. The references (Society, Deeds, Plan) and their import—colonial compliance with organizational protocols determined at the 1763 Leeds conference—doubtless mystified some auditors. Pilmore specified that American Methodism would run according to the "Large Minutes," the compilation (or Discipline) Wesley had made of his conversations with his preachers in conference over matters of doctrine and discipline, copies of which each preacher, in full connection with Wesley, carried as an operational manual. The "Large Minutes" of 1763 included a "Model Deed" and trust clause, which required a pattern of ownership for Methodist properties obliging trustees to allow Wesley "and such other persons as he shall from time to time appoint, and at all times, during his natural life, and no other persons, to have and enjoy the free use and benefit of the said premises." It provided further "that the said persons preach no other doctrine than is contained in Mr. Wesley's *Notes Upon the New Testament*, and four volumes of *Sermons*."

ORDER(S)

Pilmore and Boardman endeavored, as did their missionary successors, to make good on these commitments and bring Wesleyan order to colonial

Methodism. They discovered, for instance, that the John Street property had been legally secured "essentially wrong," not on the plan of the "Model Deed," the trustees enjoying "absolute power" without "being accountable to any one . . . contrary to the whole occonemy [economy] of the Methodists [and] . . . likely to·prove hurtful to the Work of God." They succeeded in persuading the trustees to "fix" the deed.

Wesley's appointees faced three large challenges. The ecclesiastical challenge was how to stay within the Church of England and, in general, how to sustain the Methodist commitment, as Pilmore explained it, not "to make divisions . . . or promote a Schism but to gather together in one the people of God that are scattered abroad, and revive *spiritual religion*." A second challenge, essentially theological, was how to advance Methodist doctrines, particularly those of free grace and free will, in a context where "rigid predestinarians" took pains to keep their families and servants from hearing the Methodist gospel. The third, a social challenge, was how to negotiate the social and class structure of American society and especially to make space among the Methodists and in a slaveholding context for the many "poor Affricans" who proved "obedient to the faith." Pilmore established the leadership imperatives: sustain Wesley's commitment to remain within the Church of England, do battle with the Calvinists, build a biracial fellowship (S **1769**, **1771**).

Wesley's next appointees, Francis Asbury and Richard Wright, arrived in late 1771. Asbury had explored his intentions on shipboard: "Whither am I going? To the New World. What to do? To gain honour? No, if I know my own heart. To get money? No: I am going to live to God, and to bring others so to do. In America there has been a work of God." He then needed only to participate in God's ordering. With a mandate from God, not just Wesley, Asbury would lead and direct, notwithstanding whoever else might be humanly so delegated. Though not officially in charge, Asbury judged defective the order that Boardman and Pilmore had achieved. The societies in New York and Philadelphia did not sufficiently heed Methodist discipline, and Boardman and Pilmore did not sufficiently heed the Methodist preacher's self-discipline—itinerancy. They were content "to be shut up in the cities." He exclaimed, "I have not yet the thing which I seek—a circulation of preachers, to avoid partiality and popularity."

Complaining about his colleagues' urban captivity, Asbury itinerated around New York—Westchester, Long Island, and Staten Island. By March 1772 Asbury was "much comforted" and "well pleased" when the preachers gathered in Philadelphia and Boardman appointed himself to Boston, Pilmore to Virginia, Wright to New York, and Asbury to Philadelphia. Pilmore itinerated as far south as Savannah, traveling with Robert Williams, encountering Methodist preachers John King and Robert Strawbridge, and preaching to communities already taking Methodist shape. Williams, Jesse Lee reported, would attend Anglican service, then "standing on a stump, block, or log" begin "to sing, pray, and then preach to hundreds of people." Their collective efforts "awakened" many souls and gathered the converts to the Methodist cause, according to Lee (H **68n6**). With the ordering of the appointments in conference, itineration on a continental scale, and connecting of the several spontaneous initiatives, the preachers had the blueprints for American Methodism.

On his tour, Pilmore labored for a biracial fellowship, continuing to honor the Wesleyan commitments to remain within the church and do battle with the Calvinists. The biracial struggle intensified as Pilmore worked south and dealt more extensively with the gentility and slave owners. Pilmore proved effective in starting societies. His heart lay there and not in constant itineration: "Frequent changes amongst gospel preachers, may keep up the spirits of some kinds of people, but is never likely to promote the spirit of the Gospel nor increase true religion" (H **568n8**).

LIBERTY

Asbury, on the other hand, modeled itinerancy, establishing an effective continental strategy. From the start, he also exhibited a remarkable capacity to understand the North American situation, to connect with its peoples, to speak in colloquial language, and to adapt as the unfolding political crisis brought revolution. He employed contextually apt terms, such as *power* and *liberty*, words with multiple signification to speak of the divine agency at work. Both captured the feeling with which Asbury preached *and* the effect of preaching on hearers. By *liberty*, or *freedom*, its frequent substitute, and by *power*, Asbury described a new order of reality, a new dominion, a new society. Fundamentally, liberty had to do with Arminian freedom, with prevenient grace, with universal atonement, with offers to flee the wrath to come. But it also had something to say about slavery, about the standing of all persons before God, and about the quality of human community. So in slaveholding Maryland in November 1772, Asbury reported:

> Lord's day, 8. We had a very melting time indeed, while I preached to about two hundred souls, from Rom. vi, 17, 18. We had also many people at Richard Webster's while I preached, with liberty in my soul, from 1 Cor. iv, 20: "The kingdom of God is not in word, but in power." This day I have been free from evil, happy, and joyful in my God. At the widow Bonds' there many people, both black and white, rich and poor, who were all exhorted to seek the Lord while he may be found. Some of the young women of this family are serious and thoughtful.

At another point, he noted: "I had *liberty* and *love* in preaching at five, and this day felt *power* to live to God." For a Sunday, he noted, "Preached with *power* in the morning, and spoke *freely* to a large congregation in the evening. My soul is blest with peace and *love* to God." Freedom, order, and love indeed belonged together. And when they cohered, Methodism offered the colonies a taste of the kingdom (H **568nn10–11**).

In these several entries Asbury captured much of early Methodism. It would be a biracial (S **1769, 1771**), highly emotional, affective, and expressive (S **1780b**), family-based community of love (S **1775a**). It would engage the religious sensibilities of women, widows like Phoebe Bond, who would be termed mothers in Israel (S **1775a, 1785c, 1787**). It would empower as leaders young men, like William Watters, then itinerating with Robert Williams. And it would unite male and female, rich and poor, Black and White into one people through its structures of class, society, and circuit. They would travel together toward the kingdom, a community of love and affect (melting, happy, joyful), with liberty in the soul and its own sense of power.

Liberty and order belonged together. In September 1772 Asbury carried the New York society through a series of queries and answers—not unlike those of Wesley's conferences—designed to offer the Methodist freedom through preaching but to safeguard the society's experience of God's power and its own efforts to live in love through the Wesleyan rules barring the unqualified and unruly. And so, when Asbury received a letter from Mr. Wesley, it required first "a strict attention to discipline," then appointing him "to act as assistant." Wesley also directed that Asbury rein in Robert Williams and enjoin him not to print more books without consent. At the same time

Asbury received word of his appointment (from Boardman) to Maryland for the winter.

CONFERENCING

In December 1772, exercising his role as assistant, Asbury convened a quarterly meeting, the body in the Wesleyan system charged with oversight of a circuit, the first for which records remain. Meeting at Joseph Presbury's, Gunpowder Neck, on the western shore of Maryland, it defined business with six questions. After standard queries such as "What are our collections?" and "How are the preachers stationed?" the conference asked, "Will the people be contented without our administering the sacrament?" The question posed issues of unity and authority for the little movement and specifically whether the inertias of Methodism's spontaneous beginnings or the imperatives of Wesleyan order would prevail. Should the Robert Strawbridge cohort, the planters of American Methodism, set policy, ordain themselves, and connive sacramental authority? Or should the Wesleyan principle of not separating, so zealously preached by Pilmore, Williams, and others, prevail? Pilmore and Williams were even then deeper in Anglican territory, farther south, reassuring church people of their commitments and cultivating clerical support. The evangelical Anglican priest Devereux Jarratt, whose influence radiated out from his parish in Bath, Virginia, became an early and important ally. Jarratt concluded from Williams and Methodist literature that *"he that left the church, left the Methodists."* Pilmore, who frequently preached this adage, believed it so deeply that after leaving the colonies, he eventually took orders and returned as an Episcopal priest.

Jarratt was one of several Anglican priests who interested themselves in and supported Methodist efforts. Later Asbury identified three others as especially friendly and helpful: Charles Pettigrew of North Carolina, later bishop of that diocese; Samuel Magaw of Dover and then Philadelphia; and Uzel Ogden of New Jersey (H **568n12**). All attended Methodist quarterly meetings and welcomed Methodists to the (Anglican) sacrament.

Under the question about the sacraments then lay a complex of other issues having to do with the nature and structure of the movement, its relation to the Church of England, the authority of Wesley, the duty of the preachers, and the meaning of connection. Asbury's answer to the question whether the

6

unordained preachers should administer the sacraments indicated a divided house and divergent policy: "I told them I would not agree to it at that time, and insisted on our abiding by our rules. But Mr. Boardman had given them their way at the quarterly meeting held here before, and I was obliged to connive at some things for the sake of peace" (H **568n3**).

For the quarterly conference to take up the sacraments question and resolve it in this fashion was, in a sense, presumptuous. It presumed that it had the authority to legislate. Thus began the process by which the conference achieved supremacy in Methodist polity and Methodist polity itself emerged. This early quarterly meeting exhibited two other important features. Asbury reported, "Many people attended, and several friends came many miles." Quarterly conferences would quickly become a great spiritual festival, the center really of Methodism's liturgical life (including eventually its sacramental life), the gathering that most clearly and fully exhibited Methodist community to a wider public. Already as Jesse Lee reported, the Anglican priest and Methodist sympathizer Jarratt "would frequently preach, meet the classes, hold love-feasts, and administer the Lord's supper among them."

The second development is indicated in Asbury's concluding judgment: "Great love subsisted among us in this meeting, and we parted in peace." Similarly for the next quarterly meeting (conference), in late March, Asbury reported that Strawbridge preached, "All was settled in the most amicable manner" and "The whole ended in great peace." The temper and quality of the preachers' life together in conference became increasingly important. In conferences, the Methodist people and especially the Methodist preachers would establish the bonds of their unity.

DISCIPLINE

Asbury functioned as assistant only half a year, displaced by Thomas Rankin, who arrived in June 1773, with the new title "general assistant." Asbury greeted Rankin's appearance with the notation, "To my great comfort arrived Mr. Rankin," a generous judgment, given the later tension between the two men. More to the point Asbury observed, "He will not be admired as a preacher. But as a disciplinarian, he will fill his place" (H **568n15**). Rankin came with the confidence of Wesley and a mandate. He had had prior experience in the colonies, had a decade of experience as itinerant, had been made assistant and superintendent successively of four circuits, and had served as a riding companion to Wesley. Lest his oral instructions to Rankin be unclear, Wesley followed them with a letter in late 1773 full of admonition and heady counsel on discipline. In particular, Wesley demanded that Rankin terminate improper class leaders. More good would have been accomplished, insisted Wesley, had "Brother Boardman and Pilmoor continued genuine Methodists both in doctrine and discipline. It is *your* part to supply what was wanting in them. Therefore are you sent. Let Brother Shadford, Asbury, and you go on hand in hand, and who can stand against you? Why, you are enough, trusting in Him that loves you, to overturn America" (H **568n16**).

Wesley's command with respect to a "leader" pointed to the regimens of conferencing—Christian conversation—at the grassroots level, namely, in class meetings. These small groups, a signature of Wesleyanism, quite literally constituted the people called Methodist. To be a Methodist meant to be a member of a class, so specified the "Large Minutes" and later the Methodist *Discipline* (S **1785a**; **1798**: Section II). In early American Methodism, particularly in areas of some population density, classes were divided by race and by gender. Led, often for years, by a single leader (typically a White male), classes pastored, nurtured piety, and sustained discipline and self-discipline. Converts entered the class as probationers. Under the leader's guidance and oversight, probationers moved into membership and a members' class.

The weekly class meetings provided the regular pastoring, discipline, guidance, nurture, instruction, mentoring, and encouragement that the system afforded. Within their bonds of accountability and love (stratified by gender, by race, and increasingly in North America by marital status) community and fellowship developed. From them and from their leadership came exhorters, local preachers, and traveling preachers. Guiding little bands of pilgrims toward holiness, the classes embodied and sustained the order and the goals of Wesleyanism. Creating classes, staffing them with capable leaders, and sustaining their good order were arguably a preacher's highest priorities, along with getting the system of them in order in colonial America, Rankin's charge.

Rankin indeed sought order. And he also enjoyed the distinction of establishing the third element in the Wesleyan conferencing order—the annual conference. Classes of a dozen or so provided spirituality and order for members, while quarterly meetings did so for all the local circuit leaders (stewards, class leaders, exhorters, local preachers) and annual conferences for traveling preachers. Rankin convened the first annual conference—still deemed the basic body of Methodism—in July 1773 in Philadelphia (S **1773**). He judged some adherents to be "not closely united to us" and "our discipline . . . not properly attended to, except at Philadelphia and New York; and even in those places it was on the decline" (H **568n18**). The *Minutes,* structured in the Wesleyan question-and-answer format, more resembled vows or imperatives than points for discussion. Rankin followed orders. He demanded acceptance of Wesley's authority, adherence to his doctrines and discipline, suspension of sacraments, conformity with the church, guarding of love feasts, honoring of rules about publishing, and disfellowshipping of deviants. The *Minutes* show Strawbridge as appointed, as they did also in 1775, but then for the last time. He would not abide the new discipline. William Watters, another colonist, received an appointment.

The *Minutes* posed a query that would thereafter provide an annual checkup for the movement, a gauge of its spiritual temperature, a reading of its revivalistic pulse: "What numbers are there in the society?" The answers also indicated what would be a growing pattern. Methodism centered itself in the upper South or Chesapeake region, with almost half of the 1,160 members in Maryland (500). Four of the ten appointments went to Baltimore. That area also saw the most aggressive establishment of preaching houses—Strawbridge, on Sam's Creek (1764), Leesburg (1766–68), Bush, near Aberdeen (1769), Evans (1770), Watters (1772), Fork (1773), and Gunpowder (1773). All in actual attendance, the ten and Thomas Webb, were British born. They had come to bring Wesleyan and British order just at the time that the colonies were deciding to throw off such order.

TENSIONS AND CONTROVERSIES AS REVOLUTION LOOMS

Rankin itinerated through the Methodist communities, presided over innumerable quarterly conferences, and welcomed Black participants, perhaps more than the *Minutes* actually suggest. His itinerations put him in contact with various kindred spirits, including Otterbein who had recently (May 1774) relocated to Baltimore to become pastor of its German Reformed Church (Heritage Landmark, Old Otterbein). Rankin found him a congenial and companion spirit. Otterbein had continued his established pattern of itinerating, organizing and nurturing outlying communities, and raising up leaders. Not long after arriving in Baltimore, Otterbein gathered those preachers into conference, six including himself attending what have been known as the Pipe Creek meetings. The first of these semiannual affairs met May 29, 1774. It specified a class structure for communities in Baltimore, Pipe Creek, Sam's Creek, Fredericktown, and Antietam. The *Minutes* indicate the conference concerned itself with discipline in the classes and with expansion into new communities (S **1785b**). The resemblance to Wesleyan organization (itineration, classes, discipline, conference) was more than superficial. Asbury had encountered Otterbein in early May, discussed the matter of discipline and reported that the German ministers "agreed to imitate our methods as nearly as possible." Thus began the long and complex relationship of mutual influence between the German- and English-speaking Pietist impulses. Both movements continued association with their respective "mother" churches and experienced disruptions during the Revolution. For the Wesleyans it proved severe and of their own making.

Rankin's efforts yielded unity but ironically also discord, a consequence of having British leadership in a colonial society riven with crisis over that exact point—British control. And Rankin proved unusually adept in inviting Americans to view Methodists as Tory, speaking out frequently and publicly in criticism of colonial self-indulgence, pride, and ingratitude and warning Americans of divine judgment. He also offended colonists, including members of the Provincial Congress (in Philadelphia in 1776), by speaking of the hypocrisy of slaveholders raising the banner of liberty. What "a farce it was," he noted, "for them to contend for liberty, when they themselves, kept some hundreds of thousands of poor blacks in most cruel bondage? Many confessed it was true, but it was not now the time to set them at liberty" (H **569n23**).

Wesley's publication pleading for liberty for the slaves had appeared in an American imprint not long before, in 1774. With such advocacy, liberty for the slave became a characteristic, if not necessarily a uniform or even majority, Methodist concern. However, American colonists generally did not share the priority and passion. Many had a different, solely political, liberty in mind and were willing to live with the inconsistency that Rankin, Wesley, and others detected. And some colonists found these and other Methodist actions and words to be rather more treasonous than prophetic and the little movement potentially subversive of "American" liberties. Methodism suffered politically because of its status as part of Anglicanism and as a reform run by a High Church Tory (even as it profited evangelistically from the same umbrella). Was Methodism part of the feared Anglican plot to impose an episcopate on the colonies? Was it a friend or foe to the colonial cause and American liberties?

The crisis of the American Revolution, because it disrupted control mechanisms from Wesley and the English Conference, gave the American movement an extremely short period of being ordered from abroad, of having expatriate leadership, and of being treated as a mission or colony. In short, American Methodism indigenized rapidly. The second annual conference admitted five preachers, four of them colonists, adding seven on trial, all colonists. The conference stationed future leaders Freeborn Garrettson, William Watters, and Philip Gatch. Joseph Pilmore and Richard Boardman had earlier returned to England. Well over half the appointments went to colonists.

In early 1775, John and Charles Wesley wrote Rankin and "all the preachers," counseling neutrality, peacemaking, love to all parties, and silence (politically) and "full union with each other" (H **569n25**). The third annual conference heeding Wesley's advice met in May 1775 in Philadelphia, the very time and place of the Second Continental Congress. The conference declared a "general fast for the prosperity of the work, and for the peace of America, on Tuesday the 18th of July." Unfortunately, Wesley did not heed his own counsel. He issued in 1775 the first of several publications on the American situation, *A Calm Address to Our American Colonies* (S **1775b**), a Tory tract largely extracted from Samuel Johnson's *Taxation No Tyranny*. It sold forty thousand copies in less than a month. This publication, similar public statements by both Wesleys, and intemperate loyalist actions by several preachers in America imaged Methodism publicly as a Tory movement.

COLLABORATORS, LOYALISTS, PACIFISTS, PERSECUTED, PATRIOTS

Despite that public impression, Methodists could be found along the complete spectrum on the Revolution. A few Methodists actively collaborated with the British army. Others sympathized with the loyalist cause. A number of principled loyalists returned to Britain or after the war sought refuge in Canada. A few were neutralists or pacifists. Many supported the

Revolution. And a few, including preachers, participated energetically in the Revolutionary cause. Methodists, then, ranged between the Thomases, from Webb to Ware, from Tory collaborator to American soldier.

Webb, the soldier, took advantage of itinerancy to move around the Middle Colonies for surveillance purposes. He crossed military lines. He fed information to the British command. He defied colonial authorities. He kept up epistolary contact with Lord Dartmouth and passed along military advice. He was arrested and tried by the Continental Congress, and though not convicted, he was held as a prisoner of war. Also arrested for military action, threatened with execution, and equally indiscreet in his loyalism was one of the last pair of preachers sent by Wesley, Martin Rodda, who arrived in 1774. Rodda was charged with gathering a loyalist force on the Eastern Shore of Maryland in 1777. Several other preachers, including Thomas Rankin and George Shadford, joined Webb in writing Lord Dartmouth with information about and advice on the American crisis.

Among the principled loyalists especially noteworthy are those who moved to Canada and replayed their founding roles in establishing Methodism in Canada. The Hecks and Emburys joined approximately 7,500 United Empire Loyalists to settle in Upper Canada.

The centrists included persons like Mary Evans Thorn (Parker), appointed by Pilmore a class leader, whose important memories of Philadelphia Methodism and her own spiritual pilgrimage during that period included roles of nursing and spiritual counseling for the sick and dying "whether by wounds or the plague" (S 1775a). She, her husband, and all the Wesley appointees, save Asbury, returned to England. Asbury, the consummate centrist, in March 1778 went into hiding at Thomas White's in Delaware. He did so to avoid having to take a Maryland test oath that required individuals to disavow obedience to the king, to pledge allegiance to "the State of Maryland," and to "defend" its freedom and independence. Those refusing to swear were subjected to a variety of penalties and prohibited from teaching, preaching, or traveling.

The Tory image of Methodism, exaggerated by the demands of the Maryland test, brought hardship, suffering, beatings, and imprisonment on many, including especially leaders, whose loyalties belonged either to the patriot cause or to kingdoms quite beyond this world. Philip Gatch was tarred and threatened with whipping. Caleb Pedicord bore whipping scars to his grave. Samuel Spragg escaped a mob. Some thirty-five Methodists were indicted for preaching in a six-month period on the Western Shore. Joseph Hartley, a Virginian, was arrested for preaching on the Eastern Shore of Maryland, posted bond, kept preaching, and was jailed. Also jailed were William Wrenn, Jonathan Forrest, and Freeborn Garrettson. Freeborn Garrettson has left the fullest and most graphic account of his sufferings. His *Experience and Travels of Mr. Freeborn Garrettson,* one of the first publications by and about American Methodism, reads like Paul's account of vicissitudes. A member of the gentry who on conversion had freed his slaves, Garrettson's Methodist identity made him appear a turncoat, a counterinsurgent, or even worse, a radical. In his commitments against slavery, war, and patriarchy, Garrettson experienced, witnessed for, and preached a liberty that went beyond but stood in judgment over liberty that might be bought by guns and assured politically. Proclaiming "Lord, the oppressed shall go free" proved indeed a "divine kindling" with power to scorch not just hearts but the very fabric of society. Garrettson Americanized Asbury's language of power and liberty and Pietist practice and precept.

Others less eloquent about the union of Pietist and republican terms like power and liberty simply signed on to the Revolutionary cause. Occupying the other extreme from Webb was Thomas Ware. Though his family loyalties were divided, Thomas Ware volunteered on the Revolutionary side. Not then a preacher but already under Methodist influence, he was immediately afterward appointed by Asbury to the Dover Circuit. William Duke, William Watters, and Nelson Reed took the Maryland oath, thereby committing themselves to the Revolutionary cause. Also in the Revolutionary cause but not then under Methodist influence or in a leadership role was the future leader of The Evangelical Association, Jacob Albright (1759–1808). He served in a local militia.

Jesse Lee, on the other hand, was drafted soon after beginning traveling. As "a Christian and as a preacher of the gospel," he recalled, "I could not fight. I could not reconcile it to myself to bear arms, or to kill one of my fellow creatures; however I determined to go, and to trust the Lord." He refused a gun, was put under guard, and was interrogated for his refusal to bear arms. He responded, "I could not kill a man with a good conscience, but I was a friend to our country, and was willing to do anything that I could, while I continued in the army, except that of fighting." He exercised chaplain roles (H **569n39**) serving as a noncombatant, the latter role also played by Richard Allen, who hauled supplies for Washington.

13

AMERICANIZATION

Methodists went into the American Revolution emblemed as British, Tory, and Anglican. They exited with rather more complex image problems but internally purged, transformed, and focused. While still confined in Delaware (and he, in fact, moved around considerably during his confinement), Asbury resolved:

> Tuesday, February 23, 1779: . . . I have yet been impressed with a deep concern, for bringing about the freedom of slaves in America, and feel resolved to what I can to promote it. If God in His providence hath detained me in this country, to be instrumental in so merciful and great an undertaking, I hope He will give me wisdom and courage sufficient, and enable me to give Him all the glory. I am strongly persuaded that if the Methodists will not yield on this point and emancipate their slaves, God will depart from them. (H **569n40**)

Asbury published this witness against slavery in the earliest version of his journal but suppressed it later, a suppression that belonged to a general retreat, compromise, and forgetting. Later American Methodism would indeed want to forget the freedom and liberty it had preached and the social revolution it had announced. In fact, it had been good news to many, and colonists had readily embraced it. Notwithstanding the movement's image problems and all the suppression, Methodism had prospered during the Revolution and precisely in patriot-held rather than British-held areas. Methodism had all but disappeared in New York and Philadelphia, the locales favored by Wesley's British preachers, falling to under a hundred in each city by the late 1770s and recovering to a little over five hundred combined by 1784. By that point, the little movement boasted almost fifteen thousand members. Methodism had taken hold in the Chesapeake, a land of both slavery and freedom (for statistics H **31**).

Wesley had sent over his missionaries to bring Wesleyan order to the Pietist awakenings. By 1773 they had secured the movement with six circuits and anchored it in New York, Philadelphia, and Baltimore. Ten years later the American preachers they had raised up spread across the Eastern Seaboard onto thirty-eight circuits, overwhelmingly south of the recently drawn Mason-Dixon Line. The missionaries came to connect, control, and order. A strange set of providences interposed a revolution, put the Wesleyan order to new purposes, chased away the British leadership, and left the American Methodists wandering toward a strange new freedom.

Indeed, in the late 1770s, American Methodists found themselves orphaned. Anglicanism of which it claimed to be a part was collapsing. The British Methodist leaders fled, one by one, save for Asbury (but hiding). Guidance from Wesley, tinged as it was with war-related overtones, was problematic. Were they on their own as a church? Should they begin ordinations and assume sacramental authority?

The conferences of 1777 and 1778 struggled with the Wesleyan commitments, including not to separate from the church. The official, later-published *Minutes* of 1777 so resolved, "We purpose, by the grace of God, not to take any step that may separate us from the brethren, or from the blessed work in which we are engaged." Other, manuscript minutes indicate otherwise. The conference contemplated a future without Wesley-appointed preachers and laid the groundwork for authority exercised through committee in presbyterian fashion. Over the 1778 conference the senior American-born preacher and chair of this new committee, William Watters, presided (Asbury semi-hiding at Judge Thomas White's in Delaware). Manuscript minutes indicate that the matter of the sacraments, again discussed, was again deferred and the next conference appointed for Broken Back Church in Fluvanna County (Virginia). Neither action went into the later published *Minutes*.

Two conferences occurred in 1779, the first at Kent County, Delaware, ostensibly as the *Minutes* indicated, for Asbury's safety, to accommodate preachers to the north, and as a planning or preparatory session. This conference recognized Asbury "as General Assistant in America," citing his appointment by Mr. Wesley. It vested quite considerable arbitrary power in Asbury, comparable to that enjoyed by Wesley. It made provision for successors "in case of Br. Asburys Death or absence." And it provided for its own subsequent meeting "in the Baltimore Circuit the last Tuesday in April" (H **570n7**). Finally, it warned "against a separation from the church, directly or indirectly" by all means. This Asburian gathering undertook all the actions to forestall what it clearly anticipated, namely, a further declaration of independence at the regularly called conference at Fluvanna. The following week Asbury wrote personally to John Dickins, Philip Gatch, Edward Dromgoole, and William Glendenning urging that "the preachers in the south" not separate (H **570n6**).

The regularly called conference met as called at Fluvanna (S **1779**), undeterred by the Asburian cabal and its actions. It suffered no unclarity about the

Delaware conference's acts or intent. William Watters attended both. He apparently did not preside over the latter. Philip Gatch led, a position indicated by his standing first in several key listings. The Fluvanna conference carried on the business of the movement, examined its members, collected and disbursed collections, stationed the preachers, and attended to discipline. Then it recognized the Episcopal Establishment as dissolved. Resolving, in effect, to become "dissenters," it ratified procedures by which a new church would be brought into being. The signatories to this act did not include Watters, whose sympathies lay, and subsequent allegiance would fall, with Asbury.

The church Fluvanna established combined features of Wesleyanism, Presbyterianism, and Anglicanism. They added a dose of American freedom. A committee, created through election by the preachers, took the authority that had been vested in Wesley or his general assistant—legislative and administrative authority—including presumably Wesley's power to appoint. A presbytery, similarly constituted and comprising the same four individuals, enjoyed the right to administer the sacraments, the prerogative to ordain, and apparently the obligation to determine who else received sacramental ability. The preachers undertook these acts so as to provide for the sacraments of baptism and the Lord's Supper, a gesture constituting the new entity as dissenting from the Church of England. However, the rites themselves apparently would have had an Anglican feel, "after the Church order," but shortened, made extempore, and honoring individual conscience at key points (mode of baptism, kneeling in supper). The democratic character of this scheme, limited within the conference and to the preachers, consisted in the power to elect and the right of review—to judge whether, and obligation to follow if, "the said committee shall adhere to the Scriptures" (S 1779). Wesleyan, Presbyterian, Anglican, democratic, the Fluvanna conference opened a route that American Methodism would follow, albeit very slowly.

A FIRST SCHISM

The two conferences created, in effect, a northern party and a southern party, one still Anglican and awaiting Wesley's directions, the other refining its goals. Each operated on an illegal, irregular, or theologically suspect pretext. The Fluvanna conference regularly appointed, convened, and conducted, and had defied Wesleyan precepts and its own commitments, had broken with the church, had ordained its members, and had rendered itself theologically problematic and ecclesiologically schismatic. It had made no effort to include any in the laying on of hands who might represent the wider church, longer tradition, apostolic witness, ecclesial succession, or Wesley personally. It accorded no place in its record for Asbury or any around him. The Delaware gathering (and it might be noted that both conferences occurred below the Mason-Dixon Line) honored Wesleyan precept and remained within the church but did so by usurpation. Who separated?

Winners write the history. Asbury and company did so later, letting the fact of the 1779 Fluvanna conference stand in the *Minutes* but reducing its actions from thirty-one to eight and excising those that evidenced independence. The next time around, the Asburian cabal played for keeps, reserving all legitimacy to itself. Its 1780 conference, in Baltimore at the new Lovely Lane Chapel, represented the "southern" conference only by a disciplinary action: "Quest. 20. Does this whole conference disapprove the step our brethren have taken in Virginia? Answ. Yes." And then, "Quest. 21. Do we look upon them no longer as Methodists in connection with Mr. Wesley and us till they come back? Answ. Agreed." Philip Gatch, the leader of the Fluvanna conference, along with Reuben Ellis, was present to hear the conditions, along with a more humbling set proposed by Asbury. However, the conference preferred to appoint its own deputation and agreed to send Asbury, Garrettson, and Watters to convey this action and the conditions of reinstatement—suspension of the sacraments and meeting together in Baltimore the following year. En route, Asbury continued to lobby those aligned with the other conferences whom he encountered, as he had done over the course of the year.

Emissary Watters, who enjoyed standing in both conferences, provides a poignant account of their mediation with an initially resolute southern conference (S 1780a). An equally resolute Asbury reported: "I read Mr. Wesley's thoughts against a separation: showed my private letters of instructions from Mr. Wesley; set before them the sentiments of the Delaware and Baltimore conferences; read our epistles, and read my letter to brother Gatch, and Dickins's letter in answer." All accounts of the proceedings attest the pain and emotion that both the emissaries and the southerners felt over the separation(s) but also the intransigence of the latter. Eventually while Asbury, Garrettson, and Watters prayed and prepared to depart, the southerners capitulated, agreeing to reunite, suspend the sacraments, accept Asbury's itinerating general superintendency, and write Wesley "a circumstantial letter," as

17

Garrettson termed it. Asbury curiously omitted reference to this latter critical condition (H **570n9**).

SLAVERY AND REVIVAL

In addition to its disfellowshipping of the southerners, the 1780 Asburian conference took several other actions of note. In particular, it took forceful stands on slavery:

> Does this conference acknowledge that slave-keeping is contrary to the laws of God, man, and nature, and hurtful to society; contrary to the dictates of conscience and pure religion, and doing that which we would not others should do to us and ours?—Do we pass our disapprobation on all our friends who keep slaves, and advise their freedom?
>
> Answ. Yes.

The conference required "those travelling Preachers who hold slaves to give promises, to set them free" adding in one version of the *Minutes* "*on pain of future exclusion.*" It also made provisions for enforcement, of such rigor as to be suppressed when the church published the *Minutes* in 1794. "Shall we read the minutes in every Society? and the thoughts of slave keeping, which was approved last Conference & tell the people, they must have but one year more, before we exclude them? Agreed." It further mandated that the preachers witness to the evils of slavery, hold the people accountable to free their slaves, identify "Who of our friends have freed their slaves?" and "keep a register yearly of the names of the masters, slaves, and age" (H **570nn9–11**).

The conference balanced this remarkable commitment to antislavery with troubling concessions to racism. It specified that gatherings of Black Americans should be presided over by a "helper" or "proper White person" and that "the Negroes" not be permitted "to stay late or meet by themselves." The preachers obviously did not foresee or desire the emergence of Black leadership beyond limited levels or imagine themselves and the laity trusting it. Methodists would live in this ambiguity. Asbury, for instance, reported the next year traveling with Harry Hosier but complained when Hosier refused to accompany him to Virginia and worried that Hosier might be "ruined" by the adulation of mixed congregations.

18

Another action to exercise influence for half a century regulated the middle unit in Methodist organization, the quarterly *conference* (or *meeting*), the terms being interchangeable. "Quest. 18. Shall we recommend our quarterly meetings to be held on Saturdays and Sundays when convenient? Answ. Agreed." Already the Americans were making this business meeting of the circuit into spiritual festival. Its character and existence the Leesburg version of the *Minutes* indicated,

> May it not be recommended for to begin Quarterly meeting on Saturdays 12 oclock preaching, Exhortation, Prayer. Sunday Preaching, Exhortation. Mon. Lovefeast 9, Preaching & exhortation 11. Temporal Business to be done Saturday evening & Monday morning. Ansr. Agreed.

Later in 1780, Thomas Ware described one such New Jersey event, noting its public character, the crowds, the number of preachers, the deep affections, the appeal to diverse peoples, and its ceremony, specifically, the centerpiece of this event, the love feast (S **1780b**). Freeborn Garrettson reported another on the Delmarva Peninsula, also for late 1780, where he saw "the power of God in a wonderful manner" during "breaking bread" and crowds of 1,500 one day and "near 4000" the next for preaching. Asbury recorded one, at Barratt's Chapel, Delaware, the prior week, with a crowd of "between one and two thousand people." Prior to the emergence of camp meetings, the quarterly meeting served as Methodism's public event, sometimes attracted thousands, ingathered the Methodist tribe and its leadership, sequenced the movement's sacred ceremonies, and produced conversions (H **571n13**).

Indeed, despite disruption caused by the war, continued persecution, and the aftereffects of internal discord, Jesse Lee reported "a gracious revival of religion in many places," for 1780, especially on the Eastern Shore of Maryland. Again, in 1781, he noted revival there and a "blessed revival of religion" in Virginia and parts of North Carolina. The engines of revival were the quarterly meetings, classes, family religion, and personal discipline of Methodism. And the results showed, despite the war turmoil, in the growth of the small movement: 1777—6,968; 1778—6,095 (partial count); 1779—8,577; 1780—8,504 (numbers affected by the schism); 1781—10,539; 1782—11,785; 1783—13,740 (H **571n14**). Just before his 1780 conference, Asbury became a citizen of Delaware. Although no more invested in things political, he had committed himself to the American preachers and they to him.

19

AWAITING WESLEYAN DIRECTIVES

The conference of 1781 met at Choptank in Delaware on April 16 and "adjourned to Baltimore the 24th of said month." The two sessions were "considered but one conference," as Lee put it. For precedent the *Minutes* cited Wesley's holding of an Irish conference. Thus began the "Baltimore system" of governance, multiple conference sessions whose final legislative word came from its Baltimore meeting, represented by a single set of *Minutes*. This strange pattern continued until 1787. It reflected some appreciation for the convenience of multiple conferences experienced during the division, the necessity within a far-flung movement of providing both access and unity, and the clear prominence of Baltimore as Methodism's capital. It unified the movement and unified legislation and decision making in conference (H **571n15**). The pattern also accorded with what would be the language of the *Discipline,* that a preacher was "admitted on trial," not into a particular annual conference, but "into the traveling connection."

The first action of the 1781 conference reuniting the movement also established the disciplinary and doctrinal standards of an emerging American connection as those of Wesleyanism, asking which preachers "are now determined, after mature consideration, close observation and earnest prayer, to preach the old Methodist doctrine, and strictly enforce the discipline, as contained in the Notes, Sermons, and Minutes published by Mr. Wesley . . . and firmly revolved to discountenance a separation among either preachers or people." By that action, the American preachers put themselves in a three-year limbo.

As American political independence from Britain loomed, John Wesley busied himself working for some solution to the oft-repeated American Methodist requests. The signing of the Peace of Paris and recognition of the United States prompted action. Wesley's gradual appreciation of his stature as a scriptural bishop, of his right to ordain, and of the precedents and exigencies under which elders might exercise such powers belongs to other accounts, including his own (S **1784a**). He had exhausted the obvious—Robert Lowth, bishop of London, responsible for the religious order of the colonies, rebuffed requests for regular ordinations. Wesley had been given detailed, thoughtful plans for a reformed church by trusted lieutenants, notably Joseph Benson and John Fletcher. He had seen Lady Huntingdon's connection take ordinations into their own hands. He had long been aware of authorities—including Lord Peter King, Bishop Edward Stillingfleet, dissenter Edmund Calamy, and Bishop Benjamin Hoadly—who cited instances of ordination by presbyters (elders) and argued that presbyters and bishops belonged to the same order. Wesley put to work on the case his new assistant and troubleshooter, Thomas Coke, who had earned a law degree and taken orders in the Church of England before affiliating with the Methodists.

Coke and Wesley carried on an extended discussion of how to effect ordinations for America, some of it by letter. In April 1784, Coke volunteered to serve as a deputy, outlining three reasons: to gather for Wesley "fuller Information concerning the State of the Country," to ensure "a Cement of Union remaining after yr. [your] Death between the Societies of Preachers in the two Countries," and to equip himself for appropriate oversight following Wesley's death. By August Coke had gained two compatriots for America, Richard Whatcoat and Thomas Vasey. And on September 1 and 2, despite opposition from virtually all others in his inner circle of counselors and without his brother's knowledge, Wesley, with the assistance of James Creighton, a clerical associate from Ireland, ordained Whatcoat and Vasey as deacons, the following day as elders, and Coke as a "Superintendent." In solving one problem, Wesley had created other puzzles (H **45**)—his own relation to the American preachers, his authority to ordain and therefore the legitimacy of American Methodist orders, the relation of the deputized Coke to the newly independent Americans and specifically of Coke to Asbury. What kind of church did Wesley envision? Why the curious term "superintendent"; why not "bishop"? Why, if merely "superintendent," the necessity of "ordination"? And why "ordination" if superintendents remained elders and superintendents held an office and were not a third order?

PROVISIONING AN AMERICAN CHURCH

Wesley did not send Coke empty-handed. Wesley introduced him and his plans in a letter "To Dr. COKE, Mr. ASBURY, and our Brethren in *NORTH AMERICA*" (S **1784a**). Referencing the new political and ecclesiastical situation consequent of the Revolution, Wesley announced that he had "drawn up a little Sketch" for a new church order, appointed "Dr. Coke and Mr. Francis Asbury, to be joint *Superintendents* over our Brethren in North America," and drafted a liturgy for the new church. He then exhorted

21

American Methodists to be "at full liberty, simply to follow the Scriptures and the Primitive Church." However, Wesley did not intend by "full liberty" to remove himself from the determination of how Americans might "follow the Scriptures and the Primitive Church." And he had sent as provisions, as Richard Heitzenrater has observed, revisions or analogues of documents constitutive of his Church of England. In his "liturgy," *The Sunday Service for the Methodists in North America,* he had revised the Book of Common Prayer (BCP), reducing the Thirty-nine Articles of Religion to twenty-four, and providing a psalter, *A Collection of Psalms and Hymns for the Lord's Day.* His *Sermons* and *Notes* served the boundary-setting tradition of the Anglican Book of Homilies (H **571n26**). The "little Sketch," a revised "Large Minutes," became the *Discipline* and held all these church-defining documents together.

In his journal, Coke recounted his voyage and preparation for launching the new church (S **1784b**). He met Asbury at a quarterly conference at Barratt's Chapel, Delaware (a UMC Heritage Landmark). Coke doubtless expected, as indicated in comments to John Dickins, in his initial take-charge behavior at Barratt's Chapel, and in his private disclosure of plans to Asbury, simply to announce the new order and ordain Asbury into it (H **571n27**). At most, Asbury was "respectfully to be consulted in respect to every part of the execution of it" (S **1784b, 75**). Asbury countered with precedent-setting gestures. First, he transformed a quarterly meeting into a deliberative council or conference, fifteen sitting "in Conference," according to Garrettson. Second, to this body he referred Coke's disclosure, effectively transforming pronouncements into proposals. Third, he engineered the decision to convene a conference of all the traveling preachers, appointing Garrettson to travel to issue the call. Fourth, he conveyed to the gathering of preachers the selection of the superintendents, indicating his willingness to serve "if the preachers unanimously choose me," implicitly making the selection of Coke as well as Asbury up to the impending conference (H **44–48; 572n28**). In a further presumption of authority and notwithstanding Coke's credentials and sole title then as superintendent, Asbury sent Coke on a thousand-mile circuit. For a companion on that trip Asbury sent—and the qualifiers Coke employed disclose much about the limits of Methodist egalitarianism—"his black (*Harry*) [Hosier] by name" (S **1784c**; H **572n29**).

PLANTING AN AMERICAN CHURCH

Coke indicated that he and Asbury agreed to establish a school modeled after Wesley's Kingswood academy (S **1784b**). To scout a possible site, Coke met Asbury on December 14 at Abingdon, Maryland (the future site of Cokesbury College, a UMC Heritage Landmark). From there they traveled to Perry Hall, the residence of Harry Dorsey Gough, an important way station then and thereafter for Methodist preachers and another historic site. At Perry Hall, the three ordained Britishers; their former compatriot, Asbury; and no native-born Americans completed the transformation of Wesley's pronouncements into proposals. Preparing the agenda for the Christmas Conference, they worked especially on altering the "Large Minutes" as later bishop Richard Whatcoat reported (H **572n30**). The designs that Coke brought from Wesley and polished at Perry Hall proved indispensable. However, the foundations had been well laid by Asbury and the colonists. What those colonial Pietist foundations undergirded would stand. After these first encounters of Coke and Asbury, the latter had the winning hand. Coke might have the blueprints, but Asbury had the foremen and workers. The church they made would be his.

CHAPTER II
REFORMING THE CONTINENT AND SPREADING SCRIPTURAL HOLINESS: 1792–1816

In late 1784 the preachers called Methodist, with John Wesley's blessing and guidance, established The Methodist Episcopal Church. In this national dawn, other communions broke or renegotiated ties with European authorities. To this decade United Brethren, the African Methodist Episcopal Church, Republican Methodists, and The Evangelical Association look back for defining experiences. Constitution-making sharpened identities, forced choices, demanded compromises, and produced division as Methodism struggled with matters of race, ethnicity, language, prerogative, and franchise.

THE CHRISTMAS CONFERENCE

A preachers-only assembly, effectively a constitutional convention and known as the Christmas Conference, met in Lovely Lane Chapel and Otterbein's new brick church in Baltimore. The gathering left no journal of its sessions, its chief labor being production of the first *Discipline,* cutting from and pasting into the1780 recension of Wesley's "Large Minutes" (S **1785a**). Key details—for instance, Asbury's insistence that both he and Coke be elected; the exact membership, including whether Black Americans Harry Hosier (S **1784c**) and Richard Allen were present; the origin of the church's new name, reportedly suggested by John Dickins; how business was done— emerge from the 1785 annual *Minutes* and informal accounts. "We were in great haste, and did much business in a little time," Asbury explained, entering into his *Journal* for December 24 only:

> We then rode to Baltimore, where we met a few preachers: it was agreed to form ourselves into an Episcopal Church, and to have superintendents, elders, and deacons. When the conference was seated, Dr. Coke and myself were unanimously elected to the superintendency of the Church, and my ordination followed, after being previously ordained deacon and elder (H **572n6, n1**).

Coke (S **1784b**) provides us more details, as do other participants.

In 1784, Methodists anticipated the American religious future—embracing disestablishment, offering a denominational ordering of religion, achieving autonomy from European headquarters, institutionalizing voluntarism. However, American Methodists would only slowly understand their prescience. The Christmas Conference indeed made or confirmed a number of denomination-shaping decisions. It accepted John Wesley's plan for the church, in principle if not in every detail, including his prepared liturgy, hymnbook, and revised Articles of Religion. It explicitly conceded final authority to Wesley: "During the life of Rev. Mr. Wesley, we acknowledge ourselves his Sons in the Gospel, ready in Matters belonging to Church-Government, to obey his Commands" (S **1785a**), a rubric soon to be struck. On the other hand, it chose to make decisions by debate and majority rule, thereby claiming the prerogative to approve, alter, add to, and subtract from what had been Wesley's document (the "Large Minutes"). It added to the Articles of Religion a rubric on US political autonomy and removed the "descent into hell" from the Creed. It followed Anglican, Catholic, and ancient precedent in adopting a threefold ministry of superintendents (bishops), elders, and deacons, proclaiming the new church to be episcopal and naming it "Methodist Episcopal." Balancing its deferential acknowledgment of Wesley's authority, it provided for election of superintendents by and for their accountability to the conference. It selected elders (thirteen or so) and by charging them with supervisory as well as sacramental roles created the office of presiding elder (today's district superintendent). It prohibited "Ministers or Travelling-Preachers" from drinking "spirituous Liquors." It legislated courageously and extensively against slavery, mandating that all Methodists, laity as well as preachers, emancipate their slaves (S **1785a, Q. 42–43**). But it provided for White oversight of Black American gatherings. It embraced a proposal for a college and naming it for the two superintendents (Cokesbury). It set a common salary at twenty-four pounds. It approved missionaries for Nova Scotia (Freeborn Garrettson and James Cromwell). And it recast Wesley's connectional mission statement in terms apt for the new nation and the yawning American continent. "God's Design, in raising up the Preachers called Methodists," the *Discipline* indicated was "To reform the Continent, and spread scriptural Holiness over these Lands" (S **1785a, Q. 4**).

By these several accomplishments, American Methodism appropriated the distinctives of the Wesleyan reform and linked itself with the core beliefs and polity of the church catholic. Wesley's *Sermons* lurked in the background as both the statement of its own convictions and a Wesleyan interpretation of "catholic" standards. Coke preached ordination sermons and ordained Asbury on successive days deacon, elder, and superintendent (and all references employed "ordain" for the latter office). At Asbury's ordination as superintendent, Coke made the historic case for the legitimacy of the act and an explicit case for the episcopal character of the office by delineating ten "grand characteristics of a Christian bishop." At Asbury's request, William Otterbein participated in the laying on of hands for the episcopal ordination, a fact noted by Coke (S **1784b**) but curiously omitted from Asbury's ordination certificate. Equally curious, Coke warranted the ordination on his Anglican credentials, omitting explicit reference to Wesley. What relation Methodism would strike with the other remnant of Anglicanism in the United States and what it meant by its middle name remained unclear.

OTTERBEIN IN BALTIMORE

Equally unclear was the relation between William Otterbein's Evangelical Reformed Church of Baltimore and the German Reformed Pennsylvania Coetus (synod). The Coetus first dissuaded Otterbein from accepting the Baltimore call but acquiesced after he settled there in May 1774. And though both the church and its pastor enjoyed the affiliation with the Coetus, Otterbein continued the wider itinerations, care for outlying German communities, and nurture of persons into ministry that made him as much a competitor to as agent of the Coetus. Further, Otterbein launched in May 1774 what might be seen as an alternative to the Coetus, a semiannual multidenominational gathering of preachers that met initially at Pipe Creek (Maryland). These provided mutual counsel for some eighteen class leaders and the various classes ministered to by the six attending preachers. Calling itself the "United Ministers," it continued at least through 1777. That year, the Mennonites expelled Martin Boehm for preaching false doctrine, engaging in irregular practices, and fraternizing with other religious communities—including Methodists! Increasingly, Boehm partnered with Otterbein in leading the new evangelical party developing among German pastors and people.

Under Otterbein's leadership, the Baltimore church prospered, growing steadily in membership and in 1785 erecting a brick and stone building, now the oldest in Baltimore (a UMC Heritage Landmark, Old Otterbein). That year, congregation and pastor signed a covenant that, in effect, created a denomination (albeit like Wesley's Methodism remaining within the German Reformed). The Constitution and Ordinances of the Evangelical Reformed Church of Baltimore (S **1785b**) made provision for "fraternal unity" among preachers and "churches in Pennsylvania, Maryland, and Virginia," which recognized "the superintendence of William Otterbein" and accepted this congregation's rules, practices, doctrine, and order. It retained the Reformed or Calvinist ministerial order—government by vestry, doctrine of scriptural authority, and constitution by covenant. But it repudiated predestination and irresistible grace and provided for class meetings ("special meetings" or *collegia pietatis*) to maintain order, exercise oversight, discipline members, encourage growth in the faith, and pray and sing together. Their mandated character and agenda—"to flee the wrath to come"—suggest some Wesleyan influence, as does a rule for ecumenically open Communion.

Otterbein and Asbury developed strong personal bonds. Their movements also explored unity, efforts frustrated by differences in discipline, authority, and language. With its covenantal basis for unity, the Otterbein movement instead found common ground with Pietists from other and quite different confessional backgrounds. In 1789 at Baltimore and 1791 in York, Otterbein gathered ten preachers of the Reformed tradition, six from the Mennonites, one from the Moravians, and one from the Amish, three of the group ordained. A later United Brethren (UB) narrative (H **7–9**) also claimed Lutheran adherents. The list of names placed Otterbein and Boehm first, first among equals, a fraternal rather than hierarchical basis for unity. Four others named would be prominent as their successors in the movement—George Adam Guething, John Neidig, Christian Newcomer, and John G. Pfrimmer. The "United Ministers," a fellowship of revivalists, agreed to recognize one another's ordinations, to preach in homes or barns in their neighborhoods in addition to their resident pastorates, to hold quarterly meetings in regions, and to gather at an annual conference for mutual support, theological education, and missional strategizing.

RACE, GENDER, AND GENTILITY

By precept and practice, Pietists generally and Wesleyans in particular envisioned the path to holiness as a narrow way and portrayed with some vividness the alternative, worldly path to destruction. Slavery belonged to "the world" as did the trifling, lukewarm, dull, and frivolous—jewelry, finery, balls, cards, gambling, public amusements, "hurry, fashion and company." The worldly or genteel foil for true religion proved perhaps more powerful in the Chesapeake and upper south where Methodism prospered than it did in Wesley's England. For there it defined the ethos and style of the slaveholding, code-of-honor-committed gentry. The *Discipline*, following Wesley, explicitly proscribed gentility by identifying its behavior and dress (**Q. 18** in S **1785a** but also **Q.s 15, 24, 51, 61, 66**). Slaves, poor Whites, and artisans found such denunciation of the values and lifestyle of the sometimes oppressive and patriarchal elites quite bracing and inviting. So did some "genteel." However, by converting to Methodism, elite women (and men) disavowed family, friends, culture, practices, and a lifestyle they had known all too well. So, the spirituality of women like Elizabeth McKean of St. George's, Philadelphia (S **1785c**), because of what it renounced, took on a revolutionary character. Similarly, Catherine Livingston (S **1787**), of that New York politically and socially elite family, compounded the disgrace of converting by marrying a Methodist itinerant, Freeborn Garrettson. Methodism's transvaluation of values did not then extend to granting women formal leadership status. Women held the office of class leader only briefly and sporadically. But women played immensely important roles. They used the class relations, family networks, correspondence, and home contexts for evangelization and nurture—and thus found new ways to have social influence that would benefit women in the decades to come. Such efforts yielded converts particularly within their own families and homes.

Slaves, free Black Americans, and poor Whites heard the demonization of gentility, the upending of expected social norms, as promising release from precisely the class who oppressed and exploited them. Slaves and free Black Americans, in particular, responded to Methodism's inversion of the world's values, with the full range of emotions and great expressiveness, as early itinerants like Philip Bruce reported (S **1788**). Black Americans heard and accepted Methodism's liberating word and applauded its denunciation of slavery. When in 1786 Methodism began to report membership by race, it claimed 18,791 Whites and 1,890 Blacks. The latter numbers (and its proportion) grew dramatically to 45,384 and 11,280 in 1796.

The antislavery preaching of the movement's leadership—Coke, Garrettson, Asbury, and many others—as well as their success in bringing Black Americans into Methodist fellowship, took place primarily in slaveholding areas. Methodism's initial willingness to confront the slave owner directly *and* to embrace Black Americans in "society" gave its witness a decided edge over the Quakers who preached antislavery but showed little eagerness to include African Americans in their own fellowship. Both communities contributed to significant numbers of manumissions below the Mason-Dixon Line, particularly just below it in Delaware, Maryland, and Virginia. Methodists even braved into the political sphere to petition legislatures, as did the 1785 conference, seeking rights of manumission in North Carolina. No small part of Methodism's appeal to slaves and freed persons derived from this double witness to liberty—freedom from slavery to cosmic powers of sin and death, attested by inclusion within the membership, and freedom from its collusive force, human enslavement of fellow human beings, attested by antislavery legislation and preaching.

Such advocacy, however, proved unpopular among Whites. So discovered Coke on his 1785 tour south, where his antislavery statements and reputation earned him the threat of flogging by a mob; disputes with Jesse Lee and the North Carolina Methodist slaveholder Green Hill; estrangement from Devereux Jarratt; and strained relations in conferences. The long saga of ambiguity, compromise, and retreat in Methodist race relations began early—inclusion but segregation, recognition but constraint, empowering but delimiting it. Classes were segregated, Black chapels created, separate cemeteries established—all allowed only with White oversight. Still, important Black leaders emerged. Harry Hosier (S **1784c**), for instance, traveled with key Methodist leaders—Asbury, Coke, Garrettson—and was acknowledged as the powerful team member. But Methodists had difficulty in credentialing Black leadership. Not until 1800 would The MEC permit Black leaders even the status of local deacon. African Methodists look back on the year 1787 as the beginning of their migration toward independence. Historians disagree about whether the exact incident to which the aging Richard Allen pointed (S **1792b**) can be credibly dated to 1787, but there can be no doubt that the racist and segregating spirit of which he complained was then quite alive and well (H **574n29**).

BISHOPS AND CONFERENCE

By prior understanding, Coke returned to Britain after the three 1785 American conferences (and consolidating of plans for the Cokesbury academy). He would be back in the United States in 1787, 1789, and 1791, punctuating his American visits with oversight roles in Ireland, the West Indies, and British North America. In Britain, he also embroiled himself in complicated politics over the future of Methodism after Wesley. Coke returned to the United States in 1787 with explicit, written directions from Wesley to "appoint a General Conference of all our preachers in the United States, to meet at Baltimore on 1st May 1787" and further that "Mr. Richard Whatcoat may be appointed Superintendent with Asbury" and Freeborn Garrettson be superintendent for British North America. Such directives accorded with the "binding minute" to obey Wesley's commands and with Wesley's vision of a global connection. They hardly accorded with American sensitivities.

Of Wesley's several directives, the Americans honored the most inconsequential. They met May 1 in Baltimore rather than as they had appointed at Abingdon, Maryland, on July 24. They also rescheduled two other conferences for Charleston in late March and Virginia in late April, gathering for the latter as many as three thousand at Rough Creek, Virginia. There James O'Kelly and Jesse Lee led opposition to Coke, to Wesley's exercise of authority, and to the nomination of Whatcoat. Of the May 1 meeting, Asbury noted, "We had some warm and close debates in conference; but all ended in love and peace." Thomas Ware reported, more candidly, that many preachers took great offense at the presumption of resetting the conference date, at the implicit conferring of decision making to the superintendents, at the appointment rather than election of superintendents, and at the fear that Whatcoat's elevation might produce the recall of Asbury. That fear then doomed Whatcoat's episcopal chances. The conference responded more formally by qualifying Coke's authority, stipulating in the *Annual Minutes* to the first question—Who are the superintendents?—the answer: "Thomas Coke, (when present in the States), and Francis Asbury." Confirming that on his part, Coke gave the conference a certificate promising not to exercise superintending authority when absent and limiting it when present to ordaining, presiding, and traveling. They also rescinded the binding minute of loyalty to Wesley from the *Discipline* (S **1785a, Q. 2**), sometimes described as dropping Wesley's name from the *Minutes* (H **575n35**).

Sometime after the 1787 conferences, Coke and Asbury took another action hardly to Wesley's liking. They substituted the word *bishop* for *superintendent*, an alteration ratified in the 1788 conferences and *Discipline*. The "bishops" also took it upon themselves to alter the Wesley "minute" ordering of the *Discipline,* arranging it instead as its new subtitle indicated, "under proper heads, and methodized in a more acceptable and easy manner," prefacing it with a historical account "Of the Rise of Methodism (so called) in Europe and America" (H **10**).

As The MEC's relation to Wesley evolved so did the relative power and authority of the two superintendents in the American context. While Coke enjoyed the personal relation with Wesley and seemed to be trying on Wesley's mantle and authority, Asbury consolidated influence with and power over the American itinerants. He did so by riding with them through their circuits, preaching and praying, by making the quarterly meetings and presiding in conference, by meeting classes and staying in Methodist homes, by hearing their efforts to preach and counseling with them, by filling the appointments with insight about both preachers and circuits—in short by traveling the entire connection (S **1789a**). So Asbury exhibited, daily and constantly, privately and publicly, the office of itinerating general superintendent. So he understood himself as the exemplum traveling preacher (S **1798**). Coke might write letters of counsel and direction. Coke's name might go first on *Minutes* and *Discipline*. In conference, Coke might preach and preside. And when the two superintendents traveled together, Coke might claim the pulpit. However, Asbury ran the show. Coke performed. Asbury governed.

Coke's relation with Asbury and his standing among American Methodists deteriorated further when his secret negotiations later surfaced (S **1791a**). Without Asbury's knowledge, Coke wrote and then met with Bishop William White of the newly constituted Protestant Episcopal Church about union of the two churches, outlining advantages to Episcopalians, Methodist conditions, and probable roadblocks (among them, Asbury). They worked out a scheme that predicated union on relaxation of Episcopal ministerial standards, reordinations of Methodist preachers, reconsecration of the two bishops and some continuing oversight of specifically Methodist work by the two Methodist bishops. Coke also wrote the High Church Episcopal bishop of Connecticut, Samuel Seabury, summarizing the plans. Asbury discovered the scheme, responded negatively, and resisted submission of the plan to the 1792 General Conference. That body emerged to deal with such issues of power and authority.

MULTIPLE CONFERENCES AND THE COUNCIL

Asbury's authority loomed large, quite apart from his dominating style and from his incredible appointive power. It loomed large because the countervailing authority, that of conference, fragmented as Methodism continued to expand. Lee termed the years of 1787 and 1788 the greatest revival for southern Virginia ever known, particularly in the Sussex, Brunswick, and Amelia circuits, where he claimed 4,200 converted for 1787 and comparable intensive growth in areas of Maryland and North Carolina for 1788. In 1788 Methodism added 11,481 members and nineteen circuits, extending its penetration beyond the upper south or Chesapeake, creating new circuits in South Carolina, western Pennsylvania, Kentucky, (West) Virginia, Ohio, New York, and Georgia, and establishing significant toeholds beyond the Appalachians and Alleghenies. The circuits numbered eighty-five. The number of conferences also expanded. Six were appointed for 1788, but seven held according to Lee, the last of which was in Philadelphia, not Baltimore.

For 1789, eleven conferences met, Baltimore's falling near the middle of the schedule. Thus failed a Baltimore system of governance by which the legislative acts of all the conferences were finalized at Baltimore, an early casualty of Methodist growth. The eleven conferences of 1789—through all of which legislation had to pass—established the unwieldiness of Methodism's political apparatus and prompted a short-lived, unpopular solution, a council. Proposed by the bishops to the 1789 conferences, the council was to represent "the whole connection." The representatives were "our bishops and presiding elders," that is, Asbury and his appointees. Lee, who reproduced the entirety of this legislation, complained that the council was new, dangerous, unworkable, and not genuinely representative (H **64, 575n40**).

In its first meeting, the council adopted a constitution that addressed the matter of representation and other procedural issues. It provided instead for election of members and concurrence of a majority of the conferences in legislation (plus, however, "the consent of the bishop"). Even in this revised form, many experienced the council as what Thomas Neely termed "a dangerous centralization of power" (H **575n42**). Outspoken on the issue of centralized power and leading opposition to the council was Irish-born council member James O'Kelly. Successive annual conferences vented their opposition. The southern Virginia preachers met under O'Kelly's leadership at Mecklenburg and resolved "to send no member to Council" (H **575–76n45**).

The second (1790) meeting of the council did not stem the tide of opposition. O'Kelly and Lee intensified their opposition. Nevertheless, as its *Minutes* attest, the council did show a capacity to act, to initiate, to address itself to the connection's needs, a political capacity that had been missing. It proceeded in traditional Wesleyan fashion through thirty-one policy queries and action answers. It dealt extensively with publishing—calling for book stewards in every district, identifying books to be published (including Wesley's *Sermons*), and providing counsel on American Methodism's first periodical, the *Arminian Magazine,* which lived only the two years that the council existed, 1789 and 1790. Notwithstanding the magazine's failure, these publishing initiatives and the 1789 settling of John Dickins and the publishing agency in Philadelphia—"the first publishing house in America to initiate the systematic printing and distribution of evangelical books"—constituted Methodism as a textually defined as well as an oral community, a development to which we return in the next chapter.

The council made financial provision and further rules of conduct for Cokesbury College and authorized similar schools in any districts where resources availed. It faced a variety of money and cash-flow problems. It authorized Indigenous missions, empowering the "bishop"—note the singular—to expend one salary (twenty-four pounds) for "a Teacher, or Preacher, among any of the *Indian Nations,*" an initiative not honored. And it treated what had been a major concern of the 1789 council, namely, worship, stipulating divisions within buildings and separate doors so "that men and women should sit a-part in public congregations," as "we think it primitive, prudent, and *decent.*" The 1789 council had insisted that further preaching houses be built only with conference and presiding elder support and direction, called for worship at 10:00 or 11:00 a.m. on Sundays "where we have Societies and regular Preaching," and given directions for such worship—"Singing, Prayer and reading the Holy Scriptures, with Exhortation or Reading a Sermon, in the Absence of a Preacher; and the officiating Person shall be appointed by the Elder, Deacon, or travelling Preacher, for the Time being."

GENERAL CONFERENCE

Methodism needed connectional administrative, policy-making, and legislative authority. The council demonstrated that centralized authority, countervailing that of the bishop(s), could work. Was it not needed? Without some collective voice for the preachers, was it not appropriate for the bishops to speak on behalf of Methodism to President George Washington, assuring him of Methodist support and soliciting his commitment to religious liberty (S **1789b**)? And was it surprising that four months after the second council, Bishop Coke would take it upon himself to engage in secret overtures to the Episcopalians (S **1791a**)?

A general conference had been proposed by both Lee and O'Kelly but dismissed when the plan for a council was initially introduced. By early 1791 Coke had given up on the council. Lee reiterated his proposal on July 7, 1791, submitting a scheme for a delegated or representative body. Lee's conception of delegation or representation would have to wait its time, and his notion of an annual meeting did not prevail. But he, O'Kelly, and Coke had their way. The first General Conference met in Baltimore, November 1–15, 1792. No journal from this first General Conference survives. It left its record in the *Discipline*, which it revised. Perhaps most important, it gave itself legislative power for the church, established itself as a permanent body, to convene again in four years, "to which, all the preachers in full connection were at liberty to come."

The 1792 General Conference gave impetus toward what would in the future be termed *annual conferences* by authorizing the uniting of two or more of the districts (the purview of the presiding elders) and between three and twelve circuits (the assignment of the traveling preachers) into district (annual) conferences. It defined conferences, both general and annual, by their membership—the traveling preachers in full connection. The

Discipline distinguished the presiding elder (today's district superintendent) from the eldership in general, formally recognizing what had emerged as the key conference leadership, administrative, disciplinary, and appointing office (S **1798**, section V). Appointed by the bishop and given supervisory responsibility for a district of circuits and the various levels of preachers attached to them, the presiding elder would enjoy the authority of the bishop in the bishop's absence and the power of advisory and supportive roles in the bishop's presence, notably responsibilities to preside when Methodists convened (conferenced) and to appoint, to receive, and to change Methodist leaders. The 1792 General Conference clearly worried some over the power it was lodging in the presiding eldership, for it limited the term of presiding elders in one place to four years.

REPUBLICAN, PRIMITIVE, AND AFRICAN METHODISTS

Perhaps motivating limitations on the presiding eldership were the political machinations and intense criticisms of the bishops by the presiding elder from the Virginia–North Carolina border, James O'Kelly. The second day of General Conference, O'Kelly placed a motion giving preachers who thought themselves "injured" by the bishop's appointment the "liberty to appeal to the conference" and the right, if the appeal was sustained, to another appointment. The tenor and intemperate tone of the "long" debate can be discerned in O'Kelly's account of the event (S **1792a**). O'Kelly appealed to the ideology of republicanism—the rhetoric of the Revolution, of American liberty, of democracy. This republican imagery made considerable sense to some Methodist preachers. Should not an American church conduct itself along American principles? Had they not been injured by appointments? Did not Coke and Asbury connive to increase their power? Had not the preachers been obliged to check episcopal tyranny already? Were not the preachers' liberties in danger? Would it not be better safeguarded in conference rather than episcopal hands?

Intemperately defended, the motion failed. O'Kelly walked out with a party of supporters to form a rival movement. The Republican Methodists had considerable appeal especially in lower Virginia and upper North Carolina, O'Kelly's district. For a time, Methodism seemed to be splitting in two, and actually did so at its first General Conference, foreshadowing the politicization of General Conference. The movement proposed a polity protective of liberty, grounded in Scripture alone, and explicitly antislavery as O'Kelly explained in his apologetic writings (S **1792a**). Asbury labored diligently to contain the threat on an interpersonal or relational level but also intellectually. He responded, implicitly, by editing and publishing, in Wesley-like fashion, *The Causes, Evils, and Cures of Heart and Church Divisions; Extracted from the Works of Mr. Richard Baxter and Mr. Jeremiah Burroughs.* Explicitly, at the 1796 General Conference's direction, he and Coke answered O'Kelly by carefully annotating the *Discipline* (S **1798**), defending Methodist episcopacy as essential to bedrock Methodist principles of itinerancy and connectionalism, arguing for presiding elders as providentially given extensions of these principles, and in short, defending the entire Methodist Episcopal system. Asbury also commissioned Nicholas Snethen, his "silver trumpet," to refute O'Kelly, which Snethen did with several tracts, including *A Reply to an Apology for Protesting against the Methodist Episcopal Government.* Snethen established the historiographical tradition on the Republicans as schismatic, heretical (particularly on the doctrine of the Trinity), driven by O'Kelly's megalomania, excessive in its portrayal of Asbury.

Also in 1792, William Hammett was in the process of drawing off Charleston Methodists into a church committed to following Wesley's primitive Methodism, taking that as its name, and criticizing Coke and Asbury (H **70–71**).

In the same time frame, Black Methodists under Richard Allen took important steps along the way toward independence, walking out of St. George's and establishing Bethel Church as an African congregation (S **1792b**). (Not all Black Methodists in Philadelphia followed Allen into Mother Bethel Church. A small group decided to give mother Methodism a little more time to treat them with dignity and respect and organized in 1794 as African Zoar.) Both the Allen movement and the Republican Methodists, later to take the name Christians (Disciples of Christ), held up (and managed to maintain) American Methodism's/(Wesley's) antislavery banner, championed liberty, and called for a more democratic, if not congregational, church. These issues would not go away, and the schisms cost The MEC some of its most fervent opponents of slavery, most articulate exponents of liberty, and most egalitarian spirits. William Warren Sweet estimates that the overall losses suffered in the 1790s by The MEC to the Republicans, to William Hammett,

37

and to other causes amounted to some ten thousand—roughly 20 percent of the membership total (S **p22**; H **577n63**).

DENOMINATIONALISM

The constitution-making decade produced a number of independent denominations, including The MEC. For Methodists, the decade witnessed the beginnings of multiple separations: of The Methodist Episcopals from the Church of England; of the American Methodists from Wesley; within the United States, of the Methodists from colonial Anglicans; within the Methodist camp, of Black from White; of German- and English-speaking Pietists from one another; and of Republican Methodists from the church they experienced as tyrannically ruled by bishops. The decade saw also the constituting of gender and class patterns within the churches. Liberty had many meanings.

The MEC exploded in growth from fifteen thousand in 1784 to more than ten times that in 1810 to nearly five hundred thousand adherents by 1830 (S **p22**; H **577n2**). In the decade 1800–1810 Methodism almost tripled. By 1810 Methodists constituted 7.4 percent of the population in Maryland and 8.4 percent in Delaware. The great bulk of Methodists then, as previously, lived in New York and south; 125,540 of the (MEC) 171,751 total. Increasingly, however, Methodists moved outward from the middle Atlantic and upper south. In the competitive religious free-for-all westward, Methodists, in their various permutations, weaned America from its predominantly Calvinist colonial nursing and ethnically-linguistically-racially closed confessional systems. In so doing, Methodism defined and modeled a new denominational order—voluntaristic, expansionist, oriented to the expanding nation and evangelistically open. Methodists, preaching prevenient grace and Wesley's Arminianism, altered revivalism from expectant waiting to active, aggressive invitation.

Successive MEC General Conferences from 1792 to 1816 confronted issues posed by such growth and by authority and power questions in the still imperfect new constitutional order: a quadrennial General Conference with plenary authority but fluid membership, increasingly unavailable or incapacitated bishops charged with itinerating across the connection to preside and appoint, conferences composed only of traveling preachers called together annually, presiding elders with powers derived from the bishops, an array of other officers authorized to voice concerns only within quarterly conferences, and an active people (especially women) whose piety and practice energized the whole and whose prayer and praise made up their most effective mode of communicating.

UNITED BRETHREN AND EVANGELICAL ASSOCIATION

If gender vexed early Methodism, so did race and language. Separate German-speaking "Methodist" denominations emerged despite friendly relations across linguistic lines between leaders and several efforts at comity. The United Brethren (UBC) emerged first (S **1800b**; H **7–9**) and The Evangelical Association (EA) a little later (S **1807**; H **77–79**). As with The MEC, the UBC and EA conferences addressed opportunity and problem legislatively, exercised discipline over their membership, authorized evangelistic itineration, and resolved questions of power and authority. Pietist religious practice undergirded this evolution of polity.

Lacking the Wesleyan movement's crisis over orders and sacraments and not requiring a transatlantic transfer of authority, the UBC evolved more gradually out of Reformed and Mennonite contexts and continued that evolution slowly. Martin Boehm and William Otterbein were formally elected bishops in 1800. Not until 1813 were preachers ordained, when Otterbein, after Boehm's death and anticipating his own, consecrated William Newcomer and two others, with the assistance of a Methodist elder, William Ryland. Increasingly George Adam Geeting and Christian Newcomer, and later Andrew Zeller, assumed the mantle of leadership, the latter two to be elected bishops, Geeting to be a longtime secretary. An important stage in the emergence of the United Brethren as a distinct movement and disengagement from the German Reformed occurred in the 1800 gathering of the "United Ministers" (S **1800b**). The conferees agreed to meet annually; adopted a new name, *Vereinigten Bruderschaft zu Christo* (United Brethren in Christ); approved believer's as well as infant baptism; selected their two founders, Otterbein and Boehm, as *Eltesten* (bishops); and empowered them to appoint preachers to circuits *upon consultation with pastors and circuits.* They clustered circuits around three centers, later conferences: southeastern Pennsylvania, Maryland and northern Virginia, and the Miami River valley in Ohio.

The UBC took care to designate itself as *unparteiische* (interdenominational) and to emphasize that it was only a "society." By 1804, however, the Coetus began expulsion of UBC members—first of whom was George Geeting, whom Otterbein had brought into the Reformed ministry and who had identified himself with the United Ministers. The grounds? His "disorderly conduct," a veiled reference to *unrestrained emotional worship* at meetings he led in and about his Antietam, Maryland, church. The German Reformed wanted no such *strabbler* (strugglers, or foot stampers), *knierutscher* (knee sliders), and *springbungen* (holy rollers, literally jumpers).

Newcomer, a second-generation leader, played a particularly important stabilizing role within the UBC and also in unity explorations with both The MEC and the EA, as his journal indicates (S **1813c**). Newcomer related warmly to Bishops Francis Asbury and William McKendree, much as had Otterbein and Boehm earlier. His journal also attests the vibrant spirituality, much of it eucharistic, in and through which Newcomer exercised leadership. That spiritual grounding can be seen in the Rules adopted by the UBC in 1813 (S **1813a**), which expected from preachers a renewed heart and the pursuit of holiness as preconditions for membership. In turn, the preachers built the new church "by doctrine and life, by prayer and a godly walk." The UBC set forth similar expectations for society leaders, heads of families, and members.

The UBC kept protocols for discipline simple and scriptural, a source of continuing concern and critique from Asbury and the Methodists, who implored the UBC to adapt The MEC *Discipline* for UBC usage. With Asbury's encouragement, The MEC Philadelphia Conference had translated The MEC *Discipline* into German in 1807–8, but the UBC paid it little heed, leaving it to the EA to make such a formal adoption. UBC inaction on discipline finally stopped a series of negotiations with The MEC, carried on by the Baltimore Conference and formalized in letters between the two denominations from 1809 to 1814. Of concern to Methodists as well were UBC patterns of term episcopacy and less resolute itinerancy. By 1815 when the UBC gathered for its first General Conference, unity with The MEC was off the table (S **1800b, 1813c**). If the UBC adjusted its discipline less than did The MEC, it had given more attention to doctrinal formulation than its Wesleyan colleagues and continued to do so with further confessional refinements in 1815 and 1819 (S **pp 38–40**; compare S **1785b**). The denomination continued to reflect practices as well as doctrine out of its Mennonite and Reformed past. It elected bishops for term; kept centralized power lean; selected the presiding elders (district superintendents) through ballot and appointed pastors through a stationing committee, neither by episcopal appointment; structured class meetings loosely and as voluntary; maintained a single ordination to elder; and effectively located ministerial identity in the congregation, not conference.

Like the UBC, The EA developed gradually with no single transition crisis. Competing for German-speaking members with the UBC in Pennsylvania, Maryland, and Virginia, the EA, like its leader and first bishop, Jacob Albright, emerged out of and remained in close association with the Methodists. Though catechized Lutheran, Albright found a spiritual home after his conversion experience with the Methodists and in the early 1790s professed commitment to the discipline, order, practices, and doctrine of the Methodists (S **1791b, p108**). Licensed as an exhorter by the Methodists, Albright began preaching in 1796, itinerating through German-speaking communities. Insisting that salvation came through a renewed heart, not traditions, liturgies, and catechisms, he received ridicule from the Lutherans, Reformed, and Mennonites, and in 1797 expulsion by the Lutherans. Like his Methodist compatriots, he gathered converts into classes, held camp meetings, and raised up others to preach. Albright brought together class leaders in 1803 in the EA's first formal translocal assembly. That organizing conference recognized Albright as leader, ordained him, commissioned two other preachers as associates, and constituted itself as a society. The EA met in its first regular annual conference in 1807 (S **1807**), a gathering of five itinerant preachers, three local preachers, and twenty class leaders. The society adopted the name *Neuformirten Methodisten Conferenz* (Newly Formed Methodist Conference). It elected and ordained Albright as bishop and asked him to prepare a German translation of The MEC *Discipline* "for the instruction and edification of the societies" (S **1807**), and to appoint the preachers to their circuits. Albright licensed several preachers, selected George Miller to be his chief assistant, presided at the first Communion service, and began to baptize. Although he was determined to travel widely, Albright's health failed and he died the next year (1808).

From the start the EA entertained hopes for unity either with The MEC or with the UBC. Such explorations, including the possibility of becoming the German conference of The MEC, went nowhere with Asbury over the EA's persistent use of the German language and despite affinities. In 1814,

George Miller, aging heir-apparent to Albright, retired. John Dreisbach was elected presiding elder and given oversight over the whole association (twelve preachers in the one conference in eastern Pennsylvania). In 1816 Dreisbach convened the organizing General Conference, which sustained the commitment to a German-only ministry, approved expansion into Ohio and upstate New York, authorized negotiations with the UBC, rearranged and improved the *Discipline,* and authorized a new hymnal (S **1807, p154**). The General Conference also embraced a new name, *Evangelische Gemeinschaft* (Evangelical Association), the first American church body to adopt the term *"Evangelical"* in its name.

Although *The Book of Discipline* declared the new church to be an *episcopal* church, the General Conference did not elect a bishop. For the next twenty years, two presiding elders, Dreisbach and Henry Niebel, elected for two-year terms, led the EA. A publishing house for the new church opened in New Berlin, Pennsylvania, in 1817. Sunday schools for children were introduced in 1832, a denominational newspaper, *Der Christliche Botschäfter,* began publication in 1834, and a missionary society formed in 1838. Not until 1839 was the church's second bishop, John Seybert—a bachelor known for frugality and simplicity and a former Lutheran—elected and consecrated. The new bishop began an aggressive plan of church expansion westward to Ohio and Indiana, Michigan and Illinois, even Canada. In contrast to United Brethren, Evangelicals clung firmly to the German language well into the twentieth century.

ANNUAL CONFERENCES AND GENERAL CONFERENCE (MEC)

Initially The MEC bishops called or appointed conferences mindful of traveling difficulties. The number of such borderless annual conferences swelled to seventeen in 1792 and nineteen in 1793. The 1796 General Conference addressed that chaos by specifying and establishing geographical boundaries for six annual conferences. So ordered and defined, General Conference reasoned, annual conferences would each have a share of the seasoned itinerants, would be large enough to possess the dignity needed by "every religious synod," and would facilitate more effective deployment of the itinerants. In particular, it would permit the bishops to appoint married preachers more locally and the unmarried across the continent.

The expansion of Methodism westward quickly challenged that simplification. Patterns evident from the beginning continued. The Methodist people moved west—adherents, members, "mothers in Israel," class leaders, exhorters, local preachers. These lay Methodists found one another in a new settlement and began the organizing process. Such spontaneous starts nevertheless ran by the book—the *Discipline*—under the guidance of class leader and the nearest local preacher. Other class-forming patterns began as a traveling preacher heard of settlements beyond his present itinerant rounds and appointed preaching for himself and his junior "yokefellow" wherever he could find a willing household. Thus the boundary of Methodism moved with western settlements and often as the very first phase of sociopolitical community formation. New classes and preaching places, stressing a circuit's capacity, demanded additional preachers and circuits and eventually new conferences.

Anticipating that challenge, General Conference in 1796, even as it delineated annual conference boundaries, appended a proviso to its demarcation of the Western Conference empowering the bishops with the "authority to appoint other yearly conferences in the interval of the General Conference, if a sufficiency of new circuits be anywhere formed for that purpose." General Conference reiterated that proviso up to 1832 (H **578n15**). Annual conferences marched westward with overall American settlement. So after reducing the number of conferences in the interest of communication, efficiency, and fraternal authority, the preachers in General Conference authorized their increase as the church exploded west, north, and south. Six in 1796, seven in 1800, nine in 1812, eleven in 1816, twelve in 1820 along with three provisos, seventeen in 1824, twenty-two in 1832, and twenty-nine in 1836.

The 1796 General Conference had also limited membership in annual conferences to those in or to be received into full connection. It explained: "This regulation is made that our societies and congregations may be supplied with preaching during the conferences" (H **578n18**). By 1804, having drawn these geographical and demographic boundaries, The MEC came to understand that a preacher actually belonged to a specific conference. Individual conferences, once convened primarily as instruments of mission and ministry, thereafter became social and political units, within which preachers increasingly lived out their itinerant careers.

The establishment of conferences as sociopolitical units made their representation in General Conference critical. That perception dawned slowly as annual conferences stabilized, preachers began to identify themselves with their specific conference, and General Conference sat repeatedly in one locale. By convening regularly in Baltimore, welcoming first all conference members, then those in full connection and (after 1800) those who had traveled four years, General Conferences came to be numerically overwhelmed and dominated by the two nearby annual conferences, Baltimore and Philadelphia, from which preachers could more conveniently attend. In 1804 those two overwhelmed the other five conferences, seventy to forty-two. And in 1808, they sent sixty-three and the other five a total of sixty-six preachers.

To remedy the imbalance and overrepresentation of Baltimore and Philadelphia Conferences, Jesse Lee proposed in 1804 a principle of delegation. His motion failed but the concern did not abate. A memorial for equal conference representation made the rounds of the annual conferences and was endorsed by the four more distant (New York, South Carolina, New England, and Western), with Philadelphia, Baltimore, and Virginia not concurring. At the 1808 General Conference Bishop Asbury guided the body toward eventual compromise by establishing a committee of two persons from each conference. Out of this group, Joshua Soule, Ezekiel Cooper, and Philip Bruce were commissioned to draft plans for a delegated General Conference. Soule and Cooper produced different visions. Cooper advocated a decentralized conference order, essentially that which pertains today, with a bishop for each conference, or failing that, the election of presiding elders. Soule proposed a delegated conference and explicitly limited General Conference's legislative power in several crucial areas, among them any alteration of the plan of an "itinerant general superintendency" or modification of "our present existing and established standards of doctrine." Soule's draft, with this set of "Restrictive Rules" at its heart, came eventually to be regarded as the constitution of the church (S **1808**), but it passed only after considerable debate and testing of alternatives. Cooper pressed for the election of presiding elders, an effective delimitation of the power and authority of bishops and an issue that would not go away. Lee sought delegation through seniority rather than election, a proposal brought into compromise legislation.

From their introduction the Restrictive Rules were recognized as a critical turn in the denomination's history. Soule's effort at precision left several matters ambiguous. What were the standards of doctrine? Were the Articles of Religion the intended reference as the manuscript minutes of General Conference seem to indicate or the fuller array of Wesleyan transmissions, *Sermons and Notes upon the New Testament* in particular (H **578n23**)? Who would judge the constitutionality of General Conference actions? Was it the arbiter of its own decisions? Did plenary authority lodge now in General Conference in its "full powers to make rules and regulations" or remain in the whole body of preachers? And by making bishops presiding officers and no longer members of General Conference, had the church subjected the former to the latter? How would the bishops provide guidance on a connectional level?

McKendree, the first American-born to be elected bishop, found new ways to exercise the episcopal teaching and leadership role through committees, with cabinets of presiding elders, and by setting conference agendas. Dramatically in the 1812 General Conference, and apparently without advance notice to Asbury, McKendree delivered an agenda-outlining address, setting the precedent for the Episcopal Address that thereafter began the serious work of the conference (S **1812a**). Unlike Whatcoat, who had been willing to function in an assisting role, McKendree sought collegiality and parity, expecting to have a say on appointments and initiating a genuine sharing of presidential roles by dividing the conferences.

SPIRITUALITY: IN THE HOME AND IN CAMP MEETINGS

Camp meeting origins and authorship have been and will remain contested, in part because similar multiday preaching, sacramental, and revivalistic events—including the Methodist quarterly conferences and Pennsylvania German large meetings—had long occurred in Western Christianity. Camp meeting definition emerged with the well-reported Presbyterian-initiated, multidenominational encampments in the summers of 1800 and 1801 at Cane Ridge, Kentucky. McKendree, then presiding elder of the Kentucky district, recognized immediately the value of the camp meeting. So did Bishop Asbury who, along with a number of Methodist leaders, communicated the revivalistic import of camp meetings to Bishop Coke and through the (British) *Methodist Magazine* (H **83**; **579n28**) to the Methodist world. By late 1802, Asbury had turned from observer and reporter to promoter. He directed Methodist leaders to establish camp meetings in connection with annual conferences.

More typically, Methodists structured camp meetings in relation not to annual conferences but to the staple of local Methodist religious life, quarterly meetings. They had become, as noted already, two-day, multifunction, crowd-gathering religious festivals. The quarterly meetings were camp meetings without the tents or brush arbors. Once the camp meeting emerged and had the church's blessing, routinely and for several decades, quarterly conferences across the whole church voted to hold one of their warm-weather sessions as a camp meeting, as did Smithfield (S **1811b**). Literally exploding across the North American landscape, camp meetings became a hugely successful engine of Methodist growth and a highly familiar signature of its organizational life. Preachers and presiding elders spent a considerable portion of their time, particularly in the summer, going to or conducting camp meetings. Camp meetings blossomed as much in the East where they put increasingly urbanized Methodism in touch with its fervid past, as in the frontier where they served well to command the attention and to create the community around the Methodist message and program requisite for individual transformation and corporate formation.

Jesse Lee, the first historian of American Methodism, who had traced revivals in relation to conference and quarterly conference meetings, after 1802 narrated the Methodist story as a series of camp meetings. And as he concluded his history in 1809, he did so in a short overview of the camp meeting, its staging, rules, layout, and rhythms, noting that this signature practice had "never been authorized by the Methodists, either at their general or annual conferences" (H **579n34**). Camp meetings could be celebrated for their redemptive love and experienced assurance, as Fanny Lewis did in a letter about one near Baltimore in 1803 (S **1803**). But others reacted negatively to emotionalism and display (crying, shouting, jerking, falling) and to the crowds of disorderly or disruptive persons who congregated around or outside. Methodists found it necessary to order them carefully and also to defend them against critics within and without, as did John Totten in some fifty pages of closely set type (S **1810b**).

Methodist preachers ran conferences and camp meetings, but Methodism as a whole ran predominantly in the home and as a movement of and for women whose spiritual agency was pervasive, if not always prominent (H **579nn36–38**). Indeed, as American Methodism grew in numbers and stabilized itself, as early as the 1790s in New York, a decade later elsewhere, women lost places in the offices of the church, offices to which Wesley had admitted them, most notably as class leaders. The importance of class meetings was underscored by Bishops Coke and Asbury in their commentary on the *Discipline* (S **1798**). "Christian experience," they insisted, and particularly its regular, weekly, corporate expression in class meetings constituted "the pillars of our work." The rhythms of these basic, membership aspects of Methodist life can be well seen in the schematization of class meeting times, composition, and leadership for John Street Church, New York City (S **1802**).

A number of women found ways to evade the restrictive conventions and to exercise leadership, even preaching roles. So, for instance, Fanny Newell experienced a call to preach (S **1809**), which she exercised by itinerating with her preacher husband in the years after 1818 on the Maine frontiers of Methodism. Similarly, Jarena Lee, converted under Richard Allen and married in 1811 to a preacher, Joseph Lee, experienced a call to preach that Allen initially discounted but eventually, as bishop of the African Methodist Episcopal Church (AME), embraced (S **1811a**).

The major legislative battles for women's official leadership lay decades ahead. In early nineteenth-century Methodism, the primary modality of Methodist witness, overall and for women, was through lives that testified to gospel order and to steady progress toward loving, compassionate holiness. Here polity, power, and privilege constituted no advantage, indeed, a probable disadvantage. In addition, Methodism functioned day to day, in women's sphere, in homes, on a domestic level. Classes met in homes and shops, even in New York, Baltimore, and Philadelphia where Methodism boasted church buildings that accommodated some of the meetings (S **1802**). Male itinerants entered the women's sphere and interacted predominately with women, thus blurring gender lines and boundaries of early nineteenth-century America in a way that led to great ridicule and social ostracization. Outside these cities, Methodist buildings and preaching places were the houses of their adherents and friends. And membership effectively also had a domestic character in that members belonged through their classes. Their good standing, still registered by ticket from the class leader, opened up participation on larger levels. Even the preachers were, in a sense, domesticated. As they traveled around the circuit, they stayed with families or widows, such preacher homes a centerpiece of the itinerant plan in established circuits and a project to be worked on in frontier areas.

Within a Methodism so constituted day to day on a domestic level, women exercised a variety of roles, despite, perhaps because of, the constraints on their access to office. Authorizing the informal roles were spirituality, Christlike love, and the blessing of holiness. And American Methodists, like their British counterparts, warranted and celebrated this authorization from above by publishing women's diaries, pious lives, conversion and sanctification accounts, and funeral sermons. The first of these to appear from the American Methodist press was Elizabeth Singer Rowe's *Devout Exercises of the Heart* (S **1791c**). With Wesley's encouragement and blessing, and through multiple printings on both sides of the Atlantic, the spiritual journals and letters of Hester Ann Rogers offered a model of piety for Methodist women and spiritual guidance for both women and men in the early Methodist societies. With their authority secured by the Holy Spirit, women found ample places to exhibit and vocalize their grasp of the Christian and Methodist message—and in a sense their call. In class meetings, in love feasts, with preachers around the table, with their husbands and children, on camp-meeting occasions, women interceded in prayer and praise and hymn and testimony for the movement, its members, and its leaders. Methodists claimed the importance and recognized the great variety of these informal roles with an authorizing, frequently used, biblical title, "mother in Israel" (S **1812b**). On the bedrock of spiritual influence, Methodists would create significant structures of nurture, mission, social transformation, and care.

Domesticity, spontaneity, and informality proved the rule in early Methodist spirituality and worship. One casualty of such informal piety was the liturgies and other formal worship provisions sent over in 1784 by Wesley (*The Sunday Service*). Lee reported that initially societies in "the large towns, and in some country places" read the Sunday Service and morning prayers (S **1784b** for January 22–February 6). However, he continued, after "a few years the prayer book was laid aside, and has never been used since in public worship." The preachers, he explained, were "fully satisfied that they could pray better, and with more devotion with their eyes shut, than they could with their eyes open" (H **573n12**). Unfortunately, when the Lees shut their eyes, they rather lost sight of much of what was happening in Methodism, including particularly what the women did through prayer and in sensitive areas like family and race relations.

48

THE EARLY MEC AND RACISM

By 1810, Black Methodists constituted roughly half the membership in South Carolina, more than 40 percent in Maryland, and nearly 40 percent in Delaware. In the latter two states those numbers included both free and slave, and the church had played no small part in the fight against slavery. Methodism had committed itself constitutionally, legislatively, and programmatically to antislavery. Methodists conveyed their resolve in their preaching and on the circuit life. They also took public stands. Ezekiel Cooper, an effective and articulate leader, later to be the denomination's Book Agent and, in effect, the church's official spokesperson, carried on a newspaper campaign for manumission in the *Maryland Gazette,* the *Maryland Journal,* and the *Virginia Gazette* in the early 1790s. O'Kelly witnessed against slavery in publication and through his movement. His stance and his (Republican Methodist) schism drained antislavery numbers and resolve from the movement as a whole.

Increasingly Methodism found itself facing greater resistance and opposition to its commitment from within and beyond its own ranks, the consequence of its growth and evangelistic outreach in slaveholding areas and of the waning of the societal antislavery sentiments bred during the Revolutionary epoch. Even where the antislavery commitment remained strong, Methodists found it extraordinarily difficult to translate idealism into practice, preachment into inclusive fellowship, and antislavery into interracial community. So segregated classes, virtually from the start, continued to evolve toward segregated ecclesial structure, sometimes with White leadership support, often in the face of White efforts at control, as AME narratives indicate (S **1816**), Richard Allen's biography charts (S **1792b**), and letters to Bishop Asbury attest. In 1794 Bethel Church, Philadelphia, issued a "Public Statement" of some 2,200 words explaining why its members needed separate accommodations.

Recognizing the emerging Black leadership (and the emerging segregated system), the General Conference of 1800 empowered bishops to ordain Black local deacons, though, as Jesse Lee indicated, deciding not to include that provision in the *Discipline.* Richard Allen (Philadelphia) and Daniel Coker (Baltimore) were among those first ordained. Functioning restively under White elders, the Black leaders and congregations pressed for full ordination and conference membership, providing ecclesial legitimacy and standing (H **579nn43–44**). They also spoke out publicly against slavery, as did Daniel

49

Coker (S **1810a**), and informally to bishops and conferences on their decid-edly second-class treatment by fellow Methodists.

The MEC under Asbury's leadership, though continuing to voice op-position to slavery, gradually retreated, searching for enforceable standards as southern commitment to the slave system strengthened and southern legislatures voted to prohibit manumission. The 1800 General Conference, for instance, sustained the Wesleyan witness in its pastoral letter by implor-ing a state-by-state antislavery petition to legislatures (S **1800a**), an item publicly burned in Charleston. Drafted by three clergy (Ezekiel Cooper, William McKendree, and Jesse Lee), "agreed to" by the conference, and signed by the three bishops—Asbury, Coke, and Whatcoat—the address was published in broadside format and widely distributed. Asbury had sec-ond thoughts about the wisdom of such tough talk. Six months after it was issued, he wrote in his journal: "Nothing could so effectually alarm and arm the criticism of South Carolina against the Methodists as the *Address of the General Conference*" (H **580n47**). The 1804 General Conference, conced-ing that the church's official stance caused offense in the South, published a version of the *Discipline* without the section on slavery. It made that self-censorship a policy in 1808. That General Conference also authorized "each annual conference to form their own regulations relative to buying and selling slaves." By 1816, General Conference conceded that "little can be done to abolish a practice so contrary to the principles of moral justice" and was "sorry to say that the evil appears to be past remedy." General Confer-ence resolved to adjust *Discipline*-limiting prohibition against slavehold-ers' holding office to states permitting emancipation (H **580nn48–49**). By that time, some Black Methodists decided that The MEC would simply not accommodate their needs and gathered to form the AME (S **1816**; H **91–101**). For some, Methodism's biracialism died in 1816.

A NEW DAY DAWNS

Asbury died en route to the 1816 General Conference, Coke a year ear-lier on board a ship in the Indian Ocean, and Lee in an 1816 camp meeting in Maryland. In their different ways they had modeled and enforced an itin-erant, missional form of ministry that they insisted was the primitive, apos-tolic, New Testament form. So Asbury reiterated in his several valedictories

(S **1813b**). While sitting, General Conference had Asbury's remains brought to Baltimore and interred with sermonic and ceremonial honor in the new Eutaw Street Church where it was meeting. General Conference elected Enoch George and Robert Richford Roberts to the episcopacy, entertained again the question of electing presiding elders, raised preachers' salaries to $100, condemned pew rental as a funding device, and worried over other Methodist slippage on discipline, dress, sacramental practice, and doctrine. Electing Joshua Soule as Book Editor, General Conference authorized, as had the 1812 Conference, the publication of a magazine. It appeared two years later. Variously titled, the *Methodist Magazine* was to live on for almost two centuries in print format. Among its early important communications was notice of the April 1819 formation of the Methodist Missionary Society, with the Women's Auxiliary to be constituted three months later. Another institution also continuing to the present, the Course of Study, the conference established with the directive to the bishops to prescribe a reading regimen for candidates for the ministry. Its episcopal leadership now all American-born and with new institutions in formation, The MEC looked forward to a new day.

CHAPTER III

PRINT, NURTURE, MISSIONS:
1816–50s

In treating the momentous year 1816, Nathan Bangs, Methodism's second major historian (after Lee), devoted almost thirty pages to an Asbury eulogy. After long, detailed encomium, Bangs noted that even "the sun has its spots" and ventured "with great deference" two errors in the bishop's administration, two infrastructural matters on which Asbury failed to encourage Methodist development or ensure its prosperity. The first had to do with "learning and a learned ministry," education and educational institutions, Methodism's intellectual self-promotion, and the church's place in and place for culture, science, knowledge, and literature. The second had to do with support for ministry, ministers, and ministerial families, and implicitly the great Asburian taboo, married itinerants. In the judgment of Bangs, Asbury mistakenly had kept Methodism "aloof from the world," discouraging education so as to protect piety and discouraging property (churches and parsonages) so as to safeguard itinerancy. Such concerns recur through Bangs's narrative and constituted his life's work (H **583nn1–3**).

WHICH WESLEY TO EMULATE?

Bangs's counsel and leadership guided the church, in the eyes of some contemporaries and some recent interpreters, toward softening of discipline, embrace of the world, compromise of fundamental Wesleyan practices and precepts, abandonment of the evangelistic mission to society's marginalized, and loss of Methodism's prophetic nerve. Such reactions informed pre–Civil

53

War divisions (AMEC, AMEZC, MPC, WMC, MEC-MECS, FMC), prompted various related reform efforts, and produced enduring ethical quandaries over status, authority, class, gender, race, and above all, slavery. The reformers appealed to the social holiness and innovating Wesley of field preaching and itinerancy, of General Rules, of social criticism, of antislavery. The next chapter, which covers the same period as this one, explores these political and polity developments, the reforming impulses, Methodism's countercultural edge, its appeals to revivalistic piety, its internal divisions and ensuing conflict, and its experience of radical change and discontinuity.

This chapter charts Methodism's attention to nurture, to order in congregational worship and church life, to tradition, to institutions—in short, to recovery of the churchly Wesley, Wesley as the movement's theological tutor—the Wesley of Oxford, of Kingswood, of the *Arminian Magazine,* of the *Christian Library,* of the sacraments, and of conference. These Bangs-supported initiatives reflected Methodist aspirations for respectability, progress, recognition, and refinement. Led by upwardly mobile preachers and laity in Methodism's station churches (towns and cities, South and North), the quest for order effected the denomination's evolution from side street to main street (S **pp22–23**) and toward inclusion in the Protestant establishment. The stories of both chapters—of growing societal influence and of prophetic witness—need sympathetic portrayal. The dialectic between the impulses described in these two chapters continued and continues to shape American Methodism. Institutionalization and prophetic critique thereof—the interaction in American Methodist life of the churchly and the revivalistic Wesley—subtly modulated the movement's dynamic Pietism into various scripted practices.

Connecticut-born Bangs led the recovery of the Oxford Wesley. After appointments in upper Canada, Quebec, and New York, Bangs served twice as presiding elder, before being selected Book Agent in 1820. The New York Conference elected him secretary in 1811, sent him repeatedly to General Conference, and called on him for tasks that required study or statement. He was perhaps Methodism's most visible figure between the death of Bishop Francis Asbury and the Civil War leader Bishop Matthew Simpson.

Elected to the office of Book Agent, he assumed responsibility for the publishing enterprise of the church, undertook the editing of the newly established *Methodist Magazine,* exercised the leading role creating the weekly *Christian Advocate,* championed important causes like missions and education—indeed crafted their warranting, authorizing, and constituting documents—and assumed authority to interpret signal Methodist events and developments. His editor's posts gave Bangs a connection-wide and unequaled voice. The entire church read his word and that later of other *Advocate* and magazine editors. The editor's voice proved more available, regularized, permanent, uniform, and influential than anyone else's in the church, including that of the itinerating bishops (McKendree, George, Roberts, and successors). (As an indication of the importance of Methodist media, note the following: S **1815, 1821b, 1827a, 1829, 1830b, 1834, 1841a, 1841b, 1842a.**) Methodist publishing succeeded in creating a textually defined national Wesleyan community, putting into hands and homes the Methodist witness in verse, in narrative, in doctrine, in discipline. Texts transmitted, texts inculcated, texts converted, texts sustained, texts modeled, texts bonded, texts ritualized, texts disciplined, and texts set boundaries.

APOLOGETICS AND THE COURSE OF STUDY

Even before assuming the editorial office, Bangs had established himself as Methodist spokesperson with apologetic works that appeared in 1815, 1816, 1817, and 1820: *The Errors of Hopkinsianism Detected and Refuted, The Reformer Reformed, An Examination of the Doctrine of Predestination,* and *A Vindication of Methodist Episcopacy.* These books, along with others, like Asa Shinn's *An Essay on the Plan of Salvation* of 1813, defended Wesleyan theology and Methodist ministry, orders, and episcopacy against the church's most powerful critics. In the first three, Bangs responded to Calvinists who derided its thought and the last to Episcopalians who questioned its ecclesial legitimacy.

Neither the challenges to Wesleyan Arminian theology and Methodist orders nor Methodist responses were new. Encounters and exchanges, particularly with Calvinists (Congregationalists and Presbyterians), recur through the journals of itinerants. However, for formal apologetics American Methodism had depended upon and would continue to privilege the British defense of the faith, preeminently, of course, Wesley's writings, the *Sermons* and *Notes,* which constituted official standards, and the *Works* more generally, which were sold by Methodist preachers both as imported items and under

American imprint. American Methodists continued in provincial dependence upon British theology throughout the nineteenth century. That dependence was both popular and official.

British works constituted the theological fare in the "Course of Study," recommended by Bangs on behalf of a committee, authorized by the 1816 General Conference, and detailed in conference journals (the Baltimore Conference did so at its next meeting). This first venture in more formalized preparation for ministry, a prescribed reading list, included Wesley's *Sermons* and *Notes,* John Fletcher's four volumes of *Checks to Anti-nomianism,* Joseph Benson's *Sermons on Various Occasions,* and Thomas Coke's six-volume *Commentary on the Holy Bible.* The Course of Study, with its standardized theological fare and occasional updates, would shape Methodist belief and practice for more than a century.

In confronting the Calvinists, Bangs picked up where Fletcher left off. With his anti-Calvinist works, particularly *The Errors of Hopkinsianism Detected and Refuted* and *The Reformer Reformed,* Bangs made the case for hallmark Methodist doctrines of prevenient grace, human responsibility and freedom, holiness, and moral agency against Samuel Hopkins and other Calvinists who represented the premier American theological legacy, that of Jonathan Edwards. He produced these two works with the formal approval of the New York Conference. His theological statements and the normative works on the Course of Study, thereafter obligatory for those entering ministry, addressed the concerns raised by the Committee of Safety at the 1816 General Conference: "[T]hat, in some parts of the connexion, doctrines contrary to our established articles of faith, and of dangerous tendency, have made their appearance among us, especially the ancient doctrines of *Arianism, Socinianism* and *Pelagianism*" (H **584n16**). Later apologists would defend the denomination against critics of its polity as well as detractors of its doctrine (Episcopalians and Baptists as well as Presbyterians and Congregationalists).

BOOK AGENTS

Bangs assumed the role of Book Agent in 1820, accountable to General Conference, which had authorized new publications, to the New York Conference, and to a local oversight committee. Connectional oversight of the Book Concern had presented a challenge to Methodism from the start.

The very first conference, that of 1773, had upbraided Robert Williams for printing Wesley's books on his own and stipulated conference and Wesley's approval for publishing (S **1773**). The council (under Asbury) had claimed oversight of publishing and was small enough to act effectively.

Before and after the two years of the council, a committee advised John Dickins, the church's first Book Agent, with Asbury always playing an active advising role. But conference and then General Conference reserved to itself the right to determine what would be published in the church's name. In 1796, General Conference delegated some oversight to Philadelphia, then the site of Dickins's work. Ezekiel Cooper became book agent in 1798 when Dickins died. By 1809, the *Minutes* listed John Wilson and Daniel Hitt as book agents first under "New York Conference."

Under Bangs's predecessors, the Methodist Book Concern had attempted to be an American voice. Agents printed the *Minutes* and *Disciplines*, put out official American *Hymnbooks* (S **p29**), which sold some ten thousand annually, issued the few apologetic works, and twice ventured a magazine, the *Arminian Magazine* (1789–90) and the *Methodist Magazine* (1797–98). However, for much of the magazines' content and for much of their fairly considerable publication lists, agents reprinted British works. The authoritative works (Wesley, Coke, Fletcher, Benson, Clarke), inspirational life stories, tracts, and other cheap items remained overwhelmingly British.

The sales system (also on the British model) effectively distributed Methodist literature throughout the connection, capable of radiating an American voice, could it be sounded. The system, simple but elegant, made every preacher a traveling salesman, put inventory in the itinerants' saddlebags, and gave these underpaid circuit riders high incentive (namely, commissions) to push the products. General Conference authorized the practice in 1800, permitting 18 to 25 percent to be divided between regional distributor (presiding elder) and traveling salesman (preacher). In 1812 General Conference regularized preachers' take as 18 percent. Book money augmented, sometimes rivaled, the meager salaries (quarterage) paid the preachers. The same General Conference and that of 1816 directed that the book agents recommence a magazine.

In 1818 at General Conference's behest, Joshua Soule launched the *Methodist Magazine (MQR)*, authorized as the *Methodist Missionary Magazine* and variously titled thereafter (*Methodist Magazine and Quarterly Review, Methodist Quarterly Review, Methodist Review, Religion in Life, Quarterly Review*, now again *Methodist Review*), a venture that the church sustained for almost two centuries as a print serial and now continues electronically. Soule's successor, Bangs, gave American Methodism its national voice (his voice).

Bangs transformed what had been essentially a distributing operation for British reprints and official denominational publications (*Minutes, Disciplines, Hymnbooks*) into a full-fledged publishing house capable of its own printing and binding. He expanded the serious and popular adult fare, entered the tract market, established Sunday school literature, added serials for children and youth to a diet previously limited to Wesley's *Catechism*, and effectively Americanized the Book Concern. He built, of course, on the work of his predecessors and contended from the start with regional competition that shared the innovative and Americanizing task. The greatest achievement of the Bangs years, for instance, the launching of what would be the newspaper with the widest national readership, the *Christian Advocate,* capitalized on earlier efforts (H **108–9**). The immediate and national success of the *Christian Advocate*—five thousand copies of the first issue, twenty-five thousand subscribers in two years—made it a vital authoritative Methodist voice and the most widely distributed periodical in the world. Its importance ironically derived in part from continuing competition with regional and reforming impulses (in particular, newspapers serving the reformers' cause in the 1820s–1830s, the topic of the following chapter). The *Christian Advocate* gained importance as it tilted against the reformers and critics, coordinating on a weekly basis the denomination's response to criticism and dissent.

A PRINT CHURCH

Within only a couple of years of the founding of the *Advocate,* annual conferences pressed for their own papers. General Conference responded by growing a branch of the Book Concern in Cincinnati, established as a distributing center, into a parallel operation and authorized the *Western Christian Advocate,* begun in 1834. It quickly outstripped "every religious and secular paper in the region by garnering 14,000 subscribers by 1840 and twice that number by 1860." By 1840 the number of officially recognized *Advocates* had grown to six, seven if the count includes the reformers' paper, by then voice of a distinct denomination, The Methodist Protestant Church, *Mutual Rights and Methodist Protestant.* MEC-sanctioned papers by then appeared from

New York, Cincinnati, Nashville, Pittsburgh, Richmond, and Charleston. And *Zion's Herald* had reappeared under the aegis of the New England Conference alone. Methodist papers competed with one another, with Baptist and other denominational voices, and with the secular press. They covered national and world events, scientific developments, medical remedies, farming information, obituaries, and everything Wesleyan, in short, anything and everything that would appeal to Methodists as citizens and saints and sustaining a connection-wide textual community.

The *Advocates* constituted but one aspect of the Book Concern's advance into popular literature. It became as well the engine for the church's evangelistic and missionary enterprise and for its dramatic expansion into popular nurture and family care. Methodism started with the adults, producing cheap tracts for the Methodist Tract Society, formed in 1817, then in 1823 a monthly, the *Youth's Instructor and Guardian,* and in 1827 Sunday school materials (explored below in the section on the Sunday school).

With religious literature for all ages and with the creation of a Methodist Bible Society in the mid-1820s, the church disengaged itself from the Calvinist-dominated Protestant establishment or "Evangelical United Front," the interlocking directorate of supposedly interdenominational missionary, tract, Bible, and reform societies. For the next four decades, essentially until the crisis of civil war stimulated Protestant cooperation in separate northern and southern societies, Methodists would build a Christian America in parallel with but independent of other denominations. In that missionary campaign, Methodist literature figured prominently.

The Book Concern (New York) burned in 1836, consuming critical records and important manuscripts, including the journal of Francis Asbury. That was not the only fire that this literary-cultural advance faced. By that point, a few "croakers" complained of the passing of Methodism's fervid, wild-eyed, loud-voiced, slain-in-the-spirit Asburian age. Sometimes they did so in the pulpit, through conference "semi-centennial sermons." Sometimes they "croaked" through the pages of magazines or *Advocates.* They touted nature, "the brush college" ministry, countering the Nathan Bangses in the east and the Martin Ruters in the west who had raised the banner of nurture. Nature would continue to receive its due. No camp meeting or revival would, it seems, go unnoticed by the *Advocates.* However, by 1840, the west itself would lead the denomination in cultural, educational, missional, and theological experiments. The Cincinnati Book Concern launched two important new serials for the church, a monthly *Ladies' Repository* (S **1841b, 1842a, 1872b**), the first Methodist paper to be entirely reproduced on the Web, and *Der Christliche Apologete* edited by William Nast. The one recognized the serious religious, educational, and cultural interests and capacities of Methodist women. The other translated Methodist idiom into German and, perhaps as important, mediated German theological advances into Methodist conversations.

Paralleling The MEC's German publication efforts were those of the UBC and EA, their printing ventures helping the churches negotiate into an English-language society. As with The MEC, the UBC began simply, publishing hymnbooks (in 1808) and printing the *Disciplines* (in 1815), putting the latter into English as early as 1817. Its first periodical, the *Union Messenger*, appeared through the initiative in 1834 of an individual, William Rhinehart of Virginia, stimulating his appointment that same year to head a publishing house. He immediately launched the UBC's paper, an English-language biweekly, the *Religious Telescope*, which continued until merged with the *Evangelical Messenger* in 1946. Other publications, including a history of the denomination followed (Henry Spayth's *History of the Church of the United Brethren in Christ*, 1850). For The Evangelical Association, John Dreisbach, effective successor to the denomination's founder, played the key publishing roles. With Albright's death in 1808 and the ill health of other key leaders, Dreisbach was made an elder, became conference secretary, was elected the church's first presiding elder (1814), and presided over annual conferences and the 1816 General Conference (S **1807**). Bilingual and the object of several overtures from Asbury and The MEC, Dreisbach published a catechism in 1809, several German hymnbooks, and in 1815 a corrected and enlarged *Discipline*. A successor as head of publications, W. W. Orwig, edited the EA's paper, *Der Christliche Botschäfter*, from 1837 to 1843. He also published the church's first history and was elected its third bishop. As with Bangs, these editors exercised the teaching office. The same can be said of leadership through publishing for the Methodist Protestants, the Wesleyans, The MECS, and the Free Methodists to which we turn in the next chapter. Methodism's print revolution was in full swing. Bangs, his counterparts, and his successors had created media for nurture on a geographic and demographic scale that the world had never known.

With its age-, purpose-, and taste-differentiated literary fare, with regionally based production and strategy centers, and with its incredible, nationally deployed energetic and motivated workforce of itinerant preachers and colporteurs (book peddlers), Methodism (in competition with other denominations that aspired to similar effectiveness) constituted itself a great national school and committed itself to bringing literacy to the masses. Before the era of the public school, preachers and Sunday school teachers "shouldered the principal burden of schooling." Especially in the South and West, "churches were schools and church people were schoolmasters and mistresses for a long stretch of the nineteenth century" (H **585n28**). And Sunday school libraries were the first public libraries.

PARSONAGES AND PASTORING

Nathan Bangs championed housing—housing for worship and housing for preachers. This included houses of worship and parsonages he thought key to an effective Methodist ministry on a local level and to the retention within the traveling order of the best and brightest. Celebrating a ministry of pastoral presence, Bangs urged Methodists to occupy cities, towns, and villages and to provide there its full missional repertoire—prayer meetings, classes, mission and tract societies, Sunday schools, literature, regular Sabbath worship, and sacraments. "It had been long evident to many of our ministers and people," he insisted, "that for the want of having a preacher stationed in all important places, we had lost much of the fruits of our labor." Methodist itinerants, Bangs believed, converted in revival or camp meeting only to lose the converts to denominations with a settled ministry and adequate houses for worship.

Because of inadequate houses, Methodism lost its ministry as well. The "numerous locations" of which Asbury complained owed to "the want of parsonages for the accommodation of preachers' families." Bangs entered the diagnosis and complaint as he looked back to the 1810s and exulted in the progress as he wrote of the 1830s (H **585nn29–30**). Even frontier conferences, like Mississippi, joined Bangs in advocating parsonages "on all the circuits and stations" (S **1827a**). Mary Orne Tucker in "A Pioneer Preacher's Wife" made a central motif of her autobiography the hardships of married ministers lacking parsonages (S **1838**). The 1856 General Conference (MEC) directed conferences to report on the number and value of church buildings and parsonages. An analysis in 1858 revealed that the northern church boasted 2,174 parsonages for the 5,365 traveling preachers. Perhaps surprisingly, the progress had been slower in some of the larger, older, wealthier conferences, like Baltimore (one-third) and Philadelphia (one-fourth) than in the newer conferences (H **585n33**).

More adequate buildings and a more stable and settled ministry gradually came to deliver the pastoring and nurturing that Bangs advocated, but a pastoral-style ministry posed other issues for the system. One that had been and would be perennially raised had to do with the nature and requirements of itinerancy. In 1832 General Conference determined that ministry could be too "present" and stable, complaining of the "evil of no small magnitude" of "the same preachers to be continued from year to year in town and city stations." The bishops returned to another dimension of that theme twelve years later in their 1844 address to General Conference, laying blame on preachers as well as congregations, complaining of preachers "with local views, and habits, and interests," and reducing the "itinerant system" to "the removal of the preachers once in two years from one station to another" (H **585nn34–35**).

Stationed pastors—appointed to a charge with a single congregation or society and therefore present in a community 24-7, not simply stopping by every two, four, or six weeks—took on more and more of the nurturing, "local" functions once the prerogative of the class leader. Stations emerged gradually and naturally in small towns and villages as individual societies grew large enough to support a preacher's salary. The urban circuits (S **p24**) in locales where Methodism had prospered and acquired multiple church buildings (Baltimore, New York, Philadelphia, Cincinnati) required more of a deliberate break in policy, as occurred in 1838 when, in New York City, John Street, Bedford Street, Duane Street, and Green Street separated.

Stationed preachers and preachers' wives usurped roles ascribed by *Discipline* to the class leaders. While class leaders struggled to find time for their duties, preachers and wives dedicated their entire lives to the cause. Preachers' wives (preachers marrying), discouraged by precept and practice in the early nineteenth century, became in the decades before the Civil War regular, indeed esteemed, resource persons for local church leadership (S **1838**). In station appointments, the preacher's wife evolved into a vital helpmate in ministry, increasingly an essential congregational leader, and a vocation on its own. Communities came to expect the preacher's wife to exercise a ministry, especially among other women and with the children—in teaching, in visiting, in comforting the ill and bereaved, in witnessing, in heading missionary societies, in modeling family piety, in interpreting her husband (to women and other preachers), in supporting the ministry, in negotiating the frequent moves, in short, in functioning as a sub-minister.

The class meeting's function in discipline, spiritual formation, and nurture increasingly devolved onto preacher and preacher's wife and onto the lay leadership of the missionary and tract societies and the Sunday school. Educational buildings lay ahead, but already in the 1830s and 1840s Methodists began building larger, main-street facilities, structures with two rooms and eventually two stories, plants suitable for meeting and teaching (S **p23**). Reflexively, Methodists meeting for the missionary cause or as Sunday school teachers conducted their gathering with prayers, hymns, testimony, and exhortation—offering an alternative small-group experience in the style of the class meeting. And while a missionary society (treated below) lacked the explicit disciplining oversight and the disciplinary charge of the class, it compensated with far more energizing responsibilities. It had a purpose, a cause, an explicit mandate from Jesus himself, and a role in bringing in Christ's millennial reign. Its purposes—global, even transcendent—looked beyond the group to the children, the unconverted, and the heathen. And particularly for the women, the missionary society Sunday school opened a variety of new leadership roles. These organizations had a great cause; their own heroines, the Mary Masons in home missions and the Ann Wilkinses in foreign (S **1842c**); reasons to network, to write, and to speak; and media with which to broadcast their efforts, the *Advocates,* and, after 1841, the *Ladies' Repository* (S **1841b**). Methodists have spilled much ink, from the late 1820s to the present, over the "decline" of the class meeting (S **1827a, 1841a**), often failing to notice that they "declined," in no small measure, because other structures and instrumentalities replaced some of their essential functions.

SUNDAY WORSHIP, THE SUNDAY SCHOOL, AND THE SUNDAY SCHOOL UNION

The hymnal, along with the Bible and the *Discipline,* were said to be the circuit rider's library, and the hymnbook, the guide to a member's spiritual pilgrimage. Hymnbooks shaped Methodist life together in class meetings and in corporate worship, early guidance for which specified singing, prayer, Scripture-reading, and preaching. The Methodist movements consequently kept hymnbooks in print. The MEC's *Pocket Hymn Book,* which guided home devotions, underwent several editions from its first appearance in 1785, including a supplement issued under Asbury's direction in 1808. That same year, the UBC published a second German-language hymnbook. And in 1810 the EA published the first of its several in German, its first in English appearing in 1835 some ten years later than a comparable effort by the UBC (S **pp29–30**).

Keeping Methodists singing their own hymns continued to be a challenge, even more than it had been for the Wesleys, as the lusty tunes and refrains from camp meetings made their way into regular worship (S **p35**). The 1820 MEC General Conference authorized a new hymnbook and a tune book as well. The next General Conference, that of 1824, finding considerable irregularity in Methodist worship, sacramental practice, and pastoral duties, resolved that preachers follow the order of worship prescribed in the *Discipline,* use the service prescribed for sacraments and burial, adhere to the directions for singing, employ the apostolic benediction and the Lord's Prayer uniformly in worship, and encourage the latter for private and family devotions. The delegates also instructed "superintending preachers . . . to lay out their work that there may be sufficient time allowed each preacher for the faithful and extensive discharge of all his pastoral duties in promoting family religion and instructing the children." To reinforce these expectations, they directed "that the preachers be particularly examined on these several subjects at each annual conference" (H **114–19**).

The same General Conference dealt at several points with Sunday schools. It exhorted the Book Concern to keep the price for Sunday school materials as low as possible and to "keep on hand a good assortment of books suitable" for Sunday school use. It mandated that "it shall be the duty of each travelling preacher in our connexion to encourage the establishment and progress of Sunday schools." It authorized the compilation of "a larger Catechism for the use of Sunday schools and of children in general" and directed the Book Concern to publish it. In a separate action, adopting language to be included in the *Discipline,* it enlarged the responsibilities of preachers to include forming classes for children, selecting teachers, and passing along the names of children and teachers to successors. It also addressed the training of teachers and the creation of education institutions, a topic to which we turn below.

These actions signaled Methodism's participation in the transformation of the Sunday school from a basic literacy outreach to the children of slaves, servants, the poor, and working folk to the primary mode of religious nurture, formation, and instruction for members' children. In April 1827, deciding not to continue to work through the Calvinist-dominated American Sunday School Union, The MEC founded its own Sunday School Union (SSU). It was based in New York City with Nathan Bangs, head of the Methodist Book Concern, as corresponding secretary.

Bangs and successors turned the Book Concern into an engine for the Sunday School Union, putting into children's hands in its founding year the *Child's Magazine* and a Sunday school hymnal, *Selection of Hymns for the Sunday-School Union of The Methodist Episcopal Church.* The Book Concern also published a new set of graded catechisms, replacing the older catechisms of Wesley and John Dickins and reflecting the intellectualist moral psychology then current. Drafted by the eminent British Methodist theologian Richard Watson as companion to his systematic theology, *Theological Institutes* (1823–29), also to be normative in America, these catechisms started even the youngest children (under age seven) with the Wesleyan basic doctrines of sin and salvation, provided age-adapted prayers, and taught the Lord's Prayer. Also in 1827, John P. Durbin, one of a succession of editors committed specifically to caring for Sunday school needs and one of the church's great educators, gave Methodist children (and their eager but untrained teachers) the Bible in easy format. Durbin prepared the first of what would be a series of Scripture lesson books, *Scripture Questions on the Evangelists and Acts,* counseling teachers on how to address queries also put in the *Child's Magazine.* *Scripture Questions* coached Methodist laity on a new, direct approach to Bible study. (A particularly fine catechism for German Methodists appeared in the 1860s, the work of the editor-educator William Nast [1807–99], leader of MEC missions to German Americans. And in 1858 and 1860 the book editor for The MECS, Thomas O. Summers [1812–82], produced first a two-part *Scripture Catechism* and then a collection of catechisms for the southern church. There was, however, a more notorious catechism for The MEC and MECS, one designed for slaves, which we treat in the next chapter.)

The 1828 General Conference endorsed the SSU, and the *Discipline* specifically commended Sunday schools in every pastoral appointment. The mandate seemed hardly necessary. A year's time had produced 251 auxiliary societies, 1,025 Sunday schools, 2,048 Sunday school superintendents, 10,290 teachers, 63,240 students, 60 depositories, 773,000 books, and 154,000 numbers of the *Child's Magazine* (H **588nn71–73, 76**).

Successive editors, heads of the Sunday school enterprise, bishops, and General Conferences increased the incentives for, created new resources for, and added age levels to the Sunday school. The 1840 General Conference, for instance, extended the age level to young people; required circuits and stations to establish Sunday schools; made them accountable to the official governance body on the local level, the quarterly conference; mandated preachers to exercise oversight on, visit, report about, and preach on the Sunday school; urged the appointment of Sunday school agents to travel across the connection as Sunday school promoters; and authorized a new serial. Begun in 1841, the *Sunday School Advocate* succeeded famously, its subscriptions soon surpassing the *Advocate,* itself a trendsetter in circulation (secular and religious). Daniel Kidder, who assumed responsibility for the Sunday School Union and the editorship of the *Sunday School Advocate* in the mid-1840s, boosted circulation to two hundred thousand subscribers. To encourage Sunday school libraries, Kidder published ten- to twenty-five-cent clothbound books (and even cheaper paper "Juvenile books" sold from eight to seventy-seven cents a dozen) and negotiated listing of Religious Tract Society of London items, some eight hundred Sunday school books.

MISSIONARY SOCIETIES

Methodism had been intrinsically, from the start, a missionary movement, as contemporaries themselves recognized. Even so, the Christmas Conference set apart individuals for extension efforts beyond the line of expanding circuits—in Nova Scotia and Antigua (Freeborn Garrettson among them). So Methodism used the term *"missionary"* to refer to appointments beyond its frontiers. The formalization and organization of Methodist missions really began, however, not with these official acts but with the spontaneous efforts by the convert John Stewart—part Black, part Indigenous—to evangelize among the Wyandotte in Ohio (S **1815**). From 1815 until his death in 1823 and working initially through the Black interpreter Jonathan Pointer, Stewart converted a number of Wyandottes, including several chiefs. Thus began what would be early efforts at outreach toward Cherokee, Choctaw, Creek, Potawatomi, Oneida, Menomini, Chippewa, Kaw, Shawnee, Kansas, Chickasaw, Quapaw, and Flathead peoples (see discussion in the next chapter and H **588nn89–91**).

Stewart's efforts helped Methodists recognize that in cross-cultural, multilingual, distant, or international evangelistic contexts Methodism's operative missionary scheme—conference expansion through enlarged circuits and revolving itinerants—would not work. Further, some Christianizing efforts demanded longer appointments, language skills, and other specializations. And such missionary deployments necessitated the church's invention of new organizational and financial schemes, capable of drawing together and focusing the resources of the entire connection rather than leaving all initiatives to conferences and circuits.

Stewart's example and the difficulty of reinforcing his work came to the attention of Bangs and others. Motivation came as well from the organization of interdenominational and denominational missionary efforts on both sides of the Atlantic and from the passage in Congress of a "Civilization Fund Act" encouraging educational endeavor among Indigenous peoples. So, The MEC in 1819, under Bangs's leadership, established a Missionary Society to provide "pecuniary aid . . . to enable the Conferences to carry on their missionary labours on a more extended plan" and "to extend the influence of divine truth, by means of those missionaries which may, from time to time, be approved and employed by the Bishops and Conferences for that purpose" (H **589nn92–93**).

The new society, essentially a mechanism to champion and fundraise for bishop-appointed and conference-initiated efforts, called for a network of auxiliaries. Later that same year, Mary Morgan Mason persuaded a group of women to help her found such an auxiliary.

Thus began an organizational networking across the church that would be immensely important, especially in the provision of a space for women's initiatives and for development of female leadership. In this creation of space and mechanism for women's ministry, Irish-born Mary Morgan (Mason) played a critically important role. In 1812, about a year after her arrival in New York City, Mary Morgan established a Sunday morning Bible class. From those foundations emerged the New York Sunday School Union (1816). On November 8, 1813, she was instrumental in the formation of the New York Female Assistance Society, "for the relief of the sick poor of their sex." Also in 1816 she helped to form the Asbury Female Mite Society for the relief of the wives, widows, and children of retired Methodist itinerant preachers. Married in 1817 to Thomas Mason, then assisting Joshua Soule in managing the New York City–based Methodist Book Room, she bore ten children but found time to sustain the voluntary organizations that she had birthed and to create more. She was one of the founders, in 1822, of the Asylum for Lying-in-Women and remained one of its managers for more than thirty years. In 1833, she became female superintendent of the Greene Street Sunday school and, in 1838, directress of the Female Benevolent Society for the relief of poor women. Mason made perhaps her greatest contribution, however, in leading the New York Female Missionary Society for more than forty years, which tellingly succumbed with her death in 1868 (at age sixty-six).

From 1837 to 1857, the major commitment of the Female Missionary Society was to support Mrs. Ann Wilkins, a thirty-year-old widow at the time she volunteered for missionary service in Liberia (S **1842c**). Through correspondence between Mason and Wilkins, the members of the Female Missionary Society invested themselves in the Liberian witness. Poignant connections encouraged women to join an auxiliary, their annual or life memberships supporting the missionaries in the field. The denominational societies functioned the same way, the monies raised through $2 annual or $25 life contributions making one a member. The missionary societies did not, at this point, appoint or deploy the missionaries. That remained the prerogative of the bishops—whether among the Wyandotte, for the French in Louisiana, among the slaves, in the territories, including those on the West Coast, abroad in Liberia, or elsewhere in the world. The missionary societies promoted and financed. The bishops drew on the funds raised to support missionaries whom they appointed, as they appointed others within conferences.

A NEW CONNECTIONALISM

When The MEC established a Sunday School Union in 1827, it established similar expectations about connection-wide formation of auxiliaries and other voluntary societies that would follow on the same formula. By the 1840s, the church began to experiment with other schemes of finance. One such was the practice of setting of "Times of Collections," specific Sundays when connection-wide collections would go to a given society. Here, for instance, were those for the New England Conference in 1845: "Bible 2nd S. Aug.; Sabbath School Union (MEC) Sept.; Biblical Institute 2nd. S. Oct.; Preachers' Aid 2nd. in Dec.; Missionary cause last S. Feb.; Wesleyan Education Society 1st S. April" (H **589n105**). Circuits, stations, and conferences functioned with templates for organization and operation that made Methodism a highly organized but locally and regionally staffed, directed, and energized machine. A study in simplicity, this voluntary—not bureaucratic—system, like its interdenominational and denominational competition, operated with a single executive secretary, an annual reporting meeting, and quadrennial General Conference endorsement of design and staffing. Of necessity it depended upon and welcomed the creativity, experimentation, and innovation on the local level.

Individual chapters of missionary and Sunday societies, particularly in Methodism's growing urban areas (New York, Baltimore, Boston, Philadelphia, and Chicago), did more than raise money to support distant ventures. Women's societies in particular showed what direct, hands-on missionary initiatives could accomplish in slum areas and among society's marginalized persons. One such church-related attempt attracted national interest and long served as a model for churches working in slum areas. Called Five Points Mission, it came about through the sustained efforts of the Ladies' Home Missionary Society and Methodist women who refused to accept New York's worst slum as irremediable. Beginning in 1843, the society began working among New York's slum dwellers. They besieged incoming immigrants' ships with tracts and Bibles, founded chapels along the docks, and established Sunday schools and Bible classes in poor neighborhoods, but with only limited success. At the persistent urging of new member Phoebe Palmer (see below on her holiness leadership), the society in 1848 turned to the needs of Five Points, the city's worst slum (H **127–29**).

A Sunday school with an initial attendance of seventy led to a six-day-a-week school, by the winter of 1850–51 enrolling one hundred children taught by two full-time teachers. From 772 children enrolled in 1853, attendance rose to 1,200 in 1856 and 2,500 in 1860. A monthly magazine featured stories, written with elaborate pathos, of orphans and beggars desperately in need of a loving home. As the teachers visited the tenements of the Five Points to gather their charges for school, they encountered families without food or fuel, parents without jobs, mothers sick and without medicines, houses filthy and poorly ventilated. So, by the 1860s the mission was providing four thousand hot meals a week to adult residents, operating a medical dispensary, running trade-training programs, maintaining a library, and broadening its educational programs. The expanded Five Points Mission and a related House of Industry functioned as a much-visited model for urban mission (Abraham

Lincoln stopped by on February 24, 1860). When Methodist women in Chicago organized to support a rescue mission modeled after the Five Points Mission, the editor of the *Northwestern Christian Advocate* prophesied that the cause of city missions was "destined to actuate the heart of the church with a power little dreamed of" (H **590n111**).

HOLINESS PROMOTED

Another women's initiative with enduring, transformative, and institution-creating effect was the Tuesday Meeting for the Promotion of Holiness established by two Worrall sisters, Sarah Lankford and Phoebe Palmer. It would revive American Methodism's perfectionist emphasis, create space for women to speak publicly, blossom in the holiness camp meetings of the 1850s and 1860s (S **1867b**), stimulate the revival of 1857–58, and result in the formation of a number of holiness denominations (S **1843**). Raised in a large, devout family associated with New York City's Duane Street Methodist Episcopal Church, the sisters and their spouses established in the mid-1830s a home together on New York City's Lower East Side. On May 21, 1835, Sarah Lankford received the blessing of entire sanctification while reading *An Account of the Experience of Hester Ann Rogers*. Sarah combined women's prayer meetings she had led at both the Allen Street and the Mulberry Street churches into one at their home on Tuesday afternoons. This gathering became known as the Tuesday Meeting for the Promotion of Holiness. It would continue for nearly sixty years under the leadership of one or the other of these two sisters. Phoebe, who from her conversion at eighteen had longed "for the full assurance of faith," who had been gravely ill, and who had already experienced the deaths of two infants, lost a third, a daughter Eliza, at eleven months, in a tragic nursery fire in August 1836. After her daughter's death, Phoebe Palmer intensified the quest for the deeper spiritual experience. On July 26, 1837, a date she would always refer to as her "day of days," Phoebe Palmer made "an entire surrender" to God of everything in her life, her "body, soul, and spirit; time, talents and influence," as well as "the dearest ties of nature, [her] beloved husband and child." Receiving the assurance that her consecration was accepted by God, Palmer knew this was the experience of sanctification she had been seeking.

In 1840 Phoebe Palmer assumed the leadership of the Tuesday Meeting when her sister and brother-in-law moved away from New York City. The meeting began to include men as well as women, after Professor Thomas C. Upham of Bowdoin College, a Congregational minister whose wife was a member, asked if he might also attend. He subsequently experienced entire sanctification under Phoebe Palmer's guidance. Many prominent Methodist figures became regular attenders of the Tuesday Meeting, including Nathan Bangs, Bishops Edmund S. Janes and Leonidas Hamline, and educators Stephen Olin and John Dempster. By the 1850s the meeting had become broadly evangelical, drawing ministers and laypeople from almost every Protestant denomination. Home meetings patterned after the Tuesday Meeting sprouted across the Northeast and, later, throughout the country. By 1886 some two hundred such meetings were operating in the United States and abroad.

During the 1840s, Phoebe Palmer launched a public speaking and writing vocation. Invitations came quickly. In the summer of 1840 she made her first evangelistic trip outside the city, visiting Rye, Williamsburg, and Caldwell's Landing, New York (the new home of Sarah and Thomas Lankford). Eventually her speaking itinerations would be national, indeed, transatlantic (to the British Isles on the eve of the Civil War). Reinforcing the Tuesday Meeting movement and her evangelistic efforts, Phoebe Palmer began to promote holiness through a vigorous publishing program. She became a regular contributor to the *Guide to Christian Perfection,* begun in Boston in 1839 and edited by the Reverend Timothy Merritt. This magazine, eager for responses from those who had experienced "the grace of sanctification," opened itself from the start to "the female members of the church." The magazine urged that, since "many of you have experienced the grace of sanctification, should you not then, as a thank-offering to God, give an account of his gracious dealing with your souls, that others may be partakers of this grace also?" (H **590n117**).

The practices of the Tuesday Meeting established a new template for the religious life, one that stimulated an entire holiness movement. During the 1840s, Phoebe Palmer published several books, including *The Way of Holiness* (1843), *Entire Devotion to God* (1845), and *Faith and Its Effects* (1848). In *The Way of Holiness,* Palmer described her experience of sanctification. Addressing the question "Is there not a shorter way?" she outlined the holiness theology that would become characteristic of the holiness movement as a whole (S **1843**). In Palmer's view, entire sanctification was presently available to all regenerate Christians who were ready to meet the scriptural requirements of consecrating all to God and believing God's promises. Employing "altar terminology," Palmer explained that Christ was the altar that sanctified, or made

71

acceptable, the Christian's total consecration of self. Once this consecration was complete, the seeker should exercise faith and lay claim to the scriptural promise of entire sanctification, with or without an accompanying emotional experience. And public testimony to the experience of holiness was essential to its retention. Palmer's "shorter way" gradually came to distinguish the holiness movement that ensued.

As new dimensions of her ministry unfolded, Walter Palmer began to travel with his wife and take an active part in her evangelistic meetings. By 1857–58, Phoebe and Walter found themselves at the center of a remarkable evangelical revival that was interdenominational, largely urban, and primarily led by laypeople. In her public ministry as a holiness evangelist, Phoebe Palmer had encountered some resistance; other women told her stories of their being forbidden to speak in public. As a justification for herself and them, Palmer wrote *Promise of the Father* (1859), a four hundred–page, closely argued, scripturally grounded defense of women's right to preach on the basis of the gift of the Spirit to both women and men at Pentecost (H **132–33**; S **1859b**). Although Phoebe Palmer did not press for ordination of women, she insisted that women be permitted to pray and testify in the church and even to preach Christ for the conversion of sinners. A shorter version of the argument appeared ten years later, titled *Tongue of Fire on the Daughters of the Lord* (1869). In 1872, Phoebe Palmer became ill with kidney disease and died two years later. Sixteen months later her widowed sister, Sarah, became the second Mrs. Walter Palmer. She continued the work of the Tuesday Meeting and the *Guide to Holiness* until her own death in 1896, at the age of ninety.

Tuesday Meetings, missionary societies, Sunday schools, preachers' wives, and stationed preachers affected the place of Wesley's class as the institutional foundation of religious life and of discipline. Essential on the circuit, the disciplinary function of class meetings and the once-vital leadership roles of the class leader declined or, as we have seen, were transferred and transmuted into the weekly rhythms of Sunday-oriented congregations. Pronouncements of declension, rendered with prophetic image and force, come easily to Protestants generally and to Methodists particularly. The decline of the class meeting became, therefore, a convenient Jeremiadic metaphor (along with itinerancy, holiness, and camp meetings). After all, mandated by Wesley and the *Discipline,* the class proved a highly usable and everywhere-visible symbol of change and, for many Methodists, its demise, of declension.

COLLEGIATE ENTERPRISE

Methodism's earliest experiment with higher education, the ill-fated Cokesbury College, was launched after the church's organization in 1784, and slavishly followed Wesleyan formulae. American Methodists would have their own Kingswood, thought Coke and Asbury, immodestly naming it for themselves. Cokesbury was intended to serve preachers' sons, orphans, and competent friends. It functioned at a general, modest, lower educational level as well—basic education and secondary education. It did not survive a disastrous 1795 fire.

Three decades later, Methodism started over. It established academies in 1817 in Newmarket, New Hampshire, and two years later in New York City. The next General Conference took up the matter and did so with a new sense of education's importance to denominational well-being. The 1820 report of "the committee appointed to take into consideration the propriety of recommending to the annual conferences the establishment of seminaries of learning" spoke with paranoid urgency. Almost all institutions of higher education, it insisted, were controlled by Calvinistic principles, "managed by men denying the fundamental doctrines of the gospel," oriented to be "more or less hostile to our views of the grand doctrines of Christianity," and regarded "experimental and practical godliness" as "only of secondary importance." General Conference urged annual conferences to "establish, as soon as practicable, literary institutions under their control" (H **590nn128–30**). Annual conferences responded, sometimes collaboratively, in a spate of foundings, some two hundred by the Civil War, thirty or so of which survived and flourished. Among the early conference efforts were Augusta in Kentucky (1822), McKendree in Illinois (1828), Randolph-Macon in Virginia (1830), Wesleyan University in Connecticut (1831). Dickinson and Allegheny transferred to the Methodists in the 1830s, and in the same decade, Emory in Georgia, Emory and Henry in Virginia, and Indiana Asbury University. Unusual for its day, Methodism invested in collegiate education for women from essentially the same point that it did for men, in the 1830s. Both Greensboro College in North Carolina and Wesleyan College in Georgia claim priority.

The founders of Methodist colleges intended to counter sectarianism and provide an antidote to the Presbyterian and Episcopal domination of existing institutions, including the supposedly public universities. Methodist schools would free, not bind, minds; recognize the imperative of educated leadership, both lay and ministerial; serve the community at large; command support from civic and state authorities; and, of course, admit young people from various religious communities. Denominational control would serve intellectually liberating, not constraining, purposes.

In founding schools and colleges, Methodists had several purposes in view: moral/Christian formation, the advancement of knowledge, and the training of leaders. Indeed, they were—the men's colleges, that is—the primary formal training alternative to the Course of Study for education of preachers. The colleges constituted the seminaries of their day. Wesleyan, for instance, graduated 919 over its first forty years. Of these, a third entered the Methodist ministry. That college alone produced three-quarters of the northern preachers (MEC) who earned college degrees (H **591n133**). Northern Methodists by the 1870s and 1880s could call Wesleyan "the mother of our denominational institutions" and "the crown and glory of our Church" and "mother of us all."

While the numbers and percentage of college-educated preachers remained small and the Course of Study the norm and access to ordination and conference membership, the Wesleyan ideal of a scholar pastor became the hope for station churches and the aspiring preacher. Methodism's collegiate venture reflected and contributed to the church's commitment to literacy, nurture, and culture. Increasingly, the first career of those called to ministry was teaching, not farming. An American Methodism committed to education-through-religion and religion-through-education re-created the Protestant clerical paradigm, that of the Annesleys and Wesleys, that was possible with married preachers. Pastors' sons would hear God's call, a dramatic change to the ministry profile. By the Civil War, sons of pastors constituted roughly half of those entering the Virginia Methodist and Baptist ministry (H **591n134**).

If Asbury-the-bishop incarnated Methodist connectionalism and exercised the teaching office in the early years and Bangs and the editors did so in the early nineteenth century, the college presidents constituted the key leadership and incarnated connectionalism for the pre–Civil War and Civil War decades. To that end, Methodism placed within the colleges its very best talent. The conferences appointed the brightest stars to presidencies and to faculty. From the colleges came much of the church's literary production. And if faculty members or a president left, they often went from there to a national teaching office, as editor of an *Advocate* or as bishop. The Ignatius

Fews, Augustus Longstreets, John Durbins, Wilbur Fisks, Stephen Olins, and Martin Ruters knit the church together on education's behalf.

Through the colleges, the church would carry on its larger mission of reforming the nation, joining with other denominations in common endeavor to instill Protestant commitment, republican ideals, and civic virtue in the nation's rising leaders. As with missions, Methodism did its fundraising for these colleges with the highly decentralized conference system. Conferences made the colleges a primary benevolence, legislating approval, appointing agents to solicit funds, and raising funds. The college served a vital function within this decentralized system. The conferences pressed for educational institutions out of their sense of Methodism's capacity to take its part in the larger Christian endeavor to shape a Protestant America.

THEOLOGICAL SEMINARIES AND BRUSH COLLEGES

In the Civil War era, Methodism began to think seriously about formalizing its program for ministerial education through the establishment of (postbaccalaureate) theological seminaries. New England Methodists had created a biblical institute, the Wesleyan Theological Institute in Newbury, Vermont (1839), out of which later emerged Boston University School of Theology. Garrett-Evangelical traces its history to the 1855 founding of Garrett Biblical Institute. However, James Strong gained notoriety in 1853 with a forthright case for postbaccalaureate theological education comparable to that offered at Princeton and Andover (S **1853c**). Later as a faculty member at the institution created in response to his plea, Drew Theological Seminary, and also an advocate of lay membership in General Conference (S **1864a**), Strong published a dozen volumes in biblical studies, including the still-in-print *Exhaustive Concordance of the Bible,* and was coeditor with Drew president John McClintock of the ten-volume *Cyclopaedia of Biblical, Theological, and Ecclesiastical Literature.* Strong represented and advocated a church and a ministry for an upwardly modern denomination.

Not everyone favored that initiative or embraced the vision of the church that an educated ministry would create. Indeed, Strong's advocacy elicited a round of "croaking" by those, like Peter Cartwright, who thought the "brush college" superior in forming effective preachers to either colleges or theological

75

schools. In his *Autobiography* and *Fifty Years as a Presiding Elder,* Cartwright drew together several genres—the Wesleyan journal, the western tall tale, the Hebraic jeremiad, the conference semicentennial sermon—into a highly readable account of "his" camp meeting, "brush college" Methodism. The careful reader should have been alerted by Cartwright's prefatory admissions that "my memory is greatly at fault" and that he had long ago thrown his "manuscript journals to the moles and bats." Repeatedly, in various ways, Cartwright asked, "What has a learned ministry done for the world?" Not much. By contrast, his Methodism, graphically and colorfully described in his books—that of class, circuit, camp meeting, apprenticed brush college, and Course of Study—had wrought wonders. It had "prospered in these United States without parallel in the history of the Church of Jesus Christ, since the apostolic age." A Methodism of "more than a million of members," had, Cartwright insisted, "been raised up and united in Church fellowship . . . by a body of uneducated ministers." Not one of them, he continued, "was ever trained in a theological school or Biblical institute" (H **592nn137–38**).

Cartwright and John Durbin, contemporaries, products of Kentucky Methodism, and important players in the life of the church, represented different trajectories: Durbin (editor, college president, agency head), outlined by Nathan Bangs, but Cartwright certainly not. Cartwright's rustic image, carefully cultivated, had nevertheless permitted him to hold the presiding elder's office for half a century, to be elected to thirteen General Conferences, to lead the church in founding educational institutions, to take stands against slavery, and even to run for Congress against Abraham Lincoln. Ordained deacon by Asbury and elder by McKendree, Cartwright gloried in the Methodism they embodied. Others did as well. Indeed, the semicentennial sermon, preached by order of conferences by those who, like Cartwright, had weathered a half century of itinerancy, became a nineteenth-century Methodist preaching genre. Such efforts yielded nostalgia, the jeremiad, croaking, reforming primitivism. They also pointed toward a different form of institutionalization than that advanced by Durbin (and Bangs), namely, toward a highly routinized revivalism, a highly scripted Pietism. The differences represented by Durbin and Cartwright figured in Methodist divisions to which we now turn.

CHAPTER IV
CONNECTIONAL STRAINS AND CONTESTS: 1816–50s

Division keyed Methodism's explosive growth. One year's success on a circuit or in a conference led to its division into two. From 1796 onward, the bishops were empowered "to appoint other yearly conferences in the interval of the General Conference, if a sufficiency of new circuits be anywhere formed for that purpose," a proviso reiterated up to 1832 (H 592nn3–4). Conferences marched west with overall American settlement. Distinct religious territories would emerge on the landscape much as political ones, indeed in advance of the latter. Connectional division fostered expansion. The South Carolina Conference, which at one time or another embraced Georgia and Florida and parts of North Carolina, yielded multiple conferences by division. So also the Western Conference, which covered Kentucky, Tennessee, western Virginia, and Ohio. By 1817, Missouri, Ohio, Tennessee, Genesee, and Mississippi were reporting; by 1827, Pittsburgh, Kentucky, Illinois, Holston, Maine, and Canada. By 1857, The MEC boasted forty-seven conferences, despite having "lost" those that exited to constitute other churches. Ordered division, then, expressed the Methodist connectional and appointive genius. However, even such planned divisions had their "connectional" cost. Each created a separation. Each divided the "fraternity" of the traveling preachers who constituted a conference. Each set off some members into a new conference entity from those with whom they felt deep bonds of brotherhood. Also, growth, distances, organizational complexity, new media, mission societies, and increased internal diversity strained and stressed connectional governance by male, White preachers through general, annual, and quarterly conferences.

RACIAL DIVISIONS

Increasingly, the dynamic tensions and racial-ethnic diversity within the Methodist movement posed themselves as choices—indigenization or order; liberty or uniformity; antislavery or evangelization; popularizing or connection; discipline or influence; spontaneity or formation; democracy or adherence to authority. Methodism's commitment to antislavery and its biracial character eroded, as we have noted, as the church prospered in slaveholding America. A series of grievances led to schisms along racial lines and hence the import of the AMEs tracing their founding to Richard Allen's walkouts from St. George's in 1787 and 1792 (S **1792b**). Full separation in 1816 followed requests from Allen and the Bethel Church for the prerogatives that would have accorded their ministries and that congregation fuller standing within the Methodist connection, even if on some segregated status. These prerogatives included ordination, representation, some say in appointments, property ownership, and the ability to exercise discipline. Much of the jostling occurred between the Black congregations in Philadelphia and Baltimore with White "supervising" elders, but the entire Methodist system was complicit. For instance, Asbury ordained Allen and Daniel Coker "local deacons," an action that the 1800 General Conference accepted but refused to recognize by inclusion in the *Discipline*. Coker and Allen led in the 1816 conference founding the AME, Coker initially being elected bishop but yielding to Allen (H **92–93**; S **1792b, 1816**).

A similar set of provocations to those in Philadelphia and Baltimore produced a Wilmington-based coalition, that of the African Union Church, organized in 1813. These schisms cost The MEC its Black membership and, more significantly, Black leadership. Losing that voice, articulate in sustaining the Wesleyan commitment to antislavery and unqualified affirmation that Black Americans were fully children of God (S **1810a**), The MEC found itself ever more sensitive to the concerns and counsel of its slaveholding membership. Another drain on its antislavery witness came from the earlier division, already discussed, largely among Whites, that in 1792 involving Virginia and North Carolina followers of the "Republican Methodist" James O'Kelly (S **1792a**). This schism, as much as any, made denominational leaders wary of democratizing slogans and proposals.

The New York-centered AMEZ initially sought an ongoing relation with The MEC, a middle way between separation and continued subservient status. By 1793, Wesley Chapel had six Black classes with membership of 143, James Varick among the class leaders. In 1796, he was granted permission to hold separate prayer and preaching services under supervision of a White pastor. He ran a school in his home, later in his church. In 1799 the new society selected Black trustees (including Peter Williams Sr., longstanding sexton at John Street Church) and announced a public fund drive to build an African Methodist church in the city. In 1800 the new congregation began building, and the following year Varick opened Zion African ME Church (Mother Zion). Bishop Asbury blessed the church, and the first separate Communions and baptisms led by White elders began. A year later, the new church negotiated articles of agreement with New York Conference limiting the power of trustees to maintain property for MEC but making no provision for authority in matters of church policy and program. Black deacons were ordained—James Varick, Abraham Thompson, and June Scott in 1806, and William Miller and Daniel Coker (who thereafter went to Baltimore) in 1808. This cadre's influence extended beyond Black Methodists, for instance, leading New York and New York African Americans in successive New Year's Day antislavery, antislave-trade celebrations. They also pressed for control over their facilities of the two congregations, Zion and Asbury (founded in 1814), and for elder's ordination, strategic issues after 1818 when they started a new building and found themselves competing with the AMEs who had begun to work the New York area.

By gathering twenty-two preachers in a conference (1821), they proposed to the Philadelphia and New York Annual Conferences that they set apart "a Conference for African Methodist preachers, *under the patronage of the white Methodist Bishops and Conference*" (S **1821a**; H **592n9**). The Philadelphia Conference largely assented to the memorial. However, the New York Conference, though finding it expedient to appoint "coloured preachers" who would "labour among them and take the pastoral charge of them until the next General Conference," effectively parried the request for orders and noted that setting off an annual conference was the prerogative of General Conference. William Stilwell, the White elder in charge of the two African churches and then leading his own schism from The MEC, had already advocated independence, and a committee had been working on *The Doctrines and Discipline of the African Methodist Episcopal Church in America*. Proceeding to organize on this platform and on the basis of Philadelphia's more generous posture, the New York Black Methodists met in their first conference on June 21, 1821, with two White elders, William Phoebus, as president, and Joshua Soule, as secretary. With no bishop available for that conference, elders were not ordained. The following year, however, Stilwell and two other renegade Methodist elders ordained a number of elders, among them James Varick and Christopher Rush, Zion's first two bishops. When the 1824 MEC General Conference failed to embrace this new conference, its distinct denominational identity was secured. Varick convened the first General Conference of the AMEZ Church in 1826, which reelected him to the episcopacy. Varick died the next year, just days after New York's deadline for freeing all slaves. Rush succeeded Varick as superintendent, leading the AMEZs until his health failed in 1852.

Though "bleeding Black" to the several independent African Methodisms, numbers of free Black Americans and slaves remained in The MEC, continuing efforts to achieve fuller agency and incorporation into the life of the church. Illustrative was the plea in 1832 by Philadelphia Black leaders for what AME and AMEZ had sought and what the petitioners argued would staunch further loss to those denominations, namely, fully ordained Black preachers (S **1832a**). The MEC demurred on such pleas until 1864.

GERMAN METHODISMS

The organization of the German movements, the United Brethren and The Evangelical Association, as we have noted, reflected their distinct origins in the broader evangelical movement and the specific leaven of Reformed, Lutheran, and Mennonite Pietism. Still the first conference of the former in 1789 and its formal organization in 1800 and the first conference of the latter in 1803 and its formal organization in 1807 represented failures (on both sides) to carry through on the looser comity they had enjoyed with the Methodists (S **1800b**). Efforts continued to bring the movements closer.

Christian Newcomer, who assumed leadership from Otterbein and Boehm of the UBC, indicated as early as 1803 eagerness for closer ties with the Methodists (S **1813a, 1813c**). The Baltimore Methodist Conference reciprocated, conveying through him a proposal for closer union and pressing for adoption of a *Discipline* to make that possible. Fourteen letters exploring that possibility went between Baltimore (and Philadelphia) Conferences and the United Brethren. Methodists insisted on a *Discipline* as the basis for unity. Newcomer drafted one and had it printed in 1813, ironically just as the Methodists were giving up on negotiations. In his eagerness, Newcomer and the Eastern Annual Conference over which he presided had apparently not achieved assent to the new *Discipline* by the Miami (Ohio) Annual Conference. The latter's opposition resulted in the calling of the first General Conference, thus giving this branch of the German Pietists a "Methodist-like" conference structure. However, as it settled its polity, the UBC developed a profoundly different ecclesiology than The MEC (and EA): term episcopacy, elective presiding elders (district superintendents [DSs]), single ordination, appointment of preachers by committee (not by bishop), a congregational locus for ministerial identity, loosely structured and voluntary class meetings, and a general wariness about hierarchy and centralization.

Similarly, as *Die sogenannten Albrechtsleute*, "Those Designated as Albright's People" (S **1807**), organized themselves and adopted a *Discipline* (1809), the EA received overtures from both Methodists and the UBC for unity. Each wanted accord on its own terms. For instance, in 1810 John Dreisbach encountered Asbury and Martin Boehm's son Henry. Asbury entreated him to withdraw from Albright, "go with them to Baltimore to attend their Conference; there to join them." Dreisbach counteroffered denominational unity but with German conference structures. Asbury, however, viewed German ministries as a denominational dead end, a sentiment that he registered with Dreisbach.

In 1813, the two German groups explored unity but disagreed, as had the UBC and The MEC, on ecclesiology, episcopacy, and standards for conference membership. Again, in 1816, when the EA convened in General Conference and selected its name, The Evangelical Association, the EA received another overture from the UBC about unity. Delegations from the two denominations met the following year but failed on the same issues. Gestures toward unity would be made over the years, but the conference fraternities proved difficult to unite. Differences along language and polity lines proved difficult to bridge.

WOMEN'S MINISTRIES

Gender—like race, language, caste, and culture—scripted religious roles, particularly leadership roles, and effected a unique set of division

(H **593n18**). Methodist women modeled the Christian life, converted family and friends, provided money, hosted and mentored preachers, prayed and testified in love feasts, led classes, and exhorted. They gradually lost public voice, however, including that most important local disciplinary office, class leader. The denomination's retreat did not proceed evenly, however, and a few women in the early nineteenth century claimed and exercised calls to preach. By the 1830s, particularly in The MEC, the quest for respectability and order (chapter III) led to suppression of such "public" forms, providing "domestic" alternatives instead in the "office" of preacher's wife; intracongregational organizations for gendered participation and leadership—Sunday schools, missionary and other societies; and media attentive to gender roles. The latter, in particular—the *Advocates*, Sunday school and missionary materials, published letters, notices and obituaries, and serials devoted particularly to women, *Ladies' Repository* (MEC, 1841–76) and *Southern Lady's Companion* (MECS, 1848–54)—exhibited women's religious experience (S **1841b**), championed the new religious leadership roles, including that of the preacher's wife, and defined women's religious sphere.

The vocation of preacher's wife permitted many women who had heard a call to ministry to exercise that within accepted bounds. Some women, whether traveling with itinerant husbands or within stations, effectively honored such a call, in leading, teaching, exhorting, and preaching alongside their spouses. In a number of instances before the Civil War, both within and beyond Methodism, women experienced and publicly affirmed a call to preach. Although never ordained or embraced with conference membership, these few found support for their ministries from eager hearers and encouragement from other ministers. Sometimes, a woman's preaching ministry succeeded too much, as did Sally Thompson's, resulting in trial and excommunication (S **1830a**; H **148–49**).

Other women preachers flew more successfully under the radar. Among those in The MEC was Fanny Butterfield Newell, who experienced a call to preach in a dream (S **1809**). Marrying the Reverend Ebenezer F. Newell the following year, she traveled with him around circuits in Vermont and Maine. Like Newell, the African American Jarena Lee published an account of her call and ministry, *The Life and Religious Experience of Jarena Lee*, in 1836 and in a revised version in 1849 (S **1811a**; H **150–51**). When possible, she traveled with "a Sister," that is, another woman evangelist, among them Sister

Zilpha Elaw, another Black preacher who published an account of her call and ministry (H **593–94nn27–29**).

A comparable figure among the Methodist Protestants, to whom we return below, was Hannah Pearce Reeves. She itinerated for nine years in England, moved to the United States to marry another English immigrant, William Reeves, and was married in Zanesville (Ohio), in 1831. From that point, they "labored together in the gospel ministry" until her death in 1868 (H **594n30**). In the UBC, several women were recommended or licensed to preach in the 1840s and 1850s, among them Lydia Sexton (H **151–52**). When a son became seriously ill, Lydia covenanted with God that if his life were spared, "the remainder of my days should be devoted to his [God's] service, whatever might be the inconvenience or consequences." Within a week she agreed to preach, and an appointment was "given out" for her to preach in her own home. After about a year of preaching, Lydia Sexton applied for and was granted a preacher's license. It was renewed annually, even after 1857, when the UBC General Conference legislated against women preaching. She itinerated until 1871, the last year holding the post of chaplain to the Kansas State Penitentiary. Sometimes accompanied by her husband, Lydia did the preaching, since unlike the husband in other itinerating couples, he was not ordained.

The few women who preached or exhorted, the considerable number of preachers' wives charting new forms of ministry, and the Methodist majority (women) creating and leading the various Sunday school, Tuesday Meeting, and missionary efforts all evidenced Methodism's continuing but evolving dependence on its women but its difficulty in affirming that dependence formally in the *Discipline* and recognizing their callings. Roles and opportunities that the Civil War brought would occasion the further testing of restraints and constraints.

INDIGENOUS MISSIONS

Methodism experienced a difficulty—as did other denominations—when it took the gospel across cultural lines. The Wyandotte experience, the motivation as we have noted for the development of the "sending" missionary structure, illustrates the challenges that led to that "retreat." James B. Finley, presiding elder over the Wyandotte area in northern Ohio, reinforced the efforts of John Stewart for several years by appointing itinerants as missionaries. By 1821, he had recognized that effective evangelization required more stable, full-time leadership than passing itinerants could provide and that both a school and a mission farm would serve the effort among the Wyandotte, and he selected a site in Upper Sandusky for this purpose. For these projects, he sought and gained the endorsement of Wyandotte leadership, seven chiefs assenting in a formal response witnessed by a US government agent. Finley was thereafter appointed to the Wyandotte Mission and established a school with Harriet Stubbs as "matron and instructor." He organized a church, eliciting as members four of the chiefs, Between-the-Logs, Mononcue, John Hicks, and Peacock, who with Squire Gray Eyes became an oversight committee for the school. In the next couple of years, Charles Elliott, William Walker Jr., and Lydia Barstow came as additional teachers.

In 1823, Finley, along with several Wyandotte, extended the mission among tribe members in Canada and in Michigan (the Huron Mission), forming classes in both places. Finley and successors brought Indigenous chiefs into limited levels of leadership. Chiefs Between-the-Logs and Mononcue, for instance, were early licensed to preach and in 1826 visited New York, Philadelphia, and Baltimore, along with Finley, on a preaching tour. Several other Wyandotte were licensed to preach and included in the preaching schedules. And as of 1826 fifteen functioned as class leaders. The stability and doubtless leadership development that Finley offered ended with his appointment in 1827–28 to be presiding elder again. Thereafter the Wyandotte Mission experienced successive appointments of missionaries who did not speak their language, reincorporation into a circuit, White incursions on their land, gradual migration of tribe members west, and eventually in 1842 a formal treaty relinquishing their Ohio property. Methodism neither crossed the language and culture barrier nor raised Wyandotte leaders to conference membership.

Methodism launched missions among the Creek in 1821, the Cherokee in 1822, the Choctaw in 1824, and the Chickasaw in 1835, southeastern tribes with well-developed institutions of self-government, inhabiting adjoining areas of the Carolinas, Tennessee, Georgia, and Alabama. The effort among the Cherokee—promising given significant intermarriage, cultural exchange, and earlier Protestant missions—came at the behest of Richard Riley, himself part Cherokee, who became leader of the first class. A school, meeting house, and camp meeting followed quickly. Many Cherokee were converted, including John Ross, chief of the nation for many years. By 1827 mission superintendent William McMahon claimed 675 members organized in three circuits; four schools; several licensed exhorters and local preachers; and one preacher, Turtle Fields, "eminently distinguished for his deep piety and devotion to the interests of the mission." And by 1830 the mission boasted 1,028 members and eight circuits or stations.

In 1828 the discovery of gold in Georgia Cherokee territory brought invasive and predatory actions by White settlers and a series of confiscatory laws from the Georgia legislature, in effect repudiating a Revolutionary-era treaty and Cherokee status as a sovereign nation. In 1830 Congress passed a removal bill, and the Georgia governor notified missionaries to depart or face arrest. The Cherokee resisted valiantly, and many missionaries protested against removal as well (S **1830b**; H **154–55, 594nn40–43**). Unfortunately, the Methodist missionaries found little support from their own conference, the Tennessee, which refused to interfere with "political affairs." The mission deteriorated, the membership report for 1835 being half of what it had been. By that point, the mission had two traveling preachers, Turtle Fields and John F. Boot, among the first Indigenous leaders ordained. The latter joined two other preachers with the mass deportation of more than fourteen thousand Cherokee men, women, and children on the Trail of Tears. By the 1840s an Upper and Lower Cherokee Mission could report significant leadership below annual conference level, sixteen local preachers, and sixteen exhorters plus a number of class leaders.

In 1821 William Capers of the South Carolina Conference was appointed missionary to the Creek Nation of Georgia and Alabama. Early Creek leaders included James McHenry, Samuel Checote, and George W. Steadham. The Creek and the Choctaw among whom an early mission prospered were forced to move to Indian Territory in 1836. West of the Mississippi the Cherokee, Choctaw, and Creek, as also the Chickasaw and Seminole, struggled to reconstruct their national lives. Although removal brought bitterness and distrust of Whites and their religion, the Mississippi, Tennessee, and Missouri Conferences continued to send missionaries into Oklahoma and environs. The 1844 MEC General Conference created an Indian Mission Conference that, as the church divided over slavery, became part of The Methodist Episcopal Church, South (H **156–67**; see next chapter on this division).

In the 1820s and 1830s a number of annual conferences began work with peoples of the Great Lakes region (Oneida, Chippewa, Ojibwa), in some instances commissioning a leader from one nation to launch missions in another (H **155–56**). Peter Marksman, an Ojibwa, was called by one historian "the outstanding Michigan Methodist Indian preacher of the nineteenth century" (H **595n50**; S **1842a**). By the early 1830s, urged on by Wesleyan president Wilbur Fisk, The MEC began entertaining the idea of a mission to the numerous tribes in the Pacific Northwest (including the Chinook, Salish, and Nez Percé peoples). Jason Lee, "missionary to the Flathead Indians," embraced Fisk's vision: "Live with them—learn their language—preach Christ to them—and, as the way opens, introduce schools, agriculture, and the arts of civilized life" (H **156; 595n51**).

However well intentioned, Methodist overtures functioned within the interactions of White settlers and traders with Indigenous tribes, often highly predatory, aggrandizing, and exploitive. Prejudices, stereotypes, and mistrust haunted both sides of missionary relations. Further, missions typically worked in some partnership with federal and state policies regarding Indigenous nations, another taint on its integrity. When missions succeeded and individuals or groups converted, they often found themselves alienated from their own people and not incorporated into the Methodist community. The itinerant system, which revolved White preachers in and out of missionary settings, provided little occasion for cultural understanding, skill development, strategic wisdom, and pastoral experience, much less real fluency in Indigenous languages. The mission schools, even granting the appropriateness of their civilizing agenda, suffered for lack of policy, supervision, and resources. Yet despite such severe problems and despite opposition among Indigenous people themselves, some significant Christianization occurred, often through the efforts of Indigenous preachers.

COLONIZATION AND MISSION TO THE SLAVES

The accommodation to southern sentiments and its slaveholding members had been gradual, as we have noted, the 1816 General Conference conceding that "the evil appears to be past remedy" (H **595n59**). In its own Missouri Compromise, also in 1820, The MEC effectively ended the prohibition against preachers and circuit or station leaders holding slaves. In 1824 The MEC embraced as an antislavery cause the American Colonization Society and the Liberian Mission, which dealt with slavery by exporting freedmen to evangelize Africa. Church leaders, notably Wilbur Fisk, president of Wesleyan University, and Bangs, secretary of the Missionary Society and MEC spokesperson through the *Christian Advocate,* threw their support to colonization. Other editors, save that of *Zion's Herald,* followed suit. Henry Bascom, several-time college president, later editor, still later bishop, served for two years as an agent for the American Colonization Society and set forth its aims in a repeatedly delivered speech (S **1832b**). By the 1840s annual conferences, except in the South, had endorsed the colonization cause, the bishops lined up in its favor, and much of its intelligentsia signed on as well. Donald Mathews concluded, "There was no religious denomination more closely connected with colonization than the Methodist Episcopal Church" (H **595n60**).

The retreat from antislavery, embrace of colonization, and a mission to the slave developed together. Despite the losses to the AMEs and AMEZs, The MEC retained a significant African American membership, including sizable numbers in slave states and within conferences where both slaves and free Black Americans would belong. By 1828, the year before the "Mission" really began, The MEC claimed 59,056 "Coloured" among its 421,156 members, primarily in four conferences: South Carolina, 18,460; Virginia, 9,090; Baltimore, 10,402; and Philadelphia, 8,352, for the first three of these constituting roughly a third of its membership (H **595n61**).

Among those worrying in the 1820s about the church's care of its Black membership were William Capers, superintendent of the Creek mission and a slave owner, and his friend James O. Andrew, presiding elder, not a slave owner but later a bishop and *the* slaveholder-by-marriage bishop over whom the church divided. Under their leadership and with the conviction that conversion made for a better and certainly less revolt-prone slave, first South Carolina and later other southern conferences sent missionaries—primarily at the request of planters—to preach, establish Sunday schools, catechize, and otherwise care for plantation slaves. They enjoyed the endorsement of The MEC Missionary Society and of the several *Advocates,* including that established in 1836, the *Southern Christian Advocate,* which Capers then edited. On its organization, The MECS committed itself to "Missions Among the People of Color," "furnishing the entire colored population of the South and South-west with the preaching of the gospel, the administration of the ordinances, and the moral discipline of the Christian church," which, it claimed, despite post–Nat Turner fears of slave revolts or perhaps because of fears of slave revolts, enjoyed societal affirmation. "Let it ever be the *glory* of the Methodist E. Church, South," it continued, "that she has genuine pity for the slave, effective benevolence, exulting charity, energetic, *practical zeal,* commensurate with the utmost spiritual wants of this portion of our population." The MECS expressed its commitment by deploying 127 missionaries serving 120 missions but only seventeen churches and six Sunday schools (H **595n63**).

The MECS carried on its plantation or slave mission until the Civil War, its way of nurturing the slave while ever increasing its commitment to the institution of slavery. However, as narratives by ex-slaves and interviews of ex-slaves have shown, slaves frequently found White southern efforts transparent and looked elsewhere for gospel solace, nurture, insight, and proclamation. Many experienced greater comfort from Christianized slave preachers who drew together African practices and a prophetic reading of Scripture into a highly expressive style of song and rhetoric offered during the slaves' precious time and space, from sundown to sunup and in the hush arbors. Thus emerged the "invisible institution" described by Albert Raboteau and others. After freedom, its dynamisms would animate the several Black Methodisms: AME, AMEZ, CME, and MEC.

The mission was not an inconsequential effort, by 1843 deploying seventeen missionaries working, claiming 6,556 slave members, and providing instruction to 25,025 slave children. One missionary laboring in Georgia on the Savannah River Mission reported in 1835 itinerating weekly to nine plantations, catechizing orally 165 children, praying "with the old and sick in their houses or hospitals," and lecturing or preaching "every night, and three or four times each Sabbath, beginning at sunrise" (H **595nn65–66**).

To guide the plantation mission, especially after the 1831 Nat Turner slave revolt, Capers needed an instructional resource that could be kept in White hands (preachers, planters, and spouses) but used with slaves. He created and published in 1833 *A Catechism for Little Children (and for use on) the Missions to the Slaves in South-Carolina.* Capers took this patronizing catechism (S **1833**) through several editions, expanding it for use with adult slaves and constituting it an official publication of The MECS, which kept it in print even after the Civil War.

The little catechisms cohered with a pro-slavery sentiment then increasingly part of the southern "gospel," a sentiment that enjoined Christian masters to a genuine patriarchy. Methodist leaders who enunciated such exhortations included Holland N. McTyeire, in *Duties of Christian Masters* (1859), James O. Andrews, in "Four Letters on the Religious Instruction of Negroes," which appeared in the *New Orleans Christian Advocate* (1856), William A. Smith, in *Lectures on the Philosophy and Practice of Slavery* (S **1856**), and Richard H. Rivers, in *Elements of Moral Philosophy* (1859). Capers contributed to that pro-slavery ethos and ethic after being elected bishop with the "third edition" of his catechism (1847).

GERMAN, SPANISH, AND INTERNATIONAL MISSIONS

The MEC made several efforts before the Civil War to evangelize among French speakers with only limited results. Other missions, including some across language, culture, and societal lines, succeeded and succeeded better than those to the Indigenous tribes and Black slaves in empowering communities to resource themselves. With Germans and despite the competition with the UBC, EA, Lutherans, and German Reformed, The MEC enjoyed remarkable success, due in no small measure to German-born William (Wilhelm) Nast. Trained for the Lutheran ministry and influenced at the University of Tübingen by philosophers F. C. Baur and D. F. Strauss, he came to the United States to teach, eventually instructing biblical languages at Kenyon College. Nast experienced spiritual renewal at a Methodist camp meeting, sought admission to the Ohio Conference, and in 1835 was appointed missionary to the area Germans. He created a five-week circuit of three hundred miles and twenty-two preaching places. Under his leadership came: by 1839 *Der Christliche Apologete* (a German advocate), by 1844 German districts within three annual conferences, and by 1864 four separate German conferences and a college, Baldwin-Wallace (Ohio). Nast traveled as missionary across the United States and trained others as missionaries, within ten years deploying thirty-two. From his editor's post, which he held for more than half a century, Nast produced a stream of materials for German Methodists, including catechisms, as we have noted, but also hymnals, prayer books, a translation of Wesley's standard sermons, a biography of Wesley, and biblical commentaries. By his efforts and those of his "apostles," Methodism was then exported back to Germany, capitalizing on transatlantic networks and connections.

Missions among Hispanic or Latino peoples began after the annexation of Texas, the Mexican-American War of 1846–48, and the Treaty of Guadalupe Hidalgo (H **161–62**). Benigno Cárdenas, a Mexican priest in Santa Fe, New Mexico, converted, affiliated with The MEC, and in 1853 preached "the first sermon in Spanish by a Methodist in the Southwest" (S **1853a**). Notable among early MECS leaders in Hispanic missions was Alejo Hernández who was studying for the priesthood in the 1860s, joined Benito Juárez's army of resistance against the French, also converted, and was ordained (elder in 1874). As the first Mexican ordained to the Methodist ministry, he served only four years, in Corpus Christi and in Mexico City, before dying of a stroke at age thirty-three. The establishment of the Rio Grande Mission Conference by The MECS in 1858 gave structure for such mission. The following year, Bishop George F. Pierce toured the mission area, outlined plans for a substantial missionary enterprise across the Southwest and into Mexico, and left enabling appointments "to be supplied." The Civil War led the whole endeavor to be supplied, a narrative we will resume in the next section.

Missionary experience, practice, and theory in domestic and foreign fields interplayed, as we have already seen in the relation of Indigenous and slave missions. William Taylor exemplified the mutual interaction of mission, domestic and international. After serving circuits in the Baltimore Conference and stations in Georgetown and North Baltimore, Taylor transferred to the California mission in 1849. Strategies and experience there informed evangelistic tours (1857–62) back east in the United States and Canada and then forty years of worldwide mission initiatives and advocacy of the "Pauline Method" of self-supporting missions.

The relation of the several missions owed, as well, to the extensive attention that missions garnered in the *Advocates,* later in serials like the *Missionary Advocate* (1845) and the *Heathen Woman's Friend* (1869), and through the mission societies, permitting North American Methodist women, men, and children to invest imaginatively and vicariously in conversion of various "heathen." In the 1840s and 1850s through the narratives of Melville Cox and Ann Wilkins in Liberia, Robert and Henrietta Maclay in China (and later Japan and Korea), and William and Clementina Butler in India, Methodists became emotionally involved in various missions beyond the Americas. The Lambuths, James William and Mary (McClellen), who gave "five dollars and myself for work in China," held similar fascination for The MECS (H **596n82**). Another wrinkle in the domestic-foreign missionary story was what would now be termed reverse missions, namely, Methodist evangelism in Christian Europe: Ludwig S. Jacoby to Germany in 1849, Ole P. Petersen to Norway in 1853, John P. Larsson to Sweden in 1854, and Christian B. Willerup to Denmark in 1858.

As evangelism across language, cultural, racial, and oceanic lines progressed, Methodist missionary leadership gathered coworkers into conferences. A Liberian Annual Conference emerged in 1834 and, as we have seen, an Indian (Indigenous) Mission Conference in 1844. The latter received immediate episcopacy oversight. The former requested such to successive General Conferences, beginning in 1836. Eventually Bishop Levi Scott itinerated to Liberia and in 1853 held the first annual conference, ordaining Africans (for the first time) as deacons (eleven) and elders (eight). Scott returned to endorse a proposal for missionary bishops. The 1856 MEC General Conference favored that over other options that would have recognized the Liberian Conference as a distinct and independent church. This innovation required amendment of the Third Restrictive Rule. The 1856 General Conferences ratified the rule to permit the appointment of "a Missionary Bishop or Superintendent for any of our foreign missions, limiting his jurisdiction to the same respectively" (H **596n83**). The Liberian Conference elected an African American, Francis Burns, who had been sent to Liberia by the Missionary Society, taught in the Monrovia Seminary, edited *Africa's Luminary*, and served for a decade as presiding elder, for six of those years also as president of the Liberian Conference. Burns was consecrated by Bishops Edmund Janes and Osmon Baker at the Genesee Conference in 1858, the first Black bishop. As missionary bishop, Burns was neither a general nor an itinerant superintendent, his episcopal authority limited to his assigned field. The MEC, James Kirby concludes, "not only created a new form of episcopacy, but opened a Pandora's box of questions about the nature of the episcopal office itself" (H **596n84**). Thus missions drew lines between cultures and languages. Politics drew another set of lines.

DEMOCRATIC AND ANTI-EPISCOPACY DIVISIONS

Pleas for democratizing Methodist polity that had resulted in early schisms—of O'Kelly in the Virginia area and Hammett in South Carolina (treated above)—continued in the nineteenth century. In New England, "Reformed Methodists" led by Pliny Brett, who had itinerated from 1805 to 1812, sought church government and local authority more akin to those of Congregationalism. They protested episcopacy, emphasized the attainability of entire sanctification, and repudiated war and slavery. Formally organized in 1814 at a convention in Vermont, they drew several thousand adherents across New England, New York, and Canada. By the Civil War, most of the Reformed movement had affiliated with the Methodist Protestants. Another body taking the name Primitive Methodists developed around the eccentric figure of Lorenzo Dow. He led in the export of American-style camp meeting revivalism to Britain after 1805 and import-of-the-export as a distinct denomination, beginning in 1829. The Primitives, also a critic of established MEC order, developed strength in Pennsylvania and especially in Canada. The New York Conference session that dealt with the Zion overture received word from the presiding elder that William M. Stilwell had withdrawn with a group of White Methodists. Stilwell and his uncle voiced concerns about New York Methodist use of money, the lavish renovation of the John Street Church, and the authority of other local leaders, the bishops, conference, and the *Discipline*. Appealing for their independent stance to the original charter granted to John Street, the Stilwellites enunciated democratic and primitivist principles, making the Bible alone their rule and permitting women the suffrage in matters of church governance. The movement prospered in the 1820s in the New York area, losing much of its strength to the Methodist Protestants and disappearing completely with the younger Stilwell's death in 1851.

The Methodist Protestant movement raised yet another set of democratic issues and did so in Methodism's heart, center, and capital, its site of holiest memories, its Jerusalem, the Baltimore area. There reformers in the 1820s campaigned for conference election of the episcopal lieutenants or surrogates known as presiding elders (district superintendents), for some conference role and representation for local preachers, then constituting two-thirds of the Methodist ministry, and for a lay voice in the governing of annual conferences and General Conferences. Here, as with O'Kelly, a set of legislative proposals presented the church with the question about whether and to what extent its internal life would draw on the best aspects of American democracy.

Of the three issues, that for the election of presiding elders most roiled General Conference. The presiding elder (PE) had evolved out of the circuit-supervisory and presiding roles assigned the few elders in the new MEC.

The 1786 *Discipline* specified superintending duties for elders. The 1792 *Discipline* distinguished two distinct offices, the traveling elder and the presiding elder, permitting the latter a term limit of four years in a given district and specifying his selection by the bishop (H **164–65; 597nn85–87**). Early sensitivities about the office, its authority, and the manner of selection led Bishops Asbury and Coke to give it extended defense, one of their longer apologetic expositions, in their annotated *Discipline* (S **1798**).

If the preachers had issues about the nature and episcopal authority of the office from the start, they developed more specific grievances as the years passed. With bishops itinerating connectionally, not necessarily presiding at a given conference in successive years, and leaving one conference to preside at the next, the presiding elders (PEs) exercised considerable intraconference authority, particularly as conference boundaries and membership stabilized. Bishop William McKendree formalized the PE role in appointment-making by convening them in what became known as cabinets, a practice he inaugurated as early as 1812. One of the few ways conferences exercised any comment on the bishop's selection of PEs was in their election or nonelection to General Conference.

In his Episcopal Address to the 1820 General Conference, McKendree deemed 1808 to have settled governmental and constitutional issues and presumed "that no radical change can be made for the better at present." Undeterred by this admonition, Timothy Merritt of New England and Beverly Waugh of Maryland put the issue of an elective presiding eldership before General Conference. The proposal divided the bishops (William McKendree, ill but staying nearby the conference; Enoch George; and Robert R. Roberts) as well as the body. George may have authored the proposal, as also a measure to reach compromise, a committee of six, three from each side of the issue. While the committee conferred, General Conference elected Joshua Soule to the episcopacy. John Emory drafted a consensus document for the committee providing for episcopal nomination and conference election of PEs. General Conference passed the compromise (sixty-one to twenty-five). Soule, elected but not yet consecrated as bishop and the author of the 1808 "constitution," then tendered his resignation in a stinging written challenge to the constitutionality of the measure just passed. McKendree submitted a letter of his own also pronouncing the legislation unconstitutional and himself "under no obligation to enforce or to enjoin it on others to do so" (H **597nn88–92**). These dramatic acts won the day, and the conference subsequently accepted Soule's resignation and suspended the legislation until the next General Conference.

To the subsequent round of annual conferences, McKendree submitted a letter setting forth his position on the unconstitutionality of elective presiding elders, reiterating missional points that Coke and Asbury had advanced (S **1798**), and asking that the annual conferences concur in that judgment. Seven conferences complied, but the older five northern and eastern conferences did not. Joining the cause, William Stockton, a New Jersey, later Philadelphia printer, founded what would become an important reform medium, the *Wesleyan Repository and Religious Intelligencer* (S **1821b**). Appearing first in April 1821 as a semimonthly and succeeded in 1824 by the Baltimore periodical, *The Mutual Rights of Ministers and Members of The Methodist Episcopal Church*, the paper permitted Stockton, other laity, and ministers to advocate election of presiding elders, but also lay representation and a constellation of reform measures: rights of local preachers, procedures in church trials, checks on episcopal tyranny—in short, the reform of the church. Such advocacy involved risk, particularly for preachers under appointment. In consequence, many wrote under pseudonyms.

Among those taking that risk was Nicholas Snethen, former traveling companion of Asbury, secretary of the 1800 General Conference, antislavery advocate, chaplain to the House of Representatives, and unsuccessful candidate for Congress. Snethen framed the reform cause in republican (American democratic) terms and wrote not only on behalf of the traveling preachers (the ordained, full members of conference) but also for preachers outside that fraternity, the local preachers of which he had been one. Outnumbering the traveling preachers three to one, they, with class leaders, constituted at this period the mainstay of Methodist congregational or local ministry. A diverse lot, they included gifted leaders who remained in ministry, but had "located" from the traveling ranks. The 1820 General Conference made a stab at the problem, providing the district conference for local preachers, transferring to it licensing and trial authority previously vested in the quarterly conference, and giving it some of the character of an annual conference. Separate and very unequal, this experiment was doomed, though lasting as disciplinary provision until 1836, when its functions and authority were restored to quarterly conference.

The democratic political principles that pointed toward election of PEs and rights for local preachers were invoked on behalf of the laity. Ought they to be involved in the body or bodies that acted legislatively on, for, and over them? Snethen thought so, deeming The MEC nearly as autocratic and popish as the Roman Catholic Church. And, the 1808 General Conference missed an opportunity to make the Methodist system accord with democratic and biblical practice. "WWhat scripture authority can you produce," asked Snethen, "to authorise you to govern Americans otherwise than as free men?" The reformers believed, as Bangs later noted, that responsibility ought to proceed up from the societies rather than down from General Conference (H **597nn102–4**).

The General Conference of 1824, which met again in Baltimore, evidenced the divisive bitterness that would last the decade. A resolution passed sixty-three to sixty-one deeming the votes taken in the conferences as a majority against election of PEs. Similar split votes came on elections to the episcopacy, the constitutionalists putting in Soule and the reformers putting in Elijah Hedding. General Conference also rejected petitions for representation of laity and local preachers, authorizing a circular to be conveyed by PEs to members, explaining why no change in "the present order of our Church Government" was needed or wanted (H **597n106**). While General Conference met, a number of reformers who thought differently, including seventeen members of General Conference, convened to constitute the Baltimore Union Society. The new society embraced the periodical *Mutual Rights,* employing it to encourage the formation of other such societies. The reform rocked Methodism's center, the Baltimore Conference, but gained adherents south in Virginia and North Carolina and west into Ohio and Pennsylvania. Other union societies emerged, and the Maryland and District of Columbia reformers met in a convention in November 1826, Nicholas Snethen in the chair, and issued a call for a General Convention of Reformers the next year.

The Baltimore Annual Conference, rent with the controversy, sought to suppress the movement. In 1827, under the presidency of Bishops McKendree, George, Soule, and Roberts, it denied appointment to one preacher for advocacy of *Mutual Rights* and passed a motion deeming "highly censurable" any form of "opposition to our Discipline and Church Government" (H **597n108**). The controversy escalated with exchanges in pamphlets and between *Mutual Rights* and the newly created *Christian Advocate* (New York) and the *Methodist Magazine* (MQR). In *History and Mystery of Methodist Episcopacy,* Alexander McCaine alleged that the episcopal form of government had been conspiratorially imposed and was not Wesley's intention. Irish-born McCaine was significant enough to require refutation as he served as presiding elder and had been elected as secretary of the 1820 General Conference though not a member. Respondents, including John Emory in *Defence of "Our Fathers"* and Thomas Bond in "An Appeal to the Methodists, in Opposition to the Changes Proposed in Their Church Government," argued that the reforms undercut the very genius of Methodism, itinerancy itself, the principle of sacrifice inherent in it, and "the MISSIONARY character of our ministry" (H **598nn110–11**).

Recriminations against Reformers intensified. Presiding elders in the Baltimore Conference levied charges and initiated trial proceedings against twenty-five laity and eleven local preachers, expelling the former and suspending the latter, Alexander McCaine included. In that climate, the union societies, now some twenty-four in number, met in a general convention in November 1827. The convention elected officers, established a committee of vigilance and correspondence, and drafted a memorial to General Conference, again setting forth the democratic case in church government (S **1827b**).

A NEW CHURCH

The MEC General Conference of 1828 was in no mood for democratic reform. It declared the (suspended) presiding elder legislation void, dismissed the memorials from the Reformers' convention (rejecting lay representation), confirmed the suspensions, and offered relief from these decisions only if the union societies were dissolved and *Mutual Rights* suspended (S **1828**). Having faced this challenge to its polity and constitution, the conference also initiated the first amendment of the constitution, refining procedure for amendment of the Restrictive Rules. The original version (S **1808**) required concurrence "of all the annual conferences," the dissent of a single conference functioning as a veto. The amendment substituted a majority of three-fourths of the members of annual conferences and excepted the first doctrinal restrictive rule. To the entire connection, and not to the several annual conferences as constituted bodies, would future constitutional appeals be made.

With expulsions continuing and new congregations forming, the second General Convention of Methodist Reformers met in Baltimore and laid plans for another conference and the formation of a new denomination. Articles of Association were adopted (to be worked into a *Discipline* two years later), which provided for equal lay and clergy representation in annual conferences and General Conferences and an elective presidency, but retained the "Articles of Religion, General Rules, Means of Grace, Moral Discipline, and Rites and Ceremonies in the Main of the Methodist Episcopal Church" (H **598n117**). The convention deputized agents, including Nicholas Snethen and Alexander McCaine, to travel on behalf of the cause. By the time the 1830 General Convention met, the Reformers had organized twelve annual conferences. That convention, also in Baltimore, where the movement had its greatest strength, ratified the new *Constitution and Discipline,* elected as president Francis Waters (ordained but functioning as an educator), at his prompting chose the name The Methodist Protestant Church, appointed a book committee, and authorized the transformation of *Mutual Rights* into an official church weekly. The new entity accomplished two of the three major Reformers' aims, an elective superintendency and lay representation; local preachers were not granted conference membership. The president would station preachers, though subject to revision by an annual conference committee. Its disciplinary preface traced the Reform cause back to Wesley and scriptural holiness (H **172–74**).

Over the next decades, Methodist Protestants competed with Methodist Episcopals even as new churches emerged, in each of which divisions race figured (Wesleyans, MECS, Free Methodists, CMEs). On that form of "liberty," The Methodist Protestant Church took a pass. The reforming denomination denied its "colored members" the vote and membership in General Conference and permitted each annual conference to form its own rules "for the admission and government of coloured members within its district; and to make for them such terms of suffrage as the conferences respectively may deem proper" (H **598n122**).

Methodist ambivalence on slavery betokened its growing "respectability," the adherence to it in North and South of the propertied (and slaveholding) class, the church's coming to terms with culture, its concern for and investment in the social order. Methodist Protestants, strong in what would become border states, evidenced the doubleness of Methodist acculturation. They embraced societal values of democracy but also of ambivalence on slavery. Yet they sought to transform society by bringing in converts, instilling values, and providing uplift (Sunday schools, missions, colonization, educational endeavor [founding of colleges particularly]). In reforming the continent and spreading Scripture holiness over these lands, Methodism found itself both a change agent and a changed entity (H **598nn124–25**).

97

CHAPTER V
METHODISM AND SLAVERY: 1830–60s

A revived antislavery movement of the 1830s exposed and widened a sectionally divided Methodism. In the East, immediatist William Lloyd Garrison connected abolition with an array of radical reforms. In the Midwest, Christian abolitionists, including Methodists, knit antislavery together with perfectionist evangelicalism. Abolition in both its variants pronounced slaveholding a sin and slavery evil, called Christians to repent therefrom, embraced slaves freed from and slaveholders converted from this evil, supported the Underground Railroad, and attacked the institution and all of its alliances, North and South. This aggressive, denunciatory critique enraged the South and induced southerners, Methodists included, to defend slavery, an apology that grew more explicit and vehement over the next several decades, leading Methodists to articulate a "doctrine" that the church as spiritual stood above and apart from politics. Eventually some southern Methodists joined other Protestants in issuing outright biblical and theological justifications of slavery (S **1856**; H **599n2**). Slave disquiet, slave conspiracies, and slave insurrections, most notably those of Methodist Denmark Vesey in Charleston in 1822 and of millenarian Nat Turner in Virginia in 1831, reinforced slaveholder and southern support for its peculiar institution. Defensive apologetics read the Bible for its literal sense, noted slavery's place in Old Testament and New, and drew upon Scripture for a slaveholder's ethic.

99

SECTIONALIZED METHODISM

Regionalizing changes in Methodism made the church (its conferences and laity) particularly receptive or hostile to the antislavery gospel. Of great importance were the media then available, newspapers and magazines, which we have already seen proved important in the spread of the Methodist Protestant cause. In The MEC, one national paper, *Christian Advocate and Journal* (New York), and one connectional review, the *Methodist Magazine (MQR)*, competed for Methodist Episcopal attention with regional papers the *Western Christian Advocate* (Cincinnati), *Zion's Herald* (Boston), the *Pittsburgh Christian Advocate,* and three southern papers—the *Southwestern Christian Advocate* (Nashville), the *Richmond Christian Advocate,* and the *Southern Christian Advocate* (Charleston).

Preachers, particularly those in the eastern conferences, increasingly lived out their careers in a single conference and came to view their membership as conference based. The *Minutes* reflected that regional orientation. Beginning in 1824, they were structured on a conference-by-conference rather than unified, question-by-question basis. Reinforcing that conference orientation, the reward structure—including election to General Conference and appointment to the presiding eldership—presupposed close annual conference ties and collegial support. And General Conference came to structure itself in accordance with such conference membership patterns, routinely "one from each annual conference." Of ten standing committees in 1840, four were so representative: episcopacy, boundaries, itinerancy, and *slavery.*

Bishops, too, elected in the politicized atmosphere of the Methodist Reform movement, none from the South, acquired regional commitments. Robert Richford Roberts (Philadelphia) and Enoch George (Baltimore), elected in 1816; Joshua Soule (Maine), elected but demurring in 1820 and reelected in 1824; and Elijah Hedding (New England), elected in 1824, with the aged and ill William McKendree, constituted the church's episcopal leadership. Between 1824 and division in 1844, Hedding made one tour south, and Soule one north. George and Hedding worked Philadelphia and north. Roberts and Soule, Baltimore and south. "The bishops were localized," affirmed Tigert. Kirby concurs, "McKendree was American Methodism's last real itinerant general superintendent" (H **599n6**).

Sectional media, sectional ministry, and sectional episcopacy reinforced the powerful sectional currents in the society as a whole, especially those that divided North and South. The MEC increasingly divided along regional lines, in various ways, on various issues, including (already) the knotty constitutional problems posed by the Reformers. Energizing intradenominational sectionalism were societal developments that would not stay out of the sanctuary—a revived abolitionism in the North; a southern economy tied ever more securely to the institution of slavery; fierce, sometimes violent competition between proslavery and Free-Soilers in the expansion West; and a Congress and court system embroiled over slavery and its "protection." The sectionalizing forces indeed infected the whole social order, a point eloquently made by the abolitionists as they traced out the dependency on slavery that ran through northern society. Sectional division of the churches produced intense moral warfare and principled posturing, undergirded by fears and hopes about slavery. Several popular, evangelical denominations with national constituencies divided North and South, the Presbyterians in the late 1830s, the Baptists and Methodists in the mid-1840s. The church splits elicited prophesy from prescient editors and agonized statespersons, including John C. Calhoun and Henry Clay, who wondered whether a nation could hold together if Christians could not.

Schisms anticipated, set precedent for, and established a moral and religious warrant for, and aggravated, if they did not cause, the growing division of the nation. The MEC/MECS schism will be our focus, but four divisions can be traced directly to the sectional/slavery crisis—those represented by the Wesleyan Methodist Church, The Methodist Episcopal Church, South, the Free Methodist Church, and the Colored Methodist Episcopal Church. (To some extent later holiness movements also trace their concerns with the church back to this politicizing of it.) The United Brethren Church and The Evangelical Association saw abolitionist activity but, as predominantly northern bodies, escaped some of the intensity of the struggle and did not suffer rupture. To reiterate, the church divisions prefigured, if they did not directly effect, the division of the nation (H **599nn7–9**).

METHODIST ABOLITION AND AN ANTISLAVERY CHURCH

In the New England Conference (MEC), converts to the abolitionist cause, notably La Roy Sunderland and Orange Scott, used existing

101

structures—camp meetings, quarterly conferences, rallies, letters, petitions, and elections—to attack colonization (S **1832b**), the church's acquiescence in slavery, and editors' suppression of antislavery submissions. They targeted Nathan Bangs, editor of the *Christian Advocate* (New York) after 1834, who denied abolitionists access but in articles and editorials defended the status quo. "An Appeal on the Subject of Slavery Addressed to the Members of the New England and New Hampshire Conferences" (S **1834**) charged that Bangs did "apologize for the crimes of the enslavers of the human species and attempt to justify the system." Positively it set forth the Methodist case against slavery, including a reprinting of Wesley's condemnation (H **599n12**). Scott followed up the attack of the "Appeal" with a weekly column "Slavery" that ran from January to April. Responses, criticisms, and a counter-column prompted Scott et al. to publish the "Appeal" along with a "Defense of the 'Appeal'" as a *Zion's Herald . . . Extra*. In May, abolitionists established a New England Wesleyan Anti-Slavery Society. In June, abolitionists gained six of the seven delegates to the following General Conference. They failed to pass antislavery resolutions, the questions not being put by the presiding bishop, Elijah Hedding, but did beat back motions of censure on their activities.

Bishop Hedding had a hand in a "counter-appeal" signed also by key members of the church's intelligentsia, including theologian D. D. Whedon, Wesleyan president Wilbur Fisk, and editor Abel Stevens. Hedding joined with Bishop John Emory in a pastoral letter to that conference (and also New Hampshire), published in the *Christian Advocate*, further reprimanding the abolitionists. Other conferences adhered to the bishops' position, and the subsequent General Conference acted to muffle the antislavery cause and censure two delegates for abolitionist activity. Its "pastoral address" dealt with "abolitionism" at length and exhorted the members and friends of the church "to abstain from all abolition movements and associations, and to refrain from patronizing any of their publications." The address expressed "the solemn conviction, that the only safe, Scriptural, and prudent way for us, both as ministers and as people, to take, is wholly to refrain from this agitating subject, which is now convulsing the country, and consequently the Church" (H **600n16**).

The bishops endeavored to see that the following annual conferences take this "safe, Scriptural, and prudent way." They suppressed abolition, used tactics of delay, made punitive appointments, brought charges, denied abolitionists the right to introduce memorials. Like the suppression of petition and debate in the Congress, this episcopal stance gave to abolition a second cause, "conference rights." Thereafter Scott and another reformer, George Storrs, went from conference to conference (in the North) preaching abolition and raising the conference rights banner. The bishops attempted to inhibit this abolitionizing and employed the annual review of the character of the preachers to press charges against those who "agitated" the issue. The church's papers generally followed the bishops' practice of muzzling the controversy, led in that cause by Nathan Bangs and the New York–based *Christian Advocate*.

Abolitionist ferment, however, drew active response in southern papers and conferences, where tacit acceptance of slavery turned into articulation of the doctrine that the church as spiritual should not indulge itself in politics and even an explicit proslavery rationale. Southern conferences issued resolutions condemning abolition, denying that slavery was sin, and insisting that the institution ought, as a civil matter, to be beyond the church's attention. The Georgia Annual Conference resolved "that slavery, as it exists in the United States, is *not a moral evil*" (H **600n21**). Much of the church, including some of its strongest conferences, like Baltimore, found itself torn between the two poles, fighting both explicit proslavery sentiment and abolitionism.

Bishops presiding over the southern conferences did not muzzle these defenses of slavery and attacks on abolition as their episcopal counterparts had the abolitionists. The problem, as they saw it, was not slavery but abolition. In their address to the next (1840) General Conference, the bishops called to mind the "Pastoral Address" of 1836 and its counsel "to abstain from all abolition movements," but regretted "that we are compelled to say, that in some of the northern and eastern conferences, in contravention of your Christian and pastoral counsel, and of your best efforts to carry it into effect, the subject has been agitated in such forms, and in such a spirit as to disturb the peace of the Church" (H **600n23**). In yet further concession to the slave South, the General Conference passed a resolution proposed by Emory president Ignatius Few: "*Resolved,* That it is inexpedient and unjustifiable for any preacher among us to permit colored persons to give testimony against white persons, in any state where they are denied that privilege in trials at law." In a richly symbolic gesture, the bishops refused to bring into General Conference a petition by Baltimore African American Methodists protesting this latter action (H **600nn25–26**).

Southerners won the key battles at the 1840 General Conference. Conservatives won editor elections of the northern papers, Thomas Bond over the *Christian Advocate,* Abel Stevens over *Zion's Herald,* and Charles Elliott over the *Western Christian Advocate.* Conceding defeat, Orange Scott, La Roy Sunderland, and Jotham Horton withdrew, the first stage in the formation of yet another Methodist body, the Wesleyan Methodist Connection (S **1842b**). They condemned The MEC as "not only a slave-holding, but a slavery defending, Church" and as governed by "principles not laid down in the Scriptures, nor recognized in the usages of the primitive Church—principles which are subversive of the rights both of ministers and laymen." Titling its paper *True Wesleyan,* the movement pledged itself in an organizing convention at Utica in 1843 to Wesleyan principles on slavery, to "the cause of the bleeding slave," to temperance, to "every branch of moral reform," and "to make holiness your motto" (H **600nn28–29**). These "come-outers" appealed to and recruited among northern Methodists with sympathies for the slave, some six thousand adhering initially, fifteen thousand by their first General Conference convened in 1844.

By separation, abolitionists had more transforming effect on Methodist Episcopal conferences from outside than they had had earlier as an inside reforming impulse. Northern conferences increasingly reclaimed their antislavery heritage, passing resolutions to that effect in preparation for the 1844 General Conference. "Whole conferences," reported Abel Stevens, "which once rejected antislavery resolutions now sustain them with scarce a dissent, and it cannot be doubted that soon, very soon, all our northern conferences will be of one mind on the subject." Southern conferences and papers intensified their defenses, proclaimed slavery to be no moral evil, insisted that the institution itself lay beyond the church's purview, proposed the election of a slaveholding bishop, and prepared for division, should that be necessary (H **600nn30–31**).

GENERAL CONFERENCE 1844

Slavery posed weighty issues for The MEC General Conference of 1844: the nature of sin, the relation of the church to the social and political orders, the "real" meaning of church membership, constraints on office holding and testimony for [Black] classes of people, the nature and unity of the ministerial fraternity, the relation of episcopacy and conference, the location of sovereignty, the exercise of authority, and of course, preeminently slavery itself. The MEC put the questions to itself, in memorials and petitions that poured into General Conference from annual conferences and quarterly meetings. Particularly striking were the concurrences in resolutions that had gone from annual conference to annual conference, testing for common conference resolve. The 1840 General Conference, on a motion by Nathan Bangs, had authorized the full reporting of its proceedings in the *Christian Advocate,* and that precedent, followed thereafter, has left us with a full account of the month-long drama of 1844 (H **600n35**).

At this General Conference, the conservative middle and particularly the Baltimore Conference, not the abolitionists and New Englanders, tackled slavery. Tellingly, the body rejected the South's effort to prevent the creation of a committee on slavery. Another in a series of defeats came over an appeal from the Baltimore Conference by Francis A. Harding, who "had been suspended from his ministerial standing for refusing to manumit certain slaves which came into his possession by his marriage." Baltimore had judged him, as a slaveholder, acceptable only to the slaveholding region of the conference and therefore unfit to travel (H **600nn38–39**). General Conference's concurrence foreshadowed the decision that would be made in the case of Bishop James O. Andrew, whom the conference knew to be in the same situation and whose entanglement in slavery compromised the church's symbol of itself, its principles, and its unity—a superintendency, genuinely itinerant, really general—a self-understanding on which the bishops had been eloquent, explicit, and insistent in their opening address (H **183; 601n40**).

Had Bishop Andrew's situation, making him unwelcome to itinerate nationally and preside in the North, put his exercise of superintendency in violation of the third Restrictive Rule? The Committee on Episcopacy, to which the matter had been referred, reported the facts of the situation, prompting a motion requesting his resignation. After heated exchanges, Ohio delegates proposed a substitute that recognized his slaveholding status, deemed that to "greatly embarrass the exercise of the office as an itinerant General Superintendent, if not in some places entirely prevent it," and called for him to "desist from the exercise of this office so long as this impediment remains" (S **1844a**; H **601n45**). This framing of the issue permitted constitutional questions to subsume moral and political ones. Bishop Andrew claimed the floor to speak on his own behalf. He explained his "embarrassment," the impossibility of his freeing his slaves under Georgia law, his love for "the coloured people," and his sense that he functioned properly under the *Discipline* (S **1844b**).

The constitutional issues broadened and sharpened as the debate proceeded to include the relative powers of the episcopacy and General Conference. "Has the General Conference constitutional authority to pass this resolution?" queried L. L. Hamline, editor of the *Ladies' Repository*. Indeed, Hamline insisted. It possessed the authority to remove a bishop "for anything unfitting that office, or that renders its exercise unwholesome to the Church." Enunciating what would be The MEC constitutional principle, he affirmed, General Conference's "supremacy is universal." Methodist government, he explained, differs from civil, with its separation and distribution of powers. General Conference itself possesses all three: "It has legislative, judicial, and executive supremacy." General Conference grants the bishops certain executive authority, to be sure, but does so by statute. Any powers delegated to and exercised by the bishops that are not explicitly conveyed by the Restrictive Rules can be rescinded and reclaimed by General Conference. "This conference is the sun in our orderly and beautiful system," Hamline affirmed, an image and speech that elected him to the episcopacy (H **184–85; 601n47**).

Southerners enunciated what would be constitutional principles of The MECS. William Winans explained that what limited administrative powers General Conference enjoyed were conferred and delegated. The drafter of the Restrictive Rules that were being debated, Bishop Soule, joined the southern side, rejecting the notion that bishops were but officers of General Conference. Focusing the constitutional issue on himself and his office, he affirmed that he was "a bishop of the Methodist Episcopal Church—not the bishop of the General Conference, not the bishop of any annual conference" (H **185; 601nn48–49**).

The other four bishops, sensing that division loomed, submitted a letter proposing that the matter concerning Bishop Andrew be held over until the next General Conference. New England delegates caucused, decided they no longer willingly would "buy" unity with slaves and slavery, agreed to "secede in a body, and invite Bishop Hedding to preside over them." Hedding then withdrew his signature from the bishops' initiative, announcing that what he thought would be a peace measure would not be. The motion for Andrew "to desist" then passed. On the next business day William Capers, future southern bishop, offered resolutions to divide the church, which were referred to a committee of nine (H **601nn52–55**). The southerners proposed an amicable division of the church through a constitutional amendment providing for two

General Conferences, a northern and a southern. Over the next days southerners and northerners exchanged formal position papers. The former insisted that
"the episcopacy is a co-ordinate branch, the executive department proper of the
church" and "not a mere creature" of General Conference (H 601n58). The
northerners interpreted the action in the case of Bishop Andrew followed the
recurring and basic principle of itinerancy—the examination of character—a
principle exercised in annual conference over traveling preachers and in General
Conference over bishops. It rejected "episcopacy supremacy" as "at variance
with the genius of Methodism," "the express language of the Discipline," and
"the exposition of it by all our standard writers" (H **601n60**).

As if timed to accent the emerging northern understanding of General
Conference supremacy, the Committee on Slavery reported resolutions
rescinding the proscription in church trials of testimony by "persons of
colour," stipulating that no slaveholding bishop be elected, urging that
conference take measures "entirely to separate slavery from the church," but
proposing no change in the General Rules on slavery (H **601n59**).

The Committee of Nine on the Division of the Church followed the design
outlined by Capers and reported plans for an amicable division of the church.
It provided for measures to assure peaceful delineation of a boundary between
the churches and to divide property. A key provision, an enabling constitutional
revision of one of the restrictive articles, required three-fourths majorities in
annual conferences—and assured that the debates and acrimony of General
Conference would become those of the following annual conferences (S
1844c). Peter Cartwright, who spoke immediately on the introduction of these
resolutions, "thought the proposed arrangements would create war and strife in
the border conferences." Concurring, *Christian Advocate* editor Thomas Bond
wondered if the intent of the committee had been "to provide for peace, and
love, and harmony still to be perpetuated in the great Methodist family. . . .
Why then . . . if the object is to procure peace and to prevent conflicts—why,
then, does it provide for a border warfare from Delaware to the Ohio River?"
(H **601nn61–62**). The resolutions nevertheless passed.

METHODIST EPISCOPAL CHURCH, SOUTH

The delegates from the slaveholding states met following adjournment,
called a convention to be held in Louisville, May 1, 1845, for the annual

conferences "within the slaveholding States," and issued an explanatory address "To the Ministers and Members of the Methodist Episcopal Church, in the Slaveholding States and Territories." Stating the call in terms of slavery, the address set forth a southern ecclesiology of the division (H **601n65**):

> The separation proposed is *not* schism, it is *not* secession. It is a State or family, separating into two different States of families, by mutual consent. As the "Methodist Episcopal Church" will be found North of the dividing line, so the "Methodist Episcopal Church" will be found South of the same line.

Familial feeling did not last. Annual conferences, North and South, obliged to deal with the matter, confirmed the predictions of Bond and Cartwright. Resolutions, pastoral addresses, and editorials in regional *Advocates* lobbed volleys in what would be a war—section against section, conference against conference, church against church. Southern conferences issued formal expressions of disapproval over the 1844 General Conference. They deemed the action on Andrew illegal and motivated by abolitionism. They established committees on separation or division and approved the called convention. And they passed the amendment to the sixth Restrictive Rule that would permit the division of property (particularly the Book Concern, now UMPH; and pension resources, the Chartered Fund, now Wespath).

Northern papers (*Zion's Herald,* the [New York] *Christian Advocate and Journal,* the *Western Christian Advocate,* the *Pittsburgh Christian Advocate,* and the *Northern Advocate*) entered countercriticisms (H **601n70**). The first MEC conferences to meet voted before this *Advocate* warfare was felt and acted favorably on the key constitutional issue in the division of the church, the amendment of the Restrictive Rule. By August when North Ohio met, MEC resentment was building, and that conference defeated the amendment, as did most of the following conferences. Ohio voted 132 to 1 against the change. These conferences also put their judgments before the public. Illinois explained that "we do not concur in, but strongly deprecate and oppose, any sectional division of, or separation from, the Methodist Episcopal Church." Ohio expressed pain over "the *politico-religious* aspect which the question of division has assumed at the south." So MEC (northern) conferences assumed an equal, if not more intense, politico-religious aspect. Ohio, in fact, found itself initially chaired by Bishop Joshua Soule, who had already pledged allegiance to the South. Ohio voted his presidency "inexpedient and highly improper" and forced Soule from the chair (H **602nn71–73**). Conferences, North and South, roiled with politics. And each controversial act seemed to stimulate others. The property issue alone, defeated by the votes of the northern conferences, festered for years, drawing attention from conferences as well as *Advocates*. Even its resolution ten years later, by the US Supreme Court, did not end the acrimony.

The 1845 Louisville Convention proceeded with calm deliberation to carry out the will of the several southern conferences, voting "that it is right, expedient, and necessary to erect the Annual Conferences represented in this Convention, into a distinct ecclesiastical connexion, separate from the jurisdiction of the General Conference of the Methodist Episcopal Church, as at present constituted" (H **602n74**). The convention in turn called the first General Conference for The MECS, which met in Petersburg (Virginia) in 1846. This body elected two additional bishops, Capers and Robert Payne. It undertook initiatives in higher education, established missionary machinery, authorized several *Advocates* and called for a new hymnal. The MECS adopted an adjusted *Discipline*, in a long preface narrating its history as that of American Methodism and explaining its emergence as a church (H **189–92**). And it explained all this to southern Methodists in a pastoral address.

MEC VS. MECS

The 1845 southern convention, in implementing the Plan of Separation, took action calculated to ensure further politicization, authorizing the bishops to incorporate into its conferences "any societies or stations adjoining the line of division, provided such societies or stations, by a majority of the members, according to the provisions of separation adopted by the late General Conference, request such an arrangement" (H **602n77**) Existing conference boundaries and the line drawn thereby between The MEC and The MECS did not circumscribe loyalties or sentiments about slavery. Conference boundaries crossed state lines. The northern conferences encompassed slaveholding areas. Some antislavery or more often anti-slaveholder sentiment existed in southern conferences, notably in Kentucky. Itinerants and presiding elders enjoyed close relations with circuits and congregations cut off by the new lines.

Provision for adjusting the borders and changing church loyalty created ongoing problems. Who voted? How long did such voting go on? Could small segments of a circuit go their own way? Did a redrawn line permit formerly interior circuits to vote? Territorial skirmishes erupted in the Delmarva Peninsula, western Virginia, Kentucky, Ohio, and Missouri.

In the ensuing border skirmishes, each side attempted to claim and consolidate within its borders the congregations and circuits that, in its judgment, it should have by right, by prior possession, by family relation, by convictions. Each side saw the other's comparable actions as illicit. And ironically, the border contests induced The MEC to tone down its antislavery rhetoric, indeed to quiet it, a strategy designed to hold slaveholding congregations, circuits, and districts within the northern church.

In this bitter spirit, the 1848 MEC General Conference, after having received fraternal delegations from the British and Canadian Methodists and returned their fraternal expressions, pointedly rebuffed a similar expression from The MECS. Lovick Pierce had presented its "Christian salutations," seeking "warm, confiding, and brotherly, fraternal relation" and expecting acceptance "in the same spirit of brotherly love and kindness." Instead, The MEC, noting the "serious questions and difficulties existing between the two bodies," did not "consider it proper, at present, to enter into fraternal relations with the Methodist Episcopal Church, South." Pierce responded that his communication was "final on the part of the M.E. Church, South." The 1848 MEC General Conference also undid the work of 1844. It declared that the constitutional amendment had failed. Under the guidance of a committee on the state of the church, the conference repudiated, declared "null and void," the Plan of Separation, judging that the 1844 General Conference could not legally divide the church (H **602nn83–84**). And The MEC General Conference authorized the formation of a Western Virginia Conference, a stake on territory also claimed by The MECS. In response, the southern church also organized a West Virginia Conference.

FURTHER DIVISION OVER SLAVERY

The late 1850s brought politicization around slavery and antislavery in both The MPC and The MEC, energizing laity and posing the issue of lay rights in the latter. Northerners outraged over the Fugitive Slave Law of

1850 challenged the churches' quiescence on slavery. A two-decade division within The MPC occurred, and an antislavery Methodist Church emerged when the 1858 Methodist Protestant General Conference turned down petitions to strengthen its antislavery commitments. For The MEC, the new antislavery front opened in the Genesee Conference (New York), which found itself embroiled in controversy over slavery, holiness, choirs, pew rent, secret societies—all touchstones for accommodation to the social order. The conference divided itself politically between "Nazarites" who called for return to the fraternal, revivalistic old standards, including unqualified commitment to antislavery, and those they characterized as "New School Methodists" or the "Buffalo Regency" (S **1860**). The leader of this primitivist reform impulse was B. T. Roberts. A product of small-town western New York Methodism, Roberts had gone east to college, to Wesleyan University, and developed ties to important MEC leaders, among them holiness advocates Phoebe and Walter Palmer.

Appointed in 1852 to Niagara Street, Roberts undertook a style of revival and reform that called Methodism back to what he took to be its core values, practices, and commitments—outreach to the poor, a disciplined life, the quest for holiness, camp meetings, and antislavery. His activities put him in contest with conference leaders, including the new head of the Book Concern, Thomas Carlton, previously pastor at Niagara Street and under whom the church, once Buffalo's largest, had declined and been left burdened with a huge debt. Roberts and a camp meeting network of like-minded reformers issued from the pulpit and in the press a withering critique of practices they deemed to stand in the way of revival, practices that either introduced or symbolized emerging class distinctions within the church, or both—pew rental, then the key device for funding ever more lavish churches; and secret societies, especially the Masons, the purported context within which the Genesee elite (Carlton and company) ran the conference. Through trials, harassment, and expulsions, Roberts and colleagues were forced from church editorships and from pulpits. The reformers founded their own paper, the *Northern Independent,* held laymen's conventions, garnered support for ousted ministers, and in 1860 founded the Free Methodist Church (H **602n88**).

To stem defections to the Free Methodists, The MEC General Conference passed in 1860 a "new chapter" on slavery explicitly declaring that "the buying, selling, or holding of human beings, to be used as chattels, is contrary to the laws of God and nature, inconsistent with the Golden Rule, and with that rule in our Discipline . . . to 'do no harm and to avoid evil of every kind'" (H **602n89**). Border conferences, including important East Baltimore and Philadelphia, meeting thereafter were deluged with petitions and resolutions calling for its repeal.

Laity had things to say about the fundamental social issues on which the church was then speaking. Within The MEC and The MECS, quarterly conferences did permit laity a voice. Increasingly, the laity felt restive at having their opinions and influence confined to quarterly conference as conferences embroiled themselves politically and spoke on national questions. So in episcopal Methodism the issue that Methodist Protestants championed— lay representation—resurfaced. A politicized episcopal Methodism faced but defeated resolutions for lay representation, The MEC in 1852 and The MECS in 1854. The issue would return, necessitated by the locality of quarterly conference and the divisive issues before the church (S **1864a**). The controversy in the Genesee Conference had widened to division through the holding of a succession of Laymen's Conventions, the first in 1858, the second in 1859, the third in 1860, each of them functioning politically. They issued resolutions, circulated petitions, gathered money, and organized "Bands." In 1859 a Ministers' and Laymen's Union was formed within the New York Conference, a body dedicated to preserving the status quo on the slavery issue within The MEC. In response, a rival antislavery society of the New York East Conference, also ministers and laity, pressed for change.

A laymen's convention sat concurrently with the Baltimore Conference of 1861 at Staunton (Virginia) and nudged it into an act of secession. The first item of business for this annual conference was the memorial from the "Convention of Laymen which assembled in Baltimore in December last, relating to the action on Slavery by the General Conference . . . 1861." The conference also took up memorials from Light Street, Alexandria, and Frankford Circuit. On the tenth day, after testy sessions with presiding Bishop Levi Scott, the conference put and passed a motion protesting an 1860 General Conference action on slavery (the New Chapter) (1) as unconstitutional; (2) as breaking the organic law of the Constitution of the church; (3) as destroying the unity of the church; (4) as false, heterodox, and unscriptural; (5) as misinterpreting the existing rules on slavery; and (6) as a bar to reception of members, ordination of deacons, and ordination of bishops. The conference then acted to break with The MEC.

The next (1862) Baltimore Conference met in Baltimore rather than in Virginia, that is, outside the Confederacy, and recognized the actions of the previous conference as an act of severance and those not present as withdrawing. This annual conference entertained but voted down lay delegation, thirty-four against twenty-two. It had seen the power of lay initiative, and so had the southerners who took an earlier liking to the idea. The MECS approved lay representation in 1866. Laity, they recognized, belonged in politicized and business-like conferences that legislated on social issues and stated the church's position and set policy for the whole. And with the collapse of quarterly meeting into station or small circuit, laity demanded a role on more effective conference levels, that is, annual and general. The MEC heard from its laity on the matter in 1864 (S **1864a**; chapter VII), finally conceding to lay delegation in 1872 but only on the General Conference level. Women's rights to representation and ordination lay further ahead. Politics hovered over conference activities, and conferences ordered themselves (or disordered themselves) for politics.

CHAPTER VI

A METHODIST CIVIL WAR: 1860–65

By the eve of the Civil War, membership in the Methodist denominations (UBC, EA, MPC, MEC, MECS) had reached 1.8 million (S **p22**), 5.7 percent of the total US population. Those attending and supporting the churches far exceeded actual membership, totaling closer to 3.8 million, making the Methodist family the largest US communion, surpassing both Catholics and Baptists (H **603n1**). Dispersing itself across the expanding nation and evangelizing its many peoples—The MEC had already established California and Oregon Conferences, The MECS had formed the Pacific Conference, UBC missionary efforts on the West Coast were underway, and the EA was soon to follow—Methodism embraced and reflected the nation in its many hues. With its numbers, its spread, its internal diversity, its growing prosperity, its connectional apparatus, its effective media, and its presence in city as well as town and countryside, Methodism felt itself entitled to a place in civic and religious leadership, a role in making America a Protestant nation.

That sense of civil religious entitlement would bring Methodists to the fore on both sides of the Civil War. President Lincoln's blessing on Methodists for support of the war cause (S **1864b**) could equally have been uttered by his Confederate counterpart. At the same time Methodists, North and South, betrayed the various, complex, and changing attitudes toward the two governments and the war. As public theologians, spokespersons for war, on patriotism, and on slavery, Methodists participated actively in sermons and resolutions in giving meaning(s) to the bloody sacrifices, including that of Lincoln. And for decades thereafter the war experience indelibly stamped

115

Methodism, North and South, its leaders-to-be, its institutions, its practices, and its self-understanding.

METHODIST CONFEDERACY

As the slave states seceded and despite several decades of commitment to spirituality and neutrality and explicit counsel from the southern bishops to stay above the fray, some editors, conferences, and individual ministers began to preach southern patriotism as a religious duty, the Confederate cause as one ordained by God, and the war as one for independence. Methodist preachers encouraged laity to enlist and also volunteered as regular soldiers, noncombatants, and chaplains, some seventy-two of the ordained being appointed as officers or serving in the enlisted ranks in 1861 alone (H **603nn3–4**). Conferences voted approval of secession, the Georgia Annual Conference acting a month before the state by its commitment. The 1861 Tennessee Conference requested Bishop Joshua Soule to "appoint as many preachers of this conference as he may deem proper to the chaplaincy of our army." Appoint he and the other bishops did. Methodists came to constitute almost half of the Confederate chaplaincy.

The southern Missionary Society constituted the southern army as itself a mission. The MECS bishops convened concurrently with the Missionary Society and by 1863 recognized Bishop Robert Paine as Methodist superintendent of the army and W. W. Bennett, president of Randolph-Macon, as the man in charge of publication for the army. Also in 1863, the Missionary Society drafted a nine-point enabling "Army Mission" program. Union occupation of Nashville in 1862 dispersed leadership from MECS headquarters, putting the Missionary Society into its own itineration and shutting down The Methodist Publishing House and the *Nashville Christian Advocate*. Book Editor Thomas O. Summers and Book Agent John B. McFerrin fled. Other *Advocates* took up some of the communication and publication slack, all succumbing, however, by war's end.

Methodist army missionaries, chaplains, and preachers under arms worked the camps, distributing Bibles and tracts, conducting services, holding revivals, organizing army churches, writing letters for soldiers or teaching them to read and write, nursing the wounded, praying with the maimed, burying the dead, and consoling those to be executed. Often chaplains and army missionaries accompanied regiments from their own town or region. The chaplains—poorly paid, meagerly provisioned, an afterthought within the Confederate army—worked under often indifferent, sometimes hostile, only occasionally supportive commanding officers. The lack of consistent support from officers—symbols of the elite, the genteel and planter class—would color ministerial class attitudes thereafter, encouraging greater dependence on and attention to professionals and merchants. Army service, however, permitted Methodist preachers to demonstrate and exhibit the interconnection of piety, patriotism, and manliness. Some debated even a further symbolization of male honor—whether chaplains should bear arms.

Methodists took pride in revivals and conversions within the Confederate army, a matter for self-congratulation long after the war was over, as in the 1877 volume, *A Narrative of the Great Revival in the Southern Armies During the Late Civil War Between the States of the Federal Union.* Revivalistic campaigns flourished as the carnage and casualties mounted. General "Stonewall" Jackson aided the army mission by encouraging a more regularized ministry—the appointment of more chaplains, their itineration to cover unstaffed regiments, religious services at headquarters, associations of chaplains for more cooperative endeavor, and better supplies. With Jackson's counsel, Protestants formed chaplains associations throughout the Confederate army. By associating, working together, and offering morning, noon, or tattoo (evening) services, chaplains could sustain significant revival campaigns of a week's duration and even longer—twenty-one days, thirty days, and four months and five days in a Georgia regiment. More generalized revivals occurred in the Army of Tennessee and the Army of Northern Virginia. The former produced 321 conversions and 728 church memberships in one month.

Preachers who stayed with or returned to their congregations supported families of the soldiers, visited hospitalized men, and conducted funerals and memorials for those killed. Congregations, always dominated by women, became even more so. And for southern women, the war called forth new roles and duties. Largely uninvolved in the early phases of the women's rights efforts, southern women found themselves obliged to take over and take on responsibilities abandoned as their men exited into the army. They managed the farms and plantations, oversaw the slaves, presided within the family, kept congregations going, supported the war effort with home manufactures, took over whatever schooling continued, and served as nurses.

The war encouraged southern women to have stronger interest in politics, in society, in national affairs. And it further stimulated female networking and formation of women's voluntary associations (H **603n13**). The home front saw no revivals comparable to those among the troops, and women's "religious work," which had typically reinforced the evangelization of "their" men, turned to pondering the ways of Providence, to writing letters of nurturing encouragement or condolence, to making sense of the carnage and impending defeat, and to sustaining the society's grief work. As the war progressed and casualties mounted, women took on the church's rituals for burial and the burden of mourning those killed. The new roles, enforced self-reliance, increased networking, and the defeat of a South committed to patriarchy opened new possibilities for southern women.

MILITARY DEFEAT AND MORAL VICTORY

The war wrought devastation on southern Methodism as on southern institutions generally. Church attendance dropped. Contributions shrank. Ministerial salaries went unpaid. Congregations lost their leaders. Churches were destroyed, damaged, or commandeered as Union armies advanced. The war effort, calling for sacrifice on all fronts, obliged the churches to invest in what would be a lost cause. Methodists placed college endowments in Confederate bonds, melted church bells, and sold property. Most tragically, the South as well as the North lost the members and leaders who gave their lives for the cause.

Amid the trauma of the war, Lincoln's Emancipation Proclamation, the continued critique of the South by the northern church, and looming defeat, southern Methodists joined with their Protestant counterparts in pleading that the *"moral and religious interests of the South ought to be appreciated by Christians of all nations."* They did so in an 1863 "Address to Christians Throughout the World by the Clergy of The Confederate States of America" (H **603n16**). Signed by the religious leaders of the South—Baptists, Disciples, Episcopalians, Lutherans, Presbyterians, and Methodists—it included the presidents of two MPC districts and of The MPC Lynchburg College and a who's who of The MECS, including four editors; presidents of Wofford, Randolph-Macon, and Trinity (now Duke University); prominent preachers; and three bishops, James O. Andrew, John Early, and G. F. Pierce.

118

These Christians declared that *"the war against the Confederate States has achieved no good result."* They indicated that their own commitment to the Confederacy and that of southerners generally remained firm, indeed changed "from all lingering attachment to the former Union, to a more sacred and reliable devotion to the Confederate Government." In the face of Lincoln's Emancipation Proclamation, they pledged continuing support for slavery. Deploring its abuses, they viewed the institution as "not incompatible with our holy Christianity," witnessed to their own love for the slaves "as souls for whom Christ died," and proclaimed the opportunity for Christianization of "Africans in our land" as given by "Divine Providence."

After the war's end southern Methodists would rethink to whom and what Providence had called them. That re-narration incorporated grievances over what The MEC had attempted in the South. Southern Methodists deeply resented the northern religious intrusion, The MECS especially, particularly after Bishop Edward Ames secured from Secretary of War Edwin Stanton an 1863 directive ordering officers to turn over to The MEC churches belonging to The MECS "in which a loyal minister, who has been appointed by a loyal Bishop of said Church does not officiate" (H **604n17**). Some property transfers went to northerners. In other instances, members of The MECS who had opposed secession assisted in that project. Though few, some southern Methodists, particularly in western Virginia and eastern Tennessee, favored the Union and opposed secession and the Confederacy. The most prominent dissenter and critic, William G. "Parson" Brownlow, of the Holston Conference, located and became editor successively of several Tennessee papers, the most important being the *Knoxville Whig*. Though a defender of slavery, he employed his editorials to support the Union, that is, until he was arrested and his paper was suppressed in 1861. Brownlow aided Bishop Matthew Simpson in the organization of an MEC Holston Conference. Forty preachers from Tennessee and six from elsewhere constituted that new entity in 1865, which began with one hundred churches and six thousand members. A year later it claimed another fifty churches and three times that membership. Brownlow went further in such collaboration, being elected governor that same year and US senator in 1869. His last senatorial act was the introduction of a bill for land acquisition to build (historically Black) Fisk University.

With such takeovers occurring at various places under Union army control, with portions of the church within the Union throughout the war (Kentucky, Louisville, Missouri, and western Virginia Conferences) and their continuing commitment uncertain, and with Confederate defeat looming, northerners advocated and southerners wondered whether The MECS should simply cave in, dissolve. The MECS decided not. Ministers and laity in the Missouri Conference gathered in 1865 and issued a declaration of independence (S **1865a**): "*Resolved,* That we consider the maintenance of our separate and distinct ecclesiastical organization as of paramount importance and our imperative duty." This Palmyra Manifesto, whose commitment and sentiments were embraced across the church, grounded continuation of The MECS on "our Church doctrines and discipline" and on opposition to The MEC's "prostitution of the pulpit to political purposes." So the war and reconstruction experiences solidified a Methodist version of a doctrine widely shared across southern Protestantism, that of the spirituality of the church, the legacy of its "official" policy of neutrality toward slavery. Its antipolitical political creed posited southern purity and orthodoxy in contrast to northern prostitution and heresy, the partisan, political, and social resolutions of the wartime MEC conferences extensively documented and published by southern apologists (H **202, 604nn19–20**).

The southern church, by contrast, resolved as the Mississippi Conference proclaimed, to "preach Christ and him crucified. Do not preach politics. You have no commission to preach politics" (H **604n21**). The politically fervid antipolitical political atmosphere of southern conferences continued into Reconstruction, criticizing MEC efforts on behalf of the freed slaves and worrying as well over efforts by the AME and AMEZ. "And Are We Yet Alive" sang The MECS, having relocated the hymn in its 1847 hymnal from "Christian Fellowship" and placed it first (#272) among seven conference hymns and among three for "Opening Conference." The MECS sang that hymn at its next General Conference (1850). It would be that church's theme song for the next decades as it construed the war and slavery experiences into a civil religion of the lost cause.

NORTHERN METHODIST PATRIOTISM

Surrender and emancipation ended The MECS's burden of slavery and burdened it with the "lost cause." Secession and war ended the necessity for The MEC to temper critique of slavery so as to hold on to its southern borders and furthered northern Methodism's (UBC, EA, MPC, MEC) embrace of the

Protestant crusade to Christianize America. Indeed, if one date and one action might be taken to symbolize Methodism's inclusion within the Protestant establishment, it might well be Lincoln's response and General Conference's (MEC's) 1864 formal declaration to Lincoln of its patriotism, support for the war, and endorsement of the Emancipation Proclamation (S **1864b**). General Conference took that action under the "Stars and Stripes," which it decreed by unanimous and rising vote would fly over its entire session. Northern conferences of the UBC were no less resolute in their commitment to the cause of liberty and those fighting on its behalf (S **1864c**). Indeed, from the outbreak of the war, northern conferences brought the flag into their sessions, encouraged the war effort and Methodist participation therein, supported chaplains, demanded stronger national action on slavery, and denounced the secessionists (H **604n24**). To sustain the Methodist peoples in the Union cause, preachers, editors, and bishops articulated a theology of the nation, views of Providence, and a social ethic that reworked the Wesleyan doctrines and discipline into a civil religion.

In the North as in the South, Methodists experienced opposition or indifference to the "righteous" patriotic banner, especially in the border conferences. As we noted in the last chapter, several had responded vehemently to the 1860 new disciplinary chapter on slavery, Philadelphia demanding repeal, Baltimore dividing. Kentucky and Missouri, with a small MEC and a large MECS population, proved a religious as well as military battleground. In Kentucky, The MECS conference tilted toward the Union cause, and some eighteen preachers eventually withdrew and joined The MEC. Southern Methodists in Missouri tilted toward the Confederacy and harassed preachers of The MEC until northern troops secured the state within the Union and northern Methodists could return the favor. There, too, members and preachers switched into The MEC. In Ohio, opponents of the war, southern sympathizers, supporters of the peace Democrats, and resisters to the abolitionist cause coalesced into a Copperhead church. Calling itself the Christian Union, it survived the war as a holiness denomination, the Churches of Christ in Christian Union.

The outbreak of war, however, brought much of The MEC, MPC, EA, and UBC around to support of the Union, rallied by antislavery editors placed at the helm of the *Christian Advocate* (Edward Thompson) and the *Central Christian Advocate* (Charles Elliott) by the 1860 General Conference. Gilbert Haven assumed the editorship of *Zion's Herald* only after the war but throughout contributed to it and to other papers, championing the war as God's cause, indeed as a millennial mandate, to cleanse the nation (and church) of the sin of slavery (S **1867a**). Bishop Matthew Simpson, a friend and confidant of Lincoln and eulogist at his Springfield funeral, spoke frequently and eloquently on behalf of the nation and national unity, against slavery, for the war as divinely commissioned, and in the effort to raise money for the Union cause (S **1864e**). In sermons and exhortations, waving a "battle-torn flag," he evangelized for patriotism, turned revivalism political, elicited camp meeting fervor, and brought convictions and conversions. Many northern Methodists swung during the war into crusade mentality. Conferences passed patriotic resolutions, administered oaths to themselves and their probationers, brought the flag into their sessions, and called for days of national fasting and prayer. The Philadelphia Conference virtually reversed its actions of the prior year, made loyalty a disciplinary imperative, and required an affirmative to an additional ordination question: "Are you in favor of sustaining the Union, the Government and the Constitution of the United States against the present rebellion?" Then it adopted the "Report of the Committee on the State of the Country," which denounced the "unjust and wicked rebellion" and extended a similar oath of loyalty to all conference members (H **604n28**).

The 1864 General Conference (MEC) heard Bishop Thomas A. Morris preach on the spirit of Methodism. Beginning ten affirmations with "The Spirit of Methodism is . . . ," Morris characterized Methodism as a church committed to American society, capitalism, progress, and the Union. Methodism's spirit? The spirit of truth, the spirit of revival, the spirit of enterprise, the spirit of sacrifice, the spirit of progress, the spirit of improvement, the spirit of loyalty to the civil government, the spirit of patriotism, the spirit of liberty, and the spirit of liberality (H **604n32**). Under just such commitments, General Conference (MEC) joined other Protestant denominations in petitioning Congress to amend the preamble of the Constitution to affirm God's governance of the country. It also began, belatedly, the process of revising the General Rules so that holding, buying, or selling slaves would be a bar to church membership.

Northern conferences of the UBC, for instance, that of Miami (Ohio), passed similar statements calling for the nation to carry through on the war effort, end the rebellion, and complete the overthrow of slavery with consti-tutional guarantees of freedom (S **1864c**). Similarly, having lost much of its southern and slavery-oriented territory just prior to the Civil War, Methodist

Protestantism expressed its support in its 1862 General Conference for the Emancipation Proclamation and its repudiation of disloyalty to the Union cause.

MINISTRY IN THE ARMY

Methodist laity responded to such challenges and volunteered in record numbers, perhaps some 125,000 all told. So did the preachers, both as chaplains and as soldiers. One regiment, the 73rd Illinois, even earned the designation "the preacher regiment" because of the number therein, the result of the mobilizing efforts of one minister, James Jaquess. An Ohio minister, Charles C. McCabe, recruited thousands, his sermons producing the 122nd Ohio Regiment, for which he then served as chaplain. Known as the "singing chaplain," he was captured, incarcerated in the Libby Prison in Richmond, and freed in a prisoner exchange but not before teaching other prisoners "The Battle Hymn of the Republic." Another recruiter-minister from Ohio, Granville Moody, accepted command of the 74th Ohio Regiment, preaching as well as leading and becoming known as the "gallant fighting preacher."

Methodists constituted the largest chaplains cohort within the Union armies, as on the Confederate side. Of the 2,154 regimental chaplains, 38 percent were Methodist. President Lincoln was clearer than Jefferson Davis on the necessity for chaplains, writing seven Washington ministers asking that they serve as military hospital chaplains. Congress and the War Department followed through with acts and directives establishing the office. Union chaplains worked every bit as ecumenically as their southern counterparts, partly aided by, partly competing with, the US Christian Commission. Founded in 1861 by the Young Men's Christian Association (YMCA) as a religious counterpart to another relief organization, the US Sanitary Commission, and endorsed by a YMCA-called convention of chaplains, the interdenominational Christian Commission intended to extend the revivalistic triumphs of the 1857–58 "businessmen's awakening" into the northern armies.

With strong lay leadership, aggressive fundraising, business-like revivalistic method, and rhetoric of masculine Christianity, the Christian Commission rallied northern laymen through its network of YMCA chapters to the cause of evangelizing the troops. The Christian Commission—Bishop Edmund Janes was one of its dozen commissioners and Methodists were heavily involved—effectively organized on both its recruitment and its deployment ends, placed its lay volunteers in the camps, in hospitals, and toward the front, each equipped with a handbook of duties and regulations and wearing a badge to signify his commission. Ministering to spirit and body and serving six-week stints, the lay volunteers circulated tracts, Bibles, and Scripture cards; cared for the dying, wounded, and lonely men; distributed stamps, envelopes, and stationery; wrote letters for soldiers; and led prayer meetings in "chapel tents" and YMCA rooms. By war's end the Christian Commission had deployed some five thousand volunteers, handed out 2.5 million publications, preached about fifty thousand sermons, and conducted seventy-five thousand prayer meetings. The Christian Commission enjoyed the support of President Lincoln and General Grant, and the soldiers in diaries and letters appreciatively noted its ministrations. And with such endorsement, particularly that of Grant, the commission played important roles in a revival that broke out in the Union armies in late 1863 and continued to 1865, a revival that followed very bloody battles, the converts numbering between one hundred thousand and two hundred thousand men. Sherman's troops took Charleston "singing Methodist hymns."

MOBILIZING METHODIST WOMEN

The Christian Commission and its relief effort rival, the US Sanitary Commission (USSC), depended on the involvement, labor, and resources of women. They served as volunteers, in paid capacity, sometimes within the male-dominated organizations, otherwise in auxiliaries. Black women, excluded from these organizations, formed their own, a Colored Women's Sanitary Commission (Philadelphia). Soldiers' Aid societies emerged spontaneously to gather supplies, roll bandages, collect foodstuff, prepare soldiers' wardrobes, visit the wounded, and conduct fairs and teas as fundraisers. With thousands of such emerging, a number of prominent New York women established in 1861 a coordinating agency, the Woman's Central Relief Association (WCRA), which was absorbed by and worked in tension with and in collaboration with the USSC. Male-female and local-national tensions surfaced also as the War Department pressed for efficiency, coordination, and uniformity.

Fundraising teas and fairs, which raised $100,000 in Chicago, $146,000 in Boston, $280,000 in Cincinnati, $320,000 in Pittsburgh, and $2 million in New York City, elicited and displayed northern patriotism at a point when self-doubt about and outright opposition to the war had emerged. They required considerable planning, organization, publicity, and follow-through—savvy that would thereafter be put to good use within northern Methodism. They constituted a public realm within which women held sway and dramatized their civic and patriotic commitments. And the fairs functioned to bring together women across class and religious lines. Women claimed and men could but observe "mothering" responsibilities and duties quite beyond the domestic sphere.

Women exercised civic "mothering" responsibilities within the male realm of the military as nurses, cooks, or laundresses. Some nine thousand earned the status and pension of "nurse," a role and title reserved for upper-class White women and for men. Lower-class and Black women, including Methodists whose names and efforts often went undocumented, worked in hospitals and camps without such recognition. Whether paid or volunteer, in nursing or other roles, women confronting the horrors, the carnage, the suffering, and participating in the very masculine endeavor of war found it prudent to accent their responsibilities as familial and mothering, as self-sacrificial and morally pure, and as appropriately domestic and respectable. They cared for the "boys," their boys. This empowerment by enlarging the domestic sphere had its limits. Women in all capacities worked within hierarchical military and hospital command structures. Authority and privilege adhered strictly to rules of race and gender, with Black women at the bottom. Such racist attitudes help explain why Black leaders had sought and continued to seek separate religious institutions.

NEW CARING INSTITUTIONS

In his second inaugural, President Abraham Lincoln summoned Americans "to care for him who shall have born the battle, for his widow and his orphan." In response, Methodists established, immediately and over several decades, Wesley-like institutions capable of sustained care (H **208–17**). German Americans reacted first to the command and the crisis. Since the early 1850s, Pastor William Ahrens had been urging German Methodists in America to open a *Waisenhaus* (orphanage) as the Methodist Conference in Germany had already done. Ahrens's appeals in the German Methodist newspaper, *Christliche Apologete,* bore fruit in 1864 when two German conferences opened orphanages, one on a farm near Berea, Ohio, and another in Warrenton, Missouri, to shelter Civil War and other orphans. Similarly, The Evangelical Association responded to the wartime challenge and established an orphans' asylum. An offer of one hundred acres of Ohio land added to the enthusiasm for the project, and Ebenezer Orphan Home opened in Flat Rock, Ohio, in 1866.

In 1866 a Home for Colored Orphans was founded in New Orleans by the two-year-old Black MEC Mississippi Mission Conference (see next section on Black conferences). Jennie Culver Hartzell, wife of Joseph C. Hartzell, later a bishop but then pastor of the largest White congregation in New Orleans, dramatized the needs and rallied support from northern women. She led the Woman's Home Missionary Society of The MEC to organize, support, and manage six residential homes for Black children in the South.

Southern Methodists also formed institutions for children orphaned by the war and by poverty. In 1869 a Georgia pastor, Jesse Boring, began a churchwide campaign to build Methodist orphanages across the South. The 1870 General Conference of The MECS endorsed Boring's plan and recommended each annual conference move as quickly as possible to establish an orphanage. Orphanages were established almost immediately by the North and South Georgia and Kentucky Conferences in the early 1870s; other conferences followed their lead in the 1880s. By 1900 every MECS conference had established at least one orphanage, fourteen in all.

Methodist women in San Francisco opened a home for Chinese children (Gum Moon Home) in 1870. The Woman's Missionary Society of the Pacific Coast, later the national Woman's Home Missionary Society, provided help and support for the work with finances and with volunteer workers. Shelter was provided for thirty to forty girls ranging in age from two to eighteen, and a day school accommodated more than a hundred children. In the urban East as well, Methodist women assumed much of the responsibility in the formation of children's homes. When a delegation of them visited a Philadelphia jail to distribute religious tracts in 1873, they were shocked to find dozens of young children behind bars. The women formed a committee to correct this injustice and garnered a lead gift of $10,000 in 1874. Ellen Simpson, wife of the church's most visible and powerful bishop and Lincoln confidant, helped mobilize the energy to build the best known of the nineteenth-century Methodist homes for children, The Methodist Episcopal Orphanage in Philadelphia, which opened in 1879.

Methodists founded homes for wayward children in Baltimore (1873), in New York (1885), in Chicago (1889), in Seward, Alaska (1890), in Oakland, California (1892), in Fall River, Massachusetts (1893), in San Francisco (1897), and in Washington, D.C. (1898). After its founding in 1882, the Woman's Home Missionary Society (WHMS) began building a network of child-care facilities. Mothers' Jewels Home for Children opened in 1890 in rural Nebraska. By 1916 the WHMS supervised a dozen such homes. The United Brethren opened their first orphanage in 1903 on a farm near Quincy, Pennsylvania. Methodist Protestant women opened a home for children in an abandoned school building in Denton, North Carolina, in 1910, later moved to High Point.

Women put their war-learned leadership and organizational skills to good use in and on behalf of these caring institutions. Though men were recruited as donors and trustees, women typically staffed and managed the daily operations and usually had some say in making major policy decisions. The institutions also depended on volunteer women board members, who spent large amounts of time in their orphanages caring for the children and put considerable effort into fundraising. Women orchestrated concerts, auctions, and fairs to benefit orphanages. Other sources of funding—such as dues, gifts, and bequests from individuals, and in some cases board money from parents—were crucial. Since a majority of orphans had at least one living parent, many orphanages urged surviving parents to pay a small amount toward their children's board.

Methodist women in Philadelphia, led by Jane Henry and Ellen Simpson initiated efforts to care for the aged as well. Having united to aid sick and wounded soldiers during the Civil War, they pledged to continue their work in a new way by establishing a home for the aged. In 1867 the women purchased a large townhouse and selected a dozen needy women and men, including one couple, to make it their home. By 1870, the Philadelphia women oversaw a new three-story brownstone with accommodations for one hundred guests, an infirmary, and a chapel "with stained glass windows and upholstered seats." The next year the editor of *Ladies' Repository* published a feature article on the home, complete with an engraving of the handsome building, "hoping that in many other cities, the women of our Church will catch the inspiration to go and do likewise" (H **607n67**). Homes for the aged sprang up in other cities as MEC women followed the editor's advice—in Baltimore (1868), New Haven (1874), Washington, D.C. (1889), and Chicago (1890). The Woman's Home Missionary Society began building a network of homes for retired missionaries and deaconesses. Best known and earliest was the Bancroft-Taylor Rest Home in Ocean Grove, New Jersey, which opened in 1896. MPC women organized a home for the aged in Westminster, Maryland, in 1895.

Black communities, rejected by the charitable institutions formed by White elites, organized their own institutions to care for needy older adults. As early as 1845, Stephen Smith, a local preacher and philanthropist in the AME Church, founded a Home for Aged and Infirm Colored People in Philadelphia. Methodists in two of the new all-Black MEC annual conferences (see next section on their organization, after 1864) founded homes for the aged. The first residential care program for aged Black persons in the Methodist tradition had its beginning when the pastor of Sharp Street MEC, Baltimore, Nathaniel M. Carroll, conceived the idea that there should be a home to care for indigent Black persons in his city. When Mrs. Matilda Wilson, a member of his congregation, offered her home in 1868, Pastor Carroll's dream became a reality. Two years later the Washington Conference purchased larger quarters for their new home, adopted a constitution in 1886, and secured the first charter in 1893 when eighteen guests received care. The Black conference in Louisiana opened a home for the aged in New Orleans in 1878. Otherwise in the South the churches relied on the dual, segregated system of poorhouses, along with homes for Confederate veterans and their spouses, to care for their aged and infirm.

Women of several EA churches in Philadelphia met jointly to plan a home for the aged in the spring of 1888. In August the German Home Society for Members of The Evangelical Association of North America in the City of Philadelphia was founded, incorporated, and trustees elected. Though the Evangelical General Conference in 1903 resolved to establish additional homes for the aged, the offer of the Pfeiffer family to bequeath their family home in Cedar Falls, Iowa, and the promise of a generous cash gift led to the establishment of the denomination's second elder-care facility, Western Old People's Home in 1911. In 1910 the Central Pennsylvania Conference of the United Evangelical Church (UEC) took steps toward the founding of a home for older people. Five years later property was acquired in Lewisburg, and the first building was dedicated in 1916. The UBC began elder care institutions in 1893 when a retired minister, Z. A. Colestock, offered his home in Mechanicsburg, Pennsylvania, for use as a home for the aged, later moved to a farm near Quincy and still later to a former Shaker settlement near Lebanon, Ohio.

AFRICAN AMERICAN CONFERENCES

The MEC finally acted to grant Black leaders full clergy rights only and to authorize Black annual conferences in 1864. Baltimore Black leaders had petitioned General Conference for such in 1848 and 1856 and reiterated the request in 1864. Although in one sense an empowering move, the legislation effectively made segregation denominational policy and did so in the face of eloquent challenges by Christian abolitionists like Gilbert Haven that the church model inclusivism, equality, and freedom in its organization, life, and work. The 1864 authorization, though conferring ordination and conference membership, limited the prerogatives for the new conferences, conferring on them "all the powers of other annual conferences, except a representation in the General Conference, a division of the proceeds of the Book Concern, and voting upon any constitutional question" (H **607nn78–79**).

Delaware and Washington Conferences were the first to be established. The Washington Conference included Sharp Street (1802) and eight other station churches and circuits of the Baltimore area organized into the Chesapeake District. Its second district, Potomac, gathered together twelve circuits and stations in the District of Columbia, northern Virginia, and outer Maryland areas. Conscious of its mandate to care for the interests of Black Methodism, it published its *Minutes* from the start, began church extension efforts (doubling in three years, more than tripling in ten), and assumed responsibility for the various institutions and benevolent causes, including that of education. It made an early commitment to the Centenary Biblical Institute (later Morgan College and eventually Morgan State), founded in 1867, which enjoyed as well the support of the Baltimore Conference and whose purposes included education of ministers and teachers.

In adopting the plan for Black "mission" conferences, MEC General Conference had looked beyond its own Black membership to that of The MECS. Already cooperating with other Protestants in missionary and relief organizations in the South and mindful of the challenges in educating and equipping freed slaves for citizenship and economic self-sufficiency, The MEC envisioned southern Blacks as a new field for evangelism and Black conferences as the harvest instrument. Responding to the challenge, as we shall see in the next chapter, Methodist women went south to teach, missionary preachers worked among both Blacks and Whites, new Black leaders emerged, and committed abolitionists like chaplain-then-editor-then-bishop Gilbert Haven sought to build a genuinely interracial church (S **1867a**). In a gesture in that direction, the 1868 General Conference removed the restrictions on the rights and privileges of the Black and biracial conferences (Washington and Delaware but also those established by The MEC in the South—Alabama, Georgia, Holston, Mississippi, South Carolina, Tennessee, Texas, Virginia, and North Carolina) and voted to seat delegations that had been sent as provisional.

NATIONAL CHURCHES

Charles Darwin published *On the Origin of Species* in 1859, but Methodists, like Americans generally, had too much else on their minds to take much notice. The bloody sacrifices of the war culminated, at least for northern Protestants, in the assassination of Lincoln. At Lincoln's Springfield burial, Bishop Simpson delivered the eulogy. He called Lincoln "our fallen chieftain," a "deliverer," "no ordinary man," "statesman," "an honest, temperate, forgiving man; a just man; a man of noble heart in every way." Simpson compared Lincoln to Jacob and Moses. But even those biblical types paled. Deliverance through Lincoln demanded explicit evocation of his and Christ's death on Good Friday. Fittingly, Simpson spoke of crucifixion and resurrection and of Christ as antitype for Lincoln: "We crown thee as our martyr, and Humanity enthrones thee as her triumphant son. Hero, martyr, friend, *farewell*." He then exhorted Americans to "eradicate every vestige of human slavery, to give every human being his true position before God and man, to crush every form of rebellion, and to stand by the flag which God has given us" (H **607nn84–85**).

Northern Methodist preachers echoed Simpson's "gospel." They preached on Lincoln's sacrifice in biblical terms; drew on doctrines of God, Providence, and atonement; envisioned the war as ordained in God's redemptive and emancipative plans; saw America, now saved from the sin of slavery and disunion and cleansed by the spilling of blood, as God's new Israel; spun out millennial visions of the nation's future; and prophesied triumph for American values in the South and among the freed slaves (H **608n86**). Southern Methodists wanted no part of this conflation of church and nation, of Christianity and nation, of Christ and culture, indeed imagined themselves as always having been believers in the spirituality of the church. Southern Methodist embrace of flag and culture would have to wait a war or two. Nor were there unanimity and uniformity among the people and preachers of the northern Methodist churches. However, the war had brought much of northern Methodism into mainstream Protestantism and a sense of place in American society. Civil religion and American culture became theirs as well. Indeed, as Methodism looked ahead to a centennial, it did so believing itself "the leading Church of the country," bearing "before God and man, the chief responsibility of the moral welfare of the nation" (S **1865c**). So posited editor-historian Abel Stevens affirming Methodism's connectional spirit, boosting a Centenary development fund, and demanding that the church build temples expressive of "national culture" and "advanced civilization" (S **1865b**).

The 1852 MEC General Conference had already embraced Stevens's ambition. A group of Washington Methodists presented a memorial to the Boston gathering, asking the denomination as a whole to build a major Methodist church in the nation's capital city "of convenient and prominent location, combining commodiousness in its size and attractiveness in its interior and exterior style of architecture." Regarding the success of the plan of such "high importance to the interest of the Methodism throughout the country," bishops and conference delegates pledged to promote the project in all the conferences. In March 1853 the church's seven bishops issued a pastoral letter supporting the project. Energetic booster Matthew Simpson laid the foundation stone for a large Gothic church with great fanfare in October 1854. Fundraising continued with a lead gift of $100 by President Franklin Pierce. The outbreak of the Civil War brought fundraising and construction to a halt. In 1866, the bishops appointed a prominent New York clergyman to act full time as fundraiser for the project. Construction resumed, and three years later (1869) the Metropolitan Memorial ME Church was completed at a cost of $225,000.

Dedication February 28, 1869, of what the press called "the Westminster Abbey of American Methodism," was timed to coincide with the inauguration of Methodist President Ulysses S. Grant. A third of the pews were reserved for dignitaries, including President-elect and Mrs. Grant, Vice President-elect Schuyler and Mrs. Colfax, Chief Justice Salmon Chase, and a large number of senators, representatives, and other leaders in state and church. Bishop Simpson read the opening prayers from the denomination's new (1864) liturgy for dedication of churches and preached the sermon. Descriptions of the event hit the headlines in newspapers across the country, including *The New York Times*. A lead story in *Harper's Weekly* called the new church "by far the handsomest and the most elaborate of the many fine churches in Washington" and included an engraving for the whole country to see.

This "national" church reserved one pew for each state and territory in the Union and one for the president, vice president, chief justice, and cabinet officers. President Grant occupied the President's Pew for eight years. President William McKinley sat in the same pew regularly during his term of office. (President Rutherford B. Hayes and Lucy Webb Hayes, as did President Bill Clinton and Hillary Rodham Clinton, chose to attend Washington's oldest Methodist Episcopal Church, Foundry Church, instead of Metropolitan Memorial Church. Foundry Church had built a large new church in Romanesque style at Fourteenth and G Streets in 1866.) Metropolitan Memorial Church flourished at its downtown location until the 1920s when the expansion of government buildings necessitated the acquisition of the property by the District government for the completion of Judiciary Square in 1930. The congregation relocated and built an even grander Gothic church on a new site near American University; it was dedicated in 1932.

Southern Methodists also early planned a visible presence in the nation's capital. The Washington, D.C., congregation of the Virginia Conference petitioned the 1858 General Conference for assistance in building a church that would worthily represent The MECS. The lengthy resolution, dripping with venom aimed at northern Methodists, concluded: "Every member of this body must feel that so great and influential a denomination as the Methodist Episcopal Church, South, should be represented by a large and flourishing society at the seat of the Central Government" (H **608n90**). The impending Civil War brought the plan to naught. Not till 1906 did a campaign get under way for a major MECS church in the nation's capital and another war (World War I) interfered with the speedy completion of fundraising and construction. Mount Vernon Methodist Episcopal Church, South, a monumental, white-marbled, Greek Revival–style church, which cost more than $500,000, was not completed until 1919 and came to full power under the pastorate of Clovis G. Chappell (1918–24).

The movement to establish a UBC presence in Washington began in the early 1890s when the denomination's Church Erection Society began a churchwide campaign to raise funds for a national church. Three years later Memorial United Brethren Church was completed on a "high and commanding" lot one mile north of the Capitol. Modest by Methodist standards, the small brick church of Romanesque design costing $17,000 was dedicated debt-free by Bishop Jonathan Weaver in January 1893. When rebuilt in 1905, the UBC could boast, "The Church is one of the finest in our denomination." Albright Memorial Evangelical Church in Washington was first proposed at a general missionary convention in Baltimore in 1923. Two years later the project got under way when the church's Board of Missions approved the plan, appointed a pastor as "missionary to Washington," and began a churchwide drive to raise funds. The first unit of a substantial church complex in Gothic style, the Sunday school, was completed in November 1927, a large sanctuary in 1954.

CHAPTER VII
RECONSTRUCTIONS: 1866–84

The northern church celebrated Methodist beginnings in an 1866 centenary, and both episcopal Methodisms, an 1884 centennial of American Methodist organization. They structured the year-long and longer events as occasions for taking stock, celebrating accomplishments, projecting needs, and promoting development. Between the two centennials occurred a reconciliation gesture between the two churches, the birth of the Colored Methodist Episcopal Church (CME), the founding of the Woman's Foreign Missionary Society (WFMS) and Woman's Christian Temperance Union (WCTU), substantial home missionary and educational efforts by northern Methodism among the freed slaves, the beginning of (postbaccalaureate) theological education, the inclusion of laity in governance in episcopal Methodism, testing of lay rights and ordination barriers by women, changes in membership expectations and ritual, a Methodist world ecumenical conference, exploration of unity among Methodist bodies, the reunion among Methodist Protestants, and a veritable organizational revolution from top to bottom. Symbolized by the latter and its most visible and enduring creations— the centralized board and bureaucratic denominational structures—the centennial decades, in a very real sense, closed a chapter on one Methodist century and opened one for the next.

LOOKING BACK AND LOOKING FORWARD

Some Methodists preferred the last chapter, thinking Methodism needed recommitment to holiness, revivalism, a rural style, and a gospel for the poor—not improvements expressive of bourgeoisification that catered to the church's social elite and its locally and nationally powerful. They experienced denominational centralization, development, the urban tilt, formalization, culture, and progress as pushing Methodism beyond the limits of primitive Wesleyanism and as abandoning the church's old landmarks. Such sentiments, voiced by the recently constituted and growing Free Methodists, came also to expression in yet another holiness movement, organized through the National Camp Meeting Association for the Promotion of Holiness (S **1867b**). Although holiness remained a defining Methodist commitment (S **1876a**), and Phoebe Palmer's campaigns and networks enjoyed the backing of key leadership (S **1868**), freelancing holiness evangelism as well as the plethora of new organizations raised significant issues of authority and control.

In 1867, A. E. Ballard, George C. M. Roberts, Alfred Cookman, and John Inskip called a National Camp Meeting for the Promotion of Holiness for Vineland (New Jersey). Once an evangelistic extension of the quarterly meeting but not tethered legally by the "trust clause," camp meetings had increasingly taken a life of their own. Less tightly controlled by bishops and presiding elders, camp meetings had furthered the antislavery cause into Free Methodism and rallied defenders of slavery as well. Several, notably Martha's Vineyard (Massachusetts), Round Lake (New York), Ocean Grove (New Jersey), and Pacific Grove (California), metamorphosed into popular summer vacation retreats, mixing piety and recreation, an important trajectory. The success of the 1867 event led organizers to establish a National Camp Meeting Association for the Promotion of Holiness and to call a second national "conference" for Manheim, Pennsylvania, the next year, a gathering that produced an attendance of some twenty-five thousand, including three hundred preachers, and that featured preaching by Bishop Matthew Simpson. Early support from Methodism's leadership moderated as this venture generated other associations; spawned, encouraged, and sanctioned a new style of supra-conference holiness itineration; and reinvigorated specifically holiness camp meetings across the country—camp meetings that functioned as both a preservation of earlier patterns and a prophetic judgment against a Methodism deemed to have abandoned its covenant. The issues in accountability that the camp meeting movement would pose lay ahead. In the 1860s and early 1870s the new movement gave energy to northern Methodism's holiness witness. Eventually the tension between these new associations and the church's leadership led to explicit breaks and the founding of new holiness denominations, among them, the Church of the Nazarene.

Palmer's altar theology and the renewed holiness impulse had found little resonance in southern Methodism until after Reconstruction. Then with the initial acquiescence of The MECS bishops and emerging leaders like Warren Candler and with the encouragement of the National Association, Georgia Methodists led in the rapid generation of holiness camp meetings and associations. However, early censorious missteps alienated Candler and confirmed the enmity of Emory's president Atticus Haygood. Candler and Haygood raised their voices (Candler as editor of the *Nashville Christian Advocate;* both eventually as bishops) to portray holiness associations, papers, camp meetings, and freewheeling itinerants as divisive, clannish, intemperate, and judgmental; second blessing theology as unfaithful to Methodist doctrine; and holiness cultivation of women's leadership as unbiblical. By the mid-1880s The MECS bishops began suppression of the still nascent southern holiness using punitive appointments and the threat thereof to whip the preachers into line, efforts that continued into the 1890s. The southern holiness effort and the reactions to it exposed and furthered party alignments within southern Methodism, a differentiation unthinkable during slavery. Gradually a small progressive group eager to modernize the church and the South emerged around Haygood. Institution builders in a neoconservative mode found a champion in Candler. And several styles of traditionalists held up the old landmarks—the holiness folk through their camp meetings; revivalists under the leadership of itinerating, "professional" evangelists like Sam Jones; and small-town and rural "Old Methodists" who in Georgia found leadership from politician Rebecca Latimer Felton (H **613nn69–71**).

Camp meetings ritualized Methodism's past accomplishments. The centenary prophesied a future glory (especially for northern Methodism). The 1864 MEC General Conference decided an 1866 centennial should pursue twin goals, the spiritual renewal of the church in recognition of what God had accomplished through the Methodist connection and a financial campaign to underwrite the instrumentalities (institutions) of further progress. The bishops designated twelve ministers and twelve "laymen" to plan the fundraising and decide on allocation of proceeds. They aspired to raise $2 million, identifying ten giving projects, some specific, some for general purposes (a Connectional Fund for the various church institutions). Primary beneficiaries were to be existing and proposed educational institutions in the United

States, Germany, and Ireland but also Sunday schools and missions. Profiting from the war experience in organization and mobilization, the committee divided the church into campaign districts, held subscription events in cities and large towns, sponsored centenary sermons in annual conferences, and set the first Sunday of January 1866 as a connection-wide occasion for remembrance and commitment. The *Advocates* promoted the cause and acknowledged gifts and pledges. By the time General Conference convened two years later (in 1868), $8,709,498 had been raised with more to come. Included in that effort were a $500,000 commitment by the trustees to Garrett Biblical Institute and $600,000 from robber baron Daniel Drew to establish Drew Theological Seminary. Other more local causes bear or bore their origins in this campaign in their name—"Centenary" churches and institutions. Calculating where God had brought the church in a century, Bishop Matthew Simpson counted churches valued at $29.5 million, parsonages at $4.4 million, and educational institutions at close to $7.9 million. The MEC boasted 2 publishing houses and 7 book depositories; 16 official and six unofficial papers; 2 theological seminaries; and 100 colleges and seminaries (precollegiate schools). Nine bishops, 64 annual conferences, and 7,576 itinerant and 8,602 local preachers served a little more than a million members. Outside The MEC, Simpson counted close to another million Methodists (H **608n3**).

LAY RIGHTS IN EPISCOPAL METHODISM

The muscularity of Methodism owed in no small part to the growing well-being and even wealth of its members whose philanthropy generated institution-building. Methodist laity who participated actively in the commercial, political, and social life of their communities, states, and countries chafed at their exclusion from church governance, particularly as conferences made financial decisions for which lay purses would care or addressed themselves to matters of war and policy about which laity had keen concern (S **1864a**). In earlier Methodism, laity (laymen primarily) had exercised on circuit levels important "ministerial" roles as local preachers, exhorters, class leaders, and stewards—functions significantly altered as upscale town and city congregations focused leadership on pastor, pastor's wife, and the Sunday school. The sidelining of lay "ministries" led to local preacher assemblies, organizations, and protests and to heightened sensitivity in episcopal Methodism to the several issues that had animated Methodist Protestantism.

On lay representation, The MECS moved more quickly than The MEC. The MECS had, in 1850, recognized the importance of lay concurrence in financial and secular matters. On such "interests" and on a voluntary basis it permitted annual conferences to give voice and vote to one lay steward from each district. Lay conventions had, as we noted, spoken on matters of church and state in the run-up to Civil War. And a conference of laity and ministers had issued the Palmyra Manifesto (S **1865a**) committing themselves to a postwar MECS future. In 1866, meeting for the first time since 1858, General Conference (MECS) approved a sense of the house resolution calling for lay representation in annual conferences and General Conferences. Offering the motion was Holland McTyeire, then pastor in Alabama, having fled there after serving as firebrand editor of the *Nashville Christian Advocate*. His leadership on that and other initiatives earned him election to the episcopacy at that General Conference. When subsequently ratified, The MECS's policy provided for equal lay representation in General Conference and for four laity from each presiding elder's district in annual conferences. Laity would choose their own representation. Provision was made for separate lay and clerical ballots. And only preachers would vote on matters pertaining to ministerial relations (H **609nn4–5**). Southern laity (laymen) took their seats in 1870.

Lay representation in the northern church required more of a campaign and found a campaign manager in George Crooks, who for more than twenty years nurtured the reform movement, in the Philadelphia area in the 1850s and in New York after 1857. Crooks issued a call for a March 1852 general convention to consider lay delegation in Methodist conferences (H **226–28; 609nn5–7**). The convention called for equal lay representation in annual conferences and General Conferences and offered a detailed plan for implementation. "An Address to the People," probably crafted by Crooks, circulated in pamphlet form and in the press. The 1852 General Conference (MEC) established a Committee on Lay Delegation to deal with what turned out to be the numerous petitions for and against the reform. The committee concluded that such change would not be in the best interests of the church. The committee's report was overwhelmingly adopted. Lay rights petitions went also to the next General Conference (1856), but the debate on slavery crowded out the issue. At the next General Conference (1860), recognizing

139

changes in the climate of opinion in the church, the bishops openly addressed the issue in their Episcopal Address. "We are of the opinion," they declared, "that Lay Delegation might be introduced into the General Conference with safety, and perhaps advantage."

Heeding the bishops' plea and the growing sentiment among the laity, General Conference passed a resolution expressing willingness to approve lay delegation "when the church desires it." It referred the question to a church-wide vote by "orders"—laymen over twenty-one voting in specially called meetings on a charge level and preachers in the 1862 annual conferences. By that point, George Crooks had moved to New York. Supported by laity dedicated to the cause, he founded and edited a vigorous independent Methodist newspaper (*The Methodist*) to champion lay rights, to address the issue of slavery, and to rival the crosstown, official *Christian Advocate*, which muted attention to the sensitive topics. By the time the votes were taken, secession and war concerns loomed large, and both ministry and laity voted down the proposed plan, the ministers voting three to one against and the laymen roughly two to one against.

An 1864 lay rights convention held concurrently with General Conference commissioned theological educator James Strong to make its case (S **1864a**). But the conference was unmoved, discerning "no such declaration of the popular will as to justify . . . taking action." By the time the 1868 General Conference gathered in Chicago, the demand of laity for representation had become so strong as to be irresistible. The conference not only called for another referendum on the question but also submitted a definite plan to "the godly consideration of . . . ministers and people," this time including laywomen as well as men (S **1870a**). Women organized and issued to the Methodist press an open letter to their sisters about the importance of voting in favor of lay representation. The plan was approved by a decisive vote, laywomen and laymen voting two to one for representation and the clergy in the annual conferences voting by more than three-fourths majority to change the constitution. The General Conference completed the action by voting to concur. Crooks could only regret that the plan did not allow lay members in the annual conference and that women were not included. Indeed, the 1872 lay delegation—featuring governors, senators, cabinet members, and leading industrialists—included no women then deemed "not laity" and thus ineligible (S **p31**).

The UBC introduced lay representation into its conference that same year—but into its annual conferences and not into its General Conference. Lay representation in UBC General Conferences was not added until a new constitution was adopted in 1889. The Evangelicals adopted lay representation into their conferences in 1903 at the General Conference level and 1907 at the annual conference level. So the witness of the Methodist Protestants finally prevailed.

DENOMINATIONAL ACCOUNTABILITY

Judge William Lawrence, veteran of the Ohio legislature and five-term US Congressman, presented the report of the "Special Committee on the Relationship of the Benevolent Institutions to the General Conference" (S **1872a**). The report called for putting the benevolent institutions of the denomination "under the full control of the General Conference by stipulating that boards of managers of the various agencies were to be elected by the General Conference itself" and reincorporating agencies as necessary to achieve this accountability. The enabling legislation, paralleled soon in the other Methodist churches, transformed what had been voluntary societies—the typical, widespread, parachurch organizations of the day—into truly denominational structures. Various motivations prompted the revolutionary change. An 1870 scandal, involving alleged mismanagement of funds by clergy executives in The MEC publishing house, helped further the cause of providing better oversight and opening the agencies to lay professionals. More positively, Methodist laity and ministers had participated actively in, indeed led, the Civil War relief efforts that had perfected centralized direction of locally energized and funded organizations. And they had but to read the papers to recognize the rapid incorporation of America—bringing consolidation, order, integration, efficiency, bureaucratization, and professionalization to business. Laity especially wanted similar accountability in governance and in finance in church (and state).

Recently birthed societies added to the issues of control, though one, the Board of Education, modeled the accountability being proposed. The Church Extension Society, founded in 1865, had been incorporated in Philadelphia and had begun its work with considerable fanfare and hope and would soon begin building a new church every day under the boosterism of

141

Charles C. McCabe. The Freedmen's Aid Society, also beginning what would be comparably impressive institution building throughout the South (and discussed below), had been incorporated in Ohio in 1866, "not in any respect under the jurisdiction or control of the General Conference" (S **1872a**). Only the Board of Education established in 1868 by General Conference to invest in higher education its portion of the $8 million raised during the Centenary was secured to the church by election of its board (six "laymen," six ministers).

These new societies—as for the most part they were—along with those created earlier, the Missionary Society (1819), the Sunday School Union (1827), and the Tract Society (1852) in The MEC and the Missionary Society (1845), Sunday-School Society (1854), and Tract Society (1854) of The MECS, were tied to the denominations by General Conference's election of their executives (corresponding secretaries). Other measures of accountability had been tried. And the societies had long established the imperative that auxiliaries of each be established at every level from circuit up, an important measure of connection, programming, and hence accountability. Further the executives toured the churches on behalf of their agency (H **230–32**). Still these missional, purposive, flexible, adaptive, expansive, pluriform, and decentralized societies, their executives, and hence their programs reported to a locally organized or conference-designated board of directors whose annual meeting in the headquarters city limited legal oversight to that one occasion and that city's clergy and lay leadership. Delegates to the General Conference of 1872 were disturbed to learn that "as our benevolent societies are now constituted and governed, they are practically controlled in their election of boards of managers by a few of the members who live near the places of meetings and they are really irresponsible to the church through any of its authorities" (H **609n12**). Legislation corrected that, centralizing power in the General Conference. Southern Methodists, Evangelicals, and United Brethren took steps in the same direction in the same period; The MECS just two years later.

An important disciplinary change at the denominational level moved accountability in the opposite direction, providing some check on the authority of General Conference. This was the provision for judicial review. Here the southern church took the initiative. In 1854 it had empowered the bishops, acting collectively and in writing, with the prerogative of challenging a rule or regulation and thereby obliging General Conference to muster a two-thirds majority on the question. This action, consonant with its understanding of episcopacy, The MECS confirmed and clarified in 1874. Consonant with its different understanding of conference and episcopacy, the northern church proceeded in a different fashion, generating from out of General Conference itself procedure and a body with judicial authority (see chapter X and H **232–33; 383–84**).

The impetus for order and organization affected every level of the church, including the most basic, where new official boards brought to the local church comparable efficiency and accountability (see the final section of this chapter and the 1884 "Snapshot" in H **263–74**). Similarly on regional levels, local church organization and the new centralized, accountable institutions allowed the churches to focus resources on new projects deemed beneficial to the general good, for instance, the hospitals that editor James M. Buckley advocated (S **1881a**) and that we treat in chapter VIII.

To finance an increasingly programmed Methodism, special Sundays *with special offerings* reached a scale that made them necessities for boards and agencies, but also serious rivals to ancient Christian festivals. The first was Children's Day, set for the second Sunday in June, six months removed from Christmas and at a period of the year when, without some such stimulus, Sunday school interest was in danger of flagging before the heat of summer. Begun as part of the Centenary program in 1866, Children's Day *with offering* for a Children's Educational Fund provided scholarships for higher education to "meritorious and needy Sunday School scholars of either sex, who, without such aid, be unable to obtain a complete education." Two years later, in 1868, the General Conference made the day and the fund permanent with an asking of five cents for each child enrolled. Oversight of The MEC fund was committed to the newly organized Board of Education. By 1884 The MEC General Conference ordered seven Sundays with special collections—for missions, church extension, tract distribution, Sunday school, Freedmen's Aid, higher education, and Bible distribution.

By the twentieth century, agencies found freewill special offerings too fickle and frustrating for budgeting and planning and pressed for schemes of financial planning. The 1912 MEC General Conference approved the formation of a central treasury with power to set budgets and determine "fair-share" askings called *apportionments* (S **1912b**). The 1924 General Conference strengthened the plan to unify benevolence collections, forming a World Service Commission to set goals, review budgets, and make four-year plans (it has been the General

Council on Finance and Administration, GCFA, since 1972). Stewardship Sunday, pledge cards, and duplex offering envelopes followed shortly thereafter. The Every-Member Canvass to raise church budgets emerged in stewardship education materials in the 1930s (H **609–10nn27–28**).

WOMEN'S ORGANIZATIONAL REVOLUTION

Methodist women effected their own organizational revolution, capitalizing on the networking, enlarged vision, administrative skills, and organizational experience of Civil War relief work (S **1870a**). Methodism's growing middle class increasingly enjoyed leisure due to invention of labor-saving devices and products—canned foods, store-bought clothes, washing machines. Free to pursue activities outside their homes, Methodist women turned to their churches. Petitions to the 1872 MEC General Conference sought "enlargement of [women's] Christian and benevolent activity" and requested recognition of the Ladies' and Pastors' Christian Union and the Woman's Foreign Missionary Society. Other resolutions advocated licensing and ordaining women as preachers and striking male language and inserting the word *persons* in the *Discipline* so that women could be elected stewards, Sunday school superintendents, and members of the quarterly conferences. The same year Mrs. Susanna M. D. Fry proposed through articles in the *Ladies' Repository* that The MEC establish a deaconess order (H **610nn31, 41**).

All-male General Conference had little difficulty with the Ladies' and Pastors' Christian Union (LPCU), recognizing it as a "regularly constituted society" of the church, approving its constitution, recognizing its Board of Managers, and instructing pastors of all the churches to cooperate with the new society in its important work (H **610n38**). Organized in Philadelphia in March 1868, the LPCU sought to employ the church's women in a systematic program of home evangelistic work among poor and neglected persons, under ministerial supervision. Supported by Bishop Matthew Simpson, the resident bishop of Philadelphia, it drew its vision and energy from its first corresponding secretary (chief executive), Mrs. Annie Wittenmyer, who had honed management skills in Civil War relief work, especially in supervision of army hospital kitchens under the auspices of the US Christian Commission. Recognizing that "the entire system of religious activity in the church is undergoing a change," the LPCU sought an auxiliary society in each church, with the pastor as president. Churches should subdivide the work into small districts and appoint two or more women to visit house-to-house among the unconverted, to invite unchurched persons to worship, to assist sick and poor people, and to bring children into the Sunday school. The idea caught the church's imagination. Within a year, some fifty churches in ten states had established LPCU chapters. Methodist women had already reached out to some twenty-three thousand families, appealed to nearly eleven thousand "unconverted persons," visited one thousand sick persons, helped 325 poor families, brought 419 children into the Sunday school, held meetings in 233 homes, and distributed some one hundred thousand pages of tracts (H **610n32**).

Wittenmyer proved adroitly effective and skilled in working within the limited imagination of bishops and pastors. In *Women's Work for Jesus*, Wittenmyer argued that evangelizing the unchurched masses required home visitation. Women, whose sphere was the home, were uniquely qualified to go into people's homes and "talk of Jesus, and duty and heaven." They would be welcomed where men would not. And this work could best be done by *"the systematic, voluntary labors of Christian Women, under the direction of the regular pastorate"* (H **610n35**). Wittenmyer focused on Methodist women (and church women more generally) who enjoyed sufficient leisure time to devote two or three hours a week to visitation. This great undeveloped power "might become a mighty enginery for good if properly combined and directed" (H **610n36**). When she turned her energies to temperance (becoming first president of the Woman's Christian Temperance Union, which she helped to found in 1874), Wittenmyer handed the reins of the LPCU to Mrs. Mary L. Griffith, wife of a Philadelphia Conference pastor in 1877. Griffith, who set forth her own vision of women's work within women's sphere in *Women's Christian Work,* in 1880 sent an eloquent appeal to The MEC General Conference (S **1880b**) for granting women's rights as laity, for licensing and ordaining those called, and for expunging the word *male* from the *Discipline*.

The 1872 General Conference's Committee on Woman's Work in the Church that endorsed the LPCU affirmed women as teachers of the Word of Life but with "regard to woman's preaching," it discerned, "we must wait for further developments of Providence." The committee did find women to be providentially called to missions and General Conference recognized the Woman's Foreign Missionary Society (WFMS). Women organized for-

eign missionary societies in the UBC in 1875, in The MECS in 1878, in
The MPC in 1879, and in the EA in 1883 (treated in H **238–40**). Separate
women's home missionary societies followed in 1880, MEC; 1886, MECS
(expanded in 1890); and 1893, MPC. The (UBC) Woman's Missionary Association extended its work to both foreign and home missions. All missionary work in The MECS was reorganized in 1910 into one Board of Missions, with the woman's work directed by the Woman's Missionary Council.
(Women's home missionary organizations and deaconesses will be treated in
the following chapters.)

Women organized the WFMS in Boston in March 1869 in response to
pleas by Mrs. Clementina Butler and Mrs. Lois Parker, wives of Methodist
missionaries to India (S **1869a**; H **610n41**). They urged that the gospel
could be taken to the women of India only by women and that a sending
agency, a woman's foreign missionary society, was therefore imperative. The
small assemblage of women adopted a constitution and elected "national"
officers. Setting an access-to-power pattern that would be strategically typical
in the women's missionary societies, the WFMS selected Mrs. Osmon C.
Baker (wife of Bishop Baker) as the first president and made the wives of the
other bishops vice presidents. (When in 1880, MEC women organized the
Woman's Home Missionary Society, they elected Mrs. Lucy Webb Hayes, the
US president's spouse, as president, an office she held till death in 1889.) The
WFMS chose Mrs. Harriet M. Warren, Mrs. Lois Parker, and Mrs. Jennie
Fowler Willing as corresponding secretaries. At the urging of Clementina
Butler, the WFMS fixed a membership fee at "two cents a week and a prayer"
so that no woman should have to say that she could not afford to join.

A monthly magazine, initially titled *The Heathen Woman's Friend* and
edited for twenty-five years by Mrs. Harriet M. Warren, appeared almost
immediately, in June of 1869. WFMS set its annual subscription at a modest thirty cents. The first issue summoned Methodist women to the cause of
carrying the knowledge of Christ and the blessings of Christian civilization
to sisters across the world (especially in India) and set forth the urgency of
establishing local affiliates (S **1869a**). The magazine with its stories, pictures,
and communiqués quite literally gave Methodist women the world. Through
it, they engaged and were engaged by their own public, a gendered universe.
The magazine sustained the WFMS's generating interest in India and allowed
readers to follow the careers and signal accomplishments in education and
medicine of its first two missionaries, Isabella Thoburn and Dr. Clara Swain,

sent out together in 1869 and pathmakers in their respective fields. The magazine and such high-profile single women made the case for "Woman's Work for Woman" and for unmarried women missionaries—essentially a new ministerial career for educated women (H **610n44**).

The WFMS experienced friction with the Methodist Missionary Society (often referred to as the parent board) from the start, particularly over administrative and fundraising prerogatives. Having as leaders the wives of bishops and other Methodist heavyweights served the WFMS well. The women insisted that they had organized an independent society, and they would raise and disburse their own funds for the work they had undertaken. They agreed, however, that they would "take no collections or subscriptions in any promiscuous [mixed] assembly" but would raise their funds in ways that would not interfere with the parent board and its work. By the end of its first year, the WFMS had established regional branches—Philadelphia, New York, New England, Northwestern, Western, and Cincinnati—and dispatched another missionary to India, Fannie J. Sparks.

The WCTU was the organization that most successfully expanded women's sphere, home, and mothering into a public realm and provided a context within which women could and would exercise the full array of leadership and political skills. Generated from an 1873–74 crusade against saloons that spread out nationally from spontaneous beginnings in Ohio and predicated upon a social analysis that saw drunkenness, alcoholism, saloons, and the liquor industry as the determinate factors in crime, abuse, poverty, unemployment, and corruption, the WCTU capitalized on long-standing Methodist commitments to temperance and enjoyed strong support from prominent clergy in the Methodist churches, including Bishops Matthew Simpson and Randolph S. Foster of The MEC.

The WCTU formally organized in the summer of 1874 and held its first national meeting that November, electing Wittenmyer as president and Frances Willard as corresponding (executive) secretary. Through tireless travel, networking, speaking, and writing, Willard led the WCTU in establishing chapters across the country, becoming the nation's largest women's organization. In 1879, the WCTU elected her president, an office she held till her death in 1898. From that platform Willard enunciated a vision of a transformed society, transforming the church as well. Willard proposed that America deal systemically with the systemic evil (abusive, drunken husbands/saloons/liquor industry/corrupted politicians). By adroitly employing lan-

147

guage of Sabbath, motherhood, and home and by focusing on "home protection" and legislation to achieve temperance controls, Willard articulated an increasingly grand and complex set of reforms that required the ballots of those most affected: women. Suffrage, in Willard's advocacy, became key to treating causes and symptoms, in effect the full array of what would be social-gospel interventions (S **1883b**). Willard schematized the WCTU's do-everything agenda under five major headings, "preventive, educational, evangelistic, social and legal, [and] organization," and structured the WCTU into fifty departments, each under the care of a superintendent. Ideally that structure functioned as template at every level from the local to the national, every level connected organizationally to the next. All "carefully mustered, officered, and drilled," the WCTU functioned as "womanhood's Grand Army of the Home," a "grand" exhibit as well of the organizational revolution. Through the WCTU, women gained invaluable training, achieved a sense of their own power, and moved through the church into social reform (H **611nn50–52**). Willard was one of the foremost political geniuses of her time. She was never afraid to challenge the social norms of her time, refusing to marry and bear children, stepping into the public realm with a proud voice, and always accompanied with her lifelong female partner, Anna Gordon.

SEMINARIES

After the Civil War, Methodism added postbaccalaureate theological education to its colleges and the Course of Study as a mode of preparing persons for ministry. In 1867, The MEC opened Drew Theological Seminary in Madison, New Jersey. By that point, both Boston and Garrett, founded earlier (1839 and 1854) and begun as biblical institutes so as to avoid denominational aversion to theological education, metamorphosed into BD-granting programs (the degree nomenclature changed to MDiv in the 1970s). The UBC followed suit and founded United Theological Seminary in Dayton, Ohio, in 1871. The MECS, through a gift solicited by bishops from the robber baron Cornelius Vanderbilt, founded Vanderbilt University in 1873, which added a Biblical Department in 1875 for training ministers by faculty staffed from editors at The MECS Publishing House in Nashville. (Vanderbilt University trustees and faculty broke ties with The MECS by 1910, which prompted The MECS in 1911 to establish Southern Methodist University in Dallas.) The EA established a seminary at Naperville, Illinois, in 1873 and The MPC founded what is now Wesley Theological Seminary in 1884 in Westminster, Maryland. Though the graduates from these newly founded seminaries constituted a small minority of Methodism's ministry, they raised the standard, modeled pastoral roles, and created aspirations among the various lay ministries of the church for comparable professional standing and respect. The pressures for professionalization and posturing between and among Methodism's distinct ministries lay ahead in the next century—indeed would constitute an important dynamic in denominational life.

To this point and even beyond, Methodism had looked to its quadrennially *elected* editors—of *Methodist Quarterly Reviews,* of *Advocates,* of Sunday school publications—for its doctrinal guidance, for the monitoring of important European intellectual developments, for defense of the faith against the Calvinism dominant in American evangelicalism, and for translation of its own and British doctrine into popular belief and practice. Editors, like Albert T. Bledsoe in the South, who transferred from the Baptists, and Daniel D. Whedon in the North, reoriented Methodist theology, subtly countering Calvinism generally and the long-dead Jonathan Edwards particularly with defenses of human agency, responsibility, and free will. Thus the defense of the Arminian faith foregrounded the human will rather than divine grace. Similarly, early efforts to develop an American Methodist systematic as a "rational orthodoxy," relying on Scottish commonsense philosophy, accented the capacities of the human mind to know God and God's ways. Making important efforts at a Methodist systematic were Henry B. Bascom, Thomas Ralston, and Thomas O. Summers in the South and Miner Raymond, William F. Warren, and John Miley in the North. As teacher-theologians, Summers at Vanderbilt, Raymond at Garrett, Warren at Boston, and Miley at Drew represented a new day for Methodism, the professionalizing of its theology and its capacity to engage world intellectual currents on a more sustained basis.

The theologians in the new seminaries, like Phoebe Palmer's and the holiness movement's "altar theology" and shorter way, put a premium on acts of the human will. The two theological trajectories reworked Wesleyan doctrine for the new day. The one sought to sustain the doctrine of perfection in a revivalistic context with a second conversion and a second blessing, claimed by an act of will, the shorter way. The other envisioned Methodist piety better enlivened by progress (toward reason and human ability) that

149

remembered Wesley's emphasis on education and expectations for sacramental frequency and envisioned growth through nurture.

WOMEN IN SEMINARY AND IN THE PULPIT

By credentialing themselves with a theological degree and proving their ministerial skills in the trenches, women lived into the vocation to which Palmer and later Willard believed women were called, *Woman in the Pulpit* (H **612n53**). Two graduates of Boston University School of Theology (BUST), Anna Oliver and Anna Howard Shaw, exercised successful preaching careers in The MEC before authorities clamped down. A third, New Yorker Maggie Newton Van Cott credentialed herself in the more traditional fashion as had many other women, licensed as a local preacher. Raised Episcopalian, married into the Dutch Reformed Church, Van Cott underwent a powerful conversion experience in the late 1850s, attended Methodist prayer meetings at Duane Street, and in a dream experienced a call from none other than John Wesley. Teaching Sunday school and working at the Five Points Mission, she received invitations to speak as evangelist and in 1868 devoted herself full time to evangelistic speaking. Successes earned her an exhorter's license and then a local preacher's license and an effort by the 1869 New York Conference to censure one of the responsible presiding elders. She gained supporters among prominent members of both that and the New England Conference who experienced her effectiveness. Among them, Gilbert Haven, influential editor of the equally influential New England Methodist paper, *Zion's Herald,* covered and commended her work and made a case for preaching licenses for women (S **1869b**). Daniel Curry, editor of the New York *Christian Advocate,* weighed in negatively on this "disturbing element in the Conference" and on Haven's "characteristic zeal," expressing relief that the New England Conference had not seen fit to move toward admitting her (H **612n58**). A preaching stint in California earned yet another licensing recommendation but also a ruling by Bishop Stephen Merrill that lower judicatories had no right to grant women licenses to preach. His action was appealed to the 1876 General Conference (MEC), and California also submitted a petition favoring local preacher's licenses for women, neither of which was accepted.

That same year, Anna Oliver, holder of BA and MA degrees from Rutgers Female College, New York City, graduating BD, was honored to deliver one of the BUST commencement addresses (H **243–44; 612n59**). Granted a local preacher's license by the Jamaica Plain Quarterly Conference (Boston), she subsequently assumed interim pastoral duties in First Methodist (MEC) Passaic, not far from her birthplace, New Brunswick. Assisted by the Black pastor-evangelist Amanda Smith, Oliver had the reorganized but struggling Passaic church "buzzing," as the local newspaper reported. During a year there, she increased membership 500 percent, lectured at New Jersey Methodism's Centenary College for Women, and pressed for social reforms in Passaic (care for homeless children, vocational training in the public schools, and curbs on the liquor trade). Not affirmation but reversals followed. The cabinet and bishop of the Newark Conference did not continue her in ministry, she experienced severe ill health, and her invitation to preach at the weekly meeting of the New York Methodist preachers was rescinded— the latter at the urging of then pastor, later editor, and historian James M. Buckley. In 1879 members of a heavily mortgaged Brooklyn church acquired the property at auction. They organized as an MEC church, took the precaution of obtaining a new deed without the obligatory "trust clause," and invited Oliver to become pastor. The renamed Willoughby Avenue Methodist Episcopal Church prospered under Oliver's leadership, growing from thirteen to more than a hundred by year's end and building Sunday school to two hundred. Recommended to the 1880 New England Conference for ordination and conference membership, she was not presented as a candidate by Bishop Edward Andrews. The Boston presiding elder, Lorenzo Thayer, indicated that he would appeal the ruling. The conference allowed her to speak, which she did for half an hour, making an eloquent case for pastoral work as uniquely "adapted to women," a case then subsequently published (S **1880a**). Persuaded, the conference then voted instruction to its delegates to General Conference to use their influence "to remove all distinctions of sex in the office and ordination of our ministry" (H **612n62**).

The 1880 bishop's, presiding elder's, and New England Conference's actions pertained as well to another female candidate for ordination, an 1878 BUST graduate, Anna Howard Shaw. English-born, Shaw had earned a local preacher's license in Michigan, subsequently returning to New England and pastoring two small Cape Cod churches for six years. Performing well in the ordination examination, she was duly recommended by the conference, as her narrative indicates (S **1880c**; H **612n63**).

In response to ruling against their ordinations, Shaw and Oliver elected different paths, Shaw to seek ordination elsewhere, Oliver to contest the decision. To the 1880 General Conference in Cincinnati went Thayer's appeal of the bishop's ruling, a petition from Brooklyn's Willoughby Avenue Church asking that the *Discipline* be revised so as permit the ordination of its pastor (S **front cover**), and Anna Oliver in person with a printed case including her New England speech (S **1880a**). General Conference was in no mood to change the *Discipline* "as it regards the status of women in our church" (H **612n64**). Oliver continued her ministry, sustaining Willoughby's broad-gauged social witness. However, the church's finances suffered, and it folded three years later. Her health suffered as well, and she died in 1892.

Shaw also returned to her ministry with the Cape Cod congregations and indeed pursued ordination elsewhere, namely, with the Methodist Protestants. The MPC's New York Conference accepted her candidacy and ordained her October 12, 1880 (S **1880c**). The MPC did not, however, immediately turn its New York Conference's actions into policy. Indeed, its 1884 General Conference ruled her ordination out of order. The annual conference continued, however, its recognition, and five years later another MEC woman, Eugenia St. John, sought and received MPC orders from the Kansas Conference. The 1892 MPC General Conference seated women as lay delegates and authorized annual conferences to decide for themselves whether to ordain women. The UBC General Conference in 1889 voted in favor of women's ordination, and Ella Niswonger, the church's first seminary graduate, was ordained that year. By 1901, the UBC ministerial directory listed ninety-seven women.

Shaw would eventually follow her call in a new direction, through medical school and eventually on to the women's suffrage circuit as lecturer, providing the national movement with a much-needed religious voice. Between 1904 and 1915 she served as president of the National American Woman's Suffrage Association, the largest women's rights organization in the country. Alongside her female life partner of thirty years, Lucy Elmina Anthony, a niece of the renowned Susan B Anthony, Shaw changed what it meant to be a religiously centered, politically active public voice. During World War I, Shaw was named chair of the Woman's Committee of the US Council of National Defense, the first woman to hold such a high governmental post, for which she was also the first woman to earn the Distinguished Service Medal. *This* is the legacy of Methodist women—always seeking to be bold in their ministry contexts and never fearing to follow as the Spirit of God calls them through and beyond the pulpit.

FOREIGN AND HOME MISSIONS

Missions to Central and South America followed pre–Civil War efforts among English-speakers in cities of several Latin American countries and built on Spanish-language ministry in the southwest United States (see chapter IV). By 1874, Alejo Hernández (ordained deacon in 1871), the father of border Methodism, had died, but southern Methodists had established a Mexican district, and by 1881, Santiago Tafolla had become its first Hispanic presiding elder. The same year the Woman's Missionary Society (MECS) sent two missionaries, Rebecca Toland and Annie Williams, to launch a day school, the Laredo Seminary. Nannie Holding joined them in 1883 as principal, an office that she held for close to thirty years and for which service the school was renamed in her honor. By 1885, the church constituted the Mexican Border Mission Conference, Bishop Holland McTyeire presiding at the organizing session (H **615n94**).

MEC work among Chinese Americans began in 1866 with three women from the Sixth Street Church, Sacramento, and the founding of boarding and Sunday schools to help the Chinese in their city learn English and study the Bible. The following year the California Conference launched a mission to the Chinese, sending Dr. and Mrs. Otis Gibson, former missionaries to China, to San Francisco. Gibson modeled efforts of the Sacramento Sunday school (S **1870b**; H **615n95**). Within ten years, the Gibsons established schools in principal cities in California, Oregon, and Washington, benefiting in that endeavor from active support of the national and Pacific Coast Women's Mission Society. Their collaboration included social ministries, particularly the rescue and support of Chinese women prostitutes. A Chinese and later a Japanese convert were licensed as local preachers, a beginning on indigenization (S **1886**).

The Civil War produced chaos within the diverse Oklahoma Indian Missionary Conference. After the war, Samuel Checote, under whom the Creeks rescinded laws forbidding the teaching of Christian religion, led in formation of a Creek district, translation of the Bible and hymnal into Creek, and training of Indigenous preachers. As the first Indigenous presiding elder (DS), Checote worked to bridge racial and cultural differences. He raised money for homes, schools, clinics, and churches for his people and vigorously defended the rights of the Creek Nation in petitions to Congress (S **1883a**). Indigenous women played an important role in linking home and church. Mrs. Samuel Checote made her home a center of Methodist life for both Indigenous tribe and missionaries.

President Ulysses S. Grant, a Methodist adherent, created a Board of Indian Commissioners, reorganized the appointment of missionaries to reservations, and enlisted church workers as Indian Agents, but placed them under federal control and government payroll. Grant's "Peace Policy," endorsed by Methodist editor Daniel Curry, allowed clergy of only one denomination on designated reservations. The MEC, which had little success/experience in Indigenous evangelism, received 20 percent of the reservations, twenty-one reservations in all! The MECS, which had greater experience, received none. Roman Catholics also lost, receiving seven reservations, being summarily dismissed from successful missions, with other churches, including Methodists, taking their place.

Methodists implemented an assimilationist policy in reservation schools and churches. In mission schools operated on Indigenous reservations from the late 1800s through the first half of the twentieth century, children were obliged to adopt Anglo-European culture, abandon their tribal languages, and convert to Christianity. Missionaries sought to provide moral training and wean Indians away from their "savage" customs so that they, or their children, would blend easily into the cultural institutions of Euro-American society. Mission board reports and the church press expected the Indigenous tribes would become Christian and self-respecting, hard-working citizens if freed from the binding structure of pagan tribalism and the stultifying effects of communal land control, and freed to work their own farms. By the 1890s Methodists began to take seriously the separation of church and state. Believing that appropriation of public funds for sectarian purposes was wrong, not only in principle but a violation of the letter and spirit of the US Constitution, the General Conference of 1892 requested the missionary societies no longer apply for government funds for educational purposes on Indian reservations.

Tragically, Methodists whose missionary practices showed little appreciation for Indigenous culture, indeed systematically demeaned it, were implicated in the late nineteenth-century wars, when Indigenous nations resisted the duplicitous treatment and were met with military force. In particular, in the mid-1860s disputes on the southern plains culminated in the Sand Creek, Colorado, massacre. John Chivington, an MEC pastor-colonel, led Union troops to slaughter two hundred Cheyenne and Arapaho, who had recently signed a peace treaty with the United States. Chivington received commendation from the army and was honored by Coloradans and Methodists at his death in 1894. The massacre ignited thirty years of war especially with the Plains nations—Arapaho, Comanche, Kiowa, and Sioux. The Sioux annihilation of George Custer's cavalry at the Battle of the Little Big Horn in Montana led Methodist editor Charles Fowler to agonize over Custer's defeat (S **1876c**). Another MEC editor, Joseph Hartzell, actually called for all-out war "to exterminate the savages!" The 1890 slaughter of Lakota tribesmen at Wounded Knee drew little outrage from Methodist papers. The *Western Christian Advocate* was the exception. However, Christian attitudes gradually shifted, represented in 1888 by The MEC's Woman's Home Mission Society offering an apology to Indigenous peoples and pledging to work for reforms. Beginning in 1980, The UMC General Conference has adopted a number of confessions and formal apologies for the church's implication in the "destruction of Native American people, culture, and religious practices" and explicitly for Chivington's massacre (H **615nn99–100**).

SOUTHERN AFRICAN AMERICAN METHODISMS

In 1864, The MEC authorized creation of Black annual conferences, gained access to some MECS church facilities where Union troops prevailed, and began missionary efforts among southern Blacks and Whites. In 1866, it established the Freedmen's Aid Society to elicit support for and coordinate efforts in evangelization, education, and institution building. The AME and AMEZ, effectively excluded from the South before the war, also entered the southern harvest with great energy and effectiveness, as did their Black Baptist counterparts (H **257–61; 616n114**). By war's end an MECS Black membership of more than two hundred thousand had dropped by two-thirds and by 1869 by nine-tenths (to less than twenty thousand).

Facing "an African American Exodus," the 1870 MECS General Conference, though relieved to see purging of its Black members, was frightened by the prospect of their adherence to the hostile and politically active MEC, AME, and AMEZ. So it acted to extrude its remaining Black membership. The MECS made provision for recognition, transfer of property, organization, and ordinations for a new all-Black denomination. This Colored Methodist Episcopal Church (CME) met the same year, under the presidency of MECS bishops Robert Paine and Holland N. McTyeire, created nine annual conferences, established a publishing house, and launched a journal, *The Christian Index* (S **1870c**). Paine and McTyeire consecrated William H. Miles and Richard H. Vanderhorst as bishops. The new denomination accepted The MECS paternalism and racial separatism and disavowed political Reconstruction. "Our churches," its *Discipline* affirmed, "shall in no wise be used for political purposes or assemblages." By 1874, the CME had added two bishops, ordained 607 traveling preachers, deployed 518 local preachers, established 535 Sunday schools, and garnered close to seventy-five thousand members. Emory president, later bishop, Atticus Haygood urged southern Methodists to view the end of slavery as opening a new, better day and to put race relations on a new plane (S **1880d**). However, with the end of Reconstruction many southern Protestants, Methodists included, would heed and support Jim Crow.

By contrast, The MEC began southern efforts inspired by Gilbert Haven and James Lynch. The former as columnist, then *Zion's Herald* editor, then bishop harassed a highly segregated northern Methodism and demanded that The MEC sanctify the bloody war sacrifices and live into the example of Christ and the teachings of Paul. His millennial vision of a church without caste (S **1867a**) racially integrated at all levels and in every leadership sector captured the imagination of AME editor James Lynch, who transferred his considerable talents to The MEC. Lynch went south for The MEC, organizing its Mississippi Conference, establishing educational institutions through the Freedmen's Bureau, representing the state at Republican National Conventions and the conference at General Conferences, serving as secretary of state and presiding elder until dying of pneumonia in 1872. (Among the ironies of the day, the General Conference [MEC] that year debated whether it should follow Haven's counsel and elect "colored" bishops but elected him instead.)

In places in the South, the anticaste Christian radicalism of Haven and Lynch held brief sway, and MEC women and men missionaries created interracial institutions, particularly at the conference level, as Black deacons and elders took their place within existing MEC conferences (Kentucky, Missouri) or were part of newly constituted southern MEC ventures. But even this modicum of egalitarianism proved too idealistic for White Methodists (MEC) in both the North and the South, and the small pockets of White Methodists in the South pressed for the segregation that their northern counterparts had earlier embraced. The 1868 General Conference granted Kentucky Methodists the right to divide into White and Black conferences. More such segregating requests followed, and the 1876 MEC General Conference opted for the official policy of local choice, effectively drawing the color line in the North as well as the South (H **259; 616n118**).

MEC segregation proceeded apace, but The MEC southern mission continued as well, much of it focused on building a network of Black educational institutions at all levels, from basic literacy to the formation of Black ministerial leadership and the training of a cadre of Black teachers. Working collaboratively (conspiratorially in the eyes of some in The MECS) in these efforts were the Freedmen's Aid and Southern Education Society (founded in 1866), the Board of Education, and the Woman's Home Missionary Society. By the end of its first year, this southern MEC mission had established fifty-nine schools with some five thousand students.

The Freedmen's Aid and Southern Education Society had spent, by 1892, close to $3 million, $1 million of that ($1,010,980.25 to be exact) in the prior quadrennium. Real estate it valued at $1,808,800. In the prior fiscal year, the society had disbursed monies to the following collegiate or higher-level institutions: Bennett College, Central Tennessee College, Claflin University, Clark University, Gammon Theological Seminary, George R. Smith College, Little Rock University, Morgan College, New Orleans University, Philander Smith College, Rust University, Samuel Huston College, U. S. Grant University, and Wiley College. For that year, 1892, the Freedmen's Aid and Southern Education Society claimed a total of 447 teachers and 9,310 students, though only 172 students in college. It boasted 326 persons preparing for the ministry and, over the prior quadrennium, "twelve hundred and fifty conversions . . . among the students" (H **616n121**).

"FRATERNAL" RELATIONS AMONG METHODISTS

The South was but one front on which The MEC and MECS competed. As the southern church restabilized, it reasserted itself in the altar-against-altar competition that increasingly extended west as the American population moved into new territories. In less intense ways, The MPC, EA, and UBC competed as they also moved west. But in the post–Civil War period, the churches took steps away from competition and toward unity.

Exchanges of fraternal delegates or delegations from within and beyond the Methodist family had become commonplace on General Conference as well as annual conference levels. The MEC routinely received and sent formal expressions of fraternity—with Canadian, Irish, and British Methodists; with the separate German American denominations; with the African Methodists, and with other American Protestant communions. The 1872 MEC General Conference noting the range of its exchanges and that The MECS was not among them, authorized exploration of formal fraternity and appointed a fraternal delegation to the General Conference of The MECS (H **615n103**). In response, the 1874 MECS General Conference empowered a fraternal delegation to carry the proposal of a joint commission to "adjust all existing difficulties" standing in the way of fraternal relations. The MEC reciprocated, and a Joint Commission on Fraternal Relations of three clergy and two lay-persons from each church met at Cape May, New Jersey, in August 1876 (S **1876d**). The first southern demand and the first action recalled the over-ture made by Lovick Pierce in 1848 and a staple in MECS self-understanding, that 1844 had not been a schism, namely, "there is but one Episcopal Meth-odism . . . our two General Conference jurisdictions being each rightfully and historically integral parts of the original Methodist Episcopal Church constituted in 1784." And further that each of "said Churches is a legitimate Branch of Episcopal Methodism in the United States, having a common origin in the Methodist Episcopal Church organized in 1784 . . . one Methodist family, though in distinct ecclesiastical connections" (H **615nn103–5**). The Joint Commissioners then went on to deal with the contests over property and territory between the two churches, setting out rules and procedures for adjudication of disputes.

The southern commissioners, who convened separately and kept their own record, noted that "the form of statement in a certain connection would exclude several colored organizations from the classification of Episcopal Methodisms of this country" and concluded that "the omission of reference to them could not be properly construed as an oversight" (H **615n106**). Both churches thereafter appointed fraternal delegations. Both participated, as did the array of Methodist churches, Black and White, in the first international Methodist Ecumenical Conference of 1881 at which Bishop Simpson celebrated the emerging Pan-Methodism and the family ties binding some thirty churches in twenty nations (S **1881b**). And both cooperated in the planning and mounting of the 1884 centennial of American Methodism.

The smaller Methodist bodies participated actively in this chapter in the long road to unification. Methodist Protestants had experienced schism on the eve of the Civil War, devastation during it, and loss of some congregations and preachers to The MECS thereafter. (Northern and western conferences revised the *Discipline* to include an antislavery plank.) It took until 1877 for the two wings to come together. In the interim the southern MPC received an overture concerning unity from The MECS, the latter's 1866 admission of laity into its governance, having removed one of the significant divisive issues. The northern MPC Convention went even further in explorations with the Wesleyans, publishing a joint hymnal and drawing up proposals for a new "Methodist Church" to include the nonepiscopal (MP, Free, Wesleyan, Primitive) Methodist churches. The union was not consummated, but the northern MPC conferences employed the new name until reuniting with the southern conferences in 1877. Methodist Protestants were well represented at the 1881 Methodist Ecumenical Conference.

The UBC, which had escaped formal cleavage during the Civil War, had been party to explorations of unity in the 1850s, first with the Wesleyan Methodists and then among additional smaller churches—Free Presbyterians, Free Will Baptists, Congregational, and Evangelical Association. Members of these bodies met in an Unofficial Union Convention in 1855. The UBC also responded to an invitation to the Pan-Protestant American Evangelical Alliance, sending a large delegation to its 1873 meeting. On the eve of and immediately after the Civil War, William Nast, leader of German Methodism within The MEC, made an overture to the EA about closer relations. The EA sent a delegate to the 1868 MEC General Conference. Out of these exchanges came proposals for organic unity or for transferring language conferences (MEC German ones to the EA and EA English ones to The MEC). In the 1870s and 1880s the EA and UBC again extended overtures for unity.

Neither prospect worked out. Both denominations, however, participated in the 1881 Methodist Ecumenical Conference and those that followed, eventually renamed World Methodist Conferences.

LOCAL METHODISM

Stationed ministers who were either college- or seminary-trained, or both, and vibrant Sunday schools, Bible classes, and missionary societies increasingly displaced the class meeting, absorbing some of the latter's formation and nurturing functions but not its probationary and disciplining responsibilities. The old lay offices—class leaders, stewards, and local preachers—suffered similarly, remaining official roles but seeing the local church's imagination and energy captured by Sunday school superintendents, trustees, and missionary secretaries. The lay-led class meeting, through which one came to membership and whose tickets admitted one to Communion, remained in the *Disciplines* through most of the century. However, The MEC in 1864 and MECS in 1866 introduced a ritual for "joining the church." Eventually churches held the reception rites on Communion Sundays, which The MECS encouraged pastors to offer monthly, permitting new members to take their first Communion. The rites invited the prospective member to affirm baptismal vows, renounce sin, and commit to the church's rules, doctrines, sacraments, and institutions. The pastor then extended the strong hand of fellowship.

To equip adults for the membership rite, probationer's classes came to replace the class meeting, an educational or formational process in lieu of disciplined probation. To resource such probationer's classes, The MEC in 1872 put extracts from the *Discipline* in booklet form, including the historical statement, Articles of Religion, General Rules, and Ritual. To guide probationers in digesting these standards, The MEC published in 1875 an eighty-page *Probationer's Manual*. Three years later James Porter, the retired book editor, added *Helps to Official Members of The Methodist Episcopal Church*. The most widely and longest used guide appeared first in 1883, Stephen Olin Garrison's *Probationer's Hand-Book*.

Pastor then general secretary John Vincent; his MECS counterparts, Thomas O. Summers and Atticus Haygood; and Minnesota practitioners like Sara Jane Timanus Crafts led Methodism to see the Sunday school as the great engine of formation, absorbing that dimension of and replacing the class meeting, effecting the conversion or transformation for which Methodists had looked to revivals, and eventually displacing the probationer's class as well.

As pastor in Chicago in the 1860s, Vincent spoke to Sunday school assemblies, produced model lesson plans, and organized teacher-training events, earning a national reputation that landed him as corresponding (general) secretary of the Sunday School Union in 1868. Under Vincent's leadership, Methodism developed the uniform lesson plan (the Berean), promoted national training conventions, expanded a Sunday school teacher's journal, established a system of "normal schools" to convey best practices and theory, founded Chautauqua as a Sunday school teachers' assembly (1874), and took that nationally in 1878 as the Chautauqua Literary and Scientific Circle. The uniform lesson plan featured age-graded leaflets, golden texts for devotion or memorization, pictures, teachers' materials, home readings, questions, and hymns. The uniformity and integration that this common lectionary achieved every Sunday depended on a cadre of teachers for each age group (women and men), functioning under the guidance and direction of a Sunday school superintendent, effectively the principal of a school system. And he—it was often "he" at this period—dramatized his high calling by leading the opening and closing assemblies (S **1875**).

The highly regimented Sunday school prospered in special education buildings, notably Akron Plan facilities. Lewis Miller, Akron (Ohio) Sunday school superintendent for more than thirty-five years, sought and commissioned an assembly building inspired by a school picnic in a natural amphitheater or geological punch bowl that grouped the children but naturally oriented them toward the center. His Akron Plan Sunday school opened in 1870. Two stories high and capped by a dome, the building arrayed two tiers of classrooms opening into a large semicircular room. The desks in each class faced forward so that when its windowed door opened, the students need not move to heed or hear the superintendent. Akron quickly became a Methodist pilgrimage site and the Akron Plan a distinctive American contribution to the grammar of architecture. Vincent used the *Sunday School Journal* and his 1887 book, *The Modern Sunday-School*, to promote the model. And when his church in Plainfield, New Jersey, was built in the late 1880s, Vincent had it follow the Akron Plan paired with an auditorium-style sanctuary. The combination became a standard in church building and architectural catalogs, often adapted, sometimes copied, championed, and idealized by the distinguished architect George Kramer (S **1897**) and, along with Gothic or Romanesque exteriors, announced Methodism's Main Street status.

By 1884, the American family of Methodist churches had developed a growing cluster of program boards and support services. Their administrative offices moved out of downtown church basements and into newly erected skyscrapers. Methodist Vaticans were in the making—New York, Philadelphia, Washington, and Chicago for northern Methodists; Nashville and Atlanta for southern Methodists; Baltimore and Pittsburgh for Methodist Protestants; Harrisburg for Evangelicals; and Dayton for the United Brethren. The challenges at a connectional level to which these boards responded—problems in accountability, common purpose, governance, and cohesion—were mirrored on the local level by the array of missionary, prayer, purposive, and reform societies. These denominational (men's) and women's organizations posed issues of communication, initiative, accountability, control, and authority.

The new dynamic entities did not mesh with or report to the existing authority structure, namely, the quarterly conference. And a Leaders' and Stewards' Meeting that, in some places met monthly, still functioned with the focused spiritual and fiscal agenda outlined by Wesley. In 1884, the General Conference (MEC) effected the comparable revolution at the local level to that achieved in 1872 at the general. It authorized quarterly conferences to "organize, and continue during its pleasure, an Official Board, to be composed of all the members of the Quarterly Conference," to be "presided over by the preacher in charge," to discharge many of the duties of the Leaders' and Stewards' Meeting, and to "keep a record of its proceedings" (H **616n125**). The official board brought to the local church what incorporation, consolidation, efficiency, bureaucratization, and professionalization brought to the church as a whole and, indeed, to American society, that is, corporate principles of finance, procedure, order, integration, governance, and cohesion. The change was dramatic, as Presiding Elder Morris Crawford explained, his role having been transformed as well (S **1884**). Bureaucratization at the top and corporate-like business efficiency in the local church went increasingly together.

CHAPTER VIII
RETHINKING MISSION(S): 1884–1939

Before you is an ever-widening horizon. The world lies at your feet. The nations await your coming. Will you respond to the call? The grand march for the conquest of all lands for Christ has begun. The voice of the Lord bids us go forward. We dare not accept a secondary place. With our schools and colleges, with our wealth and culture, with our social power and our vast numbers, we must have a large share in the world's evangelization.

So the 1884 Centennial Conference exhorted North American Methodists to claim the Great Commission as their own. The "Pastoral Address" presumed on shared faithfulness in doctrinal orthodoxy, continuing emphasis on the Wesleyan doctrines that relate to salvation, mission "to promote holiness," and the ongoing campaigns of morality and reform (especially temperance and Sabbath protection). The address saw prospects for Methodism's second century in its valuation of education (and modernity), its evangelistic signature, its reform spirit, its institutional strength, its global missionary reach. Evangelization of the world and reforming societal practices that stood in the way of the gospel would indeed become consuming passions of the several Methodist churches (H **619nn1–2**).

REORDERING FOREIGN MISSIONS

By the 1880s Methodist ministries outside the United States labored under overlapping, often competing authorities. Missionaries deployed under male (mission board) or female (women's missionary society) authority. Male missionaries, if ordained, remained accountable also to their American annual conferences. Missionaries established, participated in, gave leadership to, but also served within and under local ministry structures. The MEC authorized organization of mission annual conferences abroad for Liberia in 1848 and for India in 1860. In 1864, The MEC advised the bishops, whose international itinerations and occasional presidency in mission conferences constituted yet another authority system, to organize mission conferences when and where their condition "shall render such organization proper" (H **621n24**).

The 1868 General Conference granted mission conferences representation and recognized Liberia, Germany-Switzerland, and India to be "Annual Conferences endowed with all the rights, privileges, and immunities" of those in the United States (H **621n25**). This action raised to a disciplinary level the fundamental question that lay at the heart of the Methodist missionary enterprise, remains unresolved two centuries later, and indeed was latent as a policy question when John Wesley sent Thomas Coke to be joint superintendent with Francis Asbury "over our Brethren in North America" (S **1784a**). Should Methodism be either one, accountable to father Wesley and successor authority, or both, and ordered from a single country (England)? Or should the trajectory of the American movement toward indigenization, self-support, and full independence prevail? Which? Catholic uniformity and universalism, or Eastern Orthodox autocephalous churches? Reacting to the legislation, Daniel Wise, head of the Sunday School Union and former editor of *Zion's Herald,* and Daniel Curry, editor of the *Christian Advocate* (New York), went on record in articles opposing the notion that mature Methodist movements abroad should "remain ecclesiastically united to the parent Church, be governed by one discipline, superintended by our Bishops, and represented in our General Conference." An "ecumenical Methodism," they thought a bad idea (H **621n26**).

Methodist missions, like those of other churches, had nevertheless from the very start functioned as though Methodism were indeed "one" and replicated American offices, practices, polity, and institutions. And even as schools and colleges, modeled after their American counterparts, produced pastors and other leaders, US missionaries tended to run the annual conferences, constituted an informal, if not organized leadership elite, represented in their collaboration yet another authority structure, and were typically returned to the United States as General Conference delegates.

In 1884, The MEC took two actions that gestured toward indigenization—authorization for central conferences and election of William Taylor as missionary bishop for Africa. The latter responded to a memorial from the Liberian Conference requesting a bishop resident in Africa. In revivalistic campaigns from the 1870s, Taylor organized Methodist churches and trained and deployed local leaders in successive contexts—India, South Africa, England, the West Indies, Ceylon, Peru, Chile, and Brazil. Taylor's signature self-sufficient and self-supporting "Pauline Method of Missions" prospered, led into organization of the Bombay and Bengal Mission, and then to creating the South India Conference. In electing Taylor as missionary bishop, General Conference gave the Pauline method a very high platform.

The emergence of North and South India Conferences led to their initiating a proposal for a delegated body to coordinate Methodist work across India. The 1884 General Conference debated and passed provision for such a polity and governing mission entity with structure not unlike itself, the origin of the "central conference." When Bishop William Harris edited the 1884 *Discipline,* he termed the new entities "Central Mission Conferences," the title with which they would be referenced and operated for four decades (H **286–87**; **621nn27–30**). The 1884 legislation allowed for creation of a central conference either by General Conference or by "a majority vote of all the Conferences or Missions wishing to unite." In 1892 the General Conference rescinded the latter measure of self-determination, and the powers of the central conferences were limited from the start to administration and coordination. The authority to adjust the *Discipline* and to legislate for local circumstance would have to wait for a later day.

LAY MINISTRIES AT HOME

In the 1884 *Discipline* immediately before the paragraph authorizing central conferences was one recognizing the ministry of and formally establishing the Woman's Home Missionary Society (twelve years after recognition of the WFMS). Women's home missions, transformative in social gospel fashion, were stimulated by Jennie Hartzell's ministry among New Orleans freedwomen. Observing this initiative, the head of the Freedmen's Aid Society, Richard Rust, and his wife, Elizabeth, recognized the need for an organization that could work on behalf of "the poor black women and children of the Southland." At a meeting in Cincinnati on June 8, 1880, shortly after the close of the General Conference, about fifty MEC women resolved to form a Woman's Home Missionary Society "to enlist and organize the women of Methodism in behalf of the needy and destitute of all races and nationalities in this country," and with recommendation for special attention to "the Southern field" (H **621nn33–35**). They selected Elizabeth Rust as corresponding secretary and as president, Mrs. Lucy Webb Hayes, loyal Methodist and spouse of the US president. Hayes served as national president of the society until her death in 1889, presiding at its annual meetings and presenting annual reports stressing the importance of the work. Within a few years, WHMS had enlarged its mission, establishing bureaus, each headed by a secretary, to organize work with Indigenous nations on reservations, Mormons, Blacks, "illiterate Whites" in the South, Asian immigrants, and others in US missionary contexts. By the end of the first decade there were some seventy corresponding secretaries at the annual conference level, and there were reported to be "over 55,000 members in more than 1900 adult and juvenile societies. *Woman's Home Missions* had reached a circulation of 15,500" (H **621nn36–37**).

In 1886, southern Methodist women established and The MECS General Conference authorized a Woman's Department of the Board of Church Extension, subsequently the Woman's Parsonage and Home Mission Society (still later the Woman's Home Mission Society). Kentuckian Lucinda B. Helm formulated the plan and became the organization's first head. In four years, through her leadership, correspondence, publications, advocacy, and travels, thirty-six conferences and more than seven thousand women began working together to establish parsonages for the itinerant ministry in the South and the West. Helm's vision always was "nothing less than the fullest and completest organized effort for *home missions.*" In 1890 the General Conference recognized the Woman's Parsonage and Home Mission Society as an official organization of The MECS. Forced by ill health to retire in 1893, Helms continued to edit the society's journal, *Our Homes,* until her death in 1897. Another young woman from a prominent Kentucky family, Belle Harris Bennett, succeeded and served for more than twenty-five years as president of the WHMS (1896–1910) and its successor, the Woman's Missionary Council (1910–22). Her efforts established the Scarritt Bible and Training School in Kansas City in 1892, the Sue Bennett School for poor children in the mountains of Kentucky in 1897, the first church settlement house in Nashville in 1901, and the deaconess office in 1902. Bennett played a central role, as we note below, in the struggle for full laity rights for women in The MECS (H **287–89; 621–22nn38–40;** S **1910**).

The motivations for, theories concerning, organizational style of, and operating procedures of foreign and home missionary societies mutually reinforced one another. Indeed, United Brethren and Evangelicals operated with a single structure for denominational missions, and women did as well. And the Methodist Protestants established their Woman's Home Missionary Society in 1893 at the end of a session of its Woman's Foreign Missionary Society and at the latter's initiative (H **622n41**). Women in all three of these churches, consistently or sporadically, found their organization and activities subjected to denominational (that is, male) control and supervision. That prospect, recurrently advanced in the interests of efficiency and coordination, required vigilance on the part of women across Methodism, indeed across Christian communities.

*****

The Wesleyan Service Guild (WSG) was established in 1921 as auxiliary to both the WHMS and the WFMS (a "Business Women's Unit," to meet the needs of and focus the energies of a growing cadre of business and professional MEC women). Begun the prior year as an initiative of the Northwestern Branch of the Woman's Foreign Missionary Society, by May 1923 the WFMS and WHMS had elaborated protocols for the WSG as their joint auxiliary, but with its own Central Committee, constitution for local units, and monthly newsletter called *World Service Greetings*. Founder Marion Lela Norris served as its national secretary from its beginning to 1928 and also chaired its Central Committee (H **622n42**). The WSG offered working women a fourfold program: (1) development of spiritual life, (2) opportunities for world service, (3) promotion of Christian citizenship and personal service, and (4) provision for social and recreational activities. Among its mission projects was ministry to young businesswomen in Japan and with immigrant children at Campbell Settlement in Gary, Indiana. During the Depression years, WSG leaders admirably attempted to function as a support system for women facing unemployment or salary reductions and to keep them involved in guild units regardless of their financial status. On Methodist merger in 1939, the WSG became the only women's missionary organization to continue as such into the new church and as a unit within the Woman's Division of Christian Service.

*****

New youth and men's ministries emerged post-1884 as well. A Wesley Brotherhood, one of the oldest, was founded in Philadelphia in the early 1880s by pastor Thomas B. Neely. Others, variously named, followed across The MEC. Largest by the turn of the century was the Brotherhood of St. Paul—a cross between the Catholic Knights of Columbus and a Methodist men's Bible class—founded in Little Falls, New York, by former YMCA secretary then pastor, later bishop, Frederick Deland Leete. Representatives from the several organizations met in Philadelphia in 1898 to form a single Methodist Brotherhood, electing then-bishop Thomas B. Neely as honorary president. Proposals to the General Conference to adopt the organization and incorporate it into the church's official structure were not successful until 1908. UBC men established an Otterbein Brotherhood the next year (1909). The Evangelical Church delayed organizing its Albright Brotherhood until 1930 (H **620nn19–21**).

Methodists participated in and led the youth organizations—YMCA/YWCA, Christian Endeavor—birthed in the nineteenth century. Experiments in denominational youth organizations, notably the Church Lyceum, created in Philadelphia in the 1870s led in 1884 to founding of the Oxford League by John Vincent, head of the Sunday School Union, as a youth organization "modeled" on Wesley's Holy Club. Chapters of the Oxford League were to promote biblical and literary studies, to build religious piety and moral character, and to train middle-class teenagers in the works of "mercy and help." In 1889 in Cleveland, the Oxford League merged with several other competing Methodist youth organizations to form the Epworth League of The MEC. A year later the southern church organized its own Epworth League along similar lines. By 1896 more than twenty thousand local chapters had been established in local churches, North and South. The EA formed a Young People's Alliance in 1891, and the UBC formed a Young People's Union two years later (H **621n22**). Youth would grow as Christians and as loyal Methodists, league handbooks explained, by their training "in Church life and teaching; their employment in works of charity and social service, the inculcation of missionary ideals . . . and [their] direction to lives of service at home and abroad" (H **621nn22–23;** S **1893a**).

The Student Volunteer Movement (SVM) came into being in 1888 in a meeting under the auspices of the YWCA and YMCA to channel into actual service the energy for and commitment to world missions excited by those two youth organizations. One of the five organizers, Methodist John R. Mott, would chair SVM for thirty-two years, head various other missionary and ecumenical endeavors, and become Methodism's most important figure in Christianity's ecumenical world mission. SVM's watchword, "the evangelization of the world in this generation," could have served Methodism's churches as well, as the scope of their late nineteenth- and early twentieth-century missions indicate (H **622nn44–45**).

KOREAN MISSIONS AND ASIAN AMERICAN METHODISTS

In 1885 a team of Presbyterian and Methodist missionaries arrived in Korea (S **1885**)—Drew graduate Henry G. Appenzeller; his wife, Ella Dodge Appenzeller; medical doctor William Scranton; and educator Mary Scranton (H **622nn45–47**). In their first year, the Appenzellers opened a school for boys, which the Korean king named PaiChai HakDang (School to Nurture the Talent, now PaiChai University), at Chungdong, and Mary Scranton established a school for girls, Ewha HakDang (Pear Blossom School, now Ewha University). By the following year, Dr. Scranton offered Koreans a Western-style clinic that became Shibyungwon Hospital. An expanded hospital, consisting of five wards, opened the next year. They soon found out that Korean women did not want to see male doctors. In 1887 the WFMS sent Meta Howard, MD, to Korea. Under Dr. Howard's direction, the first women's hospital in Korea was established in Seoul, Po Kyu Nyo Koan Hospital, meaning "house for many sick women." A second hospital for women, the Lillian Harris Hospital, opened in another area of the city in 1893. Scranton's hospital closed in 1900, but the Harris Hospital for Women and Children prospered and laid the groundwork for the Hospital and Medical School for Women of Ewha University founded in 1928, now a leading training institute for health-care professionals in Korea.

169

Medical and educational contributions led to removal of a ban on evangelism, and Appenzeller began a ministry that in ten years gained 817 members in a dozen locations in and near Seoul. In 1890 Appenzeller began the Trilingual Press at PaiChai School, serving two purposes—disseminating the Christian message in print and providing work scholarships for students. This Korean, Chinese, and English press (later Methodist Publishing House, Seoul) published Bibles, hymnals, and Sunday school curricula. It became the home as well for several newspapers, including the *Korean Christian Advocate,* the first Korean-language Christian newspaper, and *Dongip* (the *Independence Daily*), which became the focus of PaiChai's commitment to the Korean independence movement. Appenzeller's other principal activity was participation in the translation of the Bible into Korean. He was a member of the Board of Bible Translators from 1886, a work he shared with several of the early Methodist and Presbyterian missionaries and a number of Korean translators. Appenzeller opened a bookstore in 1894, edited the *Korean Repository* and *Korea Review* to introduce Korea abroad, and was active in the scholarly Korean Asiatic Society. He died in 1902 en route to a Bible translation meeting. The mission granted licenses to preach to the first Korean national in 1888. In 1901, the first deacons were ordained. With the ordination of elders in 1908, The MEC General Conference authorized the formation of a Korea Annual Conference.

Ten years after the northern church began its mission (1895), two experienced *southern* Methodist missionaries from China, Bishop Eugene R. Hendrix and Clarence F. Reid, arrived. The following year Reid established residence in Seoul, surveyed the Korean field, and began work in both Songdo and Seoul. In 1897 Reid was made superintendent of the newly established Korea Mission by the Board of Missions of The MECS. The two Methodist churches, frustrated by slow growth in the politically charged country, soon began to work together on evangelistic strategy, including a common Korean-language hymnal and catechism, joint support for schools, and by 1910 a central theological seminary in Seoul. Both churches prospered as a result of the dramatic revivals in Wonsan in 1903 and in Pyongyang in 1907.

Over the first decades of Methodist missions, Korea remained politically volatile, threatened or dominated by either China or Japan. The client character of Korean politics affected Christianizing efforts. American missionaries did not gain the privileges in Korea enjoyed in lands under Western colonial control. Nor were the social and political elites, attentive to the political struggles and Chinese-Japanese intrigues, inclined to accept alien religion and culture that would subject them to persecution. Missions succeeded better among the poor and in the countryside. From 1905 on, many missionaries committed themselves to Korean independence and Christian leaders who grew up under the tutelage of missionaries became the backbone of the unceasing struggle to gain freedom, independence, and dignity from Japan's cruel exploitation and domination. The cause of Korean self-rule made Christianity seem less alien, indeed empowering and indigenizing.

From Appenzeller's days, conflicts emerged regarding the independence movement, the relationship between Korean religious and cultural traditions and the Christian gospel, and missionary retention of administrative and financial power in the emerging Korean churches. Korean Methodism would early (1930) establish its own autonomy (S **1931**). Conversely, the sensitive political climate may have reinforced the evangelicalism and individualism that predominate among Korean (and Korean American) Presbyterians and Methodists. Certainly from the start such notes were struck. Appenzeller put a premium on evangelism, individual conversion, conservative biblical hermeneutics, strict morals, and the social implications of Christian faith— all of which he learned at Drew.

*****

Methodist ministries among Chinese Americans and Japanese Americans, begun in the 1870s, led gradually to enabling polity structures (H **293–97; 622nn49–55**). In 1893, Chinese American churches in several communities were linked into a separate district. A decade later, in 1904, Bishop Luther Wilson presided over the formation of the Pacific Chinese (later California-Oriental) Mission Conference. Its territory extended as far east as Texas. In New York, a Cantonese ministerial student, Chu Bok, aided by the Five Points Mission, opened a school and held services in Chinese. Four years later a permanent Methodist mission in New York's Chinatown was established (now the Church of All Nations). By 1900, the EA had established a Chinese Sunday school in Chicago.

A Japanese student in an Otis Gibson mission school, Kanichi Miyama, converted, was baptized, and organized a Japanese Gospel Society. From it grew in 1879 the first Japanese Methodist Church in America, now known as Pine Street UMC. In 1881 Miyama abandoned plans for a career in

171

business and prepared himself for the ministry. Admitted "on trial" in California Conference in 1884, Miyama was appointed to work with Gibson in expanding the mission's ministry to San Francisco's Japanese American community. On this foundation, Superintendent Frederick Masters envisioned a ministry expanded to Japanese Americans on the Pacific Coast from Los Angeles to Seattle (S **1886**). Ordained elder in the California Conference in 1887, Miyama was assigned to work with the new Asian mission superintendent, M. C. Harris, a founding member of the missionary team that organized The MEC's first mission in Japan in 1873. Catering especially to university students, these leaders first rented space in Central MEC and by 1894 built, occupied, and dedicated a two-story church building on Pine Street, complete with dormitory and schoolrooms. With more than five hundred members and probationers, the church had become the second largest church in the conference! When Japanese American youth were banned from the city's high schools, Harris opened one of the first private high schools for Japanese Americans in 1898. Miyama and Harris expanded Methodism's outreach to Japanese up and down the West Coast, and eventually to Canada and Hawaii. Miyama returned to Japan in 1890 and founded Ginza Church in Tokyo and churches in Nagoya and Kamakura.

Harris had a special talent for recruiting Japanese preachers. A second, Terujiro Hasegawa, was ordained in 1889, and six others followed in the early 1890s. In 1893 nine Japanese American churches were linked on a separate district in the California Conference, and by 1900 they sought and received permission from the General Conference to organize themselves into the Pacific Japanese Mission Conference with churches in sixteen cities from San Diego to Vancouver and out to Hawaii. The MECS established Japanese missions in California in 1897 in Alameda and Sonoma Counties. As Japanese communities developed in other cities, evangelists from the Pacific Coast were sent to start missions, beginning in New York City in 1894. By 1905 the conference reported on work in California, Oregon, and Washington and overtures from Idaho, Montana, and Nebraska.

In 1904 Methodists among immigrants to Hawaii (annexed by the United States in 1898) established the first Korean Methodist congregation on American soil (eventually Christ UMC of Honolulu). By 1916 there were thirty-one Korean Methodist churches in Hawaii and thirty-five mission stations with total membership of two thousand. When Koreans emigrated to California in the early 1900s, the Japanese Methodist Mission in San Francisco organized prayer meetings in residential homes. After 1906, the year of the great earthquake and fire, mission groups divided the West Coast Asian work among them. By this comity agreement, The MECS fell heir to missions among Korean immigrants in central and northern California. San Francisco's tiny Korean American community raised funds to build the first Korean Methodist church on the mainland (later San Francisco Korean UMC) under the leadership of Ju Sam Ryang, one of the first ordained Korean preachers. Ryang opened the upper floor of the new church as a dormitory for Korean immigrants, taught English at night, and began a Korean-language Methodist paper, *Daedo* (the *Great Way*). In 1930 Ryang became the first bishop of the newly formed autonomous Korean Methodist Church. As Korean Methodists spread across the country, they planted churches across the west and then the east (one in New York in 1921 and Chicago in 1928). The MECS included both Korean American and Japanese when it organized the California Oriental Mission in 1928.

Ministries to Filipinos began with the occupation of the islands after the Spanish-American War. In 1899, Bishop James Thoburn (MEC) preached the first Protestant sermon in the Catholic Philippines. Lay missioner Nicolas Zamora and local preacher Arthur Prautch organized a congregation. By 1900 Methodists were building schools and churches in Manila, staffing them with American female and male missionaries, and recruiting local converts as preachers. The first district conference, staffed with one ordained preacher and six assistants, featured seven preaching places and 220 members on three circuits: Pandacan, Santa Cruz, and Tondo. Homer Stuntz arrived in 1901 as superintendent of the emerging mission, and a Methodist Publishing House opened in Manila, producing the first Indigenous (Tagalog) hymnal in 1902. Translations of the ritual and *Discipline* followed in 1903. Nicolas Zamora, ordained deacon in 1900, became the first Indigenous elder in 1903. The same year a training school for deaconesses opened, evolving into Harris Memorial College. By comity arrangement with other American denominations, Methodists assumed responsibility for the area in Luzon north of Manila.

Aggressive evangelism and a responsive people produced converts—6,800 in the first three years—outpacing growth in every other mission of The MEC (H **297; 622n56**). Rapid growth and expansion of circuits led to the formation of the Philippine Islands Mission Conference in 1905. Protesting modest empowerment of local leadership, Zamora led an exodus in 1908, forming the Evangelical Methodist Church. A measure of independence from

North American church governance for those who remained in The MEC came in 1944 when the Philippine Central Conference was authorized and the first Indigenous Filipino bishop, Dionisio Alejandro, elected. Migration of Filipinos to Hawaii and the continental United States led to organization of churches. By the 1930s, Filipino churches were established on the East Coast.

DEACONESS MOVEMENTS

On June 15, 1885, Lucy Rider Meyer exhorted the Chicago Methodist Episcopal Preachers' Meeting to establish a training school to prepare women for religious leadership (S **1889, 1893b**; H **625n94**). The preachers blessed her project, indicating she would have to find the money on her own. Against great financial odds, she opened the Chicago Training School for City, Home, and Foreign Missions that October and the Chicago Deaconess Home two years later. The 1888 MEC General Conference received two petitions asking that deaconess work be recognized as an official ministry of The MEC. One came from her Rock River Conference, the other from the Bengal Conference in India. The latter cited the need for deaconesses with authority to administer the sacraments to the secluded zenana women of India. The Committee on Missions, chaired by India missionary James Thoburn, brother of Isabella, the first WFMS missionary, recommended approval. Thoburn, elected missionary bishop that year, included an appeal from Lucy Rider Meyer when he spoke in advocacy (H **626n95**). General Conference established the office of deaconess, provided a plan for organizing deaconess work in The MEC, but denied deaconesses sacramental authority for the mission field in India or elsewhere.

The Chicago initiative benefited from precedents set by Methodists in Europe. In 1864, Methodist pastors in several German cities introduced *parish* deaconesses for the care of the sick, following earlier Lutheran precedent. Ten years later (1874), The MEC's conference in Germany established a deaconess order under the name *Bethanienverein* (Bethany Society). By 1884, the society had established Bethany deaconess homes and hospitals in three cities—Berlin, Frankfurt, and Hamburg—and had recruited and trained more than sixty deaconesses. Also in 1874, The Evangelical Association's conference in Germany authorized the formation of its own independent Bethany Deaconess Society in Germany. The new society opened its first hospital in 1885 in Frankfurt. In 1890, EA deaconesses were sent to Lausanne and in 1897, to Strasbourg and Vienna in nursing and childcare ministries. In 1889, the Martha and Mary Society of the German Synod of the Methodist Church in England became the third member of the Methodist family of churches to establish deaconess work in Germany (H **626nn96–98**). Beginning in the 1870s, American Methodists touted the European experiments and advocated their utility for urban and missionary settings. Among advocates were James Thoburn; Bishop Matthew Simpson;, Drew Professor John F. Hurst; pastor, later Northwestern president, and editor Bishop Charles H. Fowler; LPCU head Annie Wittenmyer; and Susanna Fry, an Ohio schoolteacher. The latter, after observing German deaconess work, set forth the case in two articles in the 1872 *Ladies' Repository* (S **1872b**; H **626nn99–104**).

An Oberlin graduate, trained further in medicine and science, experienced as teacher and administrator (H **310**), Rider Meyer served as principal and instructor in her Chicago Training School (CTS). Her husband, a secretary for the Chicago YMCA, became the school's business agent. Both the WFMS and WHMS supported the project. Methodist women donated money and furnishings and soon launched a systematic "Nickel Fund" campaign to support the school. The Meyers publicized school and cause in *The Message*, which began publication in January 1886.

Resident teachers were few in the beginning, but ministers, teachers, and physicians from the Chicago area regularly donated their time to give lectures. The course of study was comprehensive, including Bible classes, but also studies in "hygiene, in citizenship, in social and family relationships, in everything that could help or hinder in the establishment of the Kingdom of Heaven on earth." Students gained knowledge and skills for urban America by fieldwork that included house-to-house visitation among Chicago's immigrant poor and needy. Students in a rented apartment became the nucleus of a deaconess home, soon joined by Isabella Thoburn, principal of Lucknow Woman's College in India, then home on furlough.

Enabling deaconess legislation charged each annual conference to establish a nine-member Conference Board of Deaconesses, at least three of whom had to be women. These boards licensed qualified candidates twenty-five years of age or older who had served a probationary period of at least two years and were recommended by a quarterly conference. Unsalaried and living communally (S **1889, 1893b, 1902**), deaconesses were also costumed, uniformly wearing a simple, long, black dress and a bonnet with white ties at the neck. They wore it for the sake of economy, to eliminate the need for an expensive wardrobe, and for instant recognition and protection as they worked in dangerous urban neighborhoods. It also gave them greater accessibility to poor people and a sense of "sisterly union." Although receiving no salary, the single women in this sisterhood of service were provided board, their uniform, and a monthly allowance (H **627n111**). Two types of deaconess work developed, both designed to meet the needs of those in the slum neighborhoods of Chicago: nurse deaconesses and missionary deaconesses (also referred to as visitors or evangelists). To prepare students for the more technical service of the former, Rider Meyer included the basics of nursing in the course of study at CTS and called on Chicago physicians to teach them. Rider Meyer interpreted the work of these vocationally single deaconesses as that of "the Mother in the Church," the "characteristic ministry of women" to care for children and heal the sick (H **312; 627nn112–13**).

Left ambiguous in the empowering legislation of 1888 was whether the annual conferences or the WHMS could best protect and guide the deaconess project. Advocate for the latter, and the other principal leaders of the deaconess movement, was Jane Marie Bancroft (later Robinson). Daughter of an MEC pastor, Bancroft earned a PhD from Syracuse, served as dean of the Woman's College and professor of French at Northwestern. On a history fellowship, she spent two years at the universities of Zurich and Paris, studying the European deaconesses on behest of the WHMS. After presenting her report to the WHMS on her return, she published it in 1889 as *Deaconesses in Europe and Their Lessons for America,* inspiring the WHMS to undertake its own deaconess project. Married in 1891 to an active MEC layman, George O. Robinson, a Detroit lawyer and widower with four children, she continued her advocacy and leadership with spousal approval.

These two gifted, extraordinarily well-educated, and dedicated Methodist women, Lucy Rider Meyer and Jane Bancroft Robinson, vied with each other for the leadership of the deaconess movement in The MEC for nearly twenty-five years. Rider Meyer saw the order, functioning under annual conference authority, as a lifetime commitment, a religious vocation that set women apart and freed them as far as possible from the usual female commitments of marriage and family. Bancroft Robinson believed that the order should be open to women who wanted to undertake social service work for a short time before they made permanent decisions about what to do with their lives.

She believed that the WHMS ought to supervise deaconess work in order to protect its autonomy. The two sides took their case and arguments about the "original intention" of the 1888 legislation to successive General Conferences. The 1908 General Conference created a General Deaconess Board to guide all three forms of deaconess work: "the 'Church Plan,' the German Methodist, and the WHMS deaconesses." Rider Meyer and Bancroft Robinson appointed to the newly organized board, continued to maintain their own views (H **627nn118–20**).

Despite, perhaps because of, the competition, the deaconess cause initially prospered. By 1910 more than a thousand MEC deaconesses had been consecrated for service in some ninety institutions. Between 1880 and 1915, nearly sixty religious training schools opened in the United States, "primarily for lay people and most of them for women." A Training School for Colored Deaconesses was founded in Cincinnati in 1900. In 1924 The Methodist Episcopal Church consolidated the denomination's General Deaconess Board and Board of Hospitals and Homes. By that year more than two hundred deaconesses were reported to be active in the health-care work of the church. The boards worked as one until the time of reunion in 1939 when deaconess work was placed under the supervision of the Woman's Division of the Board of Missions.

Other denominations in the Methodist family had also become part of the movement: the UBC beginning deaconess work in 1897, the EA in 1903, The MPC in 1908, and The MECS in 1902. The latter's Scarritt Bible and Training School, established in 1892 in Kansas City, Missouri, relocated to Nashville in 1924. The moving spirits for the latter were Belle Harris Bennett (for whom the facility is also now named) and Mary Helm (on their roles see H **314–15** and **308–16** for fuller treatment of the deaconess movement).

HOSPITALS

Troubled that a friend's life might have been saved had he had medical care in Brooklyn, James M. Buckley, powerful editor of the *Christian Advocate* (New York), urged Methodists to catch up with Catholics, Episcopalians, and Jews and establish hospitals (S **1881a**). Bishop Matthew Simpson echoed Buckley's plea later that year in one of his addresses to the first world Methodist conference. A prosperous Methodist banker, George I. Seney, responded to Buckley with a gift of $400,000 and sixteen lots in hospital-poor Brooklyn. The Methodist Episcopal Hospital, a UMC Heritage Landmark, opened in December 1887 with a ceremony of speeches, prayers, and hymns. A coast-to-coast campaign encouraged churches and individuals to endow beds "in perpetuity" for $5,000 or for one year at $365, Methodist women organized Florence Nightingale Societies, and conferences within the region devoted one Communion offering per year to the effort. It took ten years of fundraising before all of the planned buildings were completed and equipped (H **628nn130–32**).

Methodists in other cities soon followed New York's lead. Chicago Methodists opened theirs in 1888; Cincinnati in 1889; Omaha in 1891; Kansas City, Minneapolis, and Philadelphia in 1892; Washington, D.C., in 1894; Louisville in 1895; Boston in 1896; Spokane in 1898; and Indianapolis in 1899. Southern Methodists began founding a family of hospitals early in the twentieth century: in Atlanta (Emory University Hospital), 1905; in St. Louis, 1914; in Memphis, 1921; in Houston, 1922; in Dallas, 1927; in Durham (Duke University Hospital), 1930. The Evangelicals founded five small hospitals by 1920; the United Brethren had none.

These healing ventures represented a recovery. Wesley's medical manual, *Primitive Physick*, had been among the earliest publications of the Methodists in North America. Revised at Bishop Asbury's request to suit American physicians and climate by a noted Philadelphia doctor, Henry Wilkins, in 1792, it was kept in print by the church through the 1820s and issued in pirated editions by other publishers through the 1880s. Like Wesley, Asbury and numerous other circuit riders viewed it their duty to prescribe medical remedies for sick persons. *Christian Advocates* carried Wesley-like workable remedies in regular "Health and Disease" columns. By 1830, this minister-physician tradition was ending, health care beginning its professionalization, and churches obliged increasingly to undertake physical healing on medicine's terms.

The new deaconess orders at low cost staffed several of the earliest Methodist hospitals. Deaconess societies also founded hospitals of their own. The "mother" deaconess hospital, Christ Hospital in Cincinnati, Ohio, opened its doors and its beds in 1889, an expansion of the mission of the one-year-old Elizabeth Gamble Deaconess Home and Training School founded the previous year. The Cincinnati deaconesses discovered an overwhelming demand for nursing services. Quickly outgrowing their facilities by 1892 the deaconess newsletter, *The Message*, reported that a new site would accommodate up to one hundred deaconesses and as many hospital patients. The depression of 1893 delayed construction of a new deaconess home, training school, and hospital until 1898. A School of Nursing attached to the hospital opened in 1902. In 1911 an adjacent property became the children's hospital. The 60-bed hospital grew to 400 beds when a more modern structure was occupied in 1931. In 1957 construction was begun on a new wing to house 250 additional beds (H **628n36**). Other deaconess hospitals followed, notably in Boston, Chicago, and Washington, D.C.

German American Methodists, strong in their piety and effective in their expression of faith in health and welfare ministries, founded and supported a considerable network of deaconess hospitals. The EA did so with the Evangelical Deaconess Home and Hospital in Chicago, opened in 1905 with a free dispensary, a laboratory, and a thirty-five-bed ward. MEC Germans resolved at the 1892 MEC General Conference to establish a German motherhouse in Chicago but when fundraising faltered turned to Cincinnati in 1896, thanks to a gift from Mrs. Fannie Nast Gamble, daughter of William Nast, leader of Methodism's German American movement. The MEC's Central Deaconess Board authorized pastor Christian Golder, with his deaconess sister, Louise, to rent a house in Cincinnati to found a German Methodist deaconess hospital. The order released six German nurses from Christ Hospital to assist the Golders, who purchased a well-appointed private hospital, which they reopened as Bethesda Hospital in 1898 (H **629n137**). In 1904 a maternity department opened. A much larger, state-of-the-art maternity hospital followed in 1913, a School of Nursing in 1914, absorption by the Ohio Hospital for Women and Children in 1915, and a Bethesda Home for the Aged that same year. Out of this beginning grew the Bethesda Institutions, a family of German American Methodist-sponsored hospitals, homes, and training schools in New York, Akron, Chicago, Milwaukee, Kansas City, Louisville, Detroit, Terre Haute, and Los Angeles. The order launched a denomination-wide Bethesda Society in 1897.

A signal contribution to health care among Black communities occurred with the opening in 1876 of Meharry Medical College. The renowned Nashville institution was a venture undertaken by The MEC Freedmen's Aid Society and backed financially by five Methodist Meharry brothers (from Indiana). Founded during the era when the segregated policy of "separate but equal" became national policy and dictated every aspect of society, including medical care, Meharry Medical College provided one of the few contexts within

179

which to train Black medical professionals. A teaching hospital, Hubbard Hospital, was added in 1910. Over the years Meharry expanded in depth and diversity, becoming by the 1960s America's largest private, historically Black institution educating health-care professionals and biomedical scientists. The majority of Meharry's graduates practice in medically underserved rural and inner-city areas (H **629n140**).

By the 1920s, seventy-five hospitals and clinics related to The MEC had opened to persons of any faith, many including dispensaries where medicines and supplies could be purchased under cost. To strengthen denominational ties and broaden financial support for the expanding family of hospitals, Methodists founded national organizations patterned after the Red Cross: the White Cross Society in The MEC in 1917 and the Golden Cross Society in The MECS in 1922. At the same time the UBC began a "little red Christmas stocking" program to raise money for the denomination's social welfare ministries.

However, medical services and nursing education programs lacked standardization and accreditation. Many hospitals were chronically underfunded, poorly housed, and loosely connected to various church agencies—General Deaconess Board, Woman's Home Missionary Society, Board of Home Missions, and Board of Negro Education in the case of MEC. By the 1920s church leaders established Boards of Hospitals and Homes to enforce standards—medical, curricular, architectural, and financial. During the first two years of The MEC board, eighteen of its hospitals reached the standards adopted by the Board of Hospitals and Homes and the American College of Surgeons (H **629–30nn143–47**). Over time authority shifted from hospital trustees (heavily clergy) to medical decision makers. High-salaried physicians replaced low-overhead deaconesses. And fiscal pressures led hospitals to favor paying over indigent patients, a radical shift in mission as America's cities—emerging as multiracial, multiethnic working-class centers—teemed with immigrants from abroad and the rural South, many living under slum conditions, desperately poor, despite putting both parents and young children into harsh labor.

SOCIAL CHRISTIANITY

Deaconesses represented one of several organizational ways in which Methodists addressed America's urban challenges. At the center of a number of important social-gospel initiatives was Frank Mason North (for vignettes of five other social gospelers—William Carwardine, Mary McDowell, Charles Albert Tinley, Edgar Helms, and William Bell—see H **302–8**). Typically working collaboratively, North had a leadership role in the City Evangelization Union, the Open and Institutional Church League (1894), the Methodist Federation for Social Service (1907), formulation of the Social Creed (adopted in 1908), and creation of the Federal Council of Churches (1908) and its adoption of North's expanded version of the Social Creed. In 1912, The MEC elected him one of the corresponding secretaries of the Board of Foreign Missions, a position he retained until 1924. From 1912 until 1916 he chaired the executive committee of the Federal Council of Churches, serving as the council's president (1916–20). North took an interest as well in world Methodist conferences and in efforts to reunite American Methodism. By understanding that the problems of Black Americans were not only those of rural dwellers in the Jim Crow South but also those of the waves of new Black city dwellers, North was one of the few leading MEC figures openly to support the National Association for the Advancement of Colored People (NAACP) from its foundation in 1909.

In 1891 North, then pastor in Middletown (Connecticut) and serving the community around Wesleyan University, from which he received four degrees, wrote a series of four articles on the topic of socialism and Christianity in *Zion's Herald,* New England's Methodist newspaper (S **1891**). Socialism, North insisted, devoid of its atheism and materialism, could be Christianized. Further, the "city will test the church and decide its competence," and the "problem of poverty lies very close to the problem of sin." The church recognized a prophet in its midst and appointed him the following year as head (corresponding secretary) of the New York City Mission and Church Extension Society. The same year, the New York East Conference, through a committee headed by North, broke new ground by framing a memorial to that year's General Conference, which urged a declaration of Christian duties on social concerns. General Conference took no action, but the prophetic act marks the beginning of the struggle to commit the church to a vigorous ministry of social justice in behalf of poor persons. That General Conference did authorize the City Evangelization Union, and North headed it from 1896 to 1912. For two decades in the New York City post, North engaged in building institutions; establishing the Church of All Nations; supporting mission initiatives among German, Italian, Polish, Russian, Chinese, and Japanese immigrants; working across racial lines; exhorting urban parishes to undertake ministries dealing with poverty, crime, and vice; championing urban causes through *The Christian City*; and encouraging the denomination in various ways to take on the challenges of an increasingly urban America. He put those convictions into verse in the 1903 hymn "Where Cross the Crowded Ways of Life" (H **623nn71–72**).

The open or institutional church movement represented another turn-of-the-century effort to regain ground the church had lost in the city, particularly among the working poor (H **624n78**). An open or institutional church featured, in addition to the sanctuary, an array of other rooms or an additional building that, during the week, opened the church to the community and provided for training programs, childcare, and other social services. Facilities permitted lectures, concerts, debates, clubs, and various social gatherings. In addition to flexible space, some institutional churches featured gymnasiums, swimming pools, and other recreational rooms. The church program as a whole was subdivided into special departments managed by committees. The movement consolidated in 1894 with the establishment of the Open and Institutional Church League to coordinate various programs and to pursue interdenominational cooperation (H **624nn77–79**). One of the first Methodist institutional churches, at Central MEC, New York City, reoriented that once well-to-do congregation to its changing neighborhood. Beginning in 1895, pastor S. Parkes Cadman developed a program featuring five choirs and an orchestra, kindergarten, youth club, gymnasium, game room, reading room, loan fund, employment service, soup kitchen, food and clothing dispensary, cooking and sewing classes, deaconess home, and a medical clinic (H **624–25nn80–82**). Such Methodist institutional churches—Cincinnati's Wesley Chapel, Chicago's Halstead Street Mission, Boston's Morgan Memorial Church—modeled congregation-level urban strategy and the latter birthed Goodwill Industries. The movement was promoted by the denomination's National City Evangelization Union, headed by North. From 1889 to 1916 the Union published its own newsletter, *Aggressive Methodism*, later called *The Christian City*, to promote expanded city missions and institutional churches.

MFSS AND THE SOCIAL CREED

In 1907 and anticipating the 1908 General Conference, five Methodists merged their concerns about social justice: Frank Mason North, Herbert

Welch (president of Ohio Wesleyan and later bishop), Worth Tippy (pastor of Cleveland's Epworth Memorial), Elbert Zaring (*Western Christian Advocate* editor), and Harry F. Ward (pastor of Chicago's Union Avenue). They issued calls-to-conference to prominent clergy working in the fields of church extension, religious journalism, education, and parish ministry and to interested lay leaders, social workers, businesspeople, and public officials. The conference, slated for Washington, D.C., December 3, 1907, to form "a society to stimulate wide study of social questions by the church, side by side with practical social service, and to bring the church into touch with neglected social groups." The five had in mind something like England's Wesleyan Methodist Union for Social Service whose design and activities Tippy had examined in a scouting trip earlier that year (H **321–23**). The MEC organization would "apply the sane and fervent spirit of Methodism to the social needs of the time" (H **632nn165–66**). That meeting, attended by twenty-five lay and clergy leaders—including the five conspirers—established the Methodist Federation for Social Service (MFSS). It purposed, as its mission statement declared, "to deepen within the church the sense of social obligation, to study social problems from a Christian point of view, and to promote social service in the Spirit of Christ." Welch was elected convener. Later that week the band of Methodist reformers breakfasted with progressive president Theodore Roosevelt in the White House.

Moving quickly into action, the fledgling organization drafted the first Social Creed for presentation to the 1908 MEC General Conference. Ward, the creed's principal author, replaced a lengthy and ponderous subcommittee draft with a concise, hard-hitting eleven-point statement of what Methodists stood for, drafting perhaps the preeminent summation of the social gospel. The 1908 MEC General Conference, addressed by President Theodore Roosevelt (S **1908**), recognized the MFSS as the denomination's "executive agency to rally the forces of the church in support of social reform," and adopted the creed (text H **324–25**).

During the fall of 1908, North labored over a second version of the creed, adding four affirmations concerning rights to a job, unemployment compensation, aid to dependent children, and old age disability insurance. North presented the "creed" to the Federal Council of Churches (FCC), representing most of America's Protestant churches, meeting in the fall of 1908. The FCC endorsed it wholeheartedly. The expanded statement known as "The Social Creed of the Churches" was gradually taken up by one denomination after another. Within the Methodist family, the Social Creed in either Methodist or ecumenical form was adopted by the UBC in 1912, by The MECS in 1914, and by The MPC in 1916; the EC lagged until 1934. Despite efforts to develop a common text, the social creeds of the several churches were continually modified. In 1932 North played a central role again in updating the text when the FCC creed adopted an extensive revision called "Social Ideals."

The 1936 MEC General Conference removed the Social Creed from the *Discipline,* replacing it with a statement on "the Spiritual Life of the Church." However, when the three branches of Methodism united in 1939, the Uniting Conference harmonized the separate social statements and restored the consensus creed. In addition, General Conference added several new concerns, including respect for conscientious objection to war and the recommendation that the Social Creed be presented to each congregation at least once a year (H **632nn170–71**).

RETHINKING MISSIONS

By the 1930s, American Protestants had begun to question what had been most probably their highest commitment, their most heroic enterprise, their energizing cause: missions. Diverse factors drove these misgivings, including impulses and movements covered in this chapter and the next. The maturing of "mission" churches and leadership and the building of institutions and infrastructure produced aspirations for self-government, and with it the presumption that not everything good had to come from White Europeans and Americans. Nationalist and anticolonial sentiments further linked political domination, economic exploitation, and Christian missions. At home, the social gospel and other strains of liberalism, to which we turn below, in identifying systemic problems in American society, laid groundwork for a significant and pervasive critique of Western civilization and culture. The mutual recriminations of fundamentalists and modernists added to the rhetoric of denunciation. Further criticism of an acculturated Christianity, of missions and evangelism as an Anglo-Saxon–civilizing enterprise, and of Protestantism wedded to Western culture increased in the wake of World War I in various forms of Western self-assessment, particularly the theological movement known as neoorthodoxy. The ecumenical movement, though developing out of the missionary movement, as it brought together persons from across the globe, gradually came to question the competitive confessionalism that packaged and sold the gospel in one brand or another of denominationalized Western culture. Women's groups read study books that challenged the notion that individuals and societies had to accept Western dress, names, worship practices, and architecture to be saved.

The event that gave traction to critique of missions from one angle or another was the publication in 1932 of a report of the interdenominational Laymen's Foreign Missionary Inquiry, *Re-thinking Missions*. The laymen's report held that good missionary work was accomplished by living with people and setting an example of the Christian ethic, not by revival meetings and other manipulative techniques (H **623nn58–60**). Drew President Arlo Ayres Brown participated in preparing the report, served on the Appraisal Committee, and helped publicize its findings, including through The MEC *Christian Advocate* (S **1932b**). The report's conclusions, widely unpopular, prompted debate in church conferences and papers and exposed internal struggles in the mission boards and in the fields.

A similar rethinking went on with regard to home missions. Indigenous tribes were finally granted US citizenship in 1924. A mood of cultural pluralism and realization that Indigenous nations possessed valuable cultures led nation and churches to rethink their Indigenous American policies. In 1934 President Roosevelt's new commissioner of Indian Affairs, John Collier, proposed a "New Deal" for America's Indigenous people. The Allotment Act of 1887 was repealed. The Indian Reorganization Act (IRA) dropped an assimilationist mode, recognized tribes as "sovereign" nations, reintroduced tribal government, and permitted Indigenous cultural and religious practices. Collier forced Methodists to decide what they believed to be essential to religious belief and practice and what could be adjusted in good conscience. That same year MEC mission executive Mark Dawber followed Collier's lead and proposed a controversial new mission policy of inculturation and affirmation of "Indian" life and culture, a new direction that many veteran missionaries thought wrongheaded and dangerous (S **1934a**).

METHODISM CONFLICTED: 1884–1939

Methodist leadership tended to move in a progressive direction. However, the church's prophets were few, and Methodists could be found across the full spectrum from radicalism on the one end to archconservatism (including membership in the Ku Klux Klan) on the other. Much of Methodism, however, was centrist on theological, social, and political measures and remained so for the duration of the twentieth century. Solidly in the Protestant mainstream, even prototypically Protestant, Methodists experienced the quandaries and felt the tensions with which Protestants generally and American society struggled—war and peace, labor, industry, women's rights, theological shifts, biblical interpretation, and race.

LAITY RIGHTS FOR WOMEN

After running Civil War–humanitarian enterprises and subsequently building missionary societies, the WCTU, and the Ladies' and Pastors' Christian Union (and counterparts) into significant local and national organizations, women saw no reason why such proven abilities and talent should not be recognized and applied in denominational affairs as a whole. Jennie Fowler Willing made such a case in 1870, linking women's ecclesial rights with those of their recently freed Black sisters and brothers, referencing women's churchly accomplishments, and appealing to their responsible voting participation in the denomination's 1869 referendum on lay delegation (S **1870a**; H **277**). One strategy for inclusion and participation, pursued by women in the 1870s, was to lobby for gender-neutral language in the *Discipline*. Inclusive construal of words like *layman* and *laymen* would make women eligible for all lay offices in the church—stewards, Sunday school superintendents, trustees, and quarterly conference members. Such legislation failed in the 1872 and 1876 General Conferences. In another strategy, by attending seminary and offering themselves for ordination, women tested male-limited ministry and conference membership. Another dramatic test occurred in 1880 over the question about whether a woman might be invited to *address* a General Conference—and not just any woman but the denomination's most prominent, WCTU president Frances Willard. The proposal, opposed by James Buckley, editor of the *Christian Advocate*, touched off a noisy debate that lasted two hours. Even defeated, the implacable Buckley announced that he would exhaust all parliamentary resources to prevent a woman's speaking before the conference. Buckley's statement and the inhospitable atmosphere led Willard to withdraw (H **619n6**).

The 1880 MEC General Conference did rule that women who held local church offices could be members of a quarterly conference (the governing body of the local church) and entitled to vote for delegates from a local church to the lay electoral conference. The latter in turn chose delegates to General Conference, which meant that women might be elected as lay delegates to General Conference. Would General Conference seat them? In 1888, five midwestern conferences elected women as lay delegates to General Conference (pictures S **p32**). Seventeen women were elected as reserve delegates, most of them leaders in the women's missionary societies or the WCTU. Frances Willard represented the Rock River Annual Conference and was overjoyed by the changed atmosphere that had yielded the elections.

For months before the 1888 General Conference convened at the New York City Metropolitan Opera House, Methodists debated women's laity rights and attempted to influence General Conference delegates, a controversy significant enough to be covered by the secular press. In their Episcopal Address the bishops declared that the five women could not be seated because their eligibility as delegates had not been properly determined according to The MEC constitution. With women crowding the balconies, delegates debated for almost a week over a word. Were women *laymen*? No, the majority ruled, *laymen* in church law did not include women. The clergy voted 154 to 122, the laity, more narrowly, 78 to 76 (S **1888**; H **277–83**; **619nn7–9**).

After ruling the women ineligible to be seated under the constitution, General Conference in a close vote referred the matter to the annual conferences by proposing a change to the Restrictive Rule applying to lay delegation— "and the said delegates may be men or women" (H **620n11**). In conference balloting, both laity and clergy voted in favor, but the latter not with the three-quarters required. In response in 1892, the Judiciary Committee ruled, unanimously, that women were ineligible, but on an amendment another construction of the Restrictive Rule was proposed— "and said delegates must be male members." The strategy—for this fail in the annual conference votes, thus entailing the opposite reading of *laymen*—failed, some conferences simply not balloting the question, not an outcome that gave conclusive force to the alternative reading (H **619–20nn10–11**).

Over several years Buckley continued the campaign in the *Christian Advocate* against women's lay rights (S **1890**). Other Methodist churches were not burdened with Buckley or deterred by the controversy in The MEC. The MPC and UBC led the way, granting women full laity rights in 1892 and 1893, respectively. The Methodist Protestants not only seated three laywomen delegates in 1892 but also elected Eugenia St. John as a *clergy* delegate to General Conference (H **281–82**). In 1893, the General Conference of the UBC included lay delegates for the first time. Its previous General Conference (1889) had approved the licensing and ordination of women. Clearly aware of the significance of their actions, the UBC bishops in their quadrennial address to the General Conference celebrated the several accomplishments, greeting the "sisters, who represent the loving company at the early dawn of the resurrection morning" (H **620nn14–15**). In 1896 at both The MEC and The MPC General Conferences, women appeared as elected delegates. The Methodist Protestants seated those sent. In The MEC, the debate that ensued over the four women's right to be seated was so intense and prolonged that by the time a compromise was reached, the four women had left in disgust. In 1900, The MEC finally extended women equal laity rights in adopting a new constitution. MEC women lay delegates took their seats at the 1904 General Conference in Los Angeles, twenty-four seated, thirty standing by as lay reserves.

The MECS lagged, as did the EA. Not until 1922 did Methodist women in the South gain conference rights. That year eighteen women were seated. Belle Harris Bennett led here as on other progressive causes—heading the southern church's women's home missionary organization, establishing the

Scarritt Bible and Training School, opening settlement houses to care for urban poor people, and persuading the church to recognize deaconesses. When The MECS unified its missionary endeavor and subjected the women's foreign and home missionary efforts to denominational control, Bennett acquiesced in the takeover and agreed to head the Woman's Missionary Council within the male-dominated missionary board (H **620n17**). On Bennett's recommendation and among the last acts of the soon-to-be-merged-out-of-independence, the WHMS petitioned the 1910 General Conference for full laity rights for women. Some 148 memorials, 637 petitions, and hundreds of telegrams also made the case. Bennett was invited to address the General Conference on behalf of the WHMS memorial, a first (S **1910**). Despite her eloquence, the memorial lost 188 to 74.

An even better-organized campaign and less radical appeal failed also at the 1914 General Conference, the bishops in opposition. The 1918 General Conference, half of its delegates there for the first time, had a lot on its mind—world war, possible unification with the northern church, race relations, temperance, adoption of the Social Creed, even modifying the Apostles' Creed (H **620n18**). General Conference passed legislation granting women lay rights, the bishops declaring the change a constitutional issue. To the annual conferences, the matter therefore went. All but four concurred, and women were elected and seated in 1922. Bennett, though elected, was too ill to attend and died of cancer that summer. The Evangelical Church never granted women conference rights, and former Evangelical women gained that prerogative only with the 1946 merger with the UBC.

CONFLICTS OVER HOLINESS

In the first number (in 1894) of his monthly paper, the *Peniel Herald*, Phineas Bresee announced a reoriented holiness ministry to the poor of Los Angeles out of newly constructed Peniel Hall. Bresee had served pastorates in Iowa, been presiding elder there and an Iowa delegate to General Conference (1872), before moving to Southern California. He served several large Methodist churches in the LA area, as vice chair and then chair of the board of the University of Southern California, and for a year as presiding elder of the LA district. He led the Southern California Conference delegation to the 1892 General Conference. That fall, Bishop John Vincent, presiding over conference and no friend of effusive, contentious revivalism, removed him from the district. And the presiding bishop in 1894, John Fitzgerald, refused Bresee's request for appointment to the independent Peniel city mission. Determined to pursue that course, Bresee located and within a year had generated out of the mission what was first a congregation and later a denomination, the Church of the Nazarene (H **632n6**). So Bresee joined the host of come-outers, creating a new home for hordes of such, many of them former Methodists. Others sympathetic to Bresee's cause sought to hunker down and to remain within. One such was Kentucky evangelist Henry Clay Morrison, founding and longtime editor of the *Pentecostal Herald,* who was tried but acquitted by the Kentucky Conference for "contumacious conduct" (disobedience). Later president of Asbury College and founder of Asbury Seminary, Morrison was sent five times to General Conference. Under Morrison, Asbury—College and Seminary—would become the nerve center for Methodism's holiness and conservative causes. There critique of Methodist authorities would prosper. There the question of staying in or coming out would remain live. There mainline Methodism would carry on conversations with its Wesleyan offspring.

Episcopal Methodism had experienced holiness-motivated criticism and holiness departures before. Both the Wesleyans and the Free Methodists, as we have seen, listed holiness concerns in their briefs against The MEC and, by the late nineteenth century, brought holiness critiques to the fore in their competition with The MEC. Notwithstanding the schismatic appropriation of the holiness banner, much of the intellectual and episcopal leadership of northern Methodism had emphasized and promoted the doctrine, featured it in new systematic theologies (H **633n8**), and either frequented, supported, or celebrated (or all of these) its mainspring, Palmer's enterprise—Tuesday Meetings, publications, speaking tours, and correspondence. The institutionalization of holiness (post–Civil War) in the National Camp Meeting movement initially had enjoyed episcopal blessing. By the end of the nineteenth century, however, several developments loosened Methodism's hold on holiness teaching, put distance between holiness advocates and the regular ministry, and provided alternative promotion, assembly, communication, and support systems for freelance itinerating holiness revivalists.

Non-Methodist versions of holiness increasingly emerged: notably the Oberlin perfectionism of Asa Mahan and Charles Grandison Finney; "higher Christian life" views enunciated by Presbyterian William Boardman and

Congregationalist Thomas Upham; and Keswick versions of Quaker Hannah Whitall Smith and Anglican H. W. Webb-Peploe. Composite holiness views—popularized on transatlantic speaking and preaching tours, at Bible and prophecy conventions, in new publications, and especially by Dwight L. Moody's Northfield conferences, urban revivals, and Moody Bible Institute—mixed holiness doctrines with faith healing and premillennial teachings. Such interplay, increasingly buttressed by biblicist Princeton "Calvinism" and Baconian epistemology, shaped Holiness movements Pentecostalism and Fundamentalism (H **633n9**).

The National Camp Meeting Association for the Promotion of Holiness, which began regular meetings in the 1870s with the support and encouragement of northern Methodism, stimulated the creation of more independent state and regional associations. These developed throughout rural and small-town America, especially in the South, Southwest, and Midwest. These quasi-ecclesial entities generated vocations for full-time evangelism, sometimes recognized and authorized by Methodist conferences and presiding elders, often functioning without such permission and without formal ordination. By the late 1880s, some two hundred such self-directed full-time preachers itinerated through camp meeting and other settings not subject to the authority of bishop, presiding elder, and preacher in charge. By the 1890s, the number swelled to three hundred. Increasingly, the holiness champions shrank the Christian faith and the Wesleyan message to one note and made holiness—as sanctification, as instantaneous, as a second and separate work of grace, as a second blessing—not just the main thing but the only thing. Insisting that the second blessing was the only measure of true Christian faith, they denounced more conventional, staid station-and-circuit religious practices and leadership. They zeroed in on Methodism's middle-class character, educational investments, upscale buildings, and social activities. By the 1880s some leaders, for instance, John P. Brooks, active in the Western and then the Illinois Holiness Association and editor of the *Banner of Holiness*, bid Methodists to come out of the compromised denomination as an act of faith.

The southern bishops in their address to the 1894 General Conference, while reaffirming Methodist teaching of "entire sanctification or perfect love," warned of "a party with holiness as a watchword," who had "holiness associations, holiness meetings, holiness preachers, holiness evangelists, and holiness property" and who collapsed religious experience into "only two steps, the first step out of condemnation into peace, and the next step into Christian perfection." They deplored both message and tactic, complaining especially of intrusion of freelancing holiness evangelists into circuits and stations without invitation or permission of the preacher in charge (H **633n11**).

By the 1890s, both push and pull factors produced widespread defections and created new holiness entities large and small (H **332**). Northern and southern Methodism, the United Brethren, and The Evangelical Association all lost heavily, but were not the only denominations so abandoned. In the twentieth century, the holiness denominations faced their own defections into Pentecostalism and settled after World War II into an uneasy membership in the Calvinist-dominated National Association of Evangelicals. By the 1900s, the holiness family included, in addition to the Nazarenes, the Salvation Army, the Christian and Missionary Alliance, the Church of God (Anderson), the Holiness Methodist Church, and the Pilgrim Holiness Church. In such consolidation and institutionalization endeavors, the holiness denominations tended to dampen their more radical testimony, to reduce the wingspan they had allowed women, to experience their membership's own entry into the middle class, and therefore to modulate the more radical social witness with which they began.

A METHODIST SOCIAL GOSPEL

The MEC faced a test of its commitment to the Social Creed even as it was being adopted, namely at the 1908 General Conference. The International Typographical Union (ITU) had sought an eight-hour day for its members in all future contracts. The Book Concern allied itself with an opposition movement and fired every union member at each of its several printing plants across the country. The ITU appealed to Methodist clergy on behalf of employees (S **1906**). Months later the Book Concern gave in and implemented an eight-hour workday but refused to recognize the union or rehire striking union members. Supportive clergy and union members sought signatures for printed petitions favoring unions to be sent to the 1908 General Conference. Despite its affirming the "fundamental purposes of the labor movement" to be "essentially ethical" and therefore rightfully commanding the church's support, General Conference did not order the publishing house to rehire striking workers and honor the union (H **633n3**). The MFSS began what would be a quarter-century effort to mediate the dispute. Not until November 1931, just prior to the 1932 General Conference, did the publishing house executive staff finally recognize the ITU. The Publishing House of The MECS continued to be a nonunion shop through merger with the northern church in 1939 (H **633n4**).

The MFSS declared its agenda later in 1908 at the first national conference of Methodist social workers in St. Louis: "The Socialized Church." Frank Mason North spoke on that theme, the MFSS published the several addresses and proceedings under that title (H **633n14**) and called the church to address root causes and pathologies of distress, such as lawlessness, disease, unemployment, poor housing, child labor, in short, any evil that attacks the life, health, and character of the community (H **333; 633nn15–16**).

With such analytical exhortations, the MFSS continued to engage the church on the nation's "social crisis." It published proceedings from successive national conferences (1908, 1922, 1926), as well as full-length studies of specific problems (e.g., *The Abingdon War-food Book*, with a foreword by Herbert Hoover, and John Wesley's 1773 classic "Thoughts on the Present Scarcity of Provisions"). In 1911 the MFSS launched an even more important means of communication, the long-running *Social Service Bulletin* (renamed *Social Questions Bulletin* in 1933). First edited by Harry Ward, the bulletin provided timely analysis of political and social matters, kept church leaders aware of churchly and secular issues, brought members directly in touch with the MFSS leaders, and encouraged affiliates to propagate its social service ideas and undertake local initiatives. Similar extension of the MFSS witness came as other members of the Methodist family of churches established "social justice" caucuses, boards, agencies, or commissions—The MPC in 1916, The MECS in 1926, the EC in 1930, and the UBC in 1933. The social gospel found a curricular and institutional home as the several denominations' theological schools introduced a new field, "Christian sociology." Drew did so in 1909, hiring European-trained Edwin Earp.

In 1911 Harry Ward began the first of thirty-four years as unpaid MFSS executive, an office he held while teaching Christian ethics first at Boston University School of Theology (1913–17) and then at Union Theological Seminary in New York (1918–41). Early involved with the working poor as director of a Chicago settlement house and friends with pioneer social workers Jane Addams and Mary McDowell, Ward pled labor's cause and built labor and religious coalitions that transcended race, class, party, and faith in pursuit of social equality (S **1919a**). In 1912, Ward acquired a colleague who would serve a comparably long term (thirty-two years), Francis J. Mc-Connell, elected president by the MFSS and elected bishop by The MEC the same year. McConnell gained firsthand experience with social problems and gave MFSS high connectional and national advocacy when the nation's steelworkers went on strike in 1919 deploring conditions in the mills and seeking an eight-hour day and a livable wage. McConnell, then bishop in the Pittsburgh area, became the leader and spokesperson for an ecumenical commission investigating the crisis. Their report mobilized public sympathy for the workers and against the prevailing sixty-eight-hour workweek in steel, but also made McConnell and the MFSS targets for criticism. In his 1922 book, *Christian Citizenship,* designed as a course of study for young people, McConnell insisted that the "Christian ideal" for the state was "the welfare of the people" (H **334–35**).

Colleagues with Ward and McConnell in building national coordinated social gospel programs were a number of Methodist deaconesses (H **633n19**), two of whom, Grace Scribner and Winifred Chappell, served as co-executives of MFSS and coeditors of the *Social Questions Bulletin.* Beginning in 1911, they functioned as MFSS's primary writers, with Chappell as *Bulletin* editor from 1922 to 1947. Chappell, always the friend of the poor and exploited, supported women's suffrage, labor unions, working men, and especially working women (see defense of striking mill-women of Passaic, New Jersey, S **1926**). Ward, McConnell, Scribner, and Chappell drove and directed the MFSS. Social gadflies of Methodism, they convened national conferences on Christianity and the economic order in 1922 and 1926 that portrayed the demonic side of capitalism.

DRYING UP AMERICA

The intervention in the political sphere that McConnell and company advocated had been earlier and forcefully advanced by Frances Willard and her WCTU colleagues. Willard traced pathologies in the civic, economic, transportation, and familial realms to a single source, demon rum. And though industrial concerns recurred through the Social Creed, the church put its most public focus in the early twentieth century not on the economy or the plight of workers, but on the evils of alcohol. Long demanded in congregations and Sunday schools, temperance united progressives and conservatives, southerners and northerners, women and men, and did so across the family of Methodist denominations. Temperance Sunday with its pledge card became an annual event. Since the 1880s, grape juice had been ordered for Communion services. Temperance literature of all kinds was penned, published, and promoted.

By the turn of the century, the WCTU had an ally in the temperance crusade and in moving the church beyond temperance conversions and pledges, namely, the Anti-Saloon League (established in 1895). The MEC General Conferences of 1904 and 1908 summoned the church to moral reform and the temperance cause through the agency of the state. The UBC established a Temperance Commission in 1905, adopted the Social Creed in 1909, and threw its energies behind the social reform of prohibition. By 1912, The MEC had established its own lobby and placed it in Washington, D.C. The Board of Temperance, Prohibition and Public Morals (now General Board of Church and Society) geared a vigorous prohibition campaign (S **1916**; H **336–38**). In the South and increasingly across the nation, the champion of prohibition was James Cannon Jr. (H **633n23**; **337**) Editor of the *Richmond and Baltimore Christian Advocate* from 1904 until election to the episcopacy in 1918, Cannon played a decisive role in Virginia's anti-saloon legislation of 1916. By that year, twenty-three states had gone dry, and Cannon and Anti-Saloon colleagues from across the country turned their attention to the national campaign. Cannon's nationwide speaking in and the successful conclusion of the prohibition campaign earned him the episcopacy. And he would continue to fight the cause on that platform, including advocacy abroad and opposition to wets at home, most notably that of presidential candidate Alfred E. Smith.

After passage of the Eighteenth Amendment and of the National Prohibition Enforcement Act (Volstead Act), The MEC Board led by Clarence True Wilson turned to education and enforcement. During the period between the enactment of Prohibition in 1920 and its repeal in 1933, Methodism's dominant social interest was to defend Prohibition. The Depression, which followed the failed experiment with Prohibition, put joblessness and poverty, instead of temperance, on the church's social agenda. Other ideals, like peace and unification, claimed Methodist attention as well. Methodists would then gear up for another world war without perhaps ever coming fully to terms with this last great episode of Christendom. In consequence, some later Methodists would continue to yearn and campaign for a Christian America, having not lived through or adequately analyzed Prohibition's problematic premises.

RED SCARE

During World War I, the MFSS vigorously defended the rights of conscientious objectors and political dissenters. After the war, its continued commitment to civil liberties, opposition to political oppression, and defense of labor took the MFSS increasingly into combat with the power structures of American society and earned it the enmity of the country's elites. Bishop Francis J. McConnell's investigation of the 1919 steelworkers strike brought complaint as did Ward's cautious support of the Russian Revolution in the *Social Service Bulletin* in the same year. The FBI began keeping files on Ward, and a New York State investigating committee accused him of "teaching Bolshevism." MFSS colleague Grace Scribner's weekly column on the social application of the gospel was dropped from the Methodist *Sunday School Journal*. In 1920, Ward joined other activists in founding the American Civil Liberties Union (ACLU), whose board he chaired into the 1950s. In 1929, Ward made a fact-finding trip to Russia. Thereafter "Red-baiting," reactionary attacks on the MFSS, increased, coming from various quarters, especially the Hearst press. In the 1930s, the House of Representatives' Dies Committee (forerunner of the House Un-American Activities Committee) summoned Ward to appear (H **634nn26–27**). After the stock market crash of 1929 and during the Depression, the MFSS's masthead proclaimed its commitment "to abolish the profit system in order to develop a classless society based upon the obligation of mutual service." The 1932 MEC General Conference concurred, declaring "the present industrial order is unchristian, unethical and anti-social because it is largely based on the profit motive, which is a direct appeal to selfishness," a victory for the MFSS (H **634nn28–29**). To instruct the church on moving America to a socialist order, the MFSS issued eighteen "Crisis Leaflets" over the next quadrennium. And in 1934, *Social Questions Bulletin* editor Chappell reported on her participation in organizing West Virginia miners.

To counter such prophetic actions, a Conference of Methodist Laymen gathered in Chicago in early 1935 to organize for a showdown at the 1936 General Conference. In February, the Methodist Laymen issued a pamphlet titled *Which Way America?* Not the New Deal and social security but laissez-faire capitalism! The church? Stick to regeneration of individual hearts. At the 1936 General Conference progressive causes of unification and peace loomed large, but conservatives had their day on the MFSS. General Conference reminded the church that the MFSS was not an official agency. And, as mentioned, it removed the Social Creed from the *Discipline,* replacing it with a statement on "the Spiritual life of the Church" (H **634nn30–31**).

LIBERALISM AND FUNDAMENTALISM

American Methodists were slow to embrace liberal theology and the social gospel institutionally and formally. However, to allege that Methodists ignored America's social problems, lacked machinery for dealing with them, and wanted for theory with which to energize intervention and reform is neither accurate nor fair. Indeed, as we have seen, through urban chapters of denominational and women's missionary societies, Methodists well before the Civil War had shown concern for workers, children, older persons, immigrants, temperance, and political reform. Further, in the aftermath of the Civil War, northern Methodism had addressed the educational, infrastructural, and religious needs of the "freedmen." The church's idealism also informed new missionary ventures at home and abroad. And in missions theory, but especially in temperance rhetoric, Methodism had its own sociological theory and version of a social gospel.

By the turn of the twentieth century, northern Methodism gained an intellectual resource, which for a half century would reinforce its social Christianity. Known as personal idealism, personalism, or transcendental empiricism, this philosophy had a major influence on Methodism nationally through the teaching of Boston University's Borden Parker Bowne and three generations of his successors: first, Albert C. Knudson, Edgar S. Brightman, Francis J. McConnell, and George Albert Coe; second, Walter G. Muelder, Georgia Harkness, L. Harold DeWolf, Paul Deats, S. Paul Schilling, and Peter Bertocci; and third, numerous others including Martin Luther King Jr. Bowne, trained at Halle, Göttingen, and Paris, occupied a Boston University (BU) chair in philosophy for thirty-five years, for twenty-two also dean of the graduate school. Bowne wove strands of idealism, neo-Kantianism, biblical criticism, romanticism, and rationalism together with those from his heritage (Methodism's moralism, high valuation of freedom, insistence on individual responsibility, optimism of grace, hope for perfection) into a distinctive modernist Methodist metaphysic. This tradition places at the center of theology the sacred personality of each human being in relation to the loving Personality of God. So accenting God's working through human history, the theology opened the door for countless leaders to understand their own vocation in terms of the social betterment of human life. A significant contribution to American philosophy, the personalist tradition, though focused at BU, influenced northern Methodist theology and theological education generally, especially through required reading assignments in the Course of Study (H **623nn61, 62, 65–66**).

This mainstreaming of liberalism elicited conservative consternation. Critics viewed Bowne's teaching and many books as "contrary to our present existing and established standards of doctrine." Both Bowne and his colleague in Old Testament, Hinckley G. Mitchell, were subjected to heresy charges. Complaints against Mitchell alleged that he did not believe in the Trinity, the divinity of Christ, or the Atonement. Similar fundamental charges against Bowne resulted in his trial in the New York East Conference (S **1904**). Bowne was further charged with aberrant teachings on sin, salvation, repentance, justification, regeneration, and assurance. Both men were acquitted eventually, *Advocate* editor Buckley assisting in the defense of Bowne. The decisions marked a watershed, the vindication of progressive theology that opened the way to Methodist appropriation of social gospel thought and practice (H **299–302; 623nn67–68**).

A further attack on Methodist modernism, echoing the larger fundamentalist movement, featured an intra-Drew central act. New Jersey pastor Harold Paul Sloan attacked his Drew student colleague and by then professor, Edwin Lewis, for the latter's 1922 *Methodist Review* article "The Problem of the Person of Christ." Aiding and abetting Sloan was Lewis's older Drew colleague and fellow theologian, John Faulkner. Sloan encouraged the Philadelphia Methodist Episcopal Preachers' Meeting to protest the publication of such a heretical article in a Methodist serial. It implored the Drew administration to ensure that "the objectionable teaching . . . not be repeated in the classroom as . . . instruction given to our theological students" and conveyed its denunciation to the Methodist people in the *Christian Advocate* (New York). Sloan added to the indictment when Lewis's *Jesus Christ and the Human Quest* appeared in 1924. Lewis, he asserted, denies "the incarnation in any real sense," "reduces Jesus to an extraordinary human being," and rejects his "personal pre-existence" (H **634nn32–34**).

By that point, Sloan had launched a paper, *The Call to the Colors,* later renamed *The Essentialist,* to broaden the critique and fight liberal corruption across northern Methodist theological education. Through this publication, independent preachers' meetings, petitions to General Conference, and appeals to the bishops, Sloan led a campaign, begun particularly for the 1920 conference and continued through the 1920s, to purge both seminaries and the required Course of Study of liberalism. To coordinate the efforts, Sloan helped found the Methodist League for Faith and Life in 1925. Liberals generally and personalists particularly came in for rebuke, but Harris Franklin Rall, of Garrett, and Lewis became favorite targets. In 1927, the league formally called on the bishops to rectify the situation at Drew, terming Lewis's teaching in "defiance of the law and order of the Church" and as "contravening both the second and twentieth of our Articles." Sloan took a petition, with some ten thousand signatures from churches in forty-one states, to the 1928 General Conference that charged "flagrant disloyalty to Methodist doctrinal standards in seminaries, pulpits and Sunday-school literature." The MEC bishops responded tersely to the charges and opened the 1928 General Conference opposing heresy hunting. Sloan embraced Lewis when the latter turned to neo-orthodoxy, offered a critique of liberalism, called Protestants to "re-enthrone Christ, the divine Christ" (S **1933**), and produced a *Christian Manifesto* (in 1934). The 1936 MEC General Conference, a conservative affair on several measures as we have seen, Sloan's fifth, elected him editor of the *Christian Advocate* (New York). His quadrennium of editing Methodism's mouthpiece represented a temporary setback for modernism, but perhaps even more a mellowing and mainstreaming of the church's champions of orthodoxy (H **634nn35–39**).

In southern Methodism, antimodernism took more diffuse forms. It had its own antimodernist paper, the independent *Southern Methodist,* founded in 1921. Southern conferences established affiliate branches of Sloan's League for Faith and Life and Bishops Collins Denny and Horace M. DuBose became members. In the twelve-pamphlet *Aftermath Series* (1923–24), southern Methodism had its counterpart to *The Fundamentals,* attacking higher criticism and suspect faculty and missionaries and defending blood atonement, the Resurrection, Pentateuchal dating, and ascribed biblical authorship. For straying from such standards, SMU's John A. Rice was forced to resign because of his 1920 book, *The Old Testament in the Life of Today.* Such antimodernist actions and such fundamentalist beliefs, however, Bishop Edwin Mouzon called un-Methodist and Calvinist. Claiming their term for his title, Mouzon in his 1923 *Fundamentals of Methodism,* insisted that grace and grace-produced Christian ethic, not dogma, lay at the heart of Methodism.

The modest dimensions of southern Methodist fundamentalism had less to do with episcopal scholarship than with other media or movements that channeled but also diffused its rather considerable antimodernist convictions. The exodus of holiness folk took out of southern Methodism leaders, members, and whole congregations who, had they remained, would have added to the theological chatter. Foreign missions, as well, recruited and deployed many of an evangelical and conservative bent. Three other causes functioned on antimodernist platforms and did so more effectively in the South than theological fundamentalism—temperance, unification, and the Klan. Temperance appealed to progressive aspirations but also fears of immigrants, cities, Catholics, Germans, and German theology. Especially during and in the wake of World War I, conservatives noted that from the enemy came beer and the various theological and biblical heresies. Similarly, since modernist views had found a home in the northern church, southern conservatives mounted a vigorous antimodernist-themed campaign against unification. Led by a League for the Preservation of Southern Methodism, by several of the *Advocates,* and by a number of bishops, most prominently Collins Denny and William Ainsworth, the campaign against unification appealed to regionalism, racism, and fears of modernism. So also did the Ku Klux Klan, revived in 1915 by ex-Methodist preacher William J. Simmons. The Klan, argued W. J. Cash, "summed up within itself, with precise completeness and exactness, the whole body of the fears and hates of the time. . . . It was . . . at once anti-Negro, anti-Alien, anti-Red, anti-Catholic, anti-Jew, anti-Darwin, anti-Modern, anti-Liberal, Fundamentalist, vastly Moral, militantly Protestant." It understood itself to be a religious organization and attracted individuals whose religiosity needed a host of negative referents, including small-town and rural Methodist laity and preachers (H **341–43**; **634nn41–42**; S **1922**). The Klan, it should be noted, prospered in the North as well as the South and there also drew in Methodist laity and ministry.

MECS WOMEN AND RACIAL REFORM

By the 1920s MECS women through the Woman's Missionary Council (WMC) had initiated several forms of outreach to the Black community. It collaborated with women of the CME in supporting a women's program (since 1906) at Paine College in Augusta, Georgia, an institution launched cooperatively in 1883. In 1912, it began establishing Bethlehem Centers, social settlements, the first adjacent to Paine College (H **634n43**). The witness of these Bethlehem Centers helped shape an effort by southern Methodists to seek better relations between the races and to counter the spate of lynchings, race riots, and Klan activity that followed World War I.

At its 1920 meeting in Kansas City, the WMC established a Commission on Race Relations with special concern for the needs of Black women and children. The new commission sent its chair, Carrie Parks (Mrs. Luke) Johnson, veteran in women's home mission work and pastor's daughter and wife, to a meeting of the National Association of Colored Women in Tuskegee. After the meeting Johnson and colleague Sara Estelle Haskin met in the home of Margaret Murray Washington, widow of Booker T. Washington, with ten of the leading Black women in the South. The Black women spoke of their hopes and fears for their families and their race. Mrs. Lugenia Burns Hope, wife of the Morehouse College president, concluded this eventful gathering by saying, "Women, we can achieve nothing today unless you . . . who have met us are willing to help us find a place in American life where we can be unashamed and unafraid." The impact on the two White women was considerable; as Carrie Johnson put it, "My heart broke, and I have been trying [ever since] to pass the story on to the women of my race" (H **634n45**).

With the support of the Commission on Interracial Cooperation (CIC), the major southern interracial forum, and its head Will Alexander, Johnson organized a conference of about one hundred White women leaders from various groups in the South, which convened in the YWCA in Memphis, Tennessee, on October 6–7, 1920. Carrie Parks Johnson and Estelle Haskin relayed their experience at Tuskegee and the Black women's challenge. When four distinguished Black women—Margaret Washington, Elizabeth Ross Haynes, Jennie B. Moton, and Charlotte Hawkins Brown—entered the room and with no prompting, every White woman in the room rose to her feet. Spontaneously Belle Harris Bennett began to sing "Blest Be the Tie That Binds," and the women, Black and White, joined in, many of them crying openly. The Black women described experiences of discrimination and harassment, spoke of the oppressive myth of the promiscuous Black woman, and urged the White women to control their men. "So far as lynching is concerned," Brown insisted, "if the white women would take hold of the situation, lynching would be stopped" (H **635nn46–48**). One interpreter termed the meeting a "conversion experience" for the women present, and Brown later called it "the greatest step forward since emancipation." CIC head Alexander claimed that after the Memphis meeting, southern White women were the most effective force in changing southern racial patterns and the Federal Council of Churches "the strongest force yet organized in the nation in behalf of the colored race" (H **635n49**).

Bertha Newell succeeded Johnson in 1928 as superintendent of the WMC's Bureau of Social Service (later Bureau of Christian Social Relations). Newell pressed the affiliate woman's missionary societies "to engage in more local inter-action between white women and African American women." Summer Christian Leadership Schools for members of the woman's missionary societies of the CME became one forum for this increased interaction, with White and Black women living and studying together for a week. Local White women's societies heard reports afterward and women of both races frequently continued to work together on local projects. Through the 1930s, these summer leadership schools provided a crucial opportunity for Black and White Methodist women to expe-rience enhanced mutual understanding and help (H **635nn50–51**).

The most dramatic and heroic effort toward improved race relations, and one of the most important women's crusades in American history, was that led by Texas Methodist Jessie Daniel Ames. Founding the Association of Southern Women for the Prevention of Lynching (ASWPL) in 1930, Ames considered lynching a woman's issue and called on women to repudiate the claim that lynching protected southern womanhood. (Although most Black lynchings were in the southern states, forty-six of the fifty states reported such atroci-ties taking place through the 1930s.) By 1942 more than forty-three thou-sand southern women, many of them Methodists, had signed the anti-lynching pledge, "Lynching is an indefensible crime destructive of all principles of gov-ernment, hostile to every ideal of religion and humanity, debasing and degrad-ing to every person involved. We pledge ourselves to create a new public opin-ion in the South which will not condone for any reason whatever acts of mobs or lynchers" (H **635n52**). The women's network secured pledges from law en-forcement officers not to tolerate lynchings in their counties. They thwarted potential lynchings by immediate visits to officers demanding protection for the possible victims. When a lynching was reported, the women in that vicinity who had signed the pledge investigated the crime and filed a report.

When President Harry S Truman created the first President's Committee on Civil Rights in 1946, he appointed Atlanta Methodist Dorothy Rogers Tilly, another of the unheralded White civil rights trailblazers. As a Methodist she devoted her life to improving race relations, especially in countering the KKK. In 1949, Tilly helped found the Fellowship of the Concerned, a successor to the ASWPL. Its members' presence at the trials of Black defendants brought about significant changes in courtroom justice. As lynchings declined, the fellowship became, in the 1950s, an advocate for desegregation of schools and public facilities. For her active role in this organization, Dorothy Tilly was shunned by former church friends, harassed by the Klan, accused of being a Communist, and subjected to threatening phone calls, but never dissuaded from her conviction that the church must promote racial justice.

WOMEN'S ORDINATION: ANOTHER ROUND

Active in, indeed leading the church in, major reform initiatives, women relaunched efforts for ordination and full clergy rights. The effort paralleled, interacted with, and benefited from the advancing women's rights movement and the suffrage campaign and victory. Madeline Southard, who earned a master's degree from Garrett Biblical Institute in 1919, championed the ordination cause in a 1919 article "Woman and the Ministry" in the *Methodist Review* and later (1928) in her published thesis, "The Attitude of Jesus Toward Women" (in 1928). Southard's career included a teaching stint at Methodist-related Taylor University, as lay evangelist in the United States, and as missionary in the Philippines and India. She founded the International Association of Women Preachers (IAWP), serving as president of this ecumenical organization (1919–39) and editor of its newsletter, the *Woman's Pulpit*. Elected to the 1920 General Conference by the Southwest Kansas Conference, she pursued the campaign with a memorial (petition) and letter to "fellow" delegates seeking for women the authorization to preach and "that equality of opportunity in the church that is rapidly coming to her in other fields" (S **1920**; H **635n53**). Similar memorials, asking that women be licensed to preach, came from a number of annual conferences, district superintendents, and deans and presidents of colleges, universities, and seminaries (including Garrett, Drew, and Boston). Conferences sent forty-one women as lay delegates, five of whom were Black. The 1920 MEC General Conference restored to women the authorization for local preacher's licenses, taken away in 1880.

Before the 1924 General Conference, Dr. Georgia Harkness, then associate professor of religious education at Elmira College, made a powerful case for the ministry as a vocation for women (S **1924b**). The committee considering the matter embraced "ordination of women as local preachers," providing women sacramental authority in the often marginal, rural, and missional situations to which they had been appointed. It could not recommend full clergy rights, explaining that admitting women to annual conference would introduce the "peculiar and embarrassing difficulties" of having to guarantee "to every effective minister a church and to every self-supporting church a minister." The legislation, passed after heated debate, permitted women partial ministerial status. They could be ordained but not made members of the annual conference, nor be guaranteed appointment and minimum salary, nor enjoy pension benefits. By the spring of 1927, eighty-one women had been ordained local deacons, and sixteen after two years ordained as local elder (H **635n56**). Few women deacons experienced recommendation to elders' orders in such swift succession. Madeline Southard did not receive her elders' orders until 1932, and Georgia Harkness not until 1939. Full clergy rights for women in The MEC would be delayed until 1956.

Southard's International Association of Women Preachers, later renamed the International Association of Women Ministers (IAWM), would over time gain membership from twenty-four countries and from thirty-five Christian denominations, including Roman Catholics. Especially from the 1920s through the 1950s, IAWM's annual assemblies provided social support, affirmation, and sustenance that, before the emergence of women's ministerial groups within denominations, supported otherwise relatively isolated women ministers. In addition, since its launch in 1922, the *Woman's Pulpit* constituted, until the mid-1970s, the most comprehensive repository of information about the status of gender equality in religious denominations around the world. Throughout its existence, the IAWM lived its stated purpose—to develop the spirit of fellowship among women ministers and as Southard explained, "to encourage young women whom God has called to preach" (H **635n57**).

WORSHIP AND ARCHITECTURE

The MECS counseled its members on congregational worship by including the general services of the church—Holy Communion, baptism, marriage, and burial—in its new hymnal of 1847. Northern Methodists followed, urging greater formality with their hymnal of 1878. *The Methodist*

Hymnal (1905), a joint effort of Methodists North and South, provided a full Order of Public Worship for non-Communion Sundays, a single-page order placed up front facing the title page (S **pp35, 33**; H **635n60**). "Innovations" included unison reciting of the Apostles' Creed, responsive reading of a psalm, and singing of the Gloria Patri. This 1905 order of worship, gradually adopted, continued to guide practice for the century. Aside from recovering the Psalter, the order did little to enhance the hearing of Scripture. The insertion of announcements, collection, offertory music, and a hymn between Scripture reading and sermon both reflected and encouraged the increasing likelihood that the preaching would take the Scripture lesson or part thereof as mere pretext.

Communion became more frequent in this period as most churches could count on Sunday leadership by ordained ministers. Southern Methodists led the way, mandating monthly Communion in their *Disciplines* beginning in 1870. Northern Methodists never had such a directive, but Matthew Simpson, in his celebratory *Cyclopaedia of Methodism* (1876), reported: "In cities and large towns this sacrament is usually celebrated monthly, but in country places it is seldom administered more than quarterly." In the 1870s, New Jersey Methodist Thomas Welch invented the process of canning (pasteurizing) and grape juice supplanted Communion wine, something of a reversal of the miracle at Cana. Further, in the 1890s, sanitation-minded Methodists began replacing the common cup (chalice) with individual glasses. Opponents of the "great communion innovation" *prevailed* legislatively but *failed* when it came to actual practice. Their use in congregations grew, assisted greatly by the influenza epidemic of 1918–19. By the 1920s, individual cups filled with grape juice had become almost universal in the Methodist family of churches (H **635–36nn61–64**).

Choirs, organs, trained musicians, and even paid soloists raised standards for Methodist church music. Choirs began to appear in Methodist churches in Eastern Seaboard cities and country towns as early as the 1810s. By the 1840s and 1850s, choirs, as well as pianos and organs, had become fixtures in numerous Methodist churches. By 1864 a national organization of Associated Choirs pressed for the innovations. Meeting with The MEC General Conference's blessing in a ten-day choir convention, this organization sought both to safeguard the Wesleyan practice of congregational singing and to improve musical literature and leadership (S **1864d**). The 1878 MEC *Hymnal* gave official endorsement. The preface suggested that "there should be a choir and an organ, if possible, to lead the people," and that these supports to congregational song were best situated "in front of the congregation." Organs and choir galleries in previous decades were usually at the rear of the church. Four years later The MECS publisher and theologian Thomas O. Summers defended both organs and choirs and even composed the hymn "Praise Him with Organs" for the dedication of a new organ at McKendree Church in Nashville (H **636n66**).

In an earlier era, congregations sang all their hymns to a few well-known tunes. By midcentury, some Methodists longed for a hymnal with tunes as did The MEC's Associated Choirs (S **1864d**). Three years later (1867) such a collection of hymns and tunes was published: *The Centenary Singer.* The 1878 MEC *Hymnal* interlined tunes with texts. The MECS and the UBC added tunes to their official hymnals in 1874. The EA followed in 1877. Methodists, Evangelicals, and United Brethren had expected members to buy and bring their pocket-sized hymnbooks. The 1878 MEC *Hymnal,* however, came only in a larger size, suitable for pew not pocket. Hymnbooks, once the commonly owned treasury of doctrinal teaching and devotional reading, became liturgical aids.

Worship wars, then as now, often focused on congregational song. Folk and formal styles clashed. Beginning with *The Methodist Hymnal* (MEC, 1878), there were fewer Wesley and revival hymns and more formal psalms, chorales, and hymns mostly of British origin, such as "Holy, Holy, Holy." However, unofficial "Methodist" songbooks capitalized on informal songs, spirituals, and other American folk hymns. Joseph Hillman's *The Revivalist,* first published in 1868, became popular in Sunday schools and midweek prayer meetings. Many Methodists thought the Sunday schools and prayer meetings had all the "good" songs.

When Pittsburgh Methodism's flagship, Christ MEC, was gutted by fire in 1891, the congregation set out to build a trendsetting church for the city and the denomination. The sale of the center-city site plus a sizable insurance settlement enabled the congregation to hire the nation's leading ecclesiastical architect, George Washington Kramer. On January 13, 1895, Bishop Charles H. Fowler dedicated a monumental new church. Celebrating rituals for such dedications, which began to appear in service books of The MEC in 1864 and MECS in 1870, became a proud chore for bishops. Kramer's new Christ Church featured a Romanesque exterior style and a new interior plan (auditorium-style sanctuary and Akron Plan Sunday school, discussed in chapter X), promoted as the "Ideal Church" in his 1897 book, *The What, How and Why of Church Building*. The massive, lavishly appointed church built around a large central tower, surrounded by broad transepts with curving, arcaded porticoes, was modeled after H. H. Richardson's monumental Trinity Episcopal Church, Boston (H **353, 636nn 71–72**; S **1897**). Galleries surrounded the central pulpit platform on three sides so that every hearer was as close as possible to the preacher. On the fourth side and behind the pulpit area, the space was filled with the ranks of the choir that reinforced the appeal of the preacher with its devotional singing. Such sanctuaries, often with inconspicuous Communion table, architecturally emphasized the person and personality of preacher and power and centrality of the sermon.

Kramer brought the Sunday school out of the basement where it had been crammed in old Christ Church and gave it as much attention and space as the new sanctuary. Patterned after what came to be known as the Akron Plan, the Sunday school featured two curving tiers of classrooms facing a large central auditorium. The plan efficiently gathered a large number of classes close to and in full view of the superintendent, who led the school in opening and closing worship from a platform at its center, after which doors slid closed to allow individual class sessions. The new Christ Church, built at a cost of $275,000 and dedicated debt-free, modeled the dramatic changes being made in the primary spatial components of Methodist churches between 1875 and 1925. Methodists built auditorium-style sanctuaries with Akron Plan Sunday schools by the thousands across the country, often in Romanesque style (H **636n72**).

To encourage such architectural self-expression, Methodists established departments of architecture. The MEC formed a department of architecture in its Board of Church Extension as early as 1875. Within a decade The MECS and the UBC created similar offices in their church extension agencies. The MEC board issued an annual catalog of plans prepared by Philadelphia architect Benjamin D. Price beginning in 1877. Within a few years The MECS and the UBC issued versions of the same catalog, expanded and modified each year by Price through 1889 at least (H **636–37nn73–75**). The Methodist family of denominations opened its second century by building worship-education-fellowship complexes. By the 1920s, Methodists were among the first actively and officially to repudiate the Akron Plan. A new breed of religious educators promoted instead a multiroom, public school–like Sunday school. Dramatizing the change, First MEC, Akron, tore down its famous Sunday school building in 1914 and replaced it with a freestanding public school–like educational building.

At the same time, Methodists began what would be a slow-paced recovery of Wesley's sacramental sensibilities and developed architectural ambitions that permitted a balance of Word and Table. In this recovery, Methodism, tracking cultural and larger Christian trends, embraced the "aesthetic" or Gothic architecture. The leading proponent of this second Gothic Revival was the architect and medievalist Ralph Adams Cram of Boston. New Jersey clergyman Elbert M. Conover, among the important interpreters of this movement, headed The MEC's church architecture bureau (1924–34). Conover recruited a staff of professional planners to advise building committees and local architects through printed material and slide projector lectures. In 1934 Conover became director of a newly formed Interdenominational Architecture Bureau (later a department of the National Council of Churches). He held that position until his death in 1952. From both his MEC and interdenominational posts, Conover led first Methodists and then mainline Protestants in a full-scale assault on auditorium and Akron Plan churches (S **1928**).

Well-designed church buildings, Conover insisted, in their exterior and interior, should be beautiful because "ugliness, even if consecrated, will not be forgiven." Environment should evoke reverence, inspire worship, and instill faith. Enhancing religious practice aesthetically meant attending to the centrality of the sacraments. Conover counseled, "Give to the table of the Lord the position of honor due it, with nothing but the communion rail between it and the people." It should not be overshadowed by the pulpit or crammed into a narrow passage (H **637nn84–85**).

In his illustrated lectures to church building committees and in his books Conover insisted that church architecture itself was a form of evangelism. And the best form of evangelism was a building that was distinctively a church, not a structure that could be confused with any secular building. In the churches illustrated in his widely circulated books—*Building the House of God* (1928), the *Church Building Guide* (1946), and *The Church Builder* (1948)—there is no mistaking interiors with theaters or exteriors with banks. The interiors have a divided chancel with choir stalls facing each other across the chancel. Conover did not dogmatically insist upon the re-creation of a particular Gothic style. He did believe, however, that modern church builders should be guided by the same "mystic" spirit that guided the church builders of the thirteenth and fourteenth centuries (H **637nn81–82**). So most of the plans he promoted were neo-Gothic. Notable examples include St. Mark's, New York City (1920); Trinity, Springfield, Massachusetts (1929); First, Germantown, Philadelphia (1898/1931); Chicago's Temple (1924), a skyscraper church with floors of offices and a cross-crowned Gothic spire that towered above every other building in the city; Highland Park, Dallas (1927); and First, Pasadena, California (1924). Methodism's second Gothic Revival came to a halt as the economic depression deepened in the 1930s and we pick up later architectural trends in the following chapter.

MISSION(S) IN WAR AND OF PEACE

Having blessed their respective "sacred" Civil War causes, Methodists readily rallied to support the Spanish-American War (1898) and their fellow Methodist, President William McKinley. They welcomed as well the evangelistic possibilities of McKinley's occupation of Roman Catholic Cuba and acquisition of Catholic Puerto Rico and the Philippines. Expansionist politics and Christian evangelism could work hand in hand. Mission executives jubilantly construed victory and evangelistic opportunity to uplift, civilize, and evangelize brown people in providential terms. So pronounced Adna B. Leonard, head of The MEC Missionary Society and Board of Foreign Missions (1888–1912), eight times a delegate to General Conference, and an 1885 candidate for governor of Ohio (S **1898**). MEC Bishop James Thoburn reminded a US Senate Committee on the Philippines in 1902 that "God put us in the Philippines." Following such a divine mandate, Methodists by late 1900 set about building schools and churches in Manila and recruiting converts as preachers. Homer Stuntz arrived to take superintendency of the emerging mission in 1901. Nicolas Zamora, the first native to be ordained (deacon in 1900), became the first native Indigenous elder in 1903. A comity arrangement with other American denominations assigned Methodists to an area in Luzon north of Manila. Aggressive evangelism produced converts—6,800 in the first three years—outpacing growth in every other mission of The MEC (H **638n88**).

The WFMS of The MECS established three schools for girls in Cuba beginning in 1901. Under a comity agreement, Protestant mission leaders divided Puerto Rico into four regions, one of which was assigned to the UBC and another to The MEC. UBC pastor E. L. Ortt and his wife began

Sunday school work in Ponce in 1899. The UBC continued its Puerto Rico mission until the 1931 merger of United Brethren, Disciples of Christ, and Congregational churches created the United Evangelical Church in Puerto Rico. Charles Drees, a veteran MEC missionary from Peru who was fluent in Spanish, went to San Juan in 1900 as mission superintendent, assisted by an Indigenous pastor, Manuel Andujar, and two Anglo deaconesses. Within two years the mission reported five churches with 640 members, seven Sunday schools, a "McKinley" day school, and an orphanage. The expanding mission was organized as "Porto Rico Mission Conference" in 1913 with thirty-five churches and eighteen ministers. From the earliest days of the mission, women were active in visitation and served as assistant pastors and as Christian educators.

Although some Methodists embraced the peace activism that followed in the first decade of the new century, joined peace societies, and supported arbitration as a means of dealing with international disputes, most reverted to the crusade spirit as the United States edged toward participation in World War I (H **638n90**). With American public opinion generally, Methodist attitudes gradually and generally embraced Wilsonian-idealism, crass nationalism, and anti-German sentiment. A crusade mentality supported democracy and Christianizing missions abroad and undemocratic constraints on speech and action at home. So the New York Conference published *Methodism and the Flag* enthusiastically supporting a US declaration of war, derisively condemning Christian pacifists, and including a much-publicized and often-reprinted poem by Bishop Luther B. Wilson titled "Wave, Flag of Freedom, Wave." The MECS and The MPC created War-Work Commissions. The MEC established a National War Council with headquarters at Metropolitan Church in Washington, D.C. A flyer for the organization depicted marching troops in front of a horseback-riding Francis Asbury, around whose shoulders appeared the headings: "Methodism Cooperates with Government" and "Follows Her Sons to the Trenches." Evangelicals celebrated their founder, Jacob Albright, as a Revolutionary War hero and urged his latter-day flock to follow his example.

A military draft exempted and limited conscientious objection to members of *pacifist* denominations (Friends [Quakers], Mennonites, and Church of the Brethren). The Methodist press openly attacked Quakers and other pacifists. A prominent district superintendent in the California Conference, E. P. Ryland, was dismissed for refusing to participate with his bishop and

211

cabinet in a church-sponsored war bond rally in 1917 (H **638n92**). Evangelicals, United Brethren, and German Methodists found the cornerstones of their churches painted yellow, their pastors threatened, and members insulted as un-American and un-Methodist. Postal authorities required the editor of the German-language Methodist newspaper, *Der Christliche Apologete,* to file English translations of all major articles with their office. And the church's chief editors, deeming the paper "not in full harmony with the spirit of the Church and the country" and insufficiently supportive of the Allied cause for "freedom, democracy, and humanity," required the paper's editors to sign a loyalty oath (S **1918b**).

The UBC General Conference of 1917, on the other hand, noting that "a vein of pure German blood runs through our whole church from Otterbein to the present," passed a resolution requesting "our people everywhere to refrain from any unkind criticism of their German brethren in this country." And the independent MFSS and at least one annual conference went on record opposing patriotic excesses.

The incredible mobilization—millions under arms—elicited from the churches an equally monumental effort to support their men, physically, mentally, emotionally, and spiritually. Providing an adequate supply of chaplains, for instance, required its own mobilization. Methodists channeled much of such support through national interdenominational agencies, some 325 chaplains working collaboratively with Federal Council's General Wartime Commission, established in 1917, the primary liaison between the Protestant churches and the government and involved in selection and endorsement. Methodists also channeled funds for and support of troops through the Student Christian Movement, World's Student Christian Federation, and the YMCA. The latter with its own National War Work Council proved especially vital, creating dispensary "huts" at army encampments, working with prisoners of war as well as Allied troops, and raising vast sums of money. Some five hundred Methodists worked in YMCA ministries. And one Methodist, John R. Mott, effectively led and coordinated the work of the several international agencies. Layman Mott, arguably Methodism's greatest ecumenical figure, moved relentlessly back and forth between the United States and Europe, working with counterpart ecumenists and political leaders. Later Mott was a forceful advocate for the creation of the World Council of Churches and was the preacher at the opening service of the WCC's inaugural assembly in Amsterdam in 1948. He continued such monumental efforts when the churches turned toward relief and the rebuilding of a devastated Europe. Mott shared the Nobel Peace Prize in 1946 for his work in establishing and strengthening international Christian student organizations that worked to promote peace (H **638n94**).

At war's end, when President Woodrow Wilson brought the Treaty of Versailles and League of Nations to the US Congress for ratification, the EA, The MEC, and The MECS fought for its ratification. The 1916 MEC General Conference had encouraged the nation to take the lead in an international league or federation and the church's bishops took a stand for world peace. Pastors and laity joined advocacy groups for the League of Nations and created and signed petitions urging the United States to join. The Woman's Missionary Council of The MECS in 1919 passed a resolution supporting the League, which it sent to public officials. Evelyn Riley Nicholson played a major role in shaping the churches' thinking on peace as president of The MEC's WFMS from 1920 to 1940 and member of the General Conference Committee on International Justice and Goodwill. Nicholson wrote the book *Way to a Warless World* (1924), an important voice for peace, a copy of which fittingly went in the cornerstone of The Methodist Church Center for the United Nations, which opened in 1962. By 1924, The MEC General Conference established a churchwide Commission on World Peace and adopted the "Springfield Declaration on World Peace," calling for a crusade for peace, support of the League of Nations, and US entry into the Permanent Court of International Justice (S **1924a**). Pacifist sentiment would reign, particularly in northern Methodism, until the nation found itself again in world war.

At the end of World War I, Methodists became involved in Korean efforts to throw off Japanese hegemony. United States President Wilson's declaration of the right of self-determination of peoples inspired Korean nationalists to action. In 1919, thirty six Korean leaders (sixteen of them Christian, nine Methodist) signed a declaration of independence. Methodist Syngman Rhee was elected president of a Korean provisional government. Half a million Koreans took part in unarmed demonstrations that occurred wherever the declaration was read. Japan reacted swiftly to crush the independence movement by imprisoning leaders, including many pastors, and destroying 740 buildings, including 47 churches. Of 19,525 persons arrested, 3,371 were Protestants—more than 17 percent of those arrested—an impressive figure considering that by 1919, the Protestants composed only about 1 percent of the total population. Of the 471 women arrested, Protestants accounted for more than 65 percent (309), attesting to the empowering effect of religion on Korean women. Methodists become linked with two of the most important symbols of the Korean independence movement: the martyrdom of Methodist youth Yu Kwan-sun and the massacre in the Methodist chapel at Cheamni. (H **363, 638n97**; S **1919b**). The defiant Methodist support of independence—by missionaries and converts alike—would affect growth in the decades ahead.

REUNIFICATION AND RACE

Formal conversations between The MEC and MECS began, as we noted, at an 1876 conference in Cape May, New Jersey. Each church pledged to honor the other as legitimate heir of the Christmas Conference and to exchange "fraternal delegates" (S **1876d**). The two episcopal churches joined in celebrations of the common Wesleyan heritage at the First Ecumenical (now World) Methodist Conference in London, 1881 (S **1881b**), and at a Centennial Methodist Conference in Baltimore, 1884. In 1894, The MECS General Conference proposed the exploration of closer relations and authorized the establishment of a Commission on Federation of Methodism (delegations of nine, three bishops, elders, and laity). In 1896, The MEC concurred. A Joint Commission on Federation, meeting in January 1898, recommended adjusting rivalries in overseas mission fields and crafting a common catechism, hymnbook, and order of public worship. These appeared in 1905 (S **pp29–30, 33–36**; H **638n98**). The two churches agreed to share publication facilities in Asia and both participated in emerging national and world ecumenical ventures (as we note elsewhere in this chapter). Joint celebrations of the Methodist heritage continued in 1919, 1925, 1934, and 1938 (the two hundredth anniversary of Wesley's Aldersgate conversion).

Gradually the conversations, sometimes including Methodist Protestants as well, aspired to *unification* not just *federation*. Consistently, The MECS insisted that unification be a White affair (S **1918a**). Southern Methodists entertained and suggested several ways in which Black churches could be separated off (H **638n99**). For over half a century, The MECS held out for some way of ordering the conference structure of Methodism that would (1) accord the southern White minority within a united church "the power to control its own affairs," and (2) place another minority, namely, the Black members of The MEC, into a separate ecclesial structure, preferably one as distinct as the Colored Methodist Episcopal Church. An early formulation—initially termed quadrennial conferences and providing a single quadrennial conference of Black churches—surfaced as the unification scheme from a 1911 Chattanooga Joint Commission on Federation comprising representatives of The MEC, MPC, and MECS. This Chattanooga "unity" proposal also provided, as would subsequent schemes, for fuller lay representation in annual conferences, a concession to The MPC and to advocates of lay rights within The MEC and The MECS (H **639nn100–102**).

The MPC General Conference deferred action pending resolution of issues between the two episcopal bodies. The MECS in 1914 recognized the agreement as containing the "basic principles of a genuine unification . . . by the method of reorganization" but insisted that Black Methodists be "formed into an independent organization holding fraternal relations with the reorganized and united church." Southern leaders soon added another condition, namely, the establishment of a supreme court or judiciary for the church so that no conference would have the authority to pass upon and determine the constitutionality of its own acts (a resolution of polity and authority differences that went back to 1844). The MEC, meeting in 1916, also embraced the plan "as containing the basic principles of a genuine unification," conceding at that point that its "colored membership" should be reorganized "into one or more Quadrennial or Jurisdictional Conferences" (H **639nn103–4**).

These actions led to the constitution of an (all-male) Joint Commission on Unification representing the two episcopal bodies, which met from 1916 to 1920 and left on record three volumes and more than fifteen hundred pages of debates and speeches (H **364–67; 639nn100, 105–6**). The central drama in these negotiations concerned the racial composition in any "unified" Methodism. The southern editor and commissioner A. J. Lamar made that clear, "the crux of the situation is the Status of the Colored Membership in the Methodist Episcopal Church . . . if we can't arrange that, if we come to a deadlock on that, it renders null and void everything that we have done before." The MECS proposed various schemes of segregation, including extruding Black churches completely, perhaps into combination with the CME, or placing them with either Africans or other members of color, or both, in some global separate entity. With little assistance from their White MEC counterparts, the two Black (MEC) commissioners, I. Garland Penn, executive with the Board of Education for Negroes, and Robert E. Jones, then editor of the *Southwestern Advocate,* later bishop, pled that caste be not written into the church's constitution. They viewed jurisdictions as preferable to excision, did not aspire to union with the other Black Methodist bodies, and welcomed a plan that would, at last, provide for Black episcopal leadership, even if achieved through some drawing of the color line (H **639nn108, 111**).

The Joint Commission reached agreement after five years of discussions for a scheme for six White regional conferences, one for the "colored people in the United States," and four for membership in overseas conferences. Black Methodists would be represented in General Conference, though not in the same proportions as would the White regional conferences (jurisdictions), and foreign representation was even more reduced. To these regional conferences were conferred the rights of episcopal election, plans that a few commissioners recognized as divisive and constitutionally problematic. Bishop R. J. Cooke, who had served The MEC in the South, affirmed, "We were sent here to unify the Church, . . . but with these Regional Conferences with such regional powers we are dividing the Church again." He continued, "Where is your episcopacy? Were we sent here to destroy the itinerant general superintendency?" (H **639nn112–15**).

To the 1920 MEC General Conference, the bishops posed some hard questions, asking if the plan "[made] for a real brotherhood of Christian people . . . for the real unity of all sections, races, nations, and classes within Christ's Church?" The "Church of Christ is not a racial church . . . not a national, sectional, or class church," they insisted. Hence, "plans of union that sectionalize, that nationalize, that racialize the church are not plans for Christian union" (H **639n116**). General Conference found other aspects of the plan troubling and, while reaffirming its commitment to unity, continued its commission and called for the convening of a Joint General Convention (of The MEC and The MECS) to iron out problems. Recognizing the service on behalf of unity of Robert E. Jones and his forceful advocacy, as editor, of the necessity for Black bishops (S **1912a**), General Conference elected him to the episcopacy, providing him yet another platform to pursue interracial cooperation (S **1921**). Elected along with him as among the first and long-desired Black itinerant general superintendents for service in the United States was Matthew W. Clair Sr., then presiding elder in the Washington Conference.

In The MECS cultural warfare broke out over unification, warfare that badly divided the College of Bishops, roiled annual conferences, inflamed passions in MECS *Advocates,* and politicized the entire church. Progressives supported the commission's plan. Conservatives formed organizations like the League for the Preservation of Southern Methodism. The party lines reinforced and were reinforced, as already noted, by other controversies of the 1920s and 1930s—reorganization, the Klan (S **1922**), Prohibition (S **1916**), Fundamentalism, evolution, and Al Smith's presidential campaign (H **639n118**). Each issue entailed the others. Unification came to emblematize conservative fears of Black members, the North, change, modernism, and secularism. By its temporizing action of 1920, The MEC took The MECS General Conference of 1922 off the hook. The MECS rejected the notion of such a Joint General Convention but continued a commission and authorized the calling of a special session of its General Conference if the commissioners were able to work out a viable plan.

A second Joint Commission produced in early 1923 a plan with just two White jurisdictions, one embracing The MEC, the other The MECS. With little fanfare, The MEC General Conference adopted it. The MECS did as well, but by its very tense special session General Conference gave way to cultural warfare in the conferences. New organizations emerged, the Friends of Unification and the Association to Preserve The Methodist Episcopal Church, South, by Defeating the Pending Plan of Unification. Each enjoyed backing within the church press and patronage on the College of Bishops. The southern *Advocates,* twenty for unification, six against, hoisted the battle banners. The bishops voiced their sentiments, employed their appointive power for their side of the cause, and used and abused their presiding role to sway annual conference votes. As leaned the presiding bishop, so voted the conference, with one exception (H **640n121**). The plan went down to defeat, 4,528 for and 4,108 against, far short of the required 75 percent and indicative of how badly divided the southern church found itself. Convening again two years later in regular session, The MECS accepted the recommendation of its Committee on Church Relations "that there be no agitation, discussion, or negotiation concerning unification during the ensuing quadrennium" (H **640nn120–22**).

As if to supply the controversy that the southern church had determined to avoid, the 1928 MEC General Conference seemed to concern itself throughout with the "color" of Methodism. It debated the powers and prerogatives of the central conferences, many of them in Africa and Asia. It elected bishops for such conferences, including E. Stanley Jones (who resigned his election). It brought to the podium by resolution and heard a speech from

217

Dr. I. Garland Penn, senior member of the General Conference and one of the two Black representatives on the Joint Commission of 1916–20. It was presided over by the other Black representative, Bishop Robert E. Jones. And subsequently, it passed a resolution recognizing his precedent-setting presidency "as welcome evidence of a new and better day." It paid tribute to Bishop William A. Quayle as friend to "the Negro race" and effective mediator during the East St. Louis race riot. It recognized Mrs. M. A. Camphor, delegate from Delaware and widow of African missionary Bishop Camphor. It passed a resolution calling for equal educational opportunity in the South. It recognized the service of Joseph C. Hartzell "to the African race both in the United States and in Africa." It passed a motion against US policy restricting "immigration and the rights of citizenship on grounds of race and color." It passed a resolution recognizing Melville Cox and the centenary of Liberian missions. It celebrated Mary McLeod Bethune, especially for her presidency of the National Federated Clubs of Colored Women (H **640n123**).

The MEC and The MPC continued conversations in the late 1920s and early 1930s, and The MECS rejoined in 1934, the resumption preceded by national youth gatherings, informal meetings of interested leaders, and exploratory sessions of standing commissions on union. The three churches formally authorized negotiations in General Conferences of 1932 and 1934. Yet another Joint Commission met in 1934 and 1935, accepted the principles of jurisdictional governance and full lay representation, and appointed a drafting subcommittee. The new committee's plan reverted to the 1916–20 conception of multiple (White) regional jurisdictions and one central (Black) jurisdiction. It provided for equal representation of laity and clergy in annual, jurisdictional, and General Conferences; the retention of bishops and establishment of a Council of Bishops; a Judicial Council related to General Conference and the Council of Bishops; and a new name, The Methodist Church.

The plan was criticized by key denominational leaders, especially by Methodist women, including the southern women who for a decade and a half had labored through the Commission on Interracial Co-operation for better race relations (S **1936b**). In the 1936 MEC General Conference many progressive leaders opposed the plan (S **1936a**; map, p27), including Black educator Mary McLeod Bethune (H **370–71** for brief bio). In the end The MEC General Conference voted 470 for and 83 against the plan of union. The plan passed in General Conferences of the other two churches and in annual conferences of all three, again eliciting opposition in the South and this time producing considerable anguish in Black conferences and among others committed to more genuine Methodist fraternity. Black delegates contributed thirty-six of the eighty-three "no" votes in the 1936 MEC General Conference, eleven others abstaining (S **1936a**). They sat in silence while the conference sang "We're Marching to Zion." Seven of the nineteen Black conferences defeated the proposal, a few others refusing to vote, the remainder resigning themselves to the inevitable.

In a nation becoming more sensitive to its racial inequalities and to segregation as a blight on democracy, Methodism had made more visible and constitutional the color line it had long drawn within its fraternity, a step backward that southern White Methodist women clearly recognized (S **1936b**). A united Methodism would be jurisdictioned, divided by race and region—all the Black conferences and most of its congregations gathered into one Central Jurisdiction, and White Methodism united by regions. Within the jurisdictions, the plan lodged the critical "connectional" powers—namely, the election and deployment of bishops and the election of the governing board members of the national agencies. Unity? Or federalism in a new guise?

CHAPTER X
UNIFICATIONS AND WARS: 1939–68

Methodists united in 1939, the Evangelical and United Brethren churches in 1946, and EUBs and Methodists in 1968. Methodists and EUBs joined in the multilateral and bilateral projects of the period: world, national, and state councils of churches; the Consultation on Church Union; and Second Vatican Council–inspired Protestant-Catholic conversations. The Methodist union, predicated on racism and connectionally structured segregation, rendered a strange witness for the oneness of Christ's body. So Methodists plunged after 1939 into a protracted war within. And EUBs held out for dissolution of The MC's Central Jurisdiction as key to the 1968 union. Both churches also found themselves embroiled in US wars without: World War II, Korean Conflict, cold war with the Soviets, and Vietnam. Methodism, led by its bishops, initially sought a big role in bringing peace, order, and justice to the world. The Methodist Church—its policies, practices, and governance accommodated to southern White preconditions for unity—found itself coping with internal structural stresses. Unfinished business included ordination and full conference membership for women and the proper relation between General Conference and the US-based mission boards and the churches that missions had spread across the globe.

WAR AND A NEW WORLD ORDER

The Methodist, Evangelical, and United Brethren churches stiffened their pacifist resolve even as world war loomed. The new Methodist Church urged President Roosevelt to "avoid entanglement" in the unfolding world war and called on pastors to "train our children . . . in the arts of peace." Such pacifist sentiments, undergirded by the prophetic critique of World War I, were widely held. A 1936 MEC poll conducted by Bishop James C. Baker yielded 12,854 responses, over half of whom indicated that they would not sanction war. Pacifism reigned in seminaries, women's organizations, youth and young adult ministries and publications, and some conferences. The 1935 National Council of Methodist Youth proposed and requested general agency support for a national student strike against war. The latter demurred, but mid-decade General Conferences of three churches went on record favoring peace over war. The MEC Commission on World Peace began in 1936 to register conscientious objectors (COs) with the government. Two years later, a full-page ad in the church's leading magazine called war "futile," "stupid," and "unholy." In 1939, a national Methodist Peace Fellowship formed.

Theologians like Garrett's Georgia Harkness, Bishop Francis McConnell, and Evanston pastor Ernest Tittle continued high-profile pacificist witness (H **640nn1–7**; S **1947b**)

The 1940 Methodist General Conference passed and lodged in the *Discipline* a series of resolutions pertaining to war: a "Declaration of Patriotic Principles," a long "Statement on Peace and War," one titled "Peace," and a final one, "Aggressor Nations." While pledging its patriotic loyalty and recognizing that Christians, including Methodists, differ on "what a Christian should do when his nation becomes involved in war," General Conference exhorted its leaders "to devise ways and means to keep the will to peace, vocal and determined to help keep the United States out of war" and urged that every church and conference establish a peace commission. The 1941 UBC General Conference, though making no attempt to bind the consciences of individual members, pledged itself not to officially endorse, support, or participate in war. It promised conscientious objectors the support of the church. Less than a year after Pearl Harbor, the Evangelical Church gathered for its General Conference. The 1942 conference affirmed the long-standing position of the church that "war and bloodshed are not agreeable to the Gospel of Jesus Christ," recognized the status of conscientious objectors, and approved the office and ministry of military chaplains, but added that such action was "not to be construed as implying the endorsement of war by our church" (H **640–41nn8–11**).

Sentiments within the churches, however, were shifting dramatically. The second Methodist General Conference met two and a half years after the nation was officially at war. By that point Protestants had begun to grasp the enormity of the evil with which the Allies contended, a more serious crisis, insisted *Zion's Herald* editor, L. O. Hartman, than the civilized world had ever faced. Pacifist Ernest Tittle introduced the majority report for the Committee on the State of the Church reaffirming the 1940 resolution on peace and war, applauding conscientious objectors, and offering no prayers for Allied victory. Drew Seminary dean Lynn Harold Hough offered the minority report on behalf of seventeen of the sixty-four active committee members. "Must the Christian church condemn all use of military force?" it asked. Civilization, indeed, "God himself has a stake in the struggle." The state and the Christian are duty bound to fight to correct the intolerable wrongs. We "are sending over a million young men from Methodist homes to participate in the conflict." After heated floor debate, the minority resolution prevailed by a 55 percent majority. The troubled conscience of Methodism on matters of war and peace was shared by the UBC, which met for its last General Conference during the closing year of the war. Delegates and bishops declared themselves "heartily in favor of the cessation of hostilities at the earliest possible hour, and of peace terms aimed to preserve peace and not avenge wrongs" (H **641nn12–14**).

Methodism threw itself into various war-related ministries—provision and support of chaplains, alternative service by conscientious objectors, relief efforts, and efforts to envision a postwar world. Bishop Herbert Welch urged the 1940 General Conference (MC) to "constitute an agency to respond to the vast needs of human suffering around the world" and be a "voice of conscience among Methodists to act in the relief of human suffering without distinction of race, color or creed." This Methodist Committee for Overseas Relief (MCOR) between 1940 and 1945 responded to the plight of thirty million refugees suffering in the midst of world war in China, North Africa, and Europe—providing assistance to those who had fled to camps, relocated to other countries, or resettled as refugees in the United States. Later MCOR (after merger, UMCOR) moved beyond relief to training programs to instill skills that would make communities self-supporting and self-reliant and eventually to a third emphasis: to work for the renewal of life through the alleviation of the root causes of hunger. Relief continued after the war, thanks to the Advance Program, a major churchwide "second-mile" (beyond World Service) giving program of the Board of Missions. Inaugurated in 1948, Advance contributions enabled the church to cope with disasters, heal the sick, shelter the homeless, feed the hungry, and share the faith in the postwar world, voluntarily selecting and supporting specific projects (H **641nn15–16**).

The draft legislation for World War II (1940) provided for clergy deferment, CO classification for personal religious convictions (not as in World War I solely on membership in a pacifist church), and work of national importance as an alternative to military service. During the war, more than fifteen thousand registered as COs, two-thirds from "peace churches" (Mennonites, Quakers, and Brethren) but included a considerable number of Methodists and other mainline church members. Many served without remuneration in Civilian Public Service camps. About five thousand others were sent to prison, either because they refused to register or because their objection was based on political grounds inadmissible under the law (H **376**; S **1942b**).

With little organizational support for the chaplaincy remaining from World War I, The MC Council of Bishops (COB) created a Methodist Emergency Committee in 1941. The COB charged the committee with exploring the need for rendering special aid to communities adjacent to military bases. It also bore responsibility for recruiting, endorsing, and assisting chaplains ordered to active duty. In the latter part of 1942, as the church's ministry to the military grew, the bishops established a permanent Commission on Chaplains, its functions clearly defined. Its priorities were the recruitment and careful screening of chaplains who would minister to military personnel throughout the world. A devotional booklet for servicemen, *Strength for Service to God and Country*, with a circulation of 720,000 in its first year (1942–43), set an all-time record for a single year's sales in the entire 144 years of Methodist publishing. A million copies were distributed by war's end. The booklet was revised and reprinted, in 1969 for use in Vietnam and again in 2003 for use in the second Iraq War, the latter sponsored by the Commission on United Methodist Men. Local churches close to military facilities provided spiritual, moral, and social services to training staff and trainees.

Methodists, Evangelicals, and United Brethren increasingly advocated a responsible world political organization to promote peace with justice. Leading this cause was Bishop G. Bromley Oxnam, COB secretary, member of the Commission on a Just and Durable Peace of the Federal Council of Churches (FCC), and close colleague in that initiative with John Foster Dulles, active Presbyterian layperson and later Secretary of State. With Oxnam's prodding, the COB mounted a campaign in behalf of organized peace, of an international organization to safeguard peace, and of American participation therein—the "Bishops' Crusade for a New World Order" (1943–44). Oxnam lobbied Washington personally. He wrote ferociously. He spoke everywhere. He ordered literature. He urged Methodists, young and old, to write the president, Senate, and House of Representatives on behalf of world peace, justice, brotherhood, and order. Methodism's new conversion culminated in a day of consecration, March 26, 1944, and later public commendation by Roosevelt (S **1943**).

A second Crusade for Christ (1944–48) challenged the church to raise $25 million for world rehabilitation and relief. A Crusade Scholars program supported study in the United States for international and minority students. By 1948, three hundred students had been brought to the United States as Crusade Scholars. By its half-century mark it had supported a Who's Who of Methodist (H **378**) and Christian officialdom (the latter including Makarios III, Greek Orthodox archbishop and later president of Cyprus; Graca Machal, first lady of Mozambique; Brazilian Lucia Panicett, president of its women's organization; Peruvian educator Carmel de Dias; theologian José Bonino; Emilio Castro, WCC general secretary). The church raised $27 million—in addition to oversubscribing a $24 million World Service (mission) budget. In 1948, General Conference "re-upped" with a "Quadrennial Plan for Christ and His Church," and an important feature, Advance Specials, invited congregations and conferences to over-and-above giving targeted to particular missional projects.

HOLOCAUST, JAPANESE INTERNMENT, HIROSHIMA, AND NAGASAKI

Although Methodist leaders expressed horror at Nazi attitudes and countered domestic anti-Semitism, few considered the possibility of a Jewish massacre in Germany. The Methodist press published only occasional stories about what later came to be called the Holocaust. Deceived by American propaganda during World War I, Methodists tended not to believe the worst stories about German behavior in this war. Instead they relied on the State Department for information, which was less than forthcoming about what it knew. Only later, after gazing into the pit of hell with the rest of the world, did Methodists learn the truth about the Nazi extermination campaign. In 1988, on the fiftieth anniversary of *Kristallnacht,* the beginning of the

Holocaust, United Methodist bishops in East and West Germany issued a pastoral letter.

Despite intelligence reports deeming the overwhelming majority of Japanese Americans loyal to the United States, President Franklin Roosevelt's 1942 Executive Order 9066 authorized the military to remove 120,000 Japanese Americans from their West Coast homes to hastily built relocation camps in remote areas of several western states—Idaho, Oregon, and Washington. Internment produced great hardships: loss of jobs, property, and businesses; separation of fathers from families; barracks-style living; long lines for meals and showers; and loss of privacy and other threats to family integrity—in short, concentration camp conditions. Some Methodists spoke decisively against such racism and against the policies of internment and relocation, notably the newly constituted Woman's Division (S **1942a**). Ecumenist-evangelist E. Stanley Jones detailed the life of "Barbed-Wire Christians" in the *Christian Century*. And the Methodist Youth Fellowship, gathered for convocation in 1942, after receiving a greeting from an internment camp, responded with an offering (S **1942b**; H **641–42nn22, 24, 25**). The COB in that year called attention to the plight of Japanese Americans and promoted Methodist involvement in resettlement. The 1944 MC General Conference, however, took little notice of Japanese internment.

The August 1945 news that atomic bombs had been dropped on Hiroshima and Nagasaki and that Japan had sued for peace drew simultaneous expressions of joy and fear among Methodists as among Americans generally. Among the first contributions to the ethical debate about the use of nuclear weapons came from the FCC on August 9, 1945, after the bombing of Hiroshima but before the bombing of Nagasaki. Bishop Oxnam, then president of the council, issued a statement (after conferring with FCC colleagues Dulles and others) requesting that no more bombs be dropped and fearing that continued use of nuclear weapons by a Christian nation would make them an acceptable part of modern warfare. Prominent clergy sent a letter to President Truman expressing the same sentiments. A critical mass of Methodists began to condemn nuclear weapons, the MFSA among the first Methodist organizations. And *Christian Advocate* editor Roy Smith pondered the morality of such superweapons. *Motive* editorialized "We have sinned" and later (1949) invited Albert Einstein to share his own regret for his role in opening the nuclear age.

Resolutely pacifist prewar, Methodism emerged from the traumas of World War II as chastened, realistic about the perilousness of peace, increasingly aware that wartime ally Communist Russia was no longer a partner, and troubled by the future that atomic warfare opened. The General Conferences of 1948 and 1952 passed strong resolutions on peace, world relief, and support for the United Nations. The Methodist Peace Fellowship pushed pledge cards. Shortly afterward, in 1948, the FCC appointed a commission of Christian scholars to prepare a report to the churches on the use of nuclear weapons. The report, "The Christian Conscience and Weapons of Mass Destruction," issued in 1950, gave qualified approval as a deterrent to war. Georgia Harkness, the only Methodist theologian on the commission, publicly dissented (H **642nn27–28**).

ORDERING THE NEW METHODIST CHURCH

A Council of Bishops (COB) was authorized by the *Discipline* to meet at least once a year and "plan for the general oversight and promotion of the temporal and spiritual interests of the entire Church" (H **642n31**). Under the guidance of its secretary, Oxnam, the COB indeed lived into such a charge with the New World Order mobilization for relief and peacemaking. Oxnam functioned as the COB's executive, setting agenda for meetings, ordering the proceedings, taking elaborate minutes, overseeing follow-up, arranging meetings with political figures, and in various ways energizing the COB. Fearing that the bishops would, as they subsequently did, reorient their horizons to the jurisdictions within which their primary duties were set, Oxnam arranged for a plan of visitation that would send each American bishop abroad once a quadrennium.

Had Oxnam continued to focus his energies on and pursue his interests through the COB even for the duration of his term as secretary (relinquished in 1955), the COB might well have sustained its connectional wartime prophetic and teaching office roles. But Oxnam threw himself into the public roles that his assignments to New York and then Washington offered, oversaw the church's mission enterprise, carried the torch for mainline Protestantism, labored for the Federal and National Councils of Churches, shaped denominational ministerial educational policy, presided over the Council on World

Service and Finance, fought McCarthyism (see below), and tended to the requisite episcopal appointment-making duties. For the period covered by this chapter, both the COB and the jurisdictional colleges carried on their prescribed nominating and deploying duties but devoted much of their life together to becoming family for one another, letting their gatherings function as their "conference," adjusting to jurisdictional life, and building the old-boy relationships that the 1970s would work to upend. And the regional jurisdictions adjusted their notions of what constitutes episcopal timber, recalibrated what experience and exposure counted, passed over agency executives and others with connectional experience, and increasingly elected bishops from tall-steeple churches, the district superintendency, and regional institutional leadership (H **642nn32–34**).

The case for a Judicial Council and provision for judicial review had long and different histories in the three churches. The Methodist Protestants in 1920 created a connectional Executive Committee as the last recourse for rulings of conference presidents or appeals against appointments. The MECS in 1854 empowered the bishops, acting collectively and in writing, with the prerogative of challenging a rule or regulation and thereby obliging General Conference to muster a two-thirds majority on the question. This action, consonant with its understanding of conference and episcopacy, The MECS confirmed and clarified in 1874. Consonant with its understanding of conference and episcopacy, the northern church continued after 1844 to permit General Conference to serve as the supreme court for appeals from annual conference judicial decisions and rulings on the law by presiding bishops. From 1860 to 1872 the General Conference established a Committee of Appeals and referred such matters to it. In 1876, The MEC established a Judiciary Committee, a body of twelve ("one from each General Conference District") "to consider and report their decision on all questions of law coming up to us from Judicial Conferences." In 1884, the body's authority was extended to "all records of Judicial Conference, appeals on points of law, and all proposed changes in the Ecclesiastical Code."

Both The MEC committee and the southern College of Bishops thereafter rendered "court" decisions, creating a body of *connectional* law. The MECS directed its compilation, voting in its 1866 General Conference to request the bishops "to prepare for publication a Commentary on the Discipline, embracing Episcopal decisions, with a view to produce a harmonious administration thereof." That produced Holland N. McTyeire's *Manual of the*

Discipline of The Methodist Episcopal Church, South, Including the Decisions of the College of Bishops, a volume regularly updated. The northern church proceeded later, in less formal fashion, to compile a comparable manual. In 1903 Bishop Richard J. Cooke produced *The Judicial Decisions of the General Conference of The Methodist Episcopal Church.* Another major compilation was undertaken in 1924 at the behest of General Conference (H **643nn35–44**).

A separate body entrusted with the power of judicial review—not General Conference ruling on its own legislation or the bishops collectively confirming their individual rulings—became one of The MECS's several non-negotiables, essentially from the beginning of unity discussions. In 1934, the southern General Conference created a Judicial Council, the one feature of a proposed new constitution to pass and thus removed that prerogative from its College of Bishops. The Uniting Conference created an interim Judicial Council, and the 1940 MC General Conference created the statutes for the permanent body. And of course, the 1968 EUBC-MC union continued the Judicial Council.

Elected by General Conference from slates proposed by the bishops or nominated from the floor and staggered by quadrennia so as to provide continuity, the Judicial Council, a body of nine (five clergy and four laity), succeeded in functioning as prescribed. It rules on the constitutionality of General Conference legislation, on the legality of actions taken by any connectional entity, and on decisions by bishops in annual conferences. Since 1944, General Conference entrusted the Judicial Council also with declaratory decisions on the meaning of provisions of the *Discipline* or of proposed changes. The Judicial Council elects its president, vice president, and secretary; establishes its own Rules of Practice and Procedure; hears oral arguments on cases before it; and renders and publishes its decisions, concurrences, and dissents (H **644nn46–47; 382–83** for organization and leadership).

Unification changed the experience of annual conference for much of Methodism, especially for clergy of the former MEC, for Methodist Protestants generally, and for clergy and laity where the three churches overlapped—that is, across the Bible Belt from the Delmarva Peninsula to California. Merger created essentially new conferences with White clergy members from the three denominations and dispersed former colleagues into other conferences. (We treat Black conferences in the next section of this chapter.) The MECS Baltimore Conference sent clergy into four MC conferences. In Texas, clergy members of The MEC Southern Conference, which earlier had brought together the Southern German, Gulf (northern transplants), and Swedish Mission conferences, were transferred into six MC conferences.

Stable communities of colleagues—fraternities really—became aggregations of strangers. The new West Virginia Conference brought together West Virginia conferences of the three churches and drew also from Baltimore and Holston. By 1940 415 clergy and 286 laity answered roll call. Predecessor conferences (1938) had been small: MEC, 156 ministers (plus 23 supplies); MECS, 109 clergy and 44 laity; MPC, 69 laity and 69 clergy. Fraternities of 150 had become an institution of roughly 700–800 (H **644–645nn50–55**). Northern all-clergy, all-male MEC conferences, even where left largely intact geographically, doubled in size with the addition of laity (men and women).

Something about the new conferences unsettled each predecessor church's clergy—size certainly, but also adjusting to bishops, to laity at all, to laity in equal numbers to clergy, to the increased presence of women, to strange informal rules and organizational cultures—adjustments whose cost and effect on conference life and governance were perhaps never fully appreciated because of the more overwhelming regimens, austerities, adversities, and human price imposed contemporaneously by world war.

Realigning the work and integrating the organization of the agencies of predecessor denominations into new Methodist boards and commissions posed yet another challenge. That meant, for instance, putting under the Board of Missions and Church Extensions the home and foreign mission operations of the three churches, including the several women's organizations into the board's Woman's Division of Christian Service (the latter treated below; see H **384–86** for agencies and responsibilities and for new media organizations). Protocols for the agencies, except for that of the publishing house, provided for counterpart bodies at jurisdictional, conference, and local levels, lacing the administrative and missional activities into giant corporate systems. A General Commission on World Service and Finance provided the new church financial oversight, centralized collection, and effective disbursement. A Council of Secretaries, formed in 1940, was intended to provide coordination on the program side. Decentralization reigned.

The Uniting Conference changed in a simple but fundamental way General Conference's power over its boards, stripping its authority to elect the general secretaries of the connectional agencies. The proposal honored professionalism—election of agency staff by its own board was, as one proponent put it, in accordance with "the usual practice when you are seeking experts as these boards will require to perform an expert job." Harold Paul Sloan, earlier Methodism's preeminent fundamentalist (editor of *Call to Colors,* renamed *The Essentialist*), by 1939 the editor of the *Christian Advocate* (New York), portrayed the change with a neologism, "ensmalling the church" (H **645n60**). Methodism would indeed fragment not into small groups but into centrifugal power centers: Boards and agencies were located in different cities. Bishops settled into jurisdictional colleges and ever more diocesan presidential assignments. Annual conferences experienced a large agenda in understanding who and what they were. The new Judicial Council claimed significant authority. The MC was a national church in name, but effectively regionalized (jurisdictioned). General Conferences, ostensibly the connective tissue in this new church, convened only briefly every quadrennium.

Where was the center? Who or what would connect, hold together, and coordinate the church's work and witness? By 1952, The Methodist Church grasped that it had a problem, at least with the agencies, and put in place a Coordinating Council to work at relations between and among them, expecting the Council of Secretaries and the Council of Bishops somehow to add as well toward agency collaboration. It's a wonder, in some ways, that the church responded as well as it did to the aftermath of the Depression and the world war; to the unraveling of colonialism and the transformation of mission; to the problems of race, including those it had created for itself; to the cold war, Korea, and Vietnam; and to poverty, civil rights, and feminism. In a world increasingly laced together by markets, communication, ideologies, conflicts, travel, and education, Methodism found a way of losing its traction, cohesion, or stature—of fragmenting and regionalizing itself. The MEC protagonists had wanted a unified Methodism to stand tall in American society and the world. It got instead a church slouching so as not to disturb the South's peculiar institution and MECS racial sensibilities.

JURISDICTIONS AND THE CENTRAL JURISDICTION

The 1939 union entrusted the quadrennial jurisdictional gatherings with the decisive function of electing bishops. That polity and political regionalization gradually reshaped the episcopacy, the experience brought to the office, and the perspectives with which individual bishops and the council functioned. Elections elevated fewer individuals from churchwide office and more from the district superintendency, high-steeple churches, and regional institutions. Annual conferences vied to put their own "man" in. Clergy and eventually lay power brokers instructed delegates whom to support. Conference delegations swapped commitments, a process favoring larger annual conferences when they chose to cooperate (H **646n61**).

Three jurisdictions evolved in significant fashion into full-orbed conferences, developed an ongoing apparatus, sustained intra-jurisdictional networks beyond those scripted by disciplinary mandates, evolved a distinctive regional or racial ethos, and played key roles politically in the church's struggle over racial justice. By design the two southern jurisdictions, the Southeastern and South Central, effectively carried into their operations the all-White personnel, relationships, papers, schools, camps, style, and ethos of the southern church (MECS). The Southeastern, in particular—embracing the heart of the Confederacy and constituted overwhelmingly by former MECS conferences—owned Emory University and the Lake Junaluska Assembly ("the summer capital of Southern Methodism"), developed a kind of axis between Junaluska and Atlanta, employed two executive secretaries, sponsored the Methodist portion of the *Protestant Hour,* established program committees covering the major areas of the church's life, and carried on promotional campaigns within the jurisdiction. Even this level of White consolidation and defense did not reassure some segregationists. The year after union, a Laymen's Organization for the Preservation of The Methodist Episcopal Church, South, established the Southern Methodist Church. It would be an unabashed segregationist church, a safe haven for those who shrank from contagion with the "alarming infidelity and apostasy found in the M.E. Church, North." The denomination reported thirty-one pastoral charges, forty-eight churches, and an active membership of 4,608 for 1960.

The Central Jurisdiction—as a de jure denominational policy of segregation, as a key polity structure, as a formalized practice of racial discrimination, and as a highly visible organizational self-display by a church seeking to exercise American public leadership—proved politically and symbolically problematic from the start, a sad chapter in the life of American Methodism. The church would spend the next quarter century debating this ecclesiastical apartheid and looking for a way to reorganize itself on a racially inclusive basis.

For Black Methodists, the creation of a racially segregated Central Jurisdiction was an especially humiliating disappointment but also and ironically a new resource for networking (see maps, S **26–27**; H **646nn66–67**). An artifact of White racism and a vehicle for Black empowerment, an expression of ethical failure and an instrument of social witness, an emblem of a divided community and a structure for Black fraternity and sorority, the Central Jurisdiction lived a far more complex existence than the other jurisdictions. It began the campaign to end its own life, virtually with its creation, and continued it as a quest for a fuller affirmation of Methodist inclusiveness throughout the 1950s and 1960s. Black congregations from the five geographical jurisdictions, with few exceptions, were herded into the all-Black Central Jurisdiction. New England, California, Bronx (New York), and Manhattan churches were not included. Upstate New York and Brooklyn churches, however, went into Central Jurisdiction. The jurisdiction extended even to Liberia in Africa! The Central Jurisdiction dissociated Black Methodists from their crosstown White counterparts. It created large and unwieldy conferences and forced leaders to cover great distances. Never did it garner the resources or claim the denominational attention that its proponents had envisioned. Not surprisingly, the new segregated Central Jurisdiction did not grow. The 310,000 Black members of 1939 dwindled to 250,000 by 1952. From 1940 through 1960, the five White jurisdictions grew 12.9 percent while the Black Central Jurisdiction grew only 0.3 percent!

The Central Jurisdiction did nevertheless connect Black Methodists across the entire church. It became a national enabling structure that provided for the identification, development, selection, and exercise of Black leaders. The Central Jurisdiction guaranteed Black representation on national boards and committees (denominational and Woman's). It produced national leadership for the church. It sustained in the *Central Christian Advocate* a denominational paper with a significant Black readership. It gave national attention to the denomination's Black colleges and universities (Bennett, Bethune-Cookman, Claflin, Clark, Dillard, Meharry Medical, Morristown, Paine, Philander Smith, Rust, Samuel Huston, and Wiley), relied on Gammon Theological Seminary for ministerial supply, and supported an array of institutions, including Gulfside, an assembly ground in Waveland, Mississippi.

For Black women the Central Jurisdiction's Woman's Society of Christian Service (WSCS) proved an effective vehicle for sorority, for witness, for action, and for collaboration. The Woman's Society, working with its White counterparts and through the Board of Missions, played particularly important roles, from the early 1940s, in promoting interracial concord, campaigning for African American staffing and representation in denominational missions, and protesting segregation. The Woman's Division held schools of Christian mission at both the conference and the jurisdictional levels. The Gulfside School became the school of mission for the Central Jurisdiction.

Bishops Robert Jones, Alexander Shaw, and Matthew Clair Sr. (retired) convened the 1940 session of the Central Jurisdiction. The delegates elected their first two bishops, William Hughes and Lorenzo King. Hughes, son of a "slave preacher" and secretary for "Negro Work" of the Board of Home Missions and Church Extension, died nineteen days after his consecration. King, born of slave parents in Mississippi and in his tenth year as pastor of St. Mark's in Harlem, had for the preceding ten years edited the *Southwestern Christian Advocate*, one of two Black MEC *Advocates*.

The Jurisdiction's *Central Christian Advocate* championed Black membership in The Methodist Church. Editor John Wesley Edward Bowen (1944–48) alerted Black Methodists to the challenges and opportunities in the church. Almost no issue of the paper failed to have editorial comment on racism in church and society. Bowen's education at Wesleyan and Howard Universities and years as a teacher and as a pastor gave him a steady determination to uphold Black rights, without bitterness, but also without fear. "There is no such thing as a Negro problem. . . . The real problem is the unwillingness of the white people of America to grant first class and complete citizenship to Negroes," he wrote on March 8, 1945. A year before the General and Jurisdictional Conferences of 1948, Bowen called attention (July 24, 1947) to the racial issues to be faced and urged "clear heads and sound reasoning. . . . Beware of depending too much on our feelings." His advocacy led the Central Jurisdiction to elect him bishop in 1948. Similarly, Prince Taylor, editor of the *Central Christian Advocate* in the 1950s, who applauded the Supreme Court's desegregation decision (S **1954**) in a forceful editorial, was elected to the episcopacy in 1956. Bishops Lorenzo King, Robert Brooks, and Scott Allen also edited the *Advocate* (H **647n77**).

In various ways and from the start, the Central Jurisdiction witnessed prophetically against the very racism that it emblemed and spoke out against the un-Christian and unjust character of the church's discrimination, segregation, and racial exclusivism. It did so within its own arena, through its paper, and through addresses to jurisdictional gatherings. It did so, as well, in prophetic words to the denomination. In 1951, on behalf of the Lexington Conference (the Jurisdiction's Midwestern conference), Charles F. Golden petitioned General Conference for a study commission to plan for integration, the elimination of racial discrimination, and "a racially inclusive policy at all organizational levels" (S **1951**). Golden, the first Black staff member of the Board of Missions, a member of the 1956 General Conference Commission to Study the Jurisdictional System, was elected to the episcopacy in 1960. Another important Central Jurisdiction statement came in 1962 with the issuing by its leadership of a manifesto for integration, *The Central Jurisdiction Speaks* (discussed below).

SEGREGATED METHODISM— SEGREGATED AMERICA

From the start, other churchwide organizations, embodying the church's racial diversity, witnessed against and lobbied aggressively to end segregation in the church—the unofficial Methodist Federation for Social Action (MFSA), the Methodist Student Movement (MSM), and the Woman's Division of the Board of Missions and its local affiliate, the Woman's Society of Christian Service (WSCS).

The Woman's Division led the church in its proactive struggle toward inclusiveness. It did so by its staffing policy, hiring its first Black secretary in the New York City office, Charlotte R. French, in 1941, and in 1948 electing its first Black senior staff person, Theressa Hoover (S **1973**; H **392, 400**). Also in 1941 the division adopted a policy of holding its meetings only in places where all members of its group could be entertained without any form of racial discrimination. WSCS conference and jurisdictional leaders made plans to bring together leaders of the then racially segregated annual conferences in a series of meetings and retreats. The Division's Department of Christian Social Relations and Local Church Activities (CSR/LCA) "mobilized Methodist women of all ethnic identities into one of the most sustained campaigns against racism ever witnessed in America" (H **392, 647n82–84**).

The Woman's Division memorialized the 1944 General Conference asking for a policy forbidding segregation at national meetings. The General Conference did not support the initiative, instead making Liberia a part of the Central Jurisdiction, a segregated relationship persisting for twenty years. In

1947 a Woman's Division National Seminar recommended drafting a charter of racial policies and gathering data on national, state, and local laws relating to race and color. The result, a 750-page 1951 book detailing state laws, was written by a Black lesbian feminist, Pauli Murray, whose lifetime activism began with an unsuccessful attempt to desegregate the University of North Carolina, Chapel Hill, in 1939. Her *States' Laws on Race and Color* influenced the 1954 US Supreme Court in its landmark desegregation decision *Brown v. Board of Education*. In 1952, the Woman's Division, continuing its commitment to eliminate institutional racism, at its annual meeting unanimously adopted a landmark "Charter of Racial Policies" (S **1952**). Two years later, the Woman's Division asked annual conferences to ratify the charter and to commit to its implementation. The charter was revised in 1962 and 1978. The Woman's Division also began to desegregate its schools and institutes, hospitals, and homes, and hired its first Black program staff.

Criticism of the church's institutionalized segregation came from various quarters and in various forums and on every level. Students and faculty at Methodist colleges, universities, and theological seminaries wrestled with the race issues (frequently, especially in the South, prodding reluctant administrations and trustees). Advocacy came also from the top. In November 1963, the Methodist Council of Bishops issued a pastoral statement insisting, "The Methodist Church must build and demonstrate within its own organization and program a fellowship without racial barriers [and] . . . seek to change those community patterns in which racial segregation appears, including education, housing, voting, employment and the use of public facilities" (H **393–94, 647nn86–87**). Similarly, the women of the new Evangelical United Brethren Church deplored segregation and applauded the Supreme Court's actions (S **1955**).

Methodists figured prominently in events and organizational initiatives both for and against integration (detailed H **394–96**). Among the former: Congress of Racial Equality founders James Farmer and George Houser; Branch Rickey, Brooklyn Dodger manager; all-star Jackie Robinson; sit-in leader and Vanderbilt student James Lawson and supportive dean Robert Nelson and eleven faculty; the eighty Atlanta signers of a 1957 "Ministers' Manifesto"; the twenty-eight Mississippi clergy who denounced segregation (S **1963a**); and Bishops James Mathews (White) and Charles Golden (Black) turned away from Gallaway Memorial on Easter 1964. Among the foes of integration: the White Citizen's Council–dominated official board of Galloway; Alabama governor George Wallace; and the Association of Methodist Ministers and Laymen to Preserve Established Racial Customs—a Klan-like structure operative in a number of southern conferences used to harass ministers who spoke out (H **647nn88–93**). Twelve people died in Alabama in civil rights slayings in Wallace's first term between 1963 and 1966. During at least one of the protests, Bishop Kenneth Goodson was in the governor's office with Wallace, seeking to be a moderating spirit. Bishops Nolan Harmon and Paul Hardin were among those chastised by Martin Luther King Jr. in the *Letter from Birmingham Jail.*

PROGRESS TOWARD INTEGRATION

Faced with resistance, Methodism made slow progress toward a policy and practice of fuller Christian community, though each successive General Conference received increased numbers of petitions from individual churches and conferences on the race issue. The church expressed a commitment to "the ultimate elimination of racial discrimination in The Methodist Church" in 1944. It redrew some western boundaries in 1948 to make easier the voluntary transfer of Black churches out. It eased such transfers in 1952, establishing a constitutional principle in 1956 (Amendment IX) of voluntary transfer of entire conferences or parts of conferences as well as congregations, embroiling itself in a major debate over elimination of the Central Jurisdiction, but failing to agree on a deadline.

The 1956 and 1960 General Conferences created committees to study ways of eliminating the Central Jurisdiction and in 1960 established a quadrennial program on race to create a climate for reconciliation. Alarmed that Black churches would be dropped cold into segregated systems and contexts and concerned that the process continued to honor a go-slow White timetable, Black leaders in 1960 created a broadly representative study process, involving some two hundred women, youth, pastors, district superintendents, educators, agency personnel, and other leaders, and overseen by a jurisdictional Committee of Five to frame Black expectations of merger. The 1962 manifesto, *The Central Jurisdiction Speaks,* insisted that dissolution of the Central Jurisdiction "must be sought by The Methodist Church as a whole within a framework of over-all planning, procedures, programs and Christian understanding designed to promote in demonstrable and concrete ways

237

ultimate achievement of an inclusive Methodist Church." Central Jurisdiction churches and pastors should be transferred so as to empower, involve, and engage them in their new districts and conferences, not isolated, and certainly not dumped into contexts where colleges, homes, cabinets, and other institutions remained segregated. Inclusiveness meant real change on the part of White Methodism, sensitivity to Black interests, and efforts to deal with the disparities in salaries, facilities (parsonages), pensions, and training programs (H **648nn93–94**).

White bishops in the South issued their own pastoral letter aimed at disarming fears of forced integration. "The principle of regional autonomy for which we from the first contended has been preserved," they reassured their constituents. The 1964 Pittsburgh General Conference convened in a year of extraordinary turmoil—bishops having been just refused entrance to Galloway, the NCC and other civil rights organizations then gearing up for a southern civil disobedience summer, the nation coming to terms with a presidential assassination, a church in Birmingham having been bombed, M. L. King Jr. and others having challenged Americans at the March on Washington, and Mississippi Methodists having spoken out. The Methodist Student Movement and Methodists for Church Renewal brought crisis into the hall with demonstrations demanding that the church desegregate. Following lengthy debate, the conference adopted a "Charter of Racial Policies" promising equal access to church facilities and programs and a voluntary plan to transfer all Black conferences into regional White jurisdictions and then merge Black and White annual conferences. Though rejecting a mandatory deadline to end the Central Jurisdiction, it resolved with respect to projected unity with The EUBC that "no racial structure[s] be carried over into the Constitution of the new United Church." Further, General Conference voted that clergy appointments should be made "without regard to race and color," and it lodged in the *Discipline* a resolution supporting principled civil disobedience, then a flash point of controversy across the South (H **648nn95–96**).

That June the Central Jurisdiction realigned its seventeen remaining conferences into sixteen so that Black conference lines did not cross those of the five regional jurisdictions. That summer two Black conferences merged with their White or largely White counterparts—Delaware in the Northeastern Jurisdiction and Lexington in the South Central Jurisdiction. The previous all-White Philadelphia Conference received eighteen churches; New Jersey Conference, twenty-three; West Virginia Conference, twenty-five; and Baltimore Conference, more than two hundred. That summer the first Black bishops—Prince Taylor in New Jersey and James Thomas in Iowa—were assigned to predominantly White episcopal areas. By year's end (1964) four Black conferences in the Northeastern and North Central Jurisdictions merged with White counterparts, leaving thirteen more to go, all in the South. The Central Jurisdiction met last in a special session in 1967, elected L. Scott Allen, implored the prospective United Methodist Church to make its cabinets, committees, and agencies inclusive, and adopted measures for dissolution of the remaining conferences. The final transfers and mergers were completed by 1973. Some of the jurisdiction's energy and vision live on in Black Methodists for Church Renewal, a caucus expression to jurisdictional life, as we shall see in the next chapter (H **648nn97–98**).

UNITING METHODIST WOMEN

Anticipating reunification, the six presidents of the three uniting denominations' home and foreign mission organizations called a series of planning meetings, including a retreat in Cincinnati in December 1938, attended by forty, and a larger gathering in Chicago. By the time the Uniting Conference of 1939 appointed a Joint Committee on Missions and Church Extension, the women who constituted the Woman's Section already "knew and respected and loved one another." The 1940 General Conference approved the proposed plans without a dissenting vote. Of the seventy-three women delegates to this General Conference, thirty had served on the Joint Committee on Missions. The Board of Missions and Church Extension of The Methodist Church organized in July 1940 with four divisions, one of which was the Woman's Division of Christian Service, with a membership of nearly two million. Its official (monthly) magazine, the *Methodist Woman,* united the heritages of at least four women's missionary magazines (H **648nn102–4**). The organization most closely resembled that of the Woman's Missionary Council (MECS) in several respects, notably in unifying foreign and home missionary work in one organization. Although separately incorporated, the division functioned within and in a "coordinate administrative role" of the general board. And the division possessed a distinctive Department of Christian Social Relations and Local Church Activities, one of its three departments, along with Foreign and Home Missions. Each had an executive secretary who worked in a collegial relationship with the other two executive secretaries to recommend goals, initiate program ideals, draft resolutions, plan conferences, and then coordinate and implement the programs set by the approximately fifty elected officers. The position of chair of the Woman's Division rotated on an annual basis among the executive secretaries. Louise Oldshue became the first chairperson of the Christian Social Relations department and Thelma Stevens, its executive secretary. Stevens would give distinguished leadership to this department for the next twenty-eight years (S **1972d**; H **648n105**).

Nearly every local Methodist church had one or two women's missionary groups: a Woman's Society of Christian Service for full-time homemakers and a Wesleyan Service Guild (with evening meetings) for employed women. Summer training schools equipped some ten thousand leaders to return to their churches to teach a half million members on the missional and biblical themes for the year. Thus the Woman's Division was both a grassroots and a national organization (H **648nn106–7**).

Black women first joined the professional staff of the Woman's Division as field workers assigned to the Central Jurisdiction, among them Theressa Hoover from 1948through 1958. In 1958 she became a member of the staff of Christian Social Relations. In 1965 she was named assistant general secretary and, in 1968, associate general secretary (chief executive officer) of the Women's Division of the GBGM (S **1973**; H **400** for details on others).

In 1964, the Methodist Board of Missions reorganized and transferred from the Woman's Division the work of its home and foreign mission departments to other divisions of the board. Mrs. Ann Porter Brown, the general secretary of the Woman's Division, became the first general secretary of the new unified board. This experience of integration was not, however, "as debilitating as that of women in other denominations" because organized Methodist women retained their "financial sovereignty—an essential ingredient of power and autonomy."

In the unification of The Evangelical Church and the Church of the United Brethren in Christ in 1946, the separate women's organizations of the two denominations became the Women's Society of World Service, governed at the national level by a twelve-member Women's Council, the model of The Evangelical Church. (The United Brethren women's mission organization had been separately incorporated.) By 1946, however, both United Brethren and Evangelical women had developed unified women's organizations for foreign and home missions, and both were within a general denominational board.

In the 1968 unification of The Evangelical United Brethren Church (EUBC) with The Methodist Church to form The United Methodist Church, Methodist and EUBC women merged their work for mission "with no major upheavals." Auxiliaries of this Women's Division were called the Women's Society of Christian Service and the Wesleyan Service Guild. When the Board of Missions became the Board of Global Ministries in 1972, women were able both to protect the independence of their work and to renew their grassroots organization of women for mission by creating United Methodist Women (UMW). This new structure ended the separation of women into two groups (WSCS and WSG) and encouraged active participation and leadership of women of color and of younger women. UMW would have three program areas: Christian Personhood, Christian Social Relations, and Christian Global Concerns.

The new organization for women in mission was ratified by the General Conference of 1972 and implemented at the local level by the end of 1973. In 1968, the Division successfully petitioned the Uniting Conference to create a Study Commission on the Participation of Women in The United Methodist Church. While the study commission proceeded with its work, the Women's Division created its own Ad Hoc Committee on Churchwomen's Liberation. In 1972, this committee "gave primary support" to the first conference held at the Grailville center in Ohio, "Women's Consciousness and Theology." It also played a significant role in working for the establishment of the Commission on the Status and Role of Women (COSROW) by the 1972 General Conference and in contributing to the creation of United Methodist Women (H **648n109**).

FULL CLERGY RIGHTS FOR WOMEN

Both the Methodist union of 1939 and The EUBC union of 1946 represented clergy-rights setbacks for women. The Methodists forced MPC clergywomen to yield their full clergy rights. And The EUBC made no provision to continue ordinations of women, a UBC practice and policy for a half century (since 1889). By the narrow margin of 384 to 371, the Methodist Uniting Conference defeated full conference membership for female clergy (H **648n110**). The campaign did not abate. Women continued to attend seminary. The UBC seminary had granted BD degrees to sixteen women in the decade before the 1946 union. And among Methodists, women not only attended but also occupied seminary faculty posts—Mildred Moody Eakin (at Drew, 1932–54) and Georgia Harkness (at Garrett, 1939–50 and later at Pacific School of Religion, 1950–61).

For successive General Conferences—1944, 1948, and 1952—the Methodist Woman's Division of Christian Service petitioned conference delegates to grant full clergy rights to women, as had women in The MECS since 1926 and in The MEC since 1928. The MC General Conference, meeting in 1956 in Minneapolis, received more than two thousand petitions asking for full clergy rights for women. The Committee on the Ministry brought in a compromise recommendation (by forty to thirty-two in the committee) granting full clergy rights to women but stipulating that "only unmarried women and widows may apply." A minority report would have retained the previous rules, granting women local ordination but not conference membership. The floor debate indicated the primary issue remained whether the appointment of a woman minister would be unacceptable to some churches. Motions permitting a woman to be located when she could not be placed and giving the annual conferences the right to decide the extent to which they would implement the legislation both failed. The minority report lost by a vote of 425 to 310, and by a vote of 389 to 297 the conference removed the majority report provision that married women could not apply. "Then by an overwhelming show of hands," the delegates passed the historic motion putting into the Methodist *Discipline* the following simple, but momentous words: "Women are included in all the provisions of the Discipline referring to the ministry." Alluding to this action and a compromise worked out earlier to remove obstacles in the way of ending the Central Jurisdiction, Dr. Georgia Harkness commented, "I think maybe we've had a miracle twice this week." That same evening, May 4, the General Conference saluted Harkness for the "valiant fight" she had waged for this cause throughout the years and recognized "the peculiar satisfaction" she must feel (H **649nn112–14**; H **403** on Harkness).

Although Georgia Harkness had been ordained elder in the Troy (New York–Vermont) Annual Conference, she did not apply for annual conference membership in 1956 (see H **403** on her roles as leader, teacher, theologian; and S **1924b**, S **1947** and particulars of Maud Keister Jensen and names of others admitted on trial).

In The Evangelical United Brethren Church, as in the case of The Methodist Church, women's ordination was sacrificed for unity. Although the status of those already ordained was not impaired, no provision was made for the licensing and ordination of women in the new church. A number of annual conferences did ordain women between the years 1946 and 1968, despite pre-union agreements not to do so, "at least twenty-three" to elder's orders. Some served rural churches; others collaborated as part of a clergy couple. In terms of official church policy, however, the ordination of women would have to wait until the 1968 union that formed The United Methodist Church (H **649nn117–18**).

YOUTH MINISTRIES

Following unification, in 1941, the old Epworth League became the Methodist Youth Fellowship (MYF), its clientele youth of high school age. The local church program centered on Christian nurture, recreation, projects, and outreach through morning Sunday school classes and Sunday evening social meetings. Organization and program extended beyond the local church to subdistricts, districts, annual conferences, and jurisdictions, including workshops, camps, conferences, and special events. A national conference of the fellowship brought together annually presidents of conference MYF organizations to discuss the youth program, its place in the church, and current issues of vital importance to MYF, the first of which was held on the campus of Baker University in Baldwin, Kansas, in September 1941, a gathering of future teachers, civil rights leaders, peace activists, missionaries, pastors, lay leaders, and a bishop (S **1942b**). In the 1940s and 1950s when interracial meetings were virtually unknown, especially in the South, MYFers often met together across racial lines. A similar program in The EUBC was known as Christian Endeavor (H **649nn112–20**).

Anticipating union of the separate Methodisms within two years, college and university students of each church met in a National Methodist Youth Conference (1937) in St. Louis, Missouri, and created a single student confederation to provide for student program needs—the Methodist Student Movement (MSM). With elected student leadership and sustained by campus ministry staff from the three churches, the innovative organization launched a new era in Methodist campus ministry. Upon unification in 1939, the new Board of Education established a Department of Student Work whose staff cooperatively helped direct and expand the work of the MSM. Some four hundred "preaching centers" served state, independent, and church-related campuses through near-campus churches, Wesley Foundations, and college chaplaincies. In addition to worship and study, local MSM units carried out numerous social service projects and mission programs. An MSM publication for university students, *Motive* magazine, launched in the fall of 1940, promoted theological engagement with the academy. *Motive* stimulated awareness of national and international concerns; advocated world peace and nuclear disarmament; pursued racial, social, gender, and sexual justice; and featured the arts to empower the imagination in the life of the church (H **649n121**). Dr. Martin Luther King Jr. headed the list of speakers for the eighth quadrennial conference of the MSM in the tumultuous year of 1964. By 1966 the MSM included 198 accredited Wesley Foundations at state and independent universities and 646 other campus ministry programs at Methodist-related colleges and universities.

Aggressive advocacy of antiwar positions, civil rights, and rights for homosexuals during the student revolution of the 1960s and 1970s led some in the church to lose confidence in the campus ministry. Students demanded freedom from a conservative church hierarchy. Campus ministers and national staff sought new patterns of ministry, including an ecumenically based campus ministry. United Ministries in Higher Education (UMHE) emerged in the mid-1960s, including students and staff from seven mainline churches. On the eve of The MC's union with The EUBC, in 1966, the Methodist Board of Education and the Methodist Association of College and University Ministers closed down the thirty-year ministry of the MSM and joined this ecumenical body. Leaders of several denominational student organizations formed the University Christian Movement (UCM) that same year, creating an independent, student-led Christian movement. But the high hopes that had surrounded the creation of the UCM were dissipated by the assassinations of Martin Luther King Jr. and Robert Kennedy in 1968, the escalation of the Vietnam War, and the use of police and military force against student protesters. By 1969 the UCM council opted to dissolve the movement. "The necessary creative balance between the prophetic and the pastoral had by the close of the decade been lost," concluded the movement's most recent interpreter, Robert Monk. No longer trusting its campus ministries to nurture the church's youth and train future leaders, lay and clergy, the church cut funding or otherwise neglected the campuses. The popular image of student movements and campus ministry remained under a cloud through the 1970s and beyond. A slow process of renewal began in the mid-1980s. The General Board of Higher Education and Ministry (GBHEM) again recruited national campus ministry staff and refreshed budget lines. The first national Methodist student conference since 1964 convened in 1987, providing once again opportunities for denominational fellowship and programming on a national scale. The 1992 General Conference established "Mission at the Center: A Campus Ministry Special Program" to provide grants for distinctive ministries among students. By 1997 there were 699 campus ministers and chaplains related in some way to The UMC (H **649nn122–23**).

Even as it lost trust in campus ministry, the church found a place for youth in conference governance. At the tumultuous 1970 General Conference, the renewal coalition that won gains for Black members and women included a large delegation of the church's young people who draped the convention hall with enormous signs proclaiming "YOUTH NOW." At the end of the conference young people won ten seats as nonvoting delegates, succeeded in getting the United Methodist Council on Youth Ministries out from under the Board of Education, gained self-determination in the administration of their substantial Youth Service Fund, and most important of all, won rights for youth representation on boards and agencies and in annual conferences. Conferences, for instance, gained two young people under the age of twenty-five from each district.

THE EVANGELICAL UNITED BRETHREN CHURCH

Evangelicals and United Brethren had, like their Methodist cousins, traveled a long road to the 1946 union, or perhaps we should say several roads (H **649n125**). The United Brethren created a Commission on Church Union in 1901 and began serious unity explorations with kindred churches. In 1903, the UBC entered into conversations with the Methodist Protestant and Congregational churches that produced name, constitution, and creed for a new church. The UBC bishops counseled against approval and despite the 1917 UBC General Conference concurring nevertheless committed "to fraternize with other Christian bodies and co-operate with them in the larger work of the Kingdom." In the 1920s, the UBC responded to an overture from the Reformed Church, one extended to the Evangelical Synod of North America as well to the Evangelicals (who declined). By 1929, negotiations produced a "Plan of Union" for a United Church of America. The 1929 UBC General Conference responded favorably, a stance not echoed by the very church that had concocted the plan, the Reformed Church.

By this point, the Evangelicals had healed an east-west division that went back to 1891. The western, Indianapolis-based Evangelical Association had favored the German language, greater authority for bishops, clergy-only governing conferences, and a conservative theological stance. The eastern, Philadelphia-based United Evangelical Church preferred a more collegial episcopacy, lay representation in governing conferences, and openness to biblical criticism and new theological developments. Both churches participated in early twentieth-century ecumenical ventures, including the Federal Council of Churches. By 1911, conversations to heal their own schism began and unity came in 1922 under a new name, the Evangelical Church. A small group of dissidents withdrew and formed an independent denomination, the Evangelical Congregational Church, a continuing denomination with a theological seminary in Myerstown, Pennsylvania.

In 1926, the reunited EC began union conversations with its historic partner, the United Brethren Church. The courtship between such nonidentical twins, so alike but so different, was predictably bumpy. The United Brethren, with roots in the free church heritage of the Mennonites and the mild Calvinism of western Germany, had responded to the democratic ethos of the young American republic and developed a highly participatory polity. Though the UBC continued work among German-speaking people, the use of English soon became the UBC norm. The EC, fueled by a steady influx of German immigrants, maintained a strong relationship with the fatherland and its ways. The German language remained strong among Evangelicals until the early decades of the twentieth century. The EC combined features from Episcopal Methodism with similar principles from the fatherland to give its function and structure a hierarchical and authoritarian flavor. The Evangelical Church did not welcome women delegates into its governing conferences or open its seminaries or its pulpits to women throughout its whole existence. Indeed, when unity came in 1946 with the United Brethren, the EC insisted that UBC women clergy, who had won that right almost sixty years earlier (1889), give up that right (not fully restored until union with the Methodists in 1968).

Despite the differences, the two churches had not stopped "keeping company," doing so with the various branches of Methodism. By 1934, the Evangelicals and United Brethren formed a joint commission on church union and readied a plan of union by 1941. The Plan of Union was favored by the Evangelical General Conference the following year (1942). In 1946, after the United Brethren General Conference approved the plan, the two churches—250,000 Evangelicals and 450,000 United Brethren—now both clearly identified as "churches," consummated a long-anticipated, but often despaired, union. Bishops of the uniting churches, John Stamm (EC) and Arthur Clippinger (UB), celebrated the new church as a "complete union," all conferences and congregations committing to "go forward together" (S **1947a**; H **649n127**).

The formula for union, except perhaps with regard to women in ministry, was to conjoin names, practices, and institutions of the two churches. So the denominational name. So also the *Evangelical Messenger* merged with the UBC's *Religious Telescope* to become the new church's *Telescope-Messenger*. Publishing enterprises continued initially in Harrisburg and Dayton, eventually to be focused in the latter. Three theological schools continued, the UB's in Dayton and EA's in Naperville and Reading (the last affiliated with Albright College). Between 1952 and 1954, the Dayton and Reading schools merged, favored the UBC site, and took the name "United." The latter continued there after The EUBC-Methodist merger and became an important caretaker of The EUBC heritage. Evangelical, however, would merge with the Methodists' Garrett, and the two names would be conjoined (H **649n128**).

In the first *Discipline* the two different conceptions of church membership coexisted in rituals for infant baptism and child dedication. The new church did the same with the UBC *Confession of Faith* and the EC *Articles of Faith*, publishing them side by side. As we have seen, both were originally German statements, the former reflecting Otterbein's Pietist Calvinism rooted in the Heidelberg Catechism, the latter echoing Albright's appreciation for Wesleyan discipline and holiness doctrine as captured by the creed written by George Miller (S **38–41**; H **650n129**). Miller had adapted the Methodist-Anglican Articles of Religion. He had also annexed "The Doctrine of Entire Sanctification and Christian Perfection," his own six-page digest of Wesleyan theology, the gist of which would constitute a particularly important contribution to United Methodist "Doctrinal Standards," as Article XI

247

of the *Confession of Faith of the Evangelical United Brethren Church*. This new confession the 1958 EUBC General Conference entrusted to the Board of Bishops and adopted in 1962. The bishops reduced what had been twelve paragraphs to three in Article XI—Sanctification and Christian Perfection. And as Steven O'Malley shows, the bishops brought over the Evangelical Methodist-derived *Articles'* influence in the *Confession's* treatment of the Trinity, original sin, Last Judgment, the sacraments, property, and government. Much of the *Confession,* O'Malley argues, reflects the UBC's Reformed Pietism and the Otterbein conception of the *ordo* (or *via*) *salutis,* especially in articles on reconciliation, justification, regeneration, adoption, sanctification, and good works, and in the conception of the work of Christ and the Holy Spirit (H **650n130**).

WORSHIP: EUBC AND METHODIST

Northern Methodists (MEC) initiated the first major revisions of the ritual in 1932. Since abandoning Wesley's *Sunday Service* in 1792, The MEC rite had omitted the so-called Ante-Communion, began with the offertory sentences, and thereby appended the abbreviated Communion rite to a preaching service. The 1932 revision combined word and sacrament in a unified rite, the instructions explicitly asserting that the new Communion order was "to take place of the regular order of morning worship." However, a radically *memorialist* rewriting of the inherited Prayer of Humble Access replaced the traditional "eat the flesh of thy dear Son and drink his blood" with invitation to "partake of these *memorials* of thy Son Jesus Christ." Similarly, the Eucharistic Prayer substituted "*partakers of the divine nature* through Him" for "*partakers of his most blessed body and blood,*" language retained in The MECS rite, which remained essentially that of 1792. Mainstreamed in the new common hymnal of 1935, this revised rite marked the low point of eucharistic realism in American Methodism after Wesley. And not a single eucharistic hymn remained in the new hymnal. With a few tweakings at reunion of the three Methodisms in 1939–40, this liturgy remained in place until 1964. At reunion in 1939, both northern and southern services appeared in *The Methodist Hymnal,* the long northern service more traditional liturgically and the brief southern service more traditional theologically (H **650nn132–33**).

Nolan Harmon's 1926 *Rites and Ritual of Episcopal Methodism,* a revived interest in the Wesleys, ecumenical currents, and the liturgical revival stimulated Methodist scholarship on worship and the sacraments in both Britain and America. Two liturgical caucuses encouraged liturgical reform among the Methodists. The Methodist Sacramental Fellowship (MSF) was founded in 1935 by *British* Methodists influenced by the recovery of weekly Communion in the Church of England and the wider ecumenical movement. American Methodists founded The Order of Saint Luke (OSL), a religious order dedicated to sacramental and liturgical renewal, in 1946. Both aimed to reaffirm the *catholic* faith based upon the apostolic testimony of Holy Scripture, witnessed to in the Nicene Creed, and professed by the church through the ages. Both sought to restore to modern Methodism the sacramental worship of the universal church and in particular the centrality of the Eucharist, as set forth in the lifelong teaching and practice of the Wesleys. Both groups began publishing ministries designed to put into the hands of seminarians, pastors, and layfolk liturgical works that had theological, historical, ecumenical, and practical integrity.

British Methodists published a new *Book of Services* in 1936. A decade later (1945) America Methodism published its first *Book of Worship* since 1792. The latter offered no new Communion liturgies but did feature the Christian Year, with its many teaching and worship implications. By 1960, churches increasingly celebrated Advent, kept Lent, and observed Pentecost, appreciating the ties with historic Christianity. A few Methodist churches in the 1950s began to use Communion tablecloths and pulpit and lectern hangings of appropriate color for the various seasons of the Christian Year. A second American *Book of Worship* was authorized and published in 1965. Reflecting neoorthodox and Wesleyan insistence on human rebellion and sin and the necessity of God's grace, the liturgies reclaimed penitential piety, the Psalter with its phenomenology of the human condition, the Christian Year dramatizing God's salvific work, and a one-year lectionary to walk the church through both Testaments. The revised full Communion rite approximated that of Wesley's *Sunday Service,* but with a somewhat altered pattern. Four Wesleyan eucharistic hymns found their way back into the new hymnal. A compromise on eucharistic theology retained the ambiguous "so to partake of this *sacrament* of thy Son Jesus Christ" in the Prayer of Humble Access (H **650n135**). Three services from Wesley concluded the book. The new

249

liturgies, mainstreamed in the new *Hymnal* published in 1966, were stronger theologically and sacramentally than the preceding ones.

The first order of worship for the United Brethren Church—complete with organ prelude and postlude, responsive reading, Apostles' Creed, and Gloria Patri—appeared in the *Sanctuary Hymnal* of 1914 and followed Methodist practice. A minor revision of the presider's "outline liturgy" for Communion occurred in 1925, a short introduction added before each Scripture passage. Inexplicably the invitation to the table was removed. The prayer at the table was now specifically called a "consecratory prayer," but no text was given. The UBC hymnals lacked a Communion liturgy but ten years later (1935) a new hymnal offered two. The first order was a full and formal service "based in general on the Communion in the *Book of Common Prayer* [of the Episcopal Church], revised in accordance with the usage of non-liturgical churches and adapted to meet the need of our own Communion." The compilers believed that the Lord's Supper "constitutes the loftiest service in our common worship . . . is truly a festival of thanksgiving and the occasion for penitential confession and consecration." A curious mix of Methodist prayers, gospel hymns, evangelical poetry, and responsive readings, the liturgy instructed ministers at the table to pray in Methodist memorialist fashion, "Hear us, O merciful Father, . . . grant that we, receiving this bread and wine in remembrance of his passion, may also be *partakers of the divine nature* through Jesus Christ our Lord, and so partake of these *memorials* of thy Son." The revisers shockingly omitted the sermon: "Nothing must be allowed to take the place of the supreme reality. It is believed that the Sacrament itself should be the central act of worship when we meet to remember him" (H **650nn136–38**).

Among Evangelicals, the first ever scripted order of worship, patterned after the 1914 UBC order as described above, appeared in the hymnal copyrighted in 1921. The hymnal was adopted by the United Evangelical Church in 1922, when the two groups merged. The Methodist-based full-text Communion liturgy was slightly revised (for example, the confession) in 1923 and regularly included in the denomination's official hymnals as well as the *Book of Discipline*. This rite served the church until union with the UBC in 1946.

Both the Evangelical and UBC liturgies and hymnals continued to be used in the Evangelical United Brethren Church from 1946 until 1957, when a new hymnal with Communion liturgies and a new presider's *Book of Ritual* (1959) were published. The orders of worship for non-Communion Sundays followed the more or less common Evangelical and United Brethren pattern with the fullest order "enriched" with processional and recessional hymns and choral responses throughout the service. The liturgy for Communion, though more liturgical in style, was decidedly memorialist in content. Communicants approached the table with this prayer: "Grant, therefore, gracious Lord, that we may come with confidence to the Throne of Grace; that Christ may dwell in our hearts through faith, . . . that we may be filled unto all the fullness of God." A 1952 article in The EUBC *Telescope-Messenger* might well have spoken for most Methodists as well (H **650n140**):

> [The Holy Communion] is a sacrament, an outward and visible ceremony that symbolizes inward and spiritual experience, a means through which divine grace is imparted to the believer. This means that the essence of the Lord's Supper is to be found not in its physical elements but in the mind and heart of those who participate.

*****

Church buildings of the peacetime economy of the late 1940s and after did not replicate plans of earlier periods. Large plants, for growing suburban churches, served as "seven-day-a-week-churches" requiring large parking lots. A divided chancel with both pulpit and lectern and a modest altar table against the back wall honored Conover's dictates. Generous space was provided for Christian education, staff offices, and a fellowship hall as well. Two widely different exterior styles dominated through the 1960s—red brick, white-pillared, tall-spired Colonial Revival and clean-lined, natural-finished, A-frame Modern. The pacesetter A-frame pattern of the late 1950s and 1960s sported a high roofline. The emotive power of roofs of great height frequently combined with skylights or clerestory windows to create dramatic interior light effects, often focused on the altar or pulpit. Typically the chancel remained divided though wider. The details were not Gothic, yet something of its feeling was preserved. Three of the earliest of these were featured in a photo essay in the denomination's *Together* magazine in 1958—Gretna MC in Gretna, Louisiana; Northside MC in Greenville, South Carolina; and Linwood MC in Linwood, Pennsylvania—and their numbers multiplied throughout the 1960s (H **650n144**). Another favored form for new churches became a fan-shaped plan with the congregation spread 180 degrees around table and pulpit. It was obvious that Gothic would not work for a fan-shaped church, so modern architecture won an easy victory.

A few experiments—moving the altar away from the "east" wall and celebrating Communion from behind it—signaled openness to new liturgical currents. Liturgical historian James F. White led the changes in Methodist practice and theology. His 1966 essay "Church Architecture and Church Renewal" was the first of many essays and books that contributed mightily to the field of modern church architecture (H **650n146**). Articles in popular Methodist publications in the 1960s highlighted the new developments.

A growing appreciation of symbolic representations of interaction with the divine led to new arrangements of liturgical spaces and liturgical centers. Instead of isolating the table (or altar) against the wall and a chancel-length distance away, it was placed in the midst of worshippers. Pulpit, lectern, table, and font were grouped to accent the unity of book, meal, and bath. (By the 1980s and 1990s, a new interest in the process of Christian initiation led in places to baptism by immersion or at least bigger bowls, fonts, or wading pools.) The directions of these architectural-liturgical initiatives were later summarized by James White and Susan White in their 1988 *Church Architecture: Building and Renovating for Christian Worship*: give primacy to the worshipping assembly and its functions, create one-room churches and move tables into the midst of the congregation, presume the celebrant will face the people, eliminate chancel/nave plans, reduce the number of liturgical centers, and minimize distinctions between clergy and laity. New hymnals and service books guided the trajectory: stress on the sacraments as communion with God, the lectionary as a guide to the full Bible, the church year as a way to make time meaningful, and scriptural preaching as God's word made present. In all these architectural reforms, the key word was *participation*. This latter principle had been introduced by the Second Vatican Council (1963) and reinforced by guidelines adopted by the US Roman Catholic Bishops' Committee on the Liturgy in 1978, *Environment and Art in Catholic Worship*. Written largely by the late Robert Hovda, a former Methodist who became a Catholic priest, it is a classic statement. Among "the symbols with which the liturgy deals, none is more important," it insists, than the "assembly of believers itself."

By the final decades of the century, church development moved in a different direction inspired by the megachurches of the church-growth movement. In the early years of the new millennium, The UMC tallied the second-largest percentage of denominational megachurches (9 percent) after the 20 percent of the Southern Baptists (H **651n152**). Church of the Resurrection in Leawood, Kansas, is one of the best-known United Methodist megachurches. The movement, inspired in part by Willow Creek Community Church (near Chicago), built seeker-friendly facilities resembling malls and corporate headquarters and intended not to look churchly. Anglo-Catholic liturgy, seen as a barrier to evangelizing the seeker and unchurched, was presented in common, everyday language using multisensory media. Theater seating, the latest audiovisual technology, huge projection screens, upbeat praise songs typically based on phrases in Scripture, scripted timing and transitions, charismatic or teaching sermons in some places minimized congregational worship participation. These seven-day-a-week churches engage and involve participation in other ways, such as through cell groups, affinity groups, and mission teams.

COLD AND KOREAN WARS

In the post–World War II era, the new threat of Soviet Russia as a world power and the fears engendered by communist domination of neighboring states—in eastern Europe and in Asia (especially Korea)—magnified old fears of communism and gave rise to new ones. Many Methodists, strongly committed to the UN and international means of dealing with conflict, viewed the Korean War with ambivalence. In November 1950, the Methodist Commission on World Peace urged restraint. Later that month, the Council of Bishops promised prayer for leaders of the United States and the nation's armed forces. A year later, 1951, the bishops expressed support for a negotiated settlement and urged that "every honorable concession shall be made to achieve the desired goals." Their statement continued, "We further urge that the ultimate goal of our peace-making and the stated policy of the United Nations be to secure the economic rehabilitation of an independent and united Korea." The Episcopal Address to the 1952 General Conference went further toward an endorsement of the war: "The issue of peace or war rests largely upon the people of the US who have chosen to defend the Republic of Korea through the United Nations, from the aggression of a Communist invasion." By 1952, widespread sentiment surfaced in The Methodist Church, fostered in part by the Commission on World Peace, for a new quadrennial emphasis on peace. More memorials to that year's General Conference concerned the crusade than any other issue. General Conference offered no endorsement of the war. Instead, it exhorted the COB to lead the church in peacemaking and in a new Crusade for World Order that would strengthen the UN's effectiveness as an "instrument of peace" (H **651n155**).

The US–UN action in Korea never received clear official support from The Methodist Church as it had from both the World and National Council of Churches. Instead, the church granted a tacit approval. Stronger support, as from the churches generally, went for effective US participation in the humanitarian programs of the UN. Evangelical, United Brethren, and Methodist agencies joined with many other groups in asking Congress to increase appropriations to UNICEF, the United Nations Children's Fund. Thousands of churches across the country organized their children to engage in door-to-door trick or treat for UNICEF collections, thus raising many millions of dollars to aid children and mothers in other lands. United Nations officials often commented that the churches were the largest group engaged in these supportive activities.

SOCIAL ACTIVISM AND ANOTHER "RED SCARE"

The Korean conflict, Chinese participation, fears over Russian nuclear threats, and disclosure of Communist spying intensified hysteria over collusion and fellow traveling. The FBI labeled two Methodist groups—the MFSS (after 1948, the Methodist Federation for Social *Action*, MFSA) and the Methodist Epworth League—as "tools" of the Communist Party. (The FBI discovered infiltration and suspect leaders, programs, and publications in a defunct group, Epworth having been replaced in 1941 by the MYF.) The US House Committee on Un-American Activities (HUAC) collected and republished attacks on the MFSS/A and MYF in 1952. In the Senate, Joseph McCarthy conducted similar denunciatory exposures. Clergy who rallied to the defense of Methodist social witness or questioned McCarthyism or evidenced any softening of cold war rhetoric faced charges of being tainted with communism.

Progressive bishops, reformers, and those associated with the MFSS/A became targets as anticommunists (and Methodist conservatives) equated humanitarian concerns, social reform, and support for integration with socialism and viewed reformers as dupes of or fellow travelers with Soviet Communists. In 1940 Harry Ward was hauled before the House Un-American Activities Committee. Although defended by Union Theological Seminary president Henry Sloane Coffin and Professor Reinhold Niebuhr, Ward was forced to resign his faculty post at Union Theological Seminary the following year. The retirement of Ward and of Bishop McConnell in 1944 triggered both internal dissension and external criticisms of Methodism's social justice caucus. MFSS chose the Rev. Jack McMichael, even more radical in ideas and methods than Ward and McConnell, as executive secretary. McMichael led the federation's period of greatest expansion, with some forty conference chapters and five thousand members by the end of the decade. His leadership "earned" thousands of pages of FBI files on the MFSA and McMichael. The House Un-American Activities Committee published an eighty-eight-page "exposure" of the federation's subversive nature. In 1953 McMichael appeared before the HUAC and challenged its accusations of communist subversion with such telling references to the ministry of Jesus that an aggravated committee member shouted, "Can't we leave Jesus out." McMichael replied that he absolutely could not, adding that "in a situation like this, where guilt by association seems to be the principle on which you are operating. . . . I am sure [Jesus] himself would have long ago been hauled before this committee!"

Innuendos in Rembert Gilman Smith's *Moscow over Methodism,* published in 1950 by the Methodist League Against Communism, Fascism, and Unpatriotic Pacifism and Stanley High's "Methodism's Pink Fringe," in the ever-popular *Reader's Digest,* February 1950, connected Methodist groups and leaders with ties to international communism. Walter Muelder, social ethics professor at the denomination's Boston University School of Theology and the MFSA's vice president, issued a public protest (S **1950**). So did Bishop G. Bromley Oxnam, whose reply *Reader's Digest* refused to publish. Other critics within The Methodist Church, especially the Texas-based Circuit Riders, Inc., capitalized on the prevailing McCarthyite hysteria to secure General Conference repudiation of the MFSA. Formed in 1948 with the single purpose of driving the federation out of Methodism, the group attacked the federation for its support of racial integration (H **651nn157–60**).

A storm of vilification was directed against the MFSA at the 1952 San Francisco General Conference. Delegates demanded that the MFSA stop using the name "Methodist" and vacate its offices in the Methodist building in New

York City. The MFSA was prohibited from appearing to speak for Methodists, a function rightly reserved for the General Conference itself, and certain statements made in the name of the MFSA were officially disclaimed by the denomination. Moreover, the General Conference brought the consideration of social issues more directly under its own guidance by creating a "safer," less "radical," Board of Social and Economic Relations (H **652n162**). The federation did move out of the church's office building, but defiantly did not change its name. Declassified FBI files detail how thoroughly the government had been involved in getting The Methodist Church to repudiate the MFSA. Several prominent Methodist church leaders were put under suspicion and surveillance, including Bishop G. Bromley Oxnam, MFSS executive Harry Ward, and theological school professor Georgia Harkness, among others, accused of being members of the Communist Party.

The HUAC made Bishop Oxnam, a highly respected and highly visible church leader, president of the Federal Council of Churches (1944–46), and president of the World Council of Churches (1948–54), a favorite target. The committee repeatedly released "unevaluated" reports implying that Oxnam was a member of several "subversive" organizations and either sympathized with the Communist Party or allowed himself to be used by it. Oxnam demanded a hearing before the congressional committee a year before broadcast journalist Edward R. Murrow famously took HUAC to task and at the peak of McCarthy's popularity and power. The hearing itself, a fatiguing session lasting from midafternoon till midnight on July 21, 1953, was televised across the nation. *U.S. News & World Report* reprinted the transcript of the hearing in full. The bishop, mountains of files at hand, exposed the sloppy research, unreliable reports, and deliberate falsehoods in committee records and statements, indirectly unmasking the committee's self-aggrandizing motivations in suggesting he was a Communist dupe (S **1953**). The "trial" helped diminish public respect for HUAC. Oxnam provided a brilliant defense of the rights of the individual citizen to security from unsubstantiated accusations and trial by gossip in *I Protest*, published the following year. That summer (June 28, 1953) *Parade* magazine, which accompanied countless Sunday newspapers across the country, carried a two-page article by Oxnam enticingly titled "How to Uncover Communists . . . without Throwing Mud on Innocent People" (H **652n164**).

Bishop Oxnam exonerated himself, but the MFSA lived under a cloud for a decade. Between 1953 and 1960, the MFSA operated without an executive secretary, a dedicated remnant keeping the federation alive until it blossomed again in the civil rights and antiwar movements of the 1960s. In the midst of the whirlwind, in 1951, the Board of Missions quietly launched the US-2 Program, recruiting young adults to serve as missionaries working for justice, freedom, and peace in U. communities. In fifty years the program trained about thirteen thousand young adults between the ages of twenty and thirty to serve in US-based ministries—a breakthrough of social justice concern in this period.

ECUMENICAL EFFORTS

The 1939 Methodist and 1946 EUB family unions represented key parts but just parts of the investment the churches made toward Christian unity. And the larger quest to reunite Christ's body informed the 1968 Methodist-EUB union. Methodists and EUBs worked ecumenically on various fronts—on their own global unity, in bilateral and multilateral dialogues, and in faith and order discussions—the several explorations sometimes reinforcing, sometimes competing with efforts to put the Methodist family back together. The year 1939 saw also the formation of the World Federation of Methodist Women, and two years later the creation of Church Women United brought together missionary and cooperative organizations representing some seventy American denominations. Methodists and EUBs did not take prominent roles initially, as did their holiness counterparts, in the National Association of Evangelicals (1943) but certainly did five years later in the formation of the World Council of Churches (WCC). Lay leaders John R. Mott and Charles Parlin, together with Bishop G. Bromley Oxnam, helped found the WCC. Oxnam served as its first president. Parlin headed the finance committee (1948–68) and was a member of the Central Committee (1954 58) and of the Presidium (1961–68). Through the years, Methodism's global family has contributed presidents and key leaders to the WCC (listed H **423**).

In 1948, Oxnam delivered a strong affirmation of "The Reunion of the Churches" in the Episcopal Address to General Conference. General Conference responded by forming a standing Commission on Church Union to engage in dialogue with separated churches in the United States and a Commission on the Structure of Methodism Overseas (COSMOS) to rethink links between The MC (USA) and its overseas dependent churches. The same year intercommunion and union talks with the Episcopal Church began but stalled a decade later over issues of reordination and closed Communion. In

1949, representatives of eight mainline US denominations, at a conference in Greenwich, Connecticut, unveiled the Greenwich Plan for church union. Bishop Ivan Lee Holt (MC) was elected the first president. Although the several denominations recognized the validity of one another's ordinations and appeared to have consensus on doctrine and sacramental practice, the plan foundered on polity matters.

In 1950, a successor organization to the Federal Council, the National Council of Churches (USA), representing thirty denominations from Quakers to Eastern Orthodox, organized in an assembly in Cleveland. It brought together twelve existing ecumenical and missionary agencies. Methodists played prominent leadership roles in governing body and executive staff in the council from the earliest years. During the 1950s, Professor Albert Outler (SMU faculty) and Bishop William Cannon emerged as leading Methodist voices of the ecumenical movement. In this cause Outler authored one of his most significant books, *The Christian Tradition and the Unity We Seek* (1957). Both Outler and Cannon played leading roles in the Faith and Order movement beginning at Lund, Sweden, in 1952; at the WCC third assembly (New Delhi, 1961) and fourth assembly (Uppsala, 1968); in the Consultation on Church Union in the United States beginning in 1962; and in the World Methodist Council–sponsored bilateral conversations with Roman Catholics beginning in 1966.

In 1951, the World Methodist Council (WMC), successor to the Ecumenical Methodist Conferences, was formed and decided to hold WMC Conferences at five-year rather than ten-year intervals as previously. Elmer T. Clark (MC, USA) assumed the general secretaryship. Headquartered at Lake Junaluska, North Carolina, since 1953, the WMC within sixteen years linked sixty-four member churches in 108 nations, eight of which are united churches with Methodist roots. Another intra-family Methodist project began in 1959, namely the periodic gathering of scholars in the Oxford Institutes on Methodist Theological Studies. In 1952, The Methodist Church (USA) established the Interdenominational Cooperation Fund apportionment to support ecumenical efforts around the world, witness to the Christian faith, and foster renewal of Christian unity and understanding.

In 1958, the Methodist Commission on Church Union and The EUB Commission on Church Federation and Union met jointly in Cincinnati, beginning the decade-long effort (see below). In the meanwhile, Methodists and EUBs joined the nine-communion project (including three Black

Methodist denominations) in the Consultation on Church Union (COCU). Begun in 1962, COCU produced by 1970 a plan of union, envisioning a new ecclesial body, including institutional merger. By 1963, Charles Parlin was backtracking, arguing for family-style ecumenism as the place to begin. Methodists of the world should unite first, then negotiate out of strength with Anglicans, Catholics, Lutherans, and Reformed. He saw union with The EUBC as the first step. In 1964, the Methodist delegation to the COCU plenary led by Parlin insisted on "Four Principles of Distinctive Methodist Witness": (1) bishops as itinerant general superintendents versus any notion of diocesan episcopacy, (2) a connectional system, (3) infant baptism, and (4) total abstinence as the sole interpretation of Christian temperance.

At the Second Vatican Council (1962–65), sixteen US Methodists served as observers. In the new spirit inspired by the council, the 1963 Montreal Conference of Faith and Order revisited the issue that had divided Protestants and Catholics since the sixteenth century, the interrelationship between Scripture and tradition. Understanding the church's proclamation to be rooted in the gospel, tradition, and works of the Spirit, the gathering looked toward new relations between and among Protestant, Catholic, Orthodox, Anglican, and free churches.

In 1964, the Methodist General Conference established a Commission on Ecumenical Affairs. Continued in The UMC (1968–72), it became the Ecumenical and Interreligious Concerns Division of the General Board of Global Ministries (1972–80) and later a separate commission. In 1965, Robert W. Huston was named the first full-time executive. By 1967, under Huston's guidance, Commissions on Ecumenical Affairs had been formed in sixty out of ninety conferences in the United States. In 1966, Methodism began bilateral dialogues with "separated" sisters and brothers on national and international levels: Roman Catholic (USA) 1966, Roman Catholic (international) 1967, Lutheran (USA) 1977, Lutheran (international) 1979, Anglican (international) 1988, Anglican (USA) 1988, Reformed (international) 1992, Orthodox (international) 1992. From these dialogues have come remarkable consensus statements on matters of doctrine.

THE UNITED METHODIST CHURCH

Overtures between Methodists and EUBs antedated the formation of the MEC, UBC, and EA denominations and were relaunched with the formation of The EUBC in 1946. At that first EUBC General Conference, Bishop Oxnam relayed a unity overture from The MC Council of Bishops. By the late 1950s, The EUBC began conversation with several churches, among them the Methodists, stressing a union-promising, common heritage, doctrine, worship, and polity. Explorations continued between EUBs and Methodists in the early 1960s and by 1966 had yielded a plan of union. The EUBC's Paul Washburn served as executive secretary of the joint commission, toured the church in interpreting what unity would mean, and summarized his counsel in question-and-answer format in the church's major paper (S **1966b**; H **652n167**). He reassured EUBs that they would not simply be swallowed up and that the projected new church would enhance, not undercut, their spiritual, ecumenical, ethical, strategic, and missional commitments, including the explorations represented by COCU, in which he was an active participant.

Sounding a similar concern, also in 1966, Professor Albert Outler urged Methodists to "fish or cut bait" in ecumenical waters at a second conference, Methodism in an Ecumenical Age, at Lake Junaluska, North Carolina. He warned of the dangers of world confessionalism—choose COCU or COSMOS! Outler also published that year a widely used study book for the denomination: *That the World May Believe: A Study of Christian Unity*. Many Methodists had little firsthand knowledge of the EUBs because EUB membership was concentrated in a few northern and midwestern states. To help Methodists become better acquainted with their proposed partners in denominational marriage, union negotiator-in-chief Charles Parlin wrote a study-book for church schools in 1965, and the October 1966 issue of Methodism's *Together* magazine presented fourteen pages of texts and pictures introducing The EUBC and its history, organization, and examples of its ministries in the United States and other parts of the world (H **652n168**). Both Methodists and EUBs

- had connectional systems in which local congregations were related to the general church through annual conferences under administration of bishops;

- were governed by General Conferences made up of equal numbers of lay and ministerial delegates elected by annual conferences;

- provided order for their organizational life through rules set forth in their books of *Discipline*;

- operated administratively through general boards, commissions, and other agencies that oversaw work in missions, education, publishing, pensions, evangelism, and social concerns; and

- had many congregations in rural areas and small cities and towns, struggling as members moved into the suburbs.

The differences were mostly of size, degree, and organizational complexity. The EUBC was a body of about three quarters of a million members, compared to the Methodist 10.3 million. The 4,300 EUB congregations in the United States and Canada were grouped into thirty-two annual conferences; Methodism's 38,800 churches in the United States alone were in ninety conferences. Methodism had forty-six episcopal areas, and the bishops who supervised them were elected by six jurisdictional conferences. EUBs had only seven episcopal areas, and the bishops who served them were elected by the General Conference; there were no jurisdictional conferences. EUB district superintendents (DSs) were elected by annual conferences; Methodist DSs were appointed by the bishops. Administration of all EUB general agencies was centered in Dayton, Ohio; Methodist agencies were scattered in New York, Philadelphia, Cincinnati, Nashville, Evanston, and Washington, D.C. Local church practices also differed. The EUB employed a Program Council, a gift to Methodists at union, to adapt and supplement ideas from annual conference and general agencies and develop a comprehensive and unified program for the congregation. Such councils were required in EUB congregations regardless of size. By contrast, the five commissions familiar to Methodists were optional and generally organized only in larger churches. In addition, EUB churches could organize three age-level councils (children, youth, and adults), which put the Program Council's plans into action in cooperation with the church school, Women's Society of World Service, EUB Men, and the Youth Fellowship (H **652n170**).

Missions by Evangelicals and United Brethren, begun in the mid-nineteenth century by the mid-1960s yielded 156 full-time and 12 short-term EUBC workers in Asia, Africa, and Latin America. The largest contingent served in Sierra Leone (missions begun in 1855), which enjoyed annual

261

conference status. In other countries and US territories—Brazil, Ecuador, the Dominican Republic, Puerto Rico, Japan, the Philippines, Indonesia, Hong Kong, and Nigeria—EUBC missionaries worked in *unified Protestant* ministries. Similarly, 165 EUBC home missionaries served both in their church's missions and in interdenominational projects (H **652n169**). This was not the Methodist pattern, which preferred to operate its own mission enterprise at all levels.

In late 1966 EUBs in their regular General Conference and Methodists in a special session approved the Plan and Basis of Union, both by wide margins. In 1968, EUBs and Methodists united to form The United Methodist Church (USA). Paul Washburn was among those elected bishop. The Uniting Conference adopted a major resolution, "The UMC & the Cause of Christian Unity," proclaiming a vigorous commitment to open versus closed (or family-style) ecumenism. A 1968 symposium, "Methodism's Destiny in an Ecumenical Age," gathered Methodist ecumenists from around the world at Methodist School of Theology in Delaware, Ohio. In his plenary address, Professor Outler made it clear that for him the future of theology lay in its ecumenical intention and outreach.

MISSION CHURCHES EXERCISE OPTIONS

Methodist, EUB, and UMC mission churches across the world drew on ecumenical language and aspiration for rationale and self-understanding as they charted new directions in relation to the parent denominations. Some elected to remain under the authority of General Conference as central conferences, others chose to become part of national or regional uniting churches, and still others elected autonomy and an affiliated relation (H **652nn171–72**). And these decisions would yield ecumenical and ecclesial quandaries for the twenty-first-century church. Shorn of many Methodist-EUB-planted mission churches and indeed of whole regions (all of Latin America and much of Asia), how should The UMC General Conference understand the church's global nature?

More determinative, initially, than ecumenical vision, particularly in demands for independence, were political-societal dynamics—nationalism, effects of World War II, cold war pressures, and efforts to throw off colonial yokes. By 1930, Brazilian, Mexican, and Korean Methodists had achieved autonomy, the first so as to elect its own bishops, the second to adjust to Mexican church-state legal constraints, and the third to unite Korean branches of The MEC and The MECS (H **652n173**). In 1937, Methodist missions in China merged, and in 1949 the Methodist Church of the Republic of China fled with the Nationalists to Formosa. In 1939 much of French Methodism went into a united church. In Italy, American and British Methodism united, initially (in 1946) aligning with the British conference. Japanese Methodism became part of the state-mandated Protestant church, the Kyodan, during World War II.

Recognizing the anticolonial temper that followed the war and to guide the church in this new climate, British and American Methodism took different routes with respect to their colonial expressions. British Methodism encouraged either independence or commitment to emerging united churches, or both. Hence the united or uniting churches of North and South India, Canada, and Australia.

The 1948 Methodist General Conference established the COSMOS. With more liberalized conditions under which central conferences could elect their own bishops (H **652n174**), American-birthed mission churches took different directions. The Philippines elected to remain in, while Burma (now Myanmar), Pakistan, and Liberia chose independence. The Liberians (S **1963b**), recognizing their historic status as the "first overseas African field," affirming their Methodist "faith, doctrine, practice and kinship," and celebrating the current leadership of Bishop Prince Taylor, deemed that African nationalism in general and their own "national pride and self respect" had brought them to maturity as a church. Some other West African conferences chose independence while a few East African missions elected to remain central conferences. An EUBC mission in Sierra Leone chose autonomy at first but became part of the West Africa Central Conference in 1972. All of Latin America opted for autonomy (Puerto Rico only in 1992), as did most of the Asian missions (save the Philippines). EUBC missions in Latin America became part of uniting churches. European Methodists found in either cold war pressures or their minority status, or both, reason to cling to the American church.

The Board of Missions and COSMOS guided and counseled leaders from central conferences as they wrestled with the options that the church and local circumstance presented. For instance, as overtures concerning autonomy increased and at the 1964 MC General Conference's request for guidance,

COSMOS convened some 150 representatives from churches in Asia, Africa, Latin America, and Europe in a 1966 consultation at Green Lake, Wisconsin. It outlined the possible postcolonial futures: minor adjustments keeping central conferences overseas accountable to US General Conference, formation of autonomous or joining united churches linked by a World Methodist Council of churches, or creation of a World Methodist Church with regional General Conferences. The year 1969 saw the formation of the Council of Evangelical Methodist Churches in Latin America and the Caribbean (CIEMAL), a body that would successfully guide the autonomous churches in their local mission and in relation to The United Methodist Church. As Tracey Jones, general secretary of the new denomination's board of missions, observed, both the missionary and the work of missions were radically changing (S **1969**; H **652nn175–77**).

CHAPTER XI
THE UNITED METHODIST
CHURCH: 1968–84

On April 23, 1968, in Dallas, over a table laden with symbolic documents—the Bible, hymnals, *Books of Discipline* and *Worship* and the 307-page Plan of Union—EUBC bishop Reuben Mueller and Methodist bishop Lloyd Wicke clasped hands and proclaimed their two churches joined as The United Methodist Church. Upwards of ten thousand guests and thirteen hundred delegates cheered the merger of the 10.3 million-member Methodist Church and the 750,000-member Evangelical United Brethren Church. Then the second-largest and most truly national Protestant denomination, The UMC, reached globally as attested by flags of fifty-three countries. Professor Albert Outler of Perkins likened the uniting of the two churches to Pentecost and apologized for the absence of fire and glossolalia (S **1968b**). Outler also noted that "no part of our venture in unity is really finished as yet!" To guide efforts toward full unity, General Conference authorized a special five-day session for 1970 to have as a major concern the merger and structure of the new denomination's boards and agencies. Accordingly, it created quadrennial study commissions on structure, social principles, and theology and doctrine. It also established a Program Council, authorized a *Book of Resolutions* to exhibit the church's pronouncements, and created a Commission on Religion and Race to assist in the dismantling of the Central Jurisdiction.

The spiritual exultation at the Uniting Conference inaugurated three quadrennia of difficult and divisive issues, which the drafters of the Plan of Union either could not have anticipated or preferred to postpone. No small part of Methodism's dilemmas, broadly shared across American society, concerned major national and international matters—the civil rights revolution, the women's movement, heightened ethnic consciousness, challenges of affirmative action and inclusion, the Vietnam War and its enduring social traumas, poverty and urban decay, the deindustrialization of American society, a new coalition of political conservatives and evangelicals, and continued cold war and nuclear-holocaust tensions. Also to be divisive during this period were internal church developments, including structural change, commitments to pluralism and diversity, affirmation of the "quadrilateral" as a doctrinal hermeneutic, the liberalization of teaching about divorce and remarriage, and policy on abortion, homosexuality, and inclusive language. An emergent conservative Methodism took the latter issues among its expressed concerns but derived energies as well from matters of war, race, gender, doctrine, and scriptural authority. Some commitments made in this liberating atmosphere—for instance, the reorientation of mission theology and policy toward social, political, and economic redevelopment—would be questioned more vigorously as Methodism celebrated its bicentennial.

The earlier merger on the Methodist side—that of 1939—had bought unity at the price of racial segregation and regional jurisdictions. The latter would continue into the new church, indeed, solidify further. Principled segregation in the form of the all-Black Central Jurisdiction would finally go. But how would a United Methodism honor the particular witness of the minority Evangelical United Brethren? And what would unity mean with respect to its various distinctive populations, within the United States and beyond? Diversity and pluralism would be the new church's first big challenge. Agenda item one: race!

CAUCUS AND COMMISSION

Alarmed by the disastrous riots during the summer of 1967 in Detroit and Newark, Black Methodist leaders gathered in Cincinnati in February 1968 to form Black Methodists for Church Renewal (BMCR). James Lawson, veteran of the civil rights campaign, friend and confidant of Martin Luther King Jr., and pastor of the all-Black Centenary UMC in Memphis suspected Methodists were "playing a 'mickey-mouse game'" on race. He feared that after unification, the deadening game of racism would persist in a less visible guise. Speaking for BMCR, he said bluntly, "We reject tokenism. We refuse to tolerate a cheap, meaningless fellowship not rooted in Christian acceptance, dialogue and mission. We will settle for nothing less than a church where the love of Christ rules and where a man is a man not by race, or blood, but by the will and power of God." Lawson went on to challenge the upcoming Uniting Conference "to authorize genuine urban priorities and to get the Methodist household in order" (S **1968a**). General Conference responded by establishing a Commission on Religion and Race but not without a fierce fight.

These two organizational initiatives—an advocacy/monitoring agency and a caucus (BMCR), the one establishing a toehold within the denomination's power structure, the other providing a belonging and commitment network, in various combinations and permutations—would dominate United Methodist life for the next four decades. With the formation of Good News (S **1966a**) in 1967 and of other racial-ethnic, gender, and sexual minority caucuses soon after BMCR's founding (see S **1970, 1972a, 1972d, 1973, 1976, 1978, 1985, 1988a**), United Methodism found itself both united around and divided by the several caucuses. That other mainline denominations, indeed American society, united and divided along similar lines would provide little comfort as local churches, annual conferences, and General Conferences roiled with the controversial proposals and demands that highly interested advocacy produced.

The agency-caucus axis yielded other ironies than unity in diversity and diversity in unity. Caucus advocacy aspired to ambitious transformations in society, politics, business, and religion, but in agitating conferences with resolutions and proposals, such advocacy had the effect of focusing United Methodism on itself. The caucuses pledged themselves to the renewal of United Methodism, but in many instances found common interest and sometimes collaborative effort with counterparts across denominational lines. Perhaps most ironically, a Methodism that since World War I had sought to purge itself of "foreign" language conferences and in uniting would end the scandal of a racial jurisdiction, increasingly needed non-English and racial-ethnic-sensitive ministries. And as United Methodism recognized its global character, translation and particularity reentered connectional life. In anticipation of the 1968 merger, the Rio Grande Conference voted (in 1967) to remain a separate entity. With the ending of the Central Jurisdiction, Black Methodism faced the loss of what had been an enabling structure (as well as an accommodation to White racism). Would BMCR serve in place of Black conferences and jurisdiction? With the creation of caucus (BMCR) and commission (on Religion and Race), United Methodism implicitly recognized that identity, particularity, and commitment required their own space and structure. Making that implicit recognition into explicit and affirmed denominational practice would prove a big challenge. In the course of the next three quadrennia, a newly United Methodism would find itself experiencing structural-ideological initiatives that would change the church as radically as had the innovations of the 1870s.

AFRICAN AMERICANS IN UNITED METHODISM

In many respects BMCR functioned to sustain the more positive roles of the old Central Jurisdiction, convening Black members for joyous worship and thoughtful strategizing, identifying and cultivating new leadership, and celebrating Black pride and Black culture in a predominantly White church. BMCR vigorously pressed the church to eliminate racism, to implement inclusiveness, to care for underrepresentation, and to deal with economic disparities. Although formed by activists in the civil rights movement and at the point that Black Power separatism shaped Black agendas, BMCR avoided the call to separate from the White church. Instead, as its name suggests, it looked to the renewal of Methodism as the church ended the Central Jurisdiction and brought together the ten remaining Black conferences with their White counterparts. By 1970, all the jurisdictions and many annual conferences established chapters, and BMCR's monthly tabloid, *NOW*, enjoyed wide circulation. Over the next few years BMCR chalked up an impressive record of achievements. It lobbied successfully for the Commission on Religion and Race, urged church agencies to upgrade the level of Black leadership, and secured a General Conference commitment to raise substantial funds for the church's Black colleges and their students (the continuing Black College Fund).

BMCR shared agenda and leadership with the Commission on Religion and Race whose mandate, staff, and budget were dedicated to actively and vigorously promoting the church's goal of developing a racially inclusive church (soon to champion the cause of other minorities as well). Under the leadership of its executive secretary, Woodie White (later a bishop), the commission oversaw the merger of the remaining racially structured conferences of the

Central Jurisdiction into the five geographically organized jurisdictional conferences. That would prove most challenging in South Carolina where Black and White conferences of comparable size shared the same boundaries. Nor was merger everywhere a success. Some nine thousand members in ten states refused to enter the new church, joining instead the segregationist Southern Methodist Church, formed in 1939. More positively, the 1968 Northeastern Jurisdiction elected Roy Nichols to the episcopacy, the first Black leader elected by a regional White majority jurisdiction. The same year, Black leader Theressa Hoover became associate general secretary in the Board of Global Ministries and chief executive officer of its Women's Division, a post she held until retirement in 1990. The following year, Black staff at the Board of Global Ministries formed their own Black Staff Network.

Under the quadrennial theme for the new quadrennium of "A New Church for a New World," the church pledged itself in 1968 to mobilize its energies and resources for reconciliation, witness, and renewal. It urged members to study the Sermon on the Mount "to correct the long-standing attitudes which have brought about the present crisis in the nation and around the world, especially as this crisis is prompted by racial injustice." A Fund for Reconciliation was established, with a quadrennial goal of $20 million of contributions over and above regular giving. The fund would underwrite new programs, such as the United Methodist Voluntary Service Corps to enlist young adults in local projects of reconciliation and reconstruction, and it would support other mission ventures proposed by UMC boards and agencies. In 1969 the Council of Bishops (COB) added its own voice to the theme, sending a "Message to the Church on Reconciliation" (H **655nn5–6**).

Renewal and reconciliation, however, produced conflicts over policy and money. The denomination's Nashville-based anti-union publishing house foot-dragging on a mandate to integrate its workforce at all levels drew a hard-hitting April 1968 investigative report "Practice What You Print" by New York City pastor James McGraw in *Christianity and Crisis*. BMCR called all churches, especially Black churches, to boycott purchasing publishing house products until the house joined Project Equality (H **655n7**). Pocketbook strategy internationally elicited conflict as well. The Board of Missions withdrew a $10 million investment portfolio from New York's First National City Bank in protest against the bank's involvement in a credit arrangement with the government of South Africa. The board's action drew protests by lay delegates John Satterfield of Mississippi, a former president of the American

Bar Association, and Charles Parlin of New Jersey, Wall Street lawyer and a president of the World Council of Churches.

The following year (1969) civil rights activist James Forman issued what came to be termed the "Black Manifesto" calling for reparations to African Americans from institutions that benefited from the slave labor of their ancestors. The COB in its "Message to the Church on Reconciliation" rejected the demand. However, the confrontation led denominations to allocate substantial amounts of money to minority programs and community organizations, and it helped build support within the churches for this type of funding. Later that year BMCR organized a sit-in at the Board of Missions offices in New York City. The board responded promptly and positively. In the following months $1.3 million went to programs of the National Committee of Black Churchmen, BMCR, other minority caucuses, the World Council of Churches Program to Combat Racism, and UMC Black colleges from sources the Board's National, World, and Women's divisions. Many conferences, on their own, adopted the Black church as a missional priority. Staffed through the conference budget, such programs focused on strengthening struggling congregations, ministerial training, and recruitment (H **655n9**).

Over the decade of the 1970s United Methodism dealt with problems related to racism in church life. To mainstream White leaders, at least, that problem seemed more immediately approachable than the problem of racism in society as a whole. At the 1970 special session General Conference in St. Louis, BMCR pressed the need for funding for education and economic development. Several hundred Black guests and delegates quietly encircled the delegates sitting in the arena. General Conference embraced some of BMCR's recommendations: a $2 million Minority Group Economic Empowerment Fund to be administered by the Commission on Religion and Race, a $1 million scholarship fund for minority students, and $4 million a year (to be raised) to support of the church's Black colleges.

The 1972 General Conference adopted a new Social Principles statement forthrightly condemning racism in all its forms and calling for justice for all racial-ethnic and oppressed peoples. It also made the General Commission on Religion and Race (GCORR) a permanent commission with an expanded mandate. Later that year, GBGM elected Randolph Nugent associate general secretary for the National Division, a powerful, strategic missional post. Melvin G. Talbert, a California DS, became the first Black general secretary in the denomination's history, leading the General Board of Discipleship until his election to episcopacy in 1980. Philadelphia pastor George Outen became the second Black general secretary upon his election to the General Board of Church and Society in 1976.

In November 1972, the last Black conferences, those in Mississippi and South Carolina, merged with the overlapping White conferences, albeit doing so by constituting Black districts, an evasion struck down by the Judicial Council two years later. By 1974, eighteen years after the Methodist General Conference had approved ecclesial integration, passing Amendment IX to the Constitution, and a decade after it had mandated integration, the scandal of Methodism's official policy of segregation finally ended. The prior year (1973) and ten years after guarding the University of Alabama against the "evil" of desegregation, (UM) Governor George Wallace crowned the university's first Black homecoming queen. In a television interview in 1991, Wallace expressed remorse for his former stance on segregation.

In 1974, the Women's Division of GBGM held two leadership development workshops for women of color. From this event came a talent bank for nominations, training for committees on nominations, increased presence of women of color in leadership roles, and the 1976 election of the Women's Division's first Black president, Mai H. Gray. There was publication in 1974 of two major histories of Black Methodists by Harry Richardson and James Brawley (H **454**). The same year following a Bishops' Consultation in Salisbury, Rhodesia, the six bishops in Africa issued a call for more self-determination and a larger decision-making role in missionary programs. The following year, on a visit to missionary headquarters in New York, Bishop Abel Muzorewa of Zimbabwe (then colonial Rhodesia), the second Indigenous UM African bishop (elected in 1968), made the case for African-indigenized practice and leadership, citing White missionary mistakes (S **1975**). He served as prime minister of the transitional Zimbabwe-Rhodesia (1979). Criticism of his successor, Robert Mugabe, in 1989, earned Muzorewa a year's detention but made him one of The UMC's best-known international figures (H **655n12**).

Viewing the potential for church growth or loss of ethnic churches, the 1976 and 1980 General Conferences named the Ethnic Minority Local Church as one of the church's highest missional priorities. The 1976 General Conference also adopted a fresh resolution, "The United Methodist Church and Race" (H **655n13**). By 1980 the effort to be more inclusive could be seen and felt in the presence of Black delegates and leaders at General

Conference in Indianapolis. The delegates adopted the Women's Division's "Charter for Racial Justice" as churchwide policy. And Randolph Nugent became the general secretary of the denomination's largest and most powerful board: the General Board of Global Ministries. White resentment of or opposition to such racial-ethnic empowerment—no longer tolerated in explicit form—would find alternative expression on matters of social policy, doctrine, and bureaucracy.

ASIAN AMERICAN UNITED METHODISTS

In March 1971 in Santa Monica, California, 170 Western Jurisdiction leaders of Chinese, Korean, Filipino, and Japanese American churches met and formed a jurisdictional Asian American Caucus. This first large-scale, morale uplifting Asian American convocation, supported by the annual conferences, the National Division of the Board of Missions, and the Commission on Religion and Race, included thirty youth, eleven district superintendents, the Western Jurisdiction bishops, and pastors and laypersons from practically all of the then-existing thirty-eight churches in the Western Jurisdiction. Caucus organization tested the integrative ideal with which United Methodism had come into being—the ideal expressed ethically in the commitment to end racism and the racist-inspired Central Jurisdiction, expressed structurally in ongoing board and agency consolidation, and expressed programmatically in the denomination's serial for families, *Together*.

The Immigration Act of 1965 had opened America's western door to Koreans, then Indians, Cambodians, Formosans, Hmong, Laotians, and Vietnamese. A million Asians (1960 census) exploded to 10.8 million by 2000, 43 percent growth (cf. White growth of 7 percent). Methodism, however, had for half a century been moving away from structuring itself for language and culture-specific indigenized ministries. The Oriental Provisional Conference (Chinese, Korean, and Filipino) dissolved in 1952, and the Pacific Japanese Provisional Conference reluctantly in 1964. "Unfortunately," lamented a Nisei layperson, "what started out as a great step forward in 1964, by 1966–67 was mired in disillusionment by the insensitivity of the majority of the peculiar needs of our people" (H **477, 659n90**). Integration isolated, disconnected, and demoralized ethnic congregations and leadership, and these factors weakened the church's commitment to new church development and recruitment, training, and deployment of ministers among Asian Americans. A November 1967 Japanese American gathering explored means of strengthening widely scattered local churches. They conveyed desires for unity to the COB and Board of Missions. In response the Board held consultations in three West Coast cities in October 1968.

The hearings surfaced desires for stronger theological resources for Asian American ministries, for interconference clergy appointments, and for closer relationships with Indigenous churches in Asia. Paul Hagiya, Japanese American pastor of Simpson UMC in Arvada, Colorado, informed the 1970 General Conference that integration in 1964 had been "a swallowing up process" that resulted in a "loss of zeal and strength and passion to win the Asian-American communities to Christ" (H **659n91**). Asian American leaders participated in an ethnic consultation arranged by the new Commission on Religion and Race in Chicago in October 1970. The commission also funded an office of Research and Development for Asian American ministries with the Rev. George Nishikawa, a Japanese American, as director. Data gathering revealed twenty Japanese, six Chinese, six Korean and six Filipino congregations with 5,139; 925; 786; and 548 members respectively, persistent but with little growth from the 1940s (H **659nn92–93**).

A newly formed Western Jurisdiction caucus presented its concerns to the 1972 General Conference. Acknowledging the values of their Asian heritage, they recognized "that our participation within The United Methodist Church has been only partial and limited, and that our identity as Asians has been in terms of Euro-American values and culture." They affirmed "that the Asian-American Caucus is at present the most viable means to achieve" self-determination requisite for "relevant Christian mission strategies on the local, annual conference, and national levels," exploration and appreciation of "the values of our ethnic cultural and religious heritages that make the Gospel relevant and meaningful to Asian-Americans," and liberation from "the elements of racism with The United Methodist Church and society." The caucus acknowledged "the need to understand and to cooperate with other ethnic caucus groups within The United Methodist Church" (H **659n94**).

Negotiations followed with the United Church of Christ in Japan for two ministers to supply unfilled Japanese-language pulpits. In 1972 Asian American leaders, including Roy Sano, Kathleen Thomas-Sano, and Lloyd Wake, founded and assumed leadership in the Pacific Asian American Center for Theology and Strategies. Affiliated with the Graduate Theological Union in Berkeley, PACTS pursued the development of Asian American theology and built support for church involvement in civil and human rights struggles. In 1972 the Western Jurisdiction elected Wilbur Choy, a Chinese American and the first Asian American bishop (short bio H **478**). Two additional Asian bishops followed: Roy Sano (the first Japanese American) in 1984 and Hae Jong Kim (the first Korean American) in 1992. A caucus newsletter, *Asian American News,* launched in 1973.

The third regional convocation (1974), meeting in Oakland, welcomed Asian American leaders from outside the Western Jurisdiction and named itself the National Federation of Asian American United Methodists (NFAAUM). The same year Asian American United Methodist Women gathered for the first of several consultations in Honolulu. In April 1975, the NFAAUM board of directors selected Lloyd Wake, a Japanese American pastor from San Francisco and president of the Glide Foundation, as chairperson. The Rev. Jonah Chang, a native of Taiwan and head of the office of Asian American Ministries in Oakland, was elected executive director, a position he held for ten years. A Center for Asian American Ministry opened at Claremont School of Theology in 1977. These initiatives led to some church growth and new clergy candidates. The denomination had an estimated 13,500 Asian American members in a national constituency of 10 million (H **659nn97–99**). Through convocations and engagement with the church's quadrennial missional priority (1980–84), the NFAAUM identified national priorities for leadership development, increased participation at denominational levels, and development of Asian-specific resources (H **479, 659nn100–102**).

Almost simultaneously with the formation of the NFAAUM, Koreans—the fastest-growing Asian subgroup—began their own effort at caucus formation. (The 1980 census reported that the Korean population in the United States had increased 412 percent over the previous decade and had come to number more than a half million.) Korean American Methodists formed a caucus of their own in 1973—the National Association of Korean American United Methodist Churches (NAKAUMC). At that point the Korean American congregations in The UMC numbered only twenty. By the mid-1970s, Korean Americans had established thirty congregations, and by 1977, with the blessing of the Asian American Caucus, they had persuaded United Methodist Communications to issue Korean-language editions of selected promotional resources, beginning with World Service leaflets. In 1983, the Board of Discipleship published a collection of Asian American hymns, *Hymns from the Four Winds,* the first such by any major denomination (H **480**). The Korean caucus, in what seemed the next obvious step, asked the COB to consider formation of a Korean American language "missionary/provisional" conference. NFAAUM backed the recommendation at its spring meeting just before General Conference 1984. General Conference deferred.

Particularity continued to blossom into a plethora of Asian American caucuses, among them Chinese, Filipino American, Formosan, Indochinese, Cambodian, Hmong, Laotian, Vietnamese, Japanese American, Korean American, and Southern Asian. The flowering of caucuses signaled that United Methodism would unite itself and divide itself by its several languages, cultures, and identities. Others joined Asian Americans in the flourishing of ethnicity.

LATINO/HISPANIC UNITED METHODISM

As United Methodism formed, various Hispanic conferences clarified their ecclesial political status. In 1967 the Board of Missions gave the Rio Grande Conference the option of merging with Anglo conferences or continuing as a separate conference. On this occasion, as in 1955, the conference overwhelmingly opted for its own integrity. Treated for decades as a stepchild of home-mission activity, the Hispanic churches in Texas had achieved status as a separate Rio Grande Annual Conference in 1939. Spread over the lower Rio Grande Valley with headquarters in San Antonio, Mexican American Methodists gained decision-making authority, a degree of self-determination, and the attendant opportunity for self-respect within a structure they had chosen (H **660n107**).

Elsewhere full independence seemed to be the route to self-determination. In 1967, the Puerto Rico Conference and the Methodist Church of the Caribbean and the Americas were formed. The latter brought together the Methodist churches of Antigua, Costa Rica, Guyana, Haiti, Honduras, Jamaica, the Leeward Islands, and the South Caribbean (and soon thereafter the Bahamas). In 1968 the Methodist Church of Cuba opted for autonomy, as did the United Evangelical Church of Ecuador and the Methodist churches of Chile and Argentina. In 1969 the Methodist Churches of Latin America formed a regional council, the Council of Evangelical Methodist Churches in Latin America (CIEMAL), to provide for unity under their own auspices and to labor for common ends. Through CIEMAL and a Latin American Council of Churches (organized in 1982) and to some extent in relation to GBGM and through the World Methodist Council, Latin American Methodism voiced its own concerns, often in a progressive spirit, sometimes prophetically critical of US policies in the region, notably in Nicaragua during its Sandinista phase (H **660n108**).

In the United States the Hispanic population tripled during the decade of the 1960s—pulled by economic opportunity and driven by repression and conflict—and began advocacy for civil rights and economic justice (e.g., César Chavez's 1965 organization, the United Farm Workers and José Gutierrez's 1970 national Hispanic political caucus, La Raza Unida). The population grew despite Congress's 1965 restrictions on immigrants from Mexico and Central and South America and despite the Nixon administration's 1971 bill imposing a penalty on employers hiring persons not authorized to work in the US.

United Methodism lacked structure and strategy for dealing with the explosive growth of Hispanic communities, its Spanish-language ministries geographically rather than connectionally defined (along the Rio Grande, in Puerto Rico, and in Florida). Missionary or central conferences within the United States—the nineteenth-century scheme for attending to linguistic or cultural particularity—seemed unthinkable when the church was under self-imposed mandate to close just such down (the Central Jurisdiction). Scattered Anglo UMC congregations mounted Spanish-language ministries or opened their doors to a Hispanic congregation just organizing. But could United Methodism supply trained Spanish-speaking pastors? And appoint one with a Guatemalan background to a largely Guatemalan congregation? And address needs in the urban North without bleeding the small cadre of trained leaders in the Rio Grande (H **660nn109–10**)?

Spokespersons appealed for recognition and resources to boards and agencies and within the Spanish-speaking community through a program journal, *El Interpreté* (launched in 1958 as *Acción Metodista*, retitled in 1968). Hispanic Methodists in California formed LAMAG, Latin American Action Group, led by future bishop Elias Galvan, to lobby for their interests in the West Coast area. Reporting to the 1968 Southern California–Arizona Conference, LAMAG proclaimed: "Integration seen as Angloization is an outmoded concept among Mexican Americans and can no longer be tolerated by our Latin churches." Instead LAMAG proposed a ten-point program that called for Hispanic representation at all conference levels, their participation in decisions that affected their ministries, training of their own leadership and of Anglos for Hispanic work, better salaries and facilities, and establishment of "criteria other than Anglo for measuring the success/failure of Hispanic churches" (H **483, 660n111**).

In 1970, Hispanic UMC leaders organized Metodistas Associados Representando la Causa de Hispano-Americanos (MARCHA; in English: Methodists Associated Representing the Cause of Hispanic Americans). At the 1970 special session General Conference, Elias Galvan, clergy visitor from Southern California Conference and pastor of LA's Church of All Nations, spoke on behalf of MARCHA (S **1970**; H **660n112**). Galvan told the delegates that The UMC was neglecting growing Hispanic populations, locking them into patterns of discrimination based on language and culture. Rejecting tokenism, Galvan called the new denomination "to accept the ministry to Spanish-Americans as a top priority" and to instruct the boards and agencies to appropriate funds, provide Spanish-language resources, and increase Hispanic representation on the denomination's national staff. Galvan left to the cries of "Viva MARCHA!"

Anticipating the 1972 General Conference, Roberto Escamilla, director of bilingual ministries, Board of Evangelism, writing in the *Christian Advocate,* called the Hispanic American church to become an ally in the struggle for social justice and identify more completely with the "barrio" (Spanish ghetto). He urged The UMC to recognize its responsibility to minister to migrant workers in California, Texas, Michigan, and elsewhere; to Puerto Ricans at home and in the nation's metropolitan centers; and to Cuban exiles in Florida. With Hispanic Americans in key positions in the boards and the COB, the church could develop a program adequate to the needs of youth, recruit and train Hispanic pastors and lay leaders for their roles in these new ministries, produce printed resources "written within the context of our culture," find ways to cooperate with other denominations and community groups that are struggling for justice, and proclaim the gospel with power and truth. "There is not another mission field so fertile and responsive to the gospel," he insisted, "as that which is present among Hispanic Americans." At the 1972 General Conference, Josofat Curti, MARCHA chairman and pastor of Messiah UMC in Pueblo, Colorado, echoed Escamilla's demands for Hispanic representation on the church's agencies and in the COB (H **660nn114–15**).

Among the church's responses was *Himnario Metodista,* largely a translation of British and Euro-American hymns. In 1979, however, the GBOD produced *Celebremos: Primera Parte, Colección de Coritos,* a collection of familiar choruses. *Celebremos: Segunda Parte, Colección de Himnos, Salmos y Canticos* followed in 1983 with a more global and ecumenical content, with selections from the global Latino community (Latin America, Spain, Puerto Rico, and the United States), a harvest of Hispanic music and of more current musical theology. Eighteen hymns and songs from the latter went into The UMC hymnbook of 1989. The *Book of Worship* (1992) included a Mexican Christmas Eve service, *Las Posada.* The first truly Hispanic UM hymnal and worship book, *Mil Voces Para Celebrar,* under the editorship of Raquel Mora Martinez, was ready in 1996 (H **660n116**).

In 1974, Perkins School of Theology established the Mexican American Ministry Training Program. Headed by Roy Barton, the program nurtured generations of lay and clergy leaders. With UMPH support, the program in 1981 launched *Apuntes,* a Hispanic journal of theology. In 1976 GBOD selected Roberto Escamilla as associate general secretary (H **660n118**). Hispanic women met with Latin American Methodist women in Cuernavaca, Mexico, and with Puerto Ricans in 1976 and 1977. Such events prompted Hispanic women to signal to the church that the melting pot was a myth, that its initiatives, including the Ethnic Minority Local Church, still suffered from paternalism, and that Hispanics required resources produced by Hispanics out of the Hispanic experience (S **1978**; H **486**).

Along with MARCHA, a series of national meetings fostered Hispanic unity. An early consultation meeting in Los Angeles in 1979 gave Hispanics for the first time a sense of the power and enthusiasm for their United Methodist constituency. In 1980 with MARCHA support, the first Hispanic bishop, Elias Galvan, was elected. A second bishop, Joel Martinez, was elected in 1992.

NATIVE AMERICAN UNITED METHODISM

Self-determination, always a concern for Indigenous people, received new impetus in the sociopolitical ferment of the 1960s, from the civil rights movement and from revived cultural self-consciousness among Indigenous tribal nations. The restiveness expressed itself in the American Indian Movement (AIM), organized in 1968; the 1970s celebrations of Earth Day; the 1972 Trail of Broken Treaties March on Washington, D.C.; and Vine Deloria's *God Is Red* (1973), launching Native American liberation theology.

Methodist missions historically focused on the reservation populations of the southwestern United States with little follow-up for Indigenous people who resided off their reservations. And though the church's mission with Indigenous nations included education and medical services, it had not typically extended to facing systemic and oppressive conditions affecting America's Indigenous people; to enlisting Indigenous contributors in leadership above congregational levels; to recognizing the inherent values in Indigenous life, culture, and religion; and to empowering ministries of evangelism and nurture that fit Indigenous needs as they themselves assessed these needs.

Complaints about this state of affairs prompted the Board of Missions to call a consultation just a few months before union (January 1968) to consider means of empowering the denomination's Indigenous ministries. An advisory committee formed. Only three of its dozen members were Indigenous. Thomas Roughface, a Ponca Nation pastor, spoke for the Oklahoma Indian Missionary Conference (OIMC) at the October 1970 meeting of the board: "The call for self-determination is the call to be involved in the total ministry of the Church. We [Native Americans] can no longer sit in the balconies of the Church or appear as mere observers while decisions that ultimately affect us are being made by the Church and its boards and agencies" (H **661n122**).

In 1972, the National American Indian Committee, meeting in Cherokee, North Carolina, reorganized itself into an all-Indigenous body, the Native American International Caucus (NAIC) with thirteen voting members, two staff, and five jurisdictional consultants. The word *international* signaled solidarity of America's Indigenous people with sovereignty for Indian nations, a galvanizing cause across the Indigenous peoples. Within United Methodism, NAIC sought voting rights at jurisdictional and general conferences; Indigenous leaders on boards; support for and strengthening of Indigenous ministries and local churches; sensitivity across The UMC to the customs and religious expressions of Indigenous peoples; denominational advocacy for sovereign rights of Indigenous peoples of North, Central, and South America; concerted efforts to raise education standards and salaries of pastors; and better communication among the fifty widely scattered churches outside the Oklahoma area (H **661n125**). Financial support for the new caucus came from the newly formed General Commission on Religion and Race, which reported on the status and role of the church's Indigenous constituency to the 1972 General Conference. Two representatives of the OIMC, the largest concentration of Indian Methodists with about twelve thousand church members, were seated at the opening day of the conference but without vote. Of its sixty-one ministers, one was then a seminary graduate. The Women's Division also lent its support, and in 1975 the Native American Women's Caucus was birthed at a Native American United Methodist Women Consultation in Kansas City, Missouri.

The new caucuses urged the creation of a new department for Native American ministries within the Board of Missions. Instead, a Native American staff portfolio was created, which Homer Noley, director of Native American ministries in the Nebraska Conference and a member of the Choctaw Nation, ably filled (1971–75). Noley, along with John Adams of GBCS, helped negotiate between federal officials and armed members of AIM protesting injustices at the Wounded Knee Reservation in South Dakota. (The Women's Division participated in an ecumenical support network for the standoff.) Raymond Baines of the Tlingit Nation was also appointed as ombudsman for Native American ministries.

In 1972, the Oklahoma Indian Mission became a "missionary" conference, permitting licensing and ordaining of its own ministers but not the full representational prerogatives of an annual conference (a temporizing that produced an ideological rift between national church agencies and Indigenous leaders in the field). Only in 1988, when General Conference also adopted the missional plan, "The Sacred Circle of Life: A Native American Vision," did the missionary conference finally gain the right to vote at General Conference, developments covered in the next chapter.

In 1976 NAIC asked General Conference for a comprehensive on-site study of Native American missions to make recommendations to the 1980 General Conference. NAIC also sought the formation of a General Commission on Native American ministries. Roughface, a nonvoting clergy delegate from OIMC (S **1976**), pled, "We have been the most studied species . . . give us the right to set up the machinery by which we will be able to effectively conduct our own study." General Conference did not opt for a commission but approved the formation of a study committee and established an Ethnic Minority Local Church priority (EMLC, later renamed "Racial Ethnic" and abbreviated RELC).

The new quadrennial missional priority, EMLC, spread program development, staffing, and funding sources into four general agencies and across the array of annual conferences. For Indigenous peoples, as for the other ethnic populations, it created new conference, jurisdictional, and general employment opportunities. It sensitized the denomination to its diversity. How well EMLC achieved its stated aims of strengthening congregations, enlarging the church's mission among Indigenous tribal nations, and increasing lay and clergy leadership is harder to measure. To some extent the new employment opportunities in the upper echelons drained leadership, especially clergy leadership, which otherwise would have been deployed on a congregational level. And the funding and program opportunities set up new tensions between and among general agencies, conferences (Oklahoma for Native Americans), and the caucuses (H **661n131**).

Those tensions surfaced when the study committee revisited the idea of a Native American commission, a proposal backed by NAIC but by neither OIMC nor the Commission on Religion and Race. Conflict intensified at the 1980 General Conference, where representatives of AIM—an organization not affiliated with The UMC—tried to influence the conference to take up such causes as American Indian treaty rights and to form the proposed commission. General Conference did not create a new commission, but called for existing boards and agencies to address the needs through current structure with an executive staff member in each board to be assigned the task of "advocacy, development and implementation of Native American ministries."

Despite their internal disagreements, Indigenous leaders voiced unhappiness with the perceived restrictions of comity agreements that governed tribal affairs. They appealed to General Conference to renounce these agreements as a form of denominational and governmental collusion. Such a resolution passed. General Conference, repenting for cultural and religious genocide, adopted the major resolution, "The United Methodist Church and America's Native People." Calling church and nation to "become more sharply aware and keenly conscious of the destructive impact of the unjust and injurious policies of the United States government upon the lives and culture of U.S. American Indians, Alaskan, and Hawaiian natives," the resolution exhorted congregations to "support the needs and aspirations of America's native peoples as they struggle for their survival and the maintenance of the integrity of their culture in a world intent upon their assimilation, westernization, and absorption of their lands and the termination of their traditional ways of life" (H **661n132–33**).

A newspaper to bind together scattered Indigenous peoples, *Echo of the Four Winds,* began regular publication as a bimonthly tabloid. *Echo,* along with the caucus, has built unity across the Indigenous UM communities and voiced their deeply felt concerns. A National United Methodist Native American Center (NUMNAC) opened in Oklahoma City in 1983. It relocated in 1992 to Claremont School of Theology. This center, like those for the other racial-ethnic communities and like the Multi-Ethnic Center at Drew University, helped the church focus resources for ministerial formation. Implicitly its creation recognized the church's past inadequacy to meet this basic need. It also symbolized an ongoing, institutionalized commitment to pluralism.

THE UMC AND THE VIETNAM WAR

An important UMC initiative was to publish its statements on matter of policy, concern, and commitment as a separate book, *The Book of Resolutions of The United Methodist Church: 1968.* Three of the first five resolutions dealt with war and peace (the other two with race and Project Equality). The very first, "U.S. Policy in Vietnam," commended the president for a recent effort at negotiations. These cautious statements reflected the end to the consensus that had sustained US cold war politics and divisions on a long, escalating, troubling war. Conferences roiled in debate over resolutions on the war, disarmament, the military-industrial complex, ROTC, and conscientious objection. United Methodists took their place along the whole spectrum of and at both ends of the Vietnam debate—hawk to dove.

The UMC's initial official social principles statements retained both the old Methodist Social Creed, with its embrace of "those who sincerely differ as to the Christian's duty in regard to military service," and the former EUBC statement, more strongly pacifist in tone. Just prior to union, in 1967, the COB issued a statement calling on South Vietnam and the United States to initiate a cease-fire and begin negotiations to secure "the right of self-determination for the people of South Vietnam" and "phased withdrawal of all foreign troops and bases with arrangements for asylum for those who may require it."

Methodist students, subject to the draft, proved less willing to pull their punches. The Methodist Student Movement's *Motive* openly opposed the war, supported "draft dodgers," and devoted substantial critical attention to the war. Articles, poetry, and art agonized over the war. B. J. Stiles editorialized: "In the name of God, *this* war, in *this* place, at *this* time, against *this* people, must stop" (S **1967**). The MFSA and the ecumenical Clergy and Laymen Concerned about Vietnam launched educational and lobbying efforts on behalf of conscientious objectors and urged the government to grant clemency to the seven hundred-plus young men imprisoned for resistance and the five thousand-plus who had gone abroad rather than fight. UMC boards and agencies joined the chorus—a liberal prophetic orientation that conservatives later would view as the occasion of the ideological split within and numerical decline of the church. Important in the perspective of United Methodist leaders was the social-geographical location of key agencies—particularly the GBCS and GBGM—in New York and Washington, D.C.

By 1972, with casualties continuing to mount and President Richard Nixon stepping up bombing of North Vietnam, United Methodism caught up with its prophetic leadership. Following a long debate, that year's General Conference, by a five to four majority, termed America's involvement in the war immoral, called on President Nixon to halt the bombing and withdraw all forces by year's end, urged Congress to withhold funding, and appealed to the leaders in Hanoi and Washington to release all prisoners of war (S **1972b**). General Conference also reworked the paragraph on peace in the 1972-adopted Social Principles. It declared war "incompatible with the teachings and example of Christ," rejected "war as an instrument of national foreign policy," insisted the "first moral duty of all nations" was to resolve disputes by peaceful means, called for a stop to "the militarization of society," and for reduction and control of "the manufacture, sale and deployment of armaments." [A final clause—"and that the production, possession or use of nuclear weapons be condemned"—was added in 1980.] The first four statements in the 1972 *Book of Resolutions* dealt with war, peace, and Indochina (H **655nn19–20**).

Such official acts elicited mixed reaction from church members whose sons and daughters both served and protested. Among those serving and tying United Methodism to government and the military were chaplains and the Commission on Chaplains and its successor, the Division of Chaplains within the newly formed Board of Higher Education and Ministry. For more than half a century—covering World War II, the Korean War, the Berlin buildup, the Cuban crisis, and the war in Vietnam—more than 2,600 clergy, for varying lengths of time, held special appointment by their bishops to serve as full-time chaplains. By the 1980s, more than 600 chaplains functioned in full-time ministry with more than 100 serving part-time with various institutions and the Civil Air Patrol, and about 300 in the reserve components.

MERGER COMMISSIONS—SOCIAL PRINCIPLES, STRUCTURE, DOCTRINE

The 1968 Methodist-EUB merger functioned with a unite-now-settle-differences-later principle. To be resolved? Ministry and episcopacy, doctrinal standards and social principles, the number of seminaries, and the cluster of national program boards and agencies. (Note: Worship developments from 1968 to 1984 consummating thereafter are treated in the next chapter.) To complete its work, the Uniting Conference established churchwide quadrennial study commissions. It called a special session of General Conference for 1970 to hear interim reports.

The Methodist and Evangelical United Brethren churches came to union in 1968 with strong statements on social principles that guided their life and witness. The new church ended up with not one but two statements of social principles—an aging Methodist Social Creed, originally adopted in 1908, and The EUB "Basic Beliefs Regarding Social Issues and Moral Standards." Similar at some points, they differed sufficiently at others to raise penetrating questions about their theological and ethical foundations. To address the complexities of the world situation, the commission opted for a fresh statement of social principles and a new social creed for use in services of worship.

The new statement called for responsible use of this world's natural resources. It gave vigorous support for control and limitation of population growth as well as cautious approval to abortion and to remarriage of divorced persons. It recognized the right of responsible civil disobedience and extended support for conscientious objectors to include opposition to particular wars. More explicit approval was given to the struggle for racial and social justice. The statement on human sexuality proved the most difficult of all to resolve, as we observe below.

284

The Structure Study Commission attracted the most attention during the first quadrennium and at the 1972 General Conference. Many hoped that the century-old trend of "one board after another" might be reversed and the church's bureaucracy pared. In the end, the program agencies were merely grouped into four superboards—Church and Society, Discipleship, Global Ministries, and Higher Education and Ministry—in a word, advocacy, nurture, outreach, and vocation. A quota system for board membership created space and opportunity for youth, women, ethnic ministry representatives, and former members of The EUBC.

To oversee the agency structure on its program side, the church adopted The EUBC model of a Council of Ministries (preferring that to what had been the less effective Methodist Coordinating Council) and designed it initially to function between General Conferences in interim capacity. Although the Judicial Council ruled unconstitutional its role as an interim General Conference, GCOM nevertheless retained considerable power, including the prerogatives of electing general secretaries annually, nominating the respective program board, reviewing and evaluating all programs and plans, making recommendations on budget, and coordinating the work of and minimizing the competition between the several agencies. Following Methodism's practice for well over a century, General Conference mandated for annual conference and local church what it prescribed for the connection as a whole. So congregations found themselves with new Councils of Ministry, which were to "consider, initiate, develop, and coordinate proposals for the church's strategy for mission" and to "elect teachers, counselors, and officers for the church school other than those subject to election by the Charge Conference." Mandating age-level and family coordinators and councils and work area chairs and commissions, General Conference, in effect, made it possible for every local church to experience on a day-to-day, month-to-month basis the reality that United Methodism had not pared and simplified but greatly complicated its order and procedure. Gradually over the next several quadrennia, successive General Conferences would make more and more of the structure and order permissive. However, the damage had been done. GCOM became symbolic of excessively centralized bureaucracy.

The church initially embraced but later experienced as divisive the report and recommendations of the Theological Study Commission on Doctrine and Doctrinal Standards, undertaken amid doctrinal turmoil and fragmentation (liberal, conservative, social gospel, neoorthodox, existential, ecumeni-

cal, death of God, secular city, Black, feminist, and third world theologies—
H **459**). The 1968–72 Theological Study Commission undertook its work
mindful of the theological confusion, as its chair, Albert Outler, explained,
"Somewhere in The United Methodist Church there is somebody urging every kind of theology still alive and not a few that are dead." But Outler affirmed doctrinal pluralism "as a positive theological virtue" and a Wesleyan
one: "Far from being a license to doctrinal recklessness of indifferentism," he
insisted, "the Wesleyan principle of pluralism holds in dynamic balance both
the biblical focus of all Christian doctrine and also the responsible freedom
that all Christians must have in theological reflection and public teaching"
(H **655n22**).

   Outler's commission and General Conference enshrined this "new/old"
doctrine of theological pluralism in what has become arguably the most important doctrinal guideline for United Methodism, a new, extended section
in the *Discipline*, in 1972 titled "Our Theological Task." This section functioned, per the charge to Outler and company, to indicate how the separate
theological trajectories of The EUB and Methodist churches converged in
United Methodism. The Constitution of The United Methodist Church, following the Methodist pattern, explicitly prohibited any alteration in "our
present, existing and established standards of doctrine." What were "our doctrines"? At church union, the *Discipline* simply included both the Methodist
Articles of Religion dating from 1784 and the updated Evangelical United
Brethren Confession of Faith of 1962. The Judicial Council deemed them
"congruent, if not identical in their doctrinal perspective and not in conflict."
Yet they were not identical. Nor did they explicitly reference the traditional
Wesleyan foundations (Wesley's "standard" *Sermons* and *Explanatory Notes
upon the New Testament,* for instance).

   The Uniting Conference had empowered the Theological Study Commission, if it "deems it advisable," to "undertake the preparation of a contemporary formulation of doctrine and belief, in supplementation to all anteced-
ent formulations" (H **655n23**). Sensing such a course doomed to fail, the
commission formulated a new "Part II Doctrine and Doctrinal Statements
and the General Rules" for the *Discipline*. Into part II it placed the new section "Our Theological Task" and an equally long "Historical Background,"
which reviewed doctrinal development in the predecessor churches. It sand-
wiched between these two United Methodism's several "Landmark Documents." The latter included Methodist "Articles" and "General Rules," The

EUB "Confession," and prefatory comment referencing Wesley's *Sermons* and *Explanatory Notes*. Acknowledging the bitterly polemical character of the sixteenth-century Reformation-formulated Articles of Religion, the commission urged the church henceforth to interpret the historic standards "in consonance with our best ecumenical insights and judgment" (H **655n24**). "Our Theological Task" and the "Historical Background" sustained that emphasis, enumerating basic Christian beliefs shared with other communions and reaffirming distinctive Wesleyan emphases as found in John Wesley's sermons as evangelical and catholic in character. In particular and as noted, theological pluralism among United Methodists was acknowledged and affirmed as a modern reaffirmation of what Wesley called "the catholic spirit."

A hopeful, open, ecumenical, constructive, future-oriented spirit culminated in a several-page subsection, "Theological Frontiers and New Directions." Here the church, with Outler's guidance, welcomed "all serious theological opinions developed within the framework of our doctrinal heritage and guidelines so long as they are not intolerant or exclusive toward other equally loyal opinions." "Of crucial current importance," it went on to affirm, "is the surfacing of new theological emphases focusing on the great struggles for human liberation and fulfillment. Notable among them are Black theology, female liberation theology, political and ethnic theologies, third world theology, and theologies of human rights" (H **655n25**). To keep the ongoing theological enterprise faithful to the "'marrow' of Christian truth," Outler's commission formulated what was deemed a Wesleyan theological method, the testing of claims against a fourfold norm of Scripture, tradition, experience, and reason. Introduced in the first paragraphs of the "Historical Background" and developed in "Our Theological Task" the quadrilateral was viewed as orienting United Methodism to the living core of the gospel, which it had received through the witness of the Wesleys, Albright, Otterbein, and Boehm. "This living core, as they believed, stands revealed in Scripture, illumined by tradition, vivified in personal experience, and confirmed by reason" (H **655n26**).

Adopted by General Conference toward the close of its sessions 925 to 17 without amendment and with little discussion (of the quadrilateral, theological pluralism, and affirmation of diversity), the commission's work generally met with approbation. The newly organized evangelical caucus, Good News, responded negatively. Fearing that theological pluralism would lead to doctrinal confusion, the caucus drafted its own version of United Methodist fundamentals (based not upon a unique United Methodist understanding of doctrine but in line with historic Fundamentalism in the US), which included the inspiration of Scripture, virgin birth of Christ, substitutionary atonement, physical resurrection, and return of Christ (H **655n27**). For three quadrennia Good News pressed for theological integrity, the primacy of Scripture (in the quadrilateral), definition of core beliefs, and the place of Wesley. By 1984, General Conference, in response to a flood of petitions, established a commission to review the 1972 theological statement, a development we take up in the next chapter.

The 1972 General Conference continued other union homework by establishing three commissions—to study the seminaries, ministry and ordination, and episcopacy and superintendency. Four years later the reports came in. The general church accepted major responsibility for funding ministerial education and reduced the number of seminaries by one. A new statement, "The Ministry of All Christians," the creation of a new office of diaconal minister for full-time lay professionals, and an improved candidacy plan for ordinands resulted. General Conference resolved the perennial question about whether district superintendents should be elected (EUB style) or appointed (Methodist style) in favor of the appointive pattern. Similarly, it sustained life tenure for bishops despite arguments that term episcopacy, The EUB pattern, would encourage the election of younger, female, and ethnic bishops. However, service as episcopal leaders in one geographical area was cut to a maximum of eight years.

NEW WOMEN'S ORGANIZATIONS

A United Methodist Women's Caucus formed in 1972, convened initially the prior year (S **1972d**), the creation by General Conference of the General Commission on the Status and Role of Women (COSROW), and the merger of the several women's organizations in The UMC to form United Methodist Women (UMW), the latter to be administered by the Women's Division of the General Board of Global Ministries.

Despite their preponderance in the church's membership, women constituted but 10 percent of General Conference. The number of women missionaries and of deaconesses had steadily declined (the latter from nearly 1,000 in 1939 to 366 in 1963, to 185 in 1976 and to 70 by 1997). While demand for religious educators had remained relatively constant, the percentage of women clergy (ordained as elders and full members of conference) remained small, under 1 percent (H **463**; **656n31**). On neither the professional nor the representational fronts did Methodist women seem to be making real progress, indeed, in places losing ground, at a time when a veritable social revolution for women was occurring, a revolution symbolized by activist-writer Betty Friedan's *The Feminine Mystique.* Churchwide and Division studies and consultations uncovered problems for women clergy as well as missionaries. Finding single women to be most vulnerable, one consultation called on the church "to affirm the validity and wholeness of singleness as a choice of lifestyle for clergy and laity, both women and men" (H **656nn33, 34**).

Under Theressa Hoover, the Women's Division addressed power and decision-making issues with the board as well as problems inhibiting women's fuller participation in the life of the church. An Ad Hoc Committee on Churchwomen's Liberation, working with the General Conference–authorized body, sent to the 1972 General Conference proposals that formulae be established to guarantee women's, minority, and youth membership on general church agencies. It expressed concerns about how minority-group women would fare in annual conferences and local churches as the final phases of Central Jurisdiction phaseout occurred, and it proposed other goals. Hoover voiced these matters forcefully in a hard-hitting article in 1973 in *Response,* documenting the exclusion of Black women even from the liberation causes—feminist and Black (H **656n36**; S **1973**; *Response* superseded the serials of the predecessor denominations, *World Evangel and Methodist Woman*).

The Women's Caucus (S **1972d**) represented a grassroots initiative to influence reform efforts that the Study Commission or Women's Division might formulate for the 1972 General Conference. Judy Leaming-Elmer and a group of Chicago-area women issued a call for a meeting on Thanksgiving (1971) weekend at Wheadon UMC, Evanston. The approximately twelve hundred attendees birthed a National Women's Caucus of The UMC. Meeting again the next year in anticipation of General Conference, the caucus added urgency and pressure to goals being formulated in other channels. For instance, mindful of the recommendation that boards and agencies be constituted with one-third laymen, one-third laywomen, and one-third clergy, the caucus decided to ask that committee to reconsider its formula to ensure that half the membership of these boards and agencies be women.

289

To broadcast its concerns, the caucus in 1972 launched *Yellow Ribbon*, a newsletter named in honor of badges of Victorian-era Methodist feminists.

The several efforts by caucus, Women's Division, Study Commission, and United Methodist Women across the connection led the 1972 General Conference to establish the Commission on the Status and Role of Women (COSROW). The prior year, the US Supreme Court ruled that hiring policies must be the same for women and men, and Congress passed the Equal Rights Amendment, of which the General Conference declared its support in 1972. (The ERA, as of 2019, has been ratified by two-thirds of the state legislatures but decades after the due date has passed.) The following year, the Supreme Court rendered its decision in *Roe v. Wade*, legalizing abortion, United Methodist layperson and Justice Harry Blackmun drafting the decision. Concerned with church and societal developments, Good News leader Charles Keysor warned of influence by "pagan women's libbers" on church policy and of a quota system in which women were given leadership positions solely because they are women. The 1976 General Conference, however, apprised by the commission with a careful study of women's (minimal) participation in church governance and leadership, sided with the feminists and made COSROW a *standing* (that is, permanent) commission. It required COSROWs at annual conference level "to challenge the UMC at all levels to work for full and equal participation of women in the total life of the denomination."

Among COSROW's several tasks was ridding the denomination of the policy and practice of male-exclusive language, over time a highly successful campaign. More visible and more controversial was a second feminist enterprise, the elimination of sexism from religious language. COSROW and the UM women's caucus joined other feminists in protesting the use of male-exclusive language in worship and discussion. On this cause, the church moved more cautiously, though the 1976 General Conference did approve inclusive language in official liturgies, specifically the 1976 revision of the 1972 trial-use service of Holy Communion. In 1978 COSROW adopted its own official creedal affirmation, written by Barbara Troxell (see COSROW website) and, in 1980, called The UMC to develop a statement on inclusive language and images. And in 1981, COSROW called on UM agencies to adopt sexual harassment policies, another cause that would eventually succeed. The COSROWs joined with feminists in the Women's Division and UMW to encourage church endorsement of feminist concerns, especially

ERA and abortion (on the latter, see discussion below). They succeeded in convincing the Council of Bishops in 1982 to express its support for the Equal Rights Amendment.

The campaign for full inclusion proceeded on the clergy front as well. In 1975 the first national UM clergywomen's consultation was held in Nashville (others followed in 1979, 1983, 1987, 1991, 1995, and 2002). In 1976 annual conferences sent ten clergywomen to General Conference, the first women *clergy* delegates to General Conference (ten out of the five hundred clergy delegates). In addition to approving inclusive language in worship and making COSROW a standing commission, this General Conference authorized a study of maternity/paternity leave and clergy/gender salary and passed resolutions on full personhood and on solidarity with women's rights as articulated by the International Women's Decade (H **656n40**). By 1979, the number of ordained women reached 1,000, with 886 under episcopal appointment to local churches. By 1980, women represented more than 3 percent of the total professional ministry, an increase of 75 percent over 1975, and 29 percent (736) of MDiv students (H **656n41**). As women opted for elder's orders, religious education numbers waned. Several seminaries terminated MRE programs. Despite some congregational resistance, the appointment systems assured women of employment in ministry. Gradually bishops began appointing women to the district superintendency, beginning with Margaret Henrichsen in Maine in 1967. The number grew to seven by 1980. That year the North Central Jurisdiction elected the first woman bishop, the Rev. Marjorie Swank Matthews, a long-time employee of a Michigan autoparts manufacturer, ministry being her second career, who was ordained in 1965 and then served as pastor of small churches in Michigan and New York. In 1984, jurisdictions elected two women to the episcopacy, Judith Craig and Leontine T. C. Kelly, the latter an African American, the first woman bishop of color.

The empowerment of women drew, as noted, on the larger feminist enterprise, and women representing the spectrum of feminist views came into various positions of prominence, an ascendancy to which the growing conservative impulse took exception (discussed further below). In the mid-1970s two women associated with the Good News caucus, Diane Knippers of the Good News staff and Helen Coppedge of the Good News board, gathered interested "evangelical" women and formed the Task Force on Women in the Church (WTF). The group, functioning under Good News's umbrella, launched a newsletter, *Candle,* in 1977. By 1983 *Candle* circulation reached twenty-one thousand. The newsletter critiqued the "liberal and often radical left wing bias" of UMW materials, shared inspirational faith stories of women in mission, and disseminated alternative Bible and mission study books (H **656nn42–43**). Good News and WTF would have cause for concern over the emergence of yet another caucus.

HOMOSEXUALITY: CAUSE AND CAUCUS

Before the 1968 union, Methodists and mainline Protestants had given homosexuality little sustained national attention. In the 1960s, most attention given to the diversity of human sexuality was relegated to regional and local ministry contexts among more active gay communities such as San Francisco. A summer 1970 *Religion in Life* issue carried six articles, "Ethical Concerns for the 1970s," none of which dealt with sexuality or homosexuality. Methodists were slow to appreciate post–World War II developments:

- gay rights organization and advocacy;

- implications of Alfred Kinsey's best-selling books on sexual behavior or of William Masters and Virginia Johnson's *Human Sexual Response* (1966);

- the wave of legal reform across northern, midwestern, and western states stimulated by the American Bar Association's 1961 recommendation that laws dealing with private sexual relations between consenting adults be dropped; and

- removal by health-care professionals of homosexuality from the list of mental disorders—the American Psychiatric Association in 1973 and the American Psychological Association in 1975 (H **467; 656nn45–48;** H **467**).

Early Methodist gay advocacy centered in California, specifically Glide Memorial Methodist Church in San Francisco, a church engaged in the struggle for racial and economic justice, particularly under the long tenure of pastor Cecil Williams (1963–94) and the outreach of the Rev. Ted McIlvenna, a young minister-social worker from Kansas City. The latter discovered that many male runaways were gay, driven to street hustling by the hostility and ostracism of their parents and their peers. With the backing of other Glide staff and the Glide Foundation, McIlvenna provided meeting spaces at Glide for gay organizations, reached out to other area ministers prepared to work for social justice for gays and lesbians, and garnered the support of the Rev. Clifford Crummey, Bay Area DS, who defended Glide's radical activities at the national level of Methodism (H **468; 657n49**).

A four-day Glide-sponsored consultation in May 1964 brought together lesbian and gay activists and ministers, and a few from other cities, among them B. J. Stiles, editor of *Motive,* and C. Dale White, future bishop. The San Francisco contingent continued to meet for several months and in December 1964 formed the Council on Religion and the Homosexual, a groundbreaking coalition of clergy and lesbian and gay activists. A fundraising New Year's Eve dance, broken up by police who arrested three lawyers and a ticket taker and whose photographers flashed pictures of each of the six hundred guests, electrified the movement locally, as the 1969 New York City raid on the Stonewall drag bar inaugurated the movement nationally. At trial, the judge pronounced those arrested not guilty before the defense even presented. From the pulpit of Glide Memorial Methodist, in 1963, John V. Moore preached the first sermon series on record to affirm homosexuality. In 1967, Glide Church and the Glide Foundation of San Francisco launched one of the first economic boycotts on behalf of gay rights, encouraging members and sympathizers not to buy goods and services from companies that discriminated against gays (H **468–69; 657n50**).

The Social Principles Study Commission's drafting committee, headed by Iowa bishop James Thomas, struggled over Methodism's first official statement about homosexuality or homosexual practice, convinced that the proposed Social Principles had to deal with the topic. The thirty-two-member committee published its final report, drafted by Alan Geyer, Northern New Jersey clergy and editor of the *Christian Century,* in the March 1972 *Engage,* the denomination's social-concerns magazine. The report circulated widely also in pamphlet form prior to the General Conference. This pastoral statement neither condemned nor condoned homosexual practice, but said only: "We declare our acceptance of homosexuals as persons of sacred worth, and we welcome them into the fellowship of the church. Further, we insist that society ensure their human and civil rights" (H **657nn51–53**).

A handful of openly gay men traveled to Atlanta and offered General Conference delegates and visitors the opportunity for conversation about homosexuality. Few responded positively. The legislative committee dealing with Social Principles did invite Gene Leggett, defrocked by the East Texas Conference, to speak to them about homosexuality. However, unwilling to say outright that homosexuals are welcome in the church, the committee changed the wording to read (H **657nn55–56**):

> Homosexuals, no less than heterosexuals, are persons of sacred worth, who need the ministry and guidance of the church in their struggles for human fulfillment, as well as the spiritual and emotional care of a fellowship which enables reconciling relationships with God, with others, and with self. Further, we insist that all persons are entitled to have their human and civil rights ensured.

When these two sentences reached the floor of General Conference, an extended, often emotional debate ensued, with lurid stories of kidnapping murders of young boys by homosexuals. On a floor motion, General Conference added after *civil rights ensured*: "though we do not condone the practice of homosexuality and consider this practice incompatible with Christian teaching." The debate on homosexuality seemed to be over when the section on human sexuality was approved, but then a delegate from the Philippines rose to amend the section on marriage. His amendment, adopted, read: "We do not recommend marriage between two persons of the same sex." The statement was inserted with no other reference to homosexuality in a paragraph that spoke of the "sanctity of the marriage covenant" (H **469–71; 657n58–62**).

Hostile attitudes solidified, led by *Good News* (see below). In a seven-page editorial published in the summer 1973 issue, editor Charles Keysor warned "Bible-believing" Methodists that "homosexuals, by their noisy and crude pressure tactics, are [invading] the church." Applauding the defrocking of Leggett in 1971 and forced retirement of Boston preacher William Alberts for conducting a gay marriage in Boston in 1973, Keysor urged readers to take "stronger disciplinary measures" more quickly to prevent the moral degeneration of American society. The editorial was reprinted and widely circulated by the Good News headquarters for six cents a copy or three cents for 250 or more to one address.

In early 1972, The UMC college-student magazine *Motive* devoted successive issues in their entirety to gay and lesbian rights, each headed by forthright lead editorials (S **1972a**). The advocacy prompted denominational officials to pull the plug on what had been perhaps Methodism's most creative publishing effort. In December 1973, the thirty-two-member national Council on Youth Ministries (UMCYM) announced its intention to petition the 1976 General Conference to affirm that homosexuality "not be a bar to the ordained ministry" and that "homosexuality in itself not be in any way synonymous with immorality." The council adopted a policy not to discriminate in regard to sexual orientation when hiring UMCYM staff, urged other church agencies to follow suit, and publicly stated its intention to invite representatives of a newly formed gay caucus to the council's August meeting to help plan General Conference legislation. In 1974 the UMCYM allocated $400 to the National Task Force on Gay People in the Church and called for a churchwide study of human sexuality. In several 1975 actions, it reiterated the request for a churchwide study, "in the finest Wesleyan manner of education," drawing on Scripture, tradition, experience, and reason. A position paper urged the removal of negative references to homosexuality then in the Social Principles (H **471–72**; **658nn68–70**).

In July 1975, at Wheadon UMC, Evanston, Leggett and others organized a United Methodist Gay Caucus and laid plans to be present and active at the 1976 General Conference. By 1972 the caucus took the name Affirmation after its primary goal. Spokesperson Keith Spare, of Kansas East Conference, the first openly gay man to address a General Conference, called for the body to break "a history of silence and invisibility" that perpetuates "untold suffering not only of our gay brothers and sisters and their families, but the entire Christian community." Hoping for "a grace-filled dialogue," he insisted, "we cannot ignore the inevitability of residual fears and misunderstandings" (H **658nn71–72**).

Instead, delegates voted to retain the 1972 incompatibilist stance and banned church funding of pro-gay groups or programs favoring acceptance of homosexuality. Facing the funding ban, Garrett-Evangelical Theological Seminary, fearing threat to receipts from the Ministerial Education Fund, in 1978 dismissed two openly gay students. A year later Saint Paul School of Theology placed five students on probation for distributing a pamphlet potentially read as the school's endorsement of homosexuality. In 1979, the Women's Division fired staffer Joan Clark who "came out" as a lesbian.

In other contexts, the church behaved more sympathetically. In 1977, New York City pastor Paul Abels acknowledged his homosexuality and having conducted holy unions for lesbian and gay couples in his Greenwich Village church, affirmations broadcast in the Sunday *New York Times* (H **658n75**). The New York Conference, nevertheless, declared him "appointable," and Bishop Ralph Ward reappointed Abels to Washington Square. The following November, Affirmation leaders invited some one hundred persons, gay and straight, to an "Education Conference on Homosexuality and The United Methodist Church." Speakers applauded diversity as one of The UMC's strengths and declared that the church knew no outcasts. Encouraged by the prospect of tolerance, gay and lesbian Methodists envisioned full inclusion in the church, ordination, and official rituals to bless same-sex couples living in committed, monogamous relationships. Pastor Julian Rush (Denver) joined Leggett, Huskey, and Abels in publicly "coming out." A council of regional representatives began to meet twice yearly to map strategy, launched a newsletter to link widely scattered members and friends, encouraged regional chapters, and hired two staff persons, Peggy Harmon and Michael Collins, to become Affirmation's roving ambassadors and organizers. In the following years Affirmation itself became more inclusive, adding lesbian, bisexual, and transgender concerns to the group's mission statement.

To assist United Methodists in dealing with the confusion, fear, and anger on homosexuality, the Board of Church and Society devoted its March 1980 *Engage/Social Action* to a forum on the subject of homosexuality, featuring articles by pastors, laity, graduate students, and faculty. The forum offered a petition for the upcoming 1980 General Conference to replace the "incompatibility" statement with one recognizing that "some biblical scholars, theologians, and ethicists are critically reexamining and questioning" Christian condemnation of homosexual practice and calling The UMC to seek the truth taking "seriously both the witness of our heritage and of the Spirit who is leading us" (H **474, 658nn76–77**). The forum treated the "traditional Judeo-Christian viewpoint" with an extended but less than favorable review of Charles Keysor's *What You Should Know about Homosexuality.* Keysor's resolve on biblical orthodoxy led him soon thereafter to resign his post as Good News editor and to transfer his ordination in June 1982 to the Evangelical Covenant Church of America (H **658n79**).

Contentiousness marked the 1980 General Conference. To considerable applause, North Texas Bishop W. McFerrin Stowe denounced homosexuality in the opening Episcopal Address, and Dayton resident Hazel Decker's portion of the Laity Address condemned it under cover of phrases such as "family will prevail." Bishop Melvin Wheatley, the only bishop to openly dissent to the anti-gay section of the Episcopal Address, caused a stir when he publicly stated that he did not consider homosexuality a sin. As the father of a gay son, he had been a strong supporter of Affirmation. Days later a motion from the floor to ban the ordination and appointment of self-avowed, practicing homosexuals was narrowly defeated. On the conference's last day, delegates approved a churchwide quadrennial study of human sexuality. A challenge asked the Judicial Council to rule such a study, with its inevitable reconsideration of homosexuality, out of order because the church had already defined its position on homosexuality. The council declared in October 1980 that it lacked jurisdiction to rule on the matter. So the study on human sexuality went forward and was published in 1983 (H **658–59nn80–83**).

The early 1980s witnessed several test cases on the ordination and appointment of gay pastors. In 1982, when Bishop Wheatley refused to remove Julian Rush, an "out" gay pastor from a Denver church, and proceeded to ordain a self-avowed lesbian, Joanne Carlson Brown, three churches in faraway Georgia filed charges that Wheatley's statements, appointments, and ordination had undermined "the authority of holy Scripture." The committee that investigated the charges found no "reasonable grounds" for accusing the bishop, and the charges were dropped. A year later a 3,500-member church in Colorado Springs publicly censured Wheatley, its bishop, for his active support of homosexual persons as ministers, and ten other congregations in Colorado withheld funds to their annual conferences to show their disapproval. In the meantime the Judicial Council ruled in October 1982 that nothing in UMC law prohibited the ordination of homosexual persons and that the final decision on ministerial candidates rested with the conferences (H **659nn84–87**).

To make its own case to a church with a divided mind and to anticipate action at the 1984 General Conference, Affirmation created in September 1983 an antidote to homophobia. The Reconciling Congregation Program would identify open and affirming local churches, resource education and ministries involving lesbians and gay men, and "empower local churches to advocate lesbian and gay concerns in their communities and to work as a network for such advocacy on the national level" (H **659n88**). The first reconciling congregation was New York City's Washington Square UMC with a rich tradition of hospitality to gay men and lesbians, led by the Rev. Paul Abels. Other pioneers included Wesley UMC in Fresno and Saint Paul UMC in

Denver. Volunteer coordinators Mark Bowman and Beth Richardson helped establish a permanent office in Chicago.

ELDER CARE

The 1960 Methodist General Conference had assigned its Board of Christian Social Concerns a new task—programs of research, study, and action in areas of concern, among them, medical care. A research seminar at Wesley Theological Seminary yielded *The Methodist Church and Problems of Medical Care* and a special issue of the board's magazine, *Concern*, in 1962 (H **661n135**). A policy committee chaired by Dr. Lester L. Keyser, director of Health Services of Southern Methodist University, drafted a new policy statement for the denomination. Added to the Social Creed, it affirmed (H **661n136**):

> We stand for the provision of adequate medical care for all people with special attention being given the aging, the young and minority and low income groups. We strongly favor the healing ministries of the Church and other private groups. We support our government, individuals, and foundations in required research in public health; and we support legislation to meet these needs.

The passage of Medicare and Medicaid in 1965 and of the Supplemental Security Income system in 1972 changed the roles and relative importance of institutions caring for older people, accelerating the decline of the old people's home and of the rise of personal care and nursing homes.

United Methodism responded with retirement communities continuing the service ideals of the earlier old people's homes, concentrating on residential and personal care rather than nursing care (H **492–94**). By the late 1970s and early 1980s, financial and actuarial miscalculations threatened retirement operations. Operating on the basis of prepaid contracts, which promised residents lifetime care for an initial fee, many institutions found themselves unable to cover spiraling health-care inflation and greater longevity of residents. Ironically, excellent care undid mortality projections! In 1977, Pacific Homes, a network of fourteen retirement homes and convalescent hospitals in California, Arizona, and Hawaii related to UMC's Pacific and Southwest Conference, filed for bankruptcy. In the late 1960s and the 1970s Pacific Homes's board of directors had converted from the prepaid system to a monthly fee system and worked out a plan to renegotiate new contracts with the life-care residents that would reflect actual costs and allow for the conference to set up a fund to pay the extra costs for needy residents. Nevertheless, 109 residents went to court with a class-action lawsuit (*Barr v. United Methodist Church*) seeking $250,000 in damages and fulfillment of the original life-care contracts and suing for monetary damages against a number of defendants, including the conference, two general agencies, and the denomination as a whole. Five related cases were subsequently filed by various parties.

Was The UMC or any other denomination suable as an "unincorporated association" because its thousands of units and millions of members have a common name and a common purpose? UMC officials argued that the denomination had no central headquarters, no mailing address, no CEO, and no central management. The conference and agencies pled similarly (H **494–95**). One court contended that the General Council on Finance and Administration (GCFA) and the denomination were "one and the same" and as such had to answer for any liability imposed on the denomination. In late 1979, the US Supreme Court declined to consider whether The UMC could be sued for alleged wrongdoing of one of its units, the Pacific Homes retirement network. Several other denominations and the National Council of Churches had filed amicus briefs with the court.

For the United Methodist agencies involved, the case proved a costly and time-consuming headache, and for the denomination, an "image problem." News reports accented the plaintiffs' sensational charges of "fraud" perpetrated on unsuspecting older people, giving inadequate balance to the news of the defense. Most egregiously, a 1978 CBS television *60 Minutes* report made the whole church appear heartless toward the plight of older people and a November 9, 1979, front-page *Wall Street Journal* piece declared "Predators Find Elderly Are Often Easy Prey for Array of Rip-Offs." Inflation and unanticipated longevity were the real culprits, countered the church (H **661nn139–40**).

Throughout the turmoil, Pacific Homes remained in operation, made physical improvements, attracted a waiting list of applicants, and continued to serve the housing needs of "contract residents" and those who entered the home after reorganization. In 1981, through a reorganization settlement agreement, local churches, the conference, and two agencies provided a $19.5 million loan to Pacific Homes. The loan was again restructured in 1993 with a resulting $7.5 million payment to the two conferences and repayment of other contributors. A final payment of $16.4 million in March 1999 retired the full loan amount provided to Pacific Homes, thus ending a twenty-year saga.

Frightened by this litigation, many of the church's institutions restructured their finances and renegotiated their covenants with the church's conferences and agencies. Despite and through the adversity around nursing facilities, The UMC continued exploration of principle and policy for older Americans. Viewing the aging process as part of God's plan of creation and of the good news of Christ's redemption giving hope and purpose to life, The UMC called members to help translate this message through words and deeds in church and in society. A 1976 resolution defined the "Rights of the Elderly" as adequate income; quality housing; comprehensive health insurance; long-term nursing care; and equal access to social, cultural, educational, recreational, and religious activities. A resolution, "Aging in the United States," adopted in 1988 General Conference, exhorted The UMC to be "an advocate for the elderly, for their sense of personal identity and dignity, for utilization of experience, wisdom, and skills, for health maintenance, adequate income, educational opportunities, and vocational and avocational experiences in cooperation with the public and private sectors of society." Further statements followed: "Mission and Aging of Global Population" adopted in 1992, and "Care of the Elderly" adopted in 1996. The latter committed the church to explore new approaches in health care that provide quality health care and fullness of life at affordable cost for older people, their families and friends, and society as a whole (H **661–62nn142–45**).

DIVORCE

Post–World War II America increasingly accepted divorce and liberalized divorce laws. Earlier, adultery had been the only acceptable ground, and ministers could remarry only the innocent party of a divorce. By 1940 the grounds for divorce included physical cruelty or peril. By 1960 the legalistic provisions had been removed. A cult of expressive divorce—mediated by therapists, self-help books, and other vehicles of popular culture—changed attitudes toward marriage. Divorce rates doubled between 1950 and the 1980s. The image of marriage shifted from enduring covenant to limited contract—and later, under no-fault divorce laws, to a contract that could be dissolved by either partner for any (or even no) reason whatever.

At the 1968 union, The Methodist "Social Creed" recommended "improved divorce laws," but said nothing about grounds of divorce. The EUBC "Basic Beliefs Regarding Social Issues and Moral Standards" condoned divorce only "on the ground of adultery." The 1972 Social Principles, reflecting the proliferation of no-fault divorce laws, affirmed: "We assert the sanctity of the marriage covenant. Marriage between a man and a woman has long been blessed by God and recognized by society." A few sentences later, the paragraph qualified that statement: "In marriages where the partners are . . . estranged beyond reconciliation, we recognize divorce and the right of divorced persons to remarry" (H **662nn146–47**).

Methodist, Evangelical, and United Brethren families, and even pastoral families, made their own contributions to the divorce rate. Earlier, congregations seldom accepted the leadership of a divorced pastor. Divorce led to lifting of ordination credentials, early retirement, or some other altered status that ended ministry. By the 1970s divorced pastors endeavoring to stay in the ministry challenged the (dis)appointive system. New England DS (soon bishop) C. Dale White asked, "We Protestants have held for a long time that divorce may be a caring and redemptive way to end a marriage that is doomed to remain a sickly and distorted parody of a Christian family. How can we judge clergy families any differently?" (H **662n148**).

Conferences judged variously. Some permitted divorced pastors to remain in their charges. Others moved them. Still others recommended leaves with salary and housing allowance. Most developed some support structure for clergy couples experiencing separation or divorce—counseling services, leaves of absence, and transitional funds. Churches could be reluctant to accept divorced pastors who remained single. A 1976 UMC survey showed clergy divorce still a sensitive issue in the church, but more and more divorced clergy staying in the ministry. As late as 1979, writers in *Circuit Rider* begged bishops and conferences to deal with divorce in a *pastoral* rather than a *punitive* fashion (H **662nn150–52**).

By 1976, when more than a million marriages ended in divorce in the United States, General Conference lodged a greater tolerance toward divorce and remarriage in the *Discipline*: "In marriages where the partners are, even after thoughtful consideration and counsel, estranged beyond reconciliation, we recognize divorce and the right of divorced persons to remarry." The same

301

year, the Section on Worship included four "Rituals for Divorce," in a book of experimental liturgies, *Ritual in a New Day: An Invitation*. Hoyt Hickman, who coordinated the effort, told *UM Newscope* the intent was "to bring Christ into every decision and experience of our lives, including the trauma of divorce." Calling divorce "bereavement," Hickman insisted that people should not be forced to undergo this suffering alone and faithless: "The book makes no argument as to when divorce is appropriate, but faces divorce when it is a fact" (H **662nn153–54**). This resource, the first of any denomination to offer religious services for divorcing people, produced considerable complaint. William Willimon (later bishop) termed the liturgies "cheap grace" that speak "more of our irresponsibility and unfaithfulness than our love" (H **662n155**). The rituals died a quiet death. The 1992 *Book of Worship* offered no "divorce ritual," only a prayer and suggested Scripture readings for "ministry with persons going through divorce" in the section "Healing Services and Prayer."

By 1980 the *Discipline* recognized that couples were being "estranged beyond reconciliation" and gave divorce its own heading and section. The legal fact of divorce did not, it continued, dissolve other covenantal relationships resulting from the marriage, such as "the care and nurture of the children of divorced and/or remarried persons" (H **662n156**). The new standards applied to clergy as well as laity. In 1979 the COB adopted a *Handbook on Clergy Divorce* to guide conference leadership in strengthening parsonage families and dealing responsibly with clergy divorce when it occurred. If pastors behaved responsibly throughout the crisis, did everything possible to avoid divorce, sought the best counseling available, and remained effective in ministry and emotionally capable of continuing in full service, their ministries should continue without interruption. A move, they judged, depended upon the circumstances unique to that situation. The ordained must exhibit "exemplary conduct" and faithfully keep their lifetime covenant (H **662n157**). With gradual acceptance that this episcopal guidance both provided and reflected, The UMC gradually gave up deeming divorce as a disqualifying factor for candidates for ordination or appointment for deacons, elders, and bishops.

ABORTION

Until the early 1970s, most US states prohibited abortion, except to save the mother's life. The sexual liberation and feminist movements of the 1960s insisted that a woman has the right to decide what happens in and to her body. The 1972 Social Principles, in affirming the woman's responsibility for such a crucial decision, sought middle ground: "Our belief in the sanctity of unborn human life makes us reluctant to approve abortion," but we also recognize that "devastating damage" to the mother may be caused by "an unacceptable pregnancy"; therefore, "in continuity with past Christian teaching, we recognize tragic conflicts of life with life that may justify abortion," and "we support the legal option of abortion under proper medical procedures. Therefore, a decision concerning abortion should be made only after thoughtful and prayerful consideration by the parties involved, with medical, pastoral, and other appropriate counsel." The statement continued, "Good social policy calls for the removal of abortion from the criminal code, so that women in counsel with husbands, doctors, and pastors, are free to make their own responsible decisions concerning the personal and moral questions surrounding the issue of abortion" (H **662n158**).

The Women's Division and GBCSC (GBCS) had already cooperated to provide information about abortion providers and to lobby for the repeal of antiabortion laws. A 1971 GBCS study book, *Abortion: A Human Choice,* with essays from UMC seminary faculty Allen J. Moore, Tilda Norberg, and John Swomley, was an early example of the board's abortion-rights program.

In the 1973 US Supreme Court ruling (*Roe v. Wade*), Justice Harry Blackmun, the only United Methodist on the court, crafted the court's majority opinion. Blackmun wrote "the court has recognized that a right of personal privacy does exist under the Constitution. . . . This right of privacy . . . is broad enough to encompass a woman's decision whether or not to terminate her pregnancy." Conceding the sensitive, emotional, and difficult nature of such choices, Blackmun took note that Jewish and Protestant opinion has "generally regarded abortion as a matter for the conscience of the individual and her family" (H **662n160**). He called the decision "a step that had to be taken as we go down the road toward full emancipation of women."

The ruling polarized American and United Methodist opinion. The Women's Division and women's groups in other mainline churches collaborated in creating an effective pro-choice lobby. In December 1973, sixteen Jewish and Christian religious groups met at the United Methodist Building in Washington, D.C., to discuss the Roman Catholic Church's pledge to overturn the Supreme Court decision of *Roe v. Wade*. This meeting, called by GBCS, led to the formation of the Religious Coalition for Abortion Rights (after 1993, the Religious Coalition for Reproductive Choice or RCAR). In 1974 RCAR adopted a policy position on "conscience clauses," stating publicly funded health-care institutions—unlike individuals—have no legal right to refuse to provide abortion services. RCAR rented space in the D.C. headquarters of the Board of Church and Society, remaining there until 1993. In 1975 the Council of Bishops unanimously adopted a resolution opposing amendment of the US Constitution to prohibit abortion (H **662n161**).

Other United Methodists, however, believed abortion should be prohibited. Anti-feminist campaigns reached a new peak in 1977, with abortion as a rallying issue (see next section and next chapter). Abortion opponents cheered the passage in 1977 of Representative Henry Hyde's amendment to the appropriation for the Department of Health, Education, and Welfare, forbidding the use of Medicaid funds for abortion except where the mother's life was at stake. In 1978, the bans on federal funds were extended to other appropriation bills, including medical provision for military personnel. Abortion continued to be a touchstone issue in the 1980s. The Moral Majority and President Reagan spoke repeatedly against abortion. In 1981 Congress considered the proposed Hatch Amendment, declaring that a right to abortion is not secured by the Constitution. The Hatch Amendment was defeated, having met heavy public opposition, running at over 75 percent in one 1982 poll. Antiabortion violence escalated sharply in 1984–85, including dozens of arson and bomb attacks. The militant Operation Rescue emerged in 1986 effecting the kinds of "rescues" that the government refused to do. Against such reversals the Women's Division and UMW labored. They challenged the denial of Medicaid reimbursements for abortions. The inclusive position of Methodist feminists on reproductive freedom embraced abortion rights for poor women as well as against sterilization abuse.

GOOD NEWS, A FORUM
FOR SCRIPTURAL CHRISTIANITY

Good News emerged as United Methodism was in the process of formation, its platform enunciated by Charles Keysor in a 1966 *Christian Advocate* article (S **1966a**). We delayed fuller treatment until chapter's end because—unlike many of the other caucuses that found a niche within and advocacy for its cause by a general agency—Good News found itself battling connectional authority and gradually elaborating a set of alternative, parachurch, loyal opposition, or shadow connectional structures. Also unlike other caucuses (racial-ethnic ones especially) whose creation launched careers within UMC commissions or boards for caucus leaders, Good News leaders often had enjoyed prestigious and powerful posts within the denomination and recoiled to Good News–sponsored endeavors when United Methodism refused to heed their counsel.

Keysor typified this pattern. In the mid-1950s, he had helped launch and became managing editor of *Together,* which eventually reached 1.25 million Methodists. A decade later, in 1967, then a pastor, he launched the magazine *Good News,* determined that Methodism's "silent minority" would be voiceless no more. He dreamed "that evangelical Methodists might be united in fellowship across the Church" and "that our voices may be heard as we seek to articulate historic Methodism" (H **503, 662n163**). Three years later this "virtual" fellowship gathered in Dallas—sixteen hundred registered, some three thousand for evenings—to hear invited speakers: Asbury College president Dennis Kinlaw; Bishop Gerald K. Kennedy; Ira Gallaway from the Board of Evangelism; lay evangelist Harry Denman; evangelical notables E. Stanley Jones, Oral Roberts, and Howard Ball (Campus Crusade); a couple of seminary faculty; and Asbury Seminary president Frank Stanger. Soon thereafter President Kinlaw invited Keysor to join the faculty and to bring *Good News* to Asbury. The Asbury institutional base connected the Good News caucus with an extended Wilmore conservative-evangelical family and with the family history of holiness grievance, of come-outer politics, and of true-believer conviction (H **662n164**).

Through the pages of *Good News,* with the support of an energetic and outspoken board, through connections with the burgeoning political-religious, conservative-evangelical movement, with the benefit of the larger Asbury networks, the Good News caucus began a several-decade campaign of parachurch institution building and prophetic critique of United Methodism. One early effort sought evangelical perspectives, stronger Bible content, and David C. Cook-style pedagogy in Sunday school curricula. Several years of jockeying against the "modernist" religious education establishment produced some "give" by church school editor Ewart Watts, notably a new children's series "Exploring the Bible." Demanding and being refused more, including a separate evangelical curricular track, Keysor, Riley Case, and Diane Knippers began in 1975 a separate confirmation curriculum, *We Believe.*

After a decade of such production in-house, Good News spun off Bristol Books to be an Arminian voice in the Calvinist-dominated world of conservative-evangelical-fundamentalist publishing (H **662n166**).

Good News succeeded in its aspiration to become a forum for evangelical causes. A journalistic campaign would lead to a convocation, a wider coalition, and a petition-campaign aimed at the following General Conference (flooding 1972 with some fifteen thousand petitions, three-quarters of the total received). An enlarged network, convocation(s) and coalitions would birth a closely related but independent institution offering evangelical services parallel to and competitive with the denomination's. The causes—doctrine, missions, seminaries, church funding, feminism, abortion, and homosexuality—would eventually generate an evangelical coalition: Good News, the Confessing Movement, the Mission Society for United Methodists, Aldersgate Renewal Ministries, the Foundation for Theological Education, Lifewatch, RENEW, Transforming Congregations, the Association for Church Renewal, and United Methodist Action (the latter, the United Methodist wing of the Institute of Religion and Democracy, or IRD). The next chapter treats one overriding concern, revision of the church's doctrinal statement and affirmation of theological pluralism. By 1975, as noted above, Good News built a coalition around that cause. Out of its 1975 convocation came an alternative statement of United Methodist belief, known by the meeting's locale, the Junaluska Affirmation. At the same convocation, Ed Robb, Good News vice chair, delivered a diatribe against the thirteen UMC seminaries, launching thereby another campaign (H **662n167**).

Two of the collaborative action agencies, the IRD and the Mission Society, emerged before 1984. Like Focus on the Family and the American Family Association (the latter founded in 1977 by UMC pastor Donald Wildmon), the IRD linked United Methodists with conservatives in other communions concerned about denominational and interdenominational financial support, programmatic assistance, and open advocacy for various progressive and revolutionary movements (particularly through the NCC and WCC). A stimulus to formation of the IRD was the 1979 exposé by David Jessup of involvements of and investments by the general boards of Global Ministries and Church and Society. With Good News blessing and assistance, Jessup and Ed Robb brought together or gained the endorsement of a number of persons concerned with denominational accountability. Out of this 1981 Washington, D.C., meeting came the Institute of Religion and Democracy. Supported then and thereafter by the Sarah Schaife Foundation and the Smith Richardson Foundation, the IRD quickly took its place within the emerging neoconservative, militantly free-enterprise constellation of political action groups. The IRD succeeded in feeding its findings about denominational left-leanings to *Reader's Digest* and to CBS's *60 Minutes* for late 1982 and early 1983 exposés, the article in the former titled "Do You Know Where Your Church Offerings Go?" Thus began IRD's three-front neoconservative campaign, seemingly aimed at splitting the United Methodist, Presbyterian, and Episcopal Churches (H **662n168**).

The concerns that generated the Mission Society included perceptions that GBGM had committed itself to social and political transformation, to mission rather than the sending of missionaries, and to feminism. Especially agitated over the place of the Women's Division and its new head, Peggy Billings, in GBGM decision making, Ira Gallaway, then pastor of First UMC, Peoria, Illinois, at the time the largest in the North Central Jurisdiction, and previously head of the Board of Evangelism, spelled out his concerns in a 1983 book, *Drifted Away*. The same year he joined others in founding a second mission agency that would be in the business of actually sending missionaries. The 1984 General Conference directed that mediation efforts be made between the new Mission Society and GBGM, but those proved unproductive and were soon halted (H **662nn169–70**).

More loosely knit into the conservative-evangelical political affairs were new groups committed to spiritual transformation and evangelization, among them Aldersgate Renewal Ministries, an organization reflective of a broader charismatic-Pentecostal resurgence, first gathered in 1974. The 1976 General Conference adopted "Guidelines: The UMC and the Charismatic Renewal," issued by Discipleship Resources (of GBOD) as a study book for congregations. A 1977 conference on charismatic renewal in Kansas City formed a network, initially termed the United Methodist Renewal Services Fellowship (later Aldersgate Renewal Ministries, or ARM), to pray and work together for the renewal of the church by the power of the Holy Spirit. ARM held annual national conferences, formed regional chapters, planned "Life in the Spirit" seminars, published a newsletter (*Aldersgate Journal,* later *ARM Update*), and became a self-supporting affiliate of The UMC General Board of Discipleship (GBOD). In the twenty-first century, some fifteen hundred to two thousand people would attend ARM annual meetings, and three thousand were on its support list. Since its beginning, ARM has worked with and within The

UMC as a self-advertised "non-adversarial" group that is more concerned about "lighting candles than cursing the darkness" (H **506–7; 662n171**).

SPIRITUALITY AND THE LANGUAGE OF PRAISE

The bishops, the agencies, and the connectional leaders labored to keep caucuses and causes from dividing the church. GBOD's support of Aldersgate Renewal Ministries represented such an effort, as also its Covenant Discipleship, Academy for Spiritual Formation, and "Walk to Emmaus." The latter, an adaptation of Roman Catholic Cursillo retreats, originated in Spain in 1949, and yielded some three hundred Emmaus communities by the twenty-first century. Emmaus also organizes similar programs for high school youth (called Chrysalis Flights) and for college-age young people (Chrysalis Journeys).

If such programmatic gestures looked out to United Methodism's evangelical wing, other initiatives, especially in worship and hymnody, catered to the racial-ethnic caucuses and to the churchly side of the denomination. *Songs of Zion* (1981) gathered together hymnody of the Black tradition; *Hymns from the Four Winds* (1983), Asian hymns; *Celebremos 1 and 2* (1979 and 1983), Hispanic offerings; and as subtitled, *Voices: Native American Hymns and Worship Resources* (1992). Of the four, *Songs of Zion* with its spirituals, standard evangelical hymns, and gospel songs proved to be the most popular (over one million sold) beyond the ethnic communities.

To bring order out of liturgical chaos, The UMC in 1970 authorized an ambitious twenty-one-volume Alternate Liturgies Project, the larger ecumenical and liturgical context for which its key leader, James F. White, detailed (S **1972c**). A reformed Lord's Supper appeared in English in 1972 and in Spanish in 1978. Fresh services of baptism, with provision for confirmation and renewal, followed in 1976 and new wedding and burial rites in 1979. (We revisit these new services in the next chapter at the point when they are adopted.) Here we note their use of contemporary language, adherence to classical patterns reflecting the new ecumenical and liturgical consensus, adoption of a eucharistic and eschatological tone, and provision for experimentation and wider participation. In abandoning the Wesleyan texts derived from the *Book of Common Prayer*, United Methodism drifted somewhat from

Pan-Methodism (AME, AMEZ, CME), which retained the Reformation-era, Cranmerian liturgies. Instead, The UMC became part of a new liturgical consensus, sharing worship patterns with the rest of mainstream Protestantism, indeed of English-speaking, ecumenical Christianity by:

- preaching following a set of Scripture lections for each Sunday;

- replacing altars attached to the chancel wall with freestanding tables;

- encouraging communicants to receive bread and cup either by standingor by intinction, or both, from a common cup and

- replacing the long-standing ministerial black with white robes and colorful stoles.

Revision to the imagery and phrasing for worship produced heated but fruitful debates about inclusive language, focused initially on references to humanity, but eventually raised in relation to language for God and for the divine nature. By 1974 other mainline churches and the NCC had published guides to more inclusive worship speech. The 1976 General Conference authorized GCOM to establish a task force to draw up "guidelines for eliminating sexism, racism and ageism in language content, theology, and imagery from all church resource materials and mandate that such guidelines shall be adhered to." Two years later the council approved and recommended the guidelines to the general boards and agencies and to annual conferences for their immediate use. The 1980 General Conference approved the guidelines and asked GCOM to add a section on "handicappism." GCOM complied, approved the new section in 1983, and referred the revised guidelines to the 1984 General Conference, which won approval and recommended them for immediate use (H **663nn174–75**). Guided by the Task Force on Language Guidelines, General Conference also adopted *Words that Hurt and Words that Heal.* Approved for study and referred to the general agencies for implementation in church school curriculum, clergy guidance handbooks, and worship and hymn materials, the statement counseled church members to use fewer male pronouns in reference to God; look for alternatives to words such as *Lord, King,* and *Father;* and develop more expansive and inclusive language and imagery to address and describe God, the people of God, and God's action in the world. On connectional levels, in seminaries, and in some locales, United Methodists reshaped worship accordingly. On more local levels, the guidelines and their counsel were either not known or ignored. Indeed, efforts to address concerns of caucuses on the progressive side fueled agitation on the conservative-evangelical side. The new church: United? Untied?

CHAPTER XII
FROM BICENTENNIAL TO CENTURY'S END: 1984–2000

United Methodists commemorated the bicentennial with scholarly consultations, articles and books, and celebrations at annual conferences. General Conference returned to Baltimore, "Proclaiming Grace and Freedom." To facilitate both assessment and celebration, the General Council of Ministries commissioned seventeen inquiries into the state of the connection, each a readable ninety-six pages. This *Into Our Third Century Series* took a hard look at the changing world within and beyond the church. So instructed, United Methodism became increasingly aware that it was growing outside the United States and, with mainline denominations generally, declining within the country. By 1984, United Methodism's membership, less than 11 million at merger, had dropped to near 9 million. Average worship attendance, hovering around 4 million in 1968, stood at 3.5 million. And the church school decreased from 6.2 million to 4 million, an indicator of more bad news to come (H **663nn4–6**).

Strategies and politics of diversity continued to be salient. Jurisdictional conferences in 1984 elected to the episcopacy the church's first woman of color, Leontine Kelly; its first Hispanic, Elias Galvan; another Asian American, Roy Sano; another woman, Judith Craig; and several other Black bishops— Felton May, Forrest Stith, Woodie White, and Ernest Newman, the latter the first by the Southeastern Jurisdiction. The quadrennium saw important vision statements from Hispanic and Native American leaders seeking to continue the unfinished task of developing and strengthening churches and ministries in their communities (S **1985, 1988a**). GBGM in 1986 decided to establish Korean American mission districts in each jurisdiction. The 1988 General

Conference created a National Hispanic Ministries Committee to stimulate congregational development, increase clergy recruitment and lay missioners, and develop new connective mission structures, and approved the plan to build a Methodist-related university for all of Africa (opened in 1992). Also in 1992 appeared a Native American hymn and worship book titled *Voices,* the first ever for the denomination, which included folk parables, prayers, and gospel songs from the more than twenty-five Indigenous tribal nations of The UMC. That year as well, the South Carolina Conference celebrated the assignment of a new episcopal leader, Joseph Bethea, the first Black bishop assigned to South Carolina since the dissolution of the former Central (all-Black) Jurisdiction, and his appointment of the conference's first cross-racial appointments to local churches. In 1996, General Conference adopted the resolution "Racialism: The Church's Unfinished Agenda," and the church launched two related programs, "Strengthening the Black Church for the 21st Century" and "Holy Boldness—A National Plan for Urban Ministry."

On the eve of 1984 General Conference, Good News birthed the Mission Society for United Methodists, rejecting the service-oriented, ecumenical, liberationist mission policy that Tracey Jones had enunciated for GBGM (S **1969**) and reverting to the pattern of sending evangelists. With its various political action committee (PAC) offspring, Good News succeeded in pressing its agenda in the 1984 General Conference.

A wider grassroots initiative—the Baltimore Declaration—urged the church to strengthen efforts in Christian mission: for racial justice, inclusiveness and preventing hunger; toward a nuclear freeze and arms limitation; against the ever widening gap between rich and poor nations; and for basic education and work among young people. Presented to the General Conference as a matter of personal privilege, this Baltimore Declaration was approved by the body and referred to the COB and GCOM for study and implementation (H **663n2**).

Increasingly in this period, United Methodism claimed its global nature. A signature gesture was the building of Africa University in Zimbabwe, endorsed by the General Conference of 1988 and opened in 1992. Also, 1992 saw the creation of Communities of Shalom (the Hebrew word for peace), a response of the church to "third world" conditions (poverty, despair, crime) within the United States and specifically to devastation and destruction that followed the videotaped beating of LA motorist Rodney King. A National Shalom Committee, overseen by the GBGM, offered initial training, start-up funding, technical assistance, a newsletter, brochures and videos, and biennial Shalom Summits. The UMC met its objective of organizing three hundred red Shalom sites by the year 2000. The well-being of the globe claimed attention as well. California-Pacific Conference successfully lobbied the 1992 General Conference to encourage UMC congregations "to defend creation and live as an ecologically-responsible community" (H **663n3**).

NEW DOCTRINAL STANDARDS

Good News registered its convictions for the 1984 General Conference with a deluge of petitions, swelling the total received to thirteen thousand. Among its concerns: evangelical hymns and the doctrinal statement in the *Discipline*. General Conference mandated a committee "representative of the whole church," and "a new statement which will reflect the needs of the church" and "define the scope of our Wesleyan tradition in the context of our contemporary world." The Committee on Our Theological Task construed its mandate broadly (H **514; 663nn9–10**). After three years of study and consultation, the twenty-four-member committee, with Bishop Earl Hunt as chair and Richard Heitzenrater as writer, released a draft of the statement in *Circuit Rider*.

The proposed statement reimagined the quadrilateral as the rule of Scripture within a trilateral hermeneutic of tradition, reason, and experience. It asserted the primacy of Scripture, but it argued that the Bible cannot function with a negation of tradition, reason, and experience or be read or interpreted accurately without their mediation. At the same time the revised doctrinal statement expanded the discussion of the sources and criteria of theology in a number of striking ways. It acknowledged the importance for the continuing theological task of neglected traditions, particularly traditions arising out of the sufferings and victories of the downtrodden. By emphasizing the placement of experienced oppression and liberation in theological reflection, the new statement engaged liberation theology's regard for poor, disabled, imprisoned, oppressed, and outcast people; the equality of all persons in Jesus Christ; and the openness of the gospel to human diversity. The authority of Wesley's sermons, it argued, resided not in an article in the church's constitution but in the church's continuing reference to them over three centuries as model expositions of Methodism's common heritage as Christians.

Critique came from both conservative and progressive camps. The Houston Declaration, disseminated to fifty-five thousand clergy and laity, applauded the report's stress on primacy of Scripture but assailed continuance of the quadrilateral. In "Perfect Love Casts Out Fear," progressives, including many feminist and racial-ethnic leaders, saw "no compelling reason" to change the 1972 doctrinal statement, fearing the revised statement "would move the church into a narrow sectarian and repressive stance" (on both see below and H **664nn12–13**). The Good News caucus supported the Houston critique. The MFSA, Women's Division, and COSROW supported the latter. Debate on the doctrine report at the 1988 General Conference proved strident, often more political than doctrinal, theologizing by catchword, slogan, and innuendo. However, the General Conference legislative committee, chaired by Thomas Langford, dean of Duke Divinity School, negotiated the turbulent, negative waters through a careful consideration of the document and a deliberative process. Substantive changes in the text were few. Much of the discussion focused on refinements of terminology to address concerns of the whole committee: restore traditional Trinitarian language, clarify the relationship between Scripture and the other three elements of the so-called Wesley quadrilateral, reaffirm Wesley's *Sermons* as standards, and strengthen the section on ecumenism. The process and result garnered an overwhelmingly positive approval (94 percent majority) by lay and clergy delegates. Two changes proposed from the floor of the conference drew little discussion and did not pass (H **664n15**).

The 1988 version of "Doctrinal Standards and Our Theological Task," enduring into the twenty-first century, functioned in relation to the "Doctrinal Standards," as had the predecessor statement. And as with the 1972 disciplinary statement, the hermeneutic in "Our Doctrinal Heritage" and "Our Theological Task" became far more usable and used than the standards—Articles of Religion; Confession of Faith; Wesley's *Sermons; Explanatory Notes*; and General Rules—to which it pointed. (See discussion in chapter XI and H **516**.)

The doctrine of the Trinity played a central role in "doctrine wars" and "worship wars" in the 1990s. Methodists had given up "Holy Ghost," singing to the "Holy Spirit" with the 1905 *Hymnal* and invoking the Spirit with the 1935 liturgy. The 1988 General Conference adopted a statement on "Biblical Language," which encouraged the use of diverse metaphorical images for God. Another resolution, however, mandated [no pun intended] the use of the ancient ecumenical formula "Father, Son and Holy Spirit" in baptisms and ordinations. The 2000 General Conference reviewed and expanded the 1988 statement on biblical language in theology and liturgy, but retained liturgical use of the traditional formula. Of particular force in roiling debate has been the Good News insistence that the church- and society-dividing issues of abortion and homosexuality have as much to do with doctrine as with ethics, as we will note below.

EPISCOPAL INITIATIVES

The 1939 union, as we have noted, affected episcopal authority ambiguously. Jurisdictional election and deployment regionalized the office. Momentum toward single-conference assignments further localized "itinerant general superintendency," indeed made it diocesan. On the other hand, the 1939 union provided in the council a structure for possible collective episcopal leadership. The COB, after Bishop Oxnam left his leadership post, could not sustain the connectional leadership he envisioned. One hurdle was the essential social character of their unity. The bishops made the COB into a great fraternity. They dedicated their gatherings to social and peer-support functions. They treated one another with codes of "southern" deference and courtesy. They became an extended family of diocesans and spouses gathered for dinner on the grounds.

Gradually, however, the bishops established patterns of work that would give them a united voice. Various stimuli encouraged concerted action:

- the 1968 union and the sense of a fresh start;

- a sense of crisis in the church over faltering programs and declining membership;

- the faltering of other leadership, particularly that of the boards and agencies;

- modeling by Catholic bishops of what might be achieved by collective action; and

- earlier success with various initiatives, including pastoral letters (H **664n18**).

Formation of a Committee on Episcopal Initiatives for Ministry and Mission focused the council's growing resolve to act collectively. And ecumenical wisdom pointed to the crucial dimension of *episkopé* in the church's exercise of its basic functions. The 1982 WCC publication *Baptism, Eucharist and Ministry* emphasized the leadership dimensions of the office, including that of serving "the apostolicity and unity of the Church's teaching, worship and sacramental life" and relating their Christian community "to the wider Church, and the universal Church to their community" (H **517; 664n19**).

Efforts of individual bishops exercising a representative teaching authority and gaining the ear or eye of the church showed what might be accomplished. Bishop Richard Wilke, for instance, sounded the alarm on United Methodism's hemorrhaging membership in 1986 with a title based on a traditional annual conference hymn, *And Are We Yet Alive?* Acting on his diagnosis and prescription, Wilke persuaded UMPH that church renewal could come through an intensive long-term Bible study program geared to train Christian disciples. With a small group of pastors, theologians, laypeople, Christian educators, Bible scholars, publishers, editors, and marketers, Wilke championed *DISCIPLE Bible study* (DBS), book and video instruction keyed to personal and communal reading and discussion in small groups under trained leadership. DBS aimed to develop leaders as effective followers of Christ. In 1987 UMPH conducted the first training event for pastors and leaders and over the next fifteen years put more than one million people, some beyond the United Methodist connection, through training to lead Disciple in their own congregations. The series became one of the publishing house's most successful ventures. UMPH commissioned translation of the study into French, Cantonese, Mandarin, German, Korean, Spanish, and Russian. In the course of twenty years, three additional long-term studies (DBS-IV) along with four short-term Bible studies were added. By 2006 more than 1.2 million people from thirty-four denominations had participated in DBS. To follow up on its success and its agenda, UMPH released *Christian Believer,* a study of core Christian beliefs by J. Ellsworth Kalas and Justo Gonzáles. Published in 1999, this adult study explored core Christian beliefs in the DBS family of resources in a thirty-session format examining Scripture in relation to aspects of Christian doctrine.

In 1986, the church also experienced the bishops' capacity for corporate leadership with *In Defense of Creation: The Nuclear Crisis and a Just Peace.* This biblical-theological prophecy against the nuclear arms race called the church to peacemaking and critiqued US and Soviet policies of deterrence. From a Duke Chapel kickoff service, the bishops issued a pastoral letter to be read from pulpits across the church (S **1986b**), a forty-page *Guide for Study and Action,* and a hundred-page foundation document. The "Initiatives" leaders, Dale White and C. P. Minnick, had employed as drafter Alan Geyer, executive director of the Churches' Center for Theology and Public Policy, and brought an array of other experts to testify in COB sessions. The two-year process—from the bishops' study of Scripture, of traditional postures on war and peace, and of commissioned background studies, to hearings and gathering of opinion in draft preparation, to first release, to formal presentation, to the mandated reading in its pastoral letter form, to the study of the larger statement in the congregations—represented an incredibly important experiment in episcopal exercise of the teaching office. The same process of sustained study, research, consulting, reflection, delegated writing, and pastoral exhortation informed the 1990 statement *Vital Congregations, Faithful Disciples: Vision for the Church,* drafted by Thomas Frank. In the interim, the bishops, following an established practice of pastoral letters, issued a pastoral on immigration and the plight in American society of legally undocumented people (S **1988b**).

The COB, supported by GBOD, sponsored a church growth and evangelism event in the fall of 1990 for three thousand laypersons and clergypersons. A pastoral letter for the event called congregations to be "more intentional" in responding to the command of Jesus to teach, baptize, and make disciples. Earlier in 1990, having addressed the urban crisis in a statement the prior year (H **664n25**), the bishops named Bishop Felton May to an unprecedented year-long special assignment in Washington, D.C., to provide concentrated leadership in the war on drugs and violence. At year's end, Bishop May returned to his regular post, but continued to serve as a resource person for the COB and as a liaison with The UMC and ecumenical agencies to establish an advocacy campaign to generate more realistic governmental response to the national crisis. May's experience prepared the bishops and the church to launch the aforementioned Shalom Project. Several Methodist bishops took the lead in pressuring governments to impose economic sanctions against South Africa for its policy of racial discrimination.

Thereafter followed other initiatives replicating the engagement procedures for teaching the church—on urban ministries, children and poverty, and the children of Africa. The COB addressed pastorals or released position papers on the Middle East, the ERA, racism, terrorism, AIDS, ethnic cleansing, biblical authority, ministry, and evangelism. In 1998, the COB weighed in on homosexuality and homosexual unions and the issues of discipline, order, and unity posed thereby (S **1998b**), to which we will return below. Designating a bishop the church's chief ecumenical officer, the COB enjoys ongoing staffing from the General Commission on Christian Unity and Interreligious Concerns (GCCUIC), which helps the bishops guide the denomination's ecumenical investments (COCU/CUIC, bilateral; WCC, NCC, interreligious—see below).

NATIVE AMERICAN MINISTRIES

By 1984, The UMC claimed some twenty thousand Indigenous members in 160 congregations and missions served by approximately eighty pastors. Of that total, the Oklahoma Indian Missionary Conference (OIMC) reported 8,245 members in 110 congregations, served by fifty-five pastors and four superintendents among thirty tribes in Oklahoma, Texas, and Kansas. The executive committee of the Native American International Caucus (NAIC), meeting in Oklahoma City in 1985, criticized UMC general agencies for not taking seriously Indigenous leadership and ministry (H **520, 664n28**).

The next quadrennium saw important steps toward that end. In 1987, COSROW sponsored a Native American Women's Consultation, a first, gathering 140 women in ministry from forty tribes and forty-three annual conferences in Albuquerque. In 1988, the OIMC gained full conference rights. The General Board of Church and Society (GBCS) elected its first Native American general secretary, Thom White Wolf Fassett (Seneca Nation, New York). NAIC appointed its first (part-time) executive director, Sam Wynn (Lumbee Nation, North Carolina), and presented a vision document—"The Sacred Circle of Life"—to General Conference (S **1988a**). The statement invited the church to (1) *confess* failures, past and present, (2) *develop* partner relationships and ministries of mutual trust and accountability, and (3) *implement and fund* a plan for congregational and leadership development. General Conference "received" but did not fund or staff the plan. GBGM did, however, adopt a Native American Urban Ministries Initiative targeting three cities: Denver, Seattle, and Los Angeles and the increasingly scattered and urbanized Native peoples.

To remind the church of the gifts and contributions made by Indigenous peoples to our society, General Conference added to the church's calendar a Native American Awareness Sunday, after 1992 Native American Ministries Sunday (H **521, 665nn29–30**). Resources for such services and acts of repentance and reconciliation came slowly. A long-sought NAIC and OIMC project finally came to fruition in 1992 when GBOD aided in the publication of *Voices*, a collection of Indigenous hymns and prayers. The 1992 *Book of Worship* provided hymns and liturgical resources for NAM Sunday. By the twenty-first century, NAM Sunday raised more than $350,000, half retained by conferences to develop local Indigenous ministries and the rest to missions and scholarships for Indigenous seminarians.

Responding to an NAIC request, the 1992 General Conference opened with a Service of Reconciliation and Healing to observe the five hundredth anniversary of Columbus's arrival in North America, elaborated protocols for a race-and-ethnic-sensitive retelling of that half millennium of history ("Toward a New Beginning Beyond 1992"), and adopted a "Confession to Native Americans" (H **665n32**). General Conference also adopted and funded a Native American Comprehensive Plan (NACP). By contrast to past missions developed to and for Indigenous tribes, this plan sought to honor Indigenous culture, values, traditions, and spirituality. The church pledged to work *alongside* Indigenous tribes in mission and ministry; acknowledge failures, past and present; develop partner relationships; and develop ministries of mutual trust and accountability.

Ann Saunkeah, Cherokee schoolteacher from Tulsa, became NACP director in 1997. The Rev. Thomas Roughface of the Ponca Nation became, in 1990, the OIMC superintendent, perhaps the first Indigenous leader to hold the quasi-episcopal office. In 1992, an Oklahoma City clergywoman, the Rev. Lois G. Neal, became the first Indigenous DS. One month later, Neal, a Cherokee, was named dean of the conference cabinet.

In 1994, OIMC celebrated its 150th anniversary. Two years later it adopted a capital fund campaign to plant new churches and to establish volunteers-in-mission "to continue the journey from a mission of the church to a mission *with* the church" (that is, to become autonomous and self-supporting). That year OIMC was one of only eleven conferences to pay 100 percent or more of their World Service apportionment. Also in 1996, NAIC appointed a full-time director, Alvin Deer (Kiowa-Creek Nation, Oklahoma), and Cokesbury issued *Eagle Flights: Native Americans and the Christian Faith*, a congregational study resource. The 1996 General Conference offered an ill-informed apology for the 1864 Sand Creek, Colorado, massacre led by Col. John Chivington, a Methodist pastor, which would be followed up in 2012–2016 with a quadrennial study of Sand Creek and a more intentional service of repentance. It also adopted a resolution "Concerning Demeaning Names to Native Americans," which critiqued team names and mascots that stereotyped Indigenous peoples as "violent and aggressive." In 2000, NAIC successfully petitioned General Conference to affirm the "Human Rights of Native People of the Americas." General Conference also adopted the resolution "Ecumenical Dialogues on the Native Community" (H **665n34**).

LATINO/HISPANIC MINISTRIES

In 1985, MARCHA issued "Hispanic Vision for Century III" (S **1985**). By celebrating election of Hispanic leaders, a Black woman bishop, and Japanese American bishops, the vision statement lamented little comparable progress among Hispanics through the Ethnic Minority Local Church (EMCL) missional priority, identified chronically enervating conditions, and summoned "the whole denomination" to engage in seven transformative goals. MARCHA also pledged support for the Sanctuary Movement, supported autonomy for the Methodist Church of Puerto Rico, selected laywomen as executive director and president, and held its first national Hispanic Women's Consultation. In 1986, the Rio Grande Conference selected the first Latina DS, the Rev. Minerva Carcaño. By the end of the year, three Hispanic superintendents had also been appointed outside the predominantly Hispanic Rio Grande and Puerto Rico Conferences. MARCHA had other good news to report that year: formation of fifty-seven new Hispanic congregations since 1980, increased representation on boards (twenty-two Hispanic executive staff and fifty-two members), and additional Spanish-language resources from UMPH and GBOD. The caucus held an important strategy consultation the following May in Denver (1987).

The 1988 General Conference authorized development of a comprehensive national plan for Hispanic ministries. The 1988 conference also authorized a Spanish-language translation of the full *Discipline* and adopted a resolution against establishing English as the official language of the United States, supporting a MARCHA-backed "English-plus" alternative to the

"English-only" movement. Reflecting the caucus's support of the Sanctuary Movement, the COB issued and General Conference endorsed an important pastoral letter "Undocumented Migration: To Love the Sojourner" (S **1988b**). It urged church members to join them in an effort "to correct the injustices that may be perpetuated" by the 1986 US Immigration and Control Act, to recognize God's preferential option for the "sojourner" (or stranger), and with respect to immigrants "to know them, their circumstances and needs, to love them, to embrace them and their struggle, [and] to bid them welcome to our communities, religious and civil" (H **665nn36–37**).

Over the next quadrennium, the church produced resources supportive of MARCHA's goals. Harold Recinos published *Hear the Cry: A Latino Pastor Challenges the Church* in 1989. *The United Methodist Hymnal* (1989) featured eighteen hymns of Hispanic origin, including Carlos Rosas's "Cantemos al Señor" ("Let's Sing unto the Lord"). *The United Methodist Book of Worship* (1992) included Mexican Advent and Christmas Eve liturgies, *Las Posadas,* services of preparation for the birth of the Savior and shelter for the newborn babe and the Holy Family. The National Hispanic Ministries Committee, chaired by Bishop Elias Galvan of Phoenix, assessed demographic trends, surveyed 320 Hispanic congregations about needs and ministries, and drafted a plan for 1992 General Conference.

The 1992 General Conference approved a National Hispanic Ministries Plan, the first coordinated, comprehensive Hispanic-led denominational effort to focus on the development and strengthening of Hispanic ministries in the United States. By 1999 the plan had trained 796 lay missioners and 100 pastor-mentors representing forty-six conferences. In 2000, sixty-one of the sixty-six US conferences reported some sort of Hispanic ministry. General Conference 1992 granted autonomy to the Methodist Church of Puerto Rico; began a Cuban initiative; and established a permanent church fund, "Encounter with Christ," to provide long-term support and development in Latin America and the Caribbean in areas such as evangelization and new church development; work with women, children, and youth; and community-based health care. In the jurisdictional episcopal elections that summer, The UMC elected a second Hispanic bishop, Joel Martinez, and assigned him to the Nebraska Area.

In 1994, MARCHA denounced a California immigration proposition. In 1996, General Conference concurred and adopted a fresh resolution on immigration policy, "Immigration and Refugees: To Love the Sojourner"

(H **665n38**). The UM Committee on Relief (UMCOR) launched "Justice for Our Neighbors." Modeled after a local immigration project in Virginia, the program led to the establishment of church-related legal clinics for immigrants at fourteen sites and became an ongoing program. Two important resources appeared that year, *Obras de Wesley*, a fourteen-volume scholarly translation of the modern critical edition of John Wesley's *Works* and *Mil Voces para Celebrar*, the first truly Hispanic hymnal and worship book under editorship of Raquel Mora Martínez. In 1997, The UMC and the Methodist Church of Mexico established the Mexico Border Bilateral Mission Committee. And Florida United Methodists renewed their relationship with Cuban Methodists, establishing a covenant to strengthen both ministries and sending work teams to Cuba to help rebuild churches, parsonages, and the Canaan Camp Assembly. (MARCHA was on record opposing the Cuban embargo.) A collection of hymns, *Cantos Del Pueblo*, appeared in 1997. In 1999, Jo Harris and Russ Harris published a manual for non-Hispanic churches in ministry with Hispanics, *Partners in the Mighty Works of God*. Hispanic young people, meeting in Nashville, created a Young Hispanic Methodist Movement.

In 2000, MARCHA proposed the creation of a Portuguese-language ministry. David Maldonado became the first Latino UMC theological seminary president/dean (Iliff, Denver). General Conference went on record opposing the 1996 immigration act. GBGM launched a $25 million fundraising initiative dubbed "Encounter with Christ" to help UM churches partner with Methodist churches in nineteen countries throughout Mexico, Central America, South America, and the Caribbean (H **665n39**).

KOREAN AMERICAN MINISTRIES

The 1984 General Conference charged GBGM to "consider appropriate missionary structures to strengthen Korean language ministries and new church development." The next year, Korean American Women Clergy (KAWC) gathered at its first national consultation under leadership and a National Committee on Korean-American Ministries (NCKAM) was formed under GBGM. By 1987, Korean Mission superintendents had been appointed in each jurisdiction. Korean American churches more than doubled, from 105 in 1982 to 212 in 1986. The Northeastern Jurisdiction had the largest number, the Western second. By 1987, Korean-language congregations accounted for more than half of The UMC churches formed in the United States since 1980. By the turn of the twenty-first century, the 6 congregations from 1970 had increased to about 360, in addition to which there were 260 Korean Methodist Church (KMC) congregations. By 2000, the KMC had contributed 41 percent of The UMC's approximately 500 Korean American pastors, perhaps not surprising since 95 percent were born in Korea. Only 20 of the 360 Korean American congregations were English speaking. Of the 90 Korean American clergywomen, fewer than 21 percent served Korean-language churches (H **665nn40–43**).

In the late 1980s and early 1990s, UMC Koreans competed with the KMC but struggled as well within The UMC—with officials, church organizational procedures, and cumbersome English-only ministerial education and credentialing processes; with non-Korean pastors and congregations when church facilities were shared; and with other Asian American and other ethnic groups for ecclesial, economic, and societal space and prerogative. Further, with an educated constituency of professionals, managers, health workers, and business folk and with rapidly Anglicizing children, pastors and congregations struggled to function bilingually.

In 1990, the COB named seven bishops to meet leaders of the KMC in Korea to "regularize the relationship between the two churches." Also in 1990, a Korean-language program journal, *United Methodist Family,* began publication. By 1992, the National Association of Korean American United Methodist Churches (NAKAUMC) began to lobby for a nongeographical Korean-language conference that would unite some three hundred Korean congregations across the United States, would compete more effectively with the Seoul-based KMC, and would provide something of the latter's supportive cultural and linguistic services. The caucus modeled its plan after the Spanish-speaking Rio Grande Conference. General Conference said no in 1992.

The 1992 General Conference did authorize the formation of a committee to explore development of Asian American ministries in a comprehensive manner. That summer the Northeastern Jurisdiction elected Hae Jong Kim to the episcopacy. In 1994, GBGM published *A Manual on Shared Facilities* to ease tensions between congregations sharing the same building, offering suggestions on leadership responsibilities, property, and budgets. The General Commission on Religion and Race also began offering resources for facility sharing at the same time. NAKAUMC laid out a more formal proposal for Korean American missionary conferences in an open letter to delegates to the

1996 General Conference (S **1996a**). Some Korean American clergywomen and GBGM lobbied against the plan, and General Conference again rejected it. General Conference did approve the proposed comprehensive plan for Asian American ministries that had been formulated over the quadrennium. Funded at $900,000, it addressed congregational development, leadership training, community outreach ministry, and language resources development (H **527**).

In April 1998, the GBGM commissioned the first group of Korean American "mission pastors" to develop new congregations. The next month, the first national Korean American United Methodist Mission Convocation met in Los Angeles. It offered sessions on sensitivity training, ministry with second-generation Korean Americans, and development of leadership roles for the growing number of Korean American clergywomen, many of whom served non-Korean or multicultural ministries. Also in 1998, United Methodist Communications launched a bimonthly magazine for Korean UMC pastors and lay leaders: *United Methodists in Service*. The 2000 General Conference responded to and approved several Korean and Asian Caucus proposals, funding ministries for more than fifteen Asian-language groups, underwriting a Council on Korean American Ministries, and adopting a bilingual Korean-English hymnal as an official church resource.

ABORTION POLICY

In 1987, nine United Methodists, led by North Carolina pastor Paul Stallsworth, formed "a national organization to help United Methodists deal with our church's inability to minister to the problems of our pro-abortion society," as he later explained (H **665n45**). This Taskforce on United Methodists on Abortion and Sexuality, an unofficial antiabortion caucus, contests UMC involvement in the Religious Coalition for Abortion Rights (RCAR) and presses to circumscribe or eliminate the church's sanction of abortion. Under such guidance, the 1988 General Conference added to the "Abortion" section of the Social Principles the proviso "We cannot affirm abortion as an acceptable measure of birth control, and we unconditionally reject it as a means of gender selection" (H **665n46**).

In 1990, Stallsworth and colleagues launched a newsletter, *Lifewatch,* and the same year convened thirty UMC leaders, primarily from the Southeast.

They issued the Durham Declaration (S **1990**), calling on the church to address abortion theologically, and offered a first attempt to do just that. By affirmation of faith and proclamation of the message of salvation in Jesus Christ, they summoned United Methodists to "let the children come to me" and to rely on God's sufficient grace "to meet the massive test" of abortion. Comparing the cause to antislavery, they accused the denomination of treating in political terms what has fundamentally to do with God's creation and ought to be constitutive of the church's mission. The declaration urged United Methodists "to become a church that hospitably provides a safe refuge for the so-called 'unwanted child' and mother." Although the document pledged "to offer the hope of God's mercy and forgiveness" to women who obtain elective abortions, it contrasted with the church's existing teaching on abortion by giving no indication that abortion is ever a justifiable option for Christians. Signers of the declaration included four retired bishops and also theologians Stanley Hauerwas, William Willimon (later bishop), Geoffrey Wainwright, and Thomas Oden (H **529; 665n47**).

The 1992 General Conference debated but affirmed United Methodist participation in the Religious Coalition for Abortion Rights, an 84 percent majority. Delegates were assured that neither GBGM nor GBCS had supported RCAR financially, although both boards had seats on the RCAR board. At the end of 1993, RCAR moved to larger quarters in Washington, D.C. With opponents taking terrorist actions at birth control clinics, some UMC clergy rallied support for Planned Parenthood and pro-choice options. And the 1996 General Conference defeated a "rights of the unborn" addendum to its pro-choice-with-stipulations stance on abortion. Delegates also voted to continue support for the Religious Coalition for Reproductive Choice (RCRC, previously RCAR).

Antiabortion strategy, in church as in state, chipped away at language protective of choice. The 2000 General Conference added: "We oppose the use of late-term abortion known as dilation and extraction (partial-birth abortion) and call for an end of this practice except when the physical life of the mother is in danger and no other medical procedure is available, or in the case of severe fetal anomalies incompatible with life" (H **665n49**). Less conciliatory than Stallsworth and *Lifewatch,* the IRD and its UM *Action* continued to vilify the Women's Division, GBCS, and progressive church leaders generally on abortion and other culture war issues. By 2016, The UMC would withdraw its participation in RCAR/RCRC (although individual annual conferences have recommitted their support). As the votes on LGBTQ+ affirmation have grown closer with each General Conference, the votes on whether or not to support abortion as a legal right have grown further apart, with more votes opting to restrict The UMC's language. What was once a few sentences in the early 1970s is now a 2½ page statement on abortion, with qualification after qualification leading ultimately to a confused declaration of a woman's right to an abortion but only under the narrowest of circumstances.

HOMOSEXUALITY

Prohibition against ordination of gay men and lesbians became a key Good News agenda item for and the central "gay issue" at the 1984 General Conference. The delegates approved "fidelity in marriage and celibacy in singleness" as a standard for all ordained clergy. When consulted, the Judicial Council declared that the "seven last words," as the statement became labeled, did not forbid gay and lesbian clergy. General Conference then clarified the prohibition: "Since the practice of homosexuality is incompatible with Christian teaching, self-avowed practicing homosexuals are not to be accepted as candidates, ordained as ministers, or appointed to serve in The United Methodist Church" (H **665n50**). What did "self-avowed practicing homosexuals" mean? Did the absence of a comma separating "self-avowed" and "practicing" mean orientation alone did not bar ordination? In April 1987, the COB complained that "unless 'self-avowed' homosexuals admit that they are 'practicing' that lifestyle, the decision to ordain them rests with the clergy members of each annual conference, not a bishop or the Council of Bishops" (H **665n51**). Confusion reigned.

Affirmation and RCP (see chapter XI) mounted efforts to rescind the restrictions, make the church more welcoming to gays and lesbians, and articulate a unifying theology for the cause and develop resources through which to transmit it. It commissioned position papers and in 1985 launched a quarterly, *Manna for the Journey,* later renamed *Open Hands.* At successive General Conferences, beginning with that of 1988, RCP has coordinated a public reconciling witness. By the early 1990s, fifty congregations, four annual conferences, and one general agency (GCCUIC) had committed themselves to hospitality, healing, and hope. In 1996 a Reconciling Parents Network, MoSAIC (Methodist Students for an All-Inclusive Church), and United Methodists of Color for a Fully Inclusive Church formed. These groups, organized with the support of the national RCP office, functioned independently, a relationship that prompted RCP in 2000 to rename itself the Reconciling Ministries Network (H **665n52**).

To clarify the church's mind in a different direction, conservative pastors and seminary professors gathered in Houston in December 1987 to strategize and adopt an agenda for the upcoming conference. Conferees endorsed a three-part (previously mentioned Houston Declaration) declaration bemoaning a "crisis of faith." Commenting in turn on "the Primacy of Scriptures," "The Trinity," and "The Ordained Ministry," the declaration devoted one section entirely to homosexuality, labeled homosexual practice as sinful, urged support of ministries that helped gay men and lesbians change their lifestyle, even if their orientation was immutable, and called it "unacceptable in the context of the Christian faith" for gays and lesbians to "be ordained to ministry or continue in representative positions within the Church." Host church pastor Bill Hinson and Duke's Geoffrey Wainwright led the drafting. The declaration went to all UMC clergy and local church lay leaders, a mailing of more than fifty-five thousand. Another lay statement, "A Call to Action," was released to the church in early March (H **665–66nn53–54**).

A progressive rebuttal, "Perfect Love Casts Out Fear," issued in December by fifty pastors and seminary professors and signed by more than one hundred other church leaders, charged that the Houston statement presented "truths as Wesleyan which are anathema to the spirit of Wesley and Methodism." Proclaiming the "diversity of our people is the glory of this UMC," the progressives maintained, "they do not speak for us. They do not speak for us as women. They do not speak for persons of color. They do not speak for Wesley. We pray that they do not speak for the General Conference." "The Bible," they noted, "does not have a great deal to say about homosexuality . . . knows nothing of sexual orientation." Houston, they observed, ignored the contexts (adultery, promiscuity, violence, idolatry) of biblical statements (H **531; 666n55**).

The COB issued its own "statement of concern" during their November 1987 meeting. It called upon all United Methodists to "join with us in being faithful to the standards, 'fidelity in marriage and celibacy in singleness,' which have been adopted through the struggles of our covenant community of faith over the years." And in his COB presidential, Bishop Earl Hunt urged colleagues to lead the church in "warfare against evil," beginning with racism and sexual immorality, especially homosexuality. "I believe the intercession of episcopal leadership on this issue is warranted," he exhorted, "because of the involvement of basic principles of historic Christian teaching." That year, ironically, retired bishop Finis Crutchfield of Houston, died allegedly of AIDS. When the Crutchfield family implied that the virus had been acquired through Crutchfield's acts of pastoral care to persons with AIDS, the Texas gay community broke its silence and outed Crutchfield as a gay man who lived a double life—a heterosexual bishop and a sexually active gay man with multiple sex partners (H **666n57**).

The 1988 General Conference reaffirmed The UMC's negative legislation on gay and lesbian issues by a wide margin. However, it added to the incompatible statement (as italicized): "Although we do not condone the practice of homosexuality, and consider this practice to be incompatible with Christian teaching, *we affirm that God's grace is available to all. We commit ourselves to be in ministry for and with all persons*." By a narrow margin, General Conference approved a four-year study of homosexuality, called for earlier by the church's youth. An addition to the Social Principles statement urged The UMC "to take the leadership role in bringing together the medical, theological, and social science disciplines to address this most complex issue"—human sexuality (H **666nn58–60**). Delegates proved able to separate AIDS from the intense debate on homosexuality, including only oblique allusions in the denomination's first comprehensive treatment: "AIDS and the Healing Ministry of the Church." In the best tradition of Methodist activism, the statement directed church agencies and congregations to develop a plan for ministry to persons with AIDS and to act to change public policy, especially in the area of civil rights for persons with AIDS. A second resolution, "Resources for AIDS Education," mandated an education program through the entire church by the several general boards concerned with the AIDS issue. Affirmation served as a key resource behind the scenes in developing The UMC's response to the AIDS epidemic (H **666nn61–62**).

To counter the highly successful RCP (now Reconciling Ministries Network), conservatives in the California–Nevada Conference, led by Robert Kuyper, in October 1988 formed the Transforming Congregation Program (TCP). Kuyper described TCP in *Good News* as a theological and medical concern and homosexuality as a sin that can be forgiven and a sickness that can be cured. Good News adopted the movement as one of its task forces and supported its development of TCP by providing a $10,000 start-up grant.

That provided a stipend for Bakersfield pastor Kuyper as national coordinator and a part-time secretary. In 1996, TCP became a separate ministry, and in 1998 the organization hired layman Jim Gentile as full-time executive director (H **666n64**).

The study committee created by the 1988 General Conference gathered testimony in biblical studies, theology, ethics, and the sciences; heard grassroots members; and debated whether to lift or reinforce the church's ban on ordained practicing homosexuals. After its four years of information gathering, the study committee agreed to disagree about what the church can and cannot affirm with regard to homosexuality. It reported to General Conference, eight "Things the Church Can Responsibly Teach" and ten "Things the Church Cannot Responsibly Teach" on the subject of homosexuality (S **1992**; H **533–34**; **666n65**). The majority of the committee concluded certain assertions to be true:

- the seven biblical references and allusions cannot be taken as definitive for Christian teaching about homosexual practices because they represent cultural patterns of ancient society and not the will of God;

- the scientific evidence is sufficient to support the contention that homosexuality is not pathological or otherwise an inversion, developmental failure, or deviant form of life as such, but is rather a human variant, one that can be healthy and whole;

- the emerging scholarly views in biblical studies, ethics, and theology support a view that affirms homosexual relationships that are covenantal, committed, and monogamous; and

- the witness to God's grace of lesbian and gay Christians in the life of the church supports these conclusions (H **666n66**).

The 1992 General Conference "received" the report, rejected its recommendations, but directed that it be made available for congregations to study. General Conference added two sections in the Social Principles supporting the human and civil rights of gay men and lesbians. Later in 1992, charges against Jeanne Knepper, a lesbian, led to one of the first cases to go to the

Judicial Council. The council ruled that she continue to be appointed by a bishop to ministry in the denomination.

At the 1996 General Conference, fifteen bishops broke ranks and spoke out against church policies. Despite this admonition and other lobbying efforts favoring change, the 1996 General Conference reaffirmed The UMC's exclusionary rules and added a prohibition in the Social Principles regarding same-sex unions: "Ceremonies that celebrate homosexual union shall not be conducted by our ministers and shall not be conducted in our churches." The 1996 prohibition against **holy unions** "remedied" the 1972 Social Principles that permissively declared "we do not recommend marriage between two persons of the same sex" (H **666nn68–69**). Since this legislation did not specifically prohibit holy *unions,* such services had been celebrated, usually quietly, by UMC clergy from the early 1970s: Cecil Williams in San Francisco, William Alberts in Boston, and Paul Abels in New York. Bans began around 1990 when Bishop Joseph Yeakel forbade a Washington, D.C., congregation from holding such a service, stating it would violate church law. Two conferences, Minnesota and Troy (upstate New York and Vermont), endeavored to allow congregations or pastors discretion on such unions, actions appealed to the Judicial Council. The Judicial Council ruled in October 1993 that only the General Conference had the authority to establish the church's rites and rituals. Thus the decisive action by the 1996 General Conference. During the same year, the US Congress passed and President Bill Clinton signed the Defense of Marriage Act, defining marriage as being "between a man and a woman."

Holy unions heightened conflict within The UMC. Progressives issued a "Statement of Conscience," dated January 1, 1997, along with the document "In All Things Charity," drafted by fifteen clergy and signed by thirteen hundred UMC clergy across the nation who vowed to continue to celebrate holy unions. Later that year signers and their Affirmation friends formed a web-based Covenant Relationship Network (CORNET) to support the right of UMC clergy to perform holy unions. Conservatives countered with "The More Excellent Way: God's Plan Reaffirmed," a manifesto urging those who seek acceptance of homosexuality in all its forms to find other venues than "UM pulpits, boards, agencies, educational institutions and other affiliated entities" to express their views (H **667nn72–74**).

In 1997, Jimmy Creech, pastor of First UMC, Omaha, performed a covenant service for two women despite his bishop's request that he refrain from doing so. Charges were successfully brought against him, and after his second holy union and church trial in North Carolina, Creech's ministerial credentials were revoked. Jimmy Creech defended his disobedience at his trial (S **1998a**) and as a layperson continued to proclaim that "the church, not gays had sinned" and to campaign for same-sex unions. Later that spring the Council of Bishops issued a pained pastoral statement on holy unions in hopes of healing the rift (S **1998b**; H **667n76**). In August, the Judicial Council determined the disciplinary prohibition against same-sex unions to be enforceable, notwithstanding the law's curious placement in the Social Principles, a matter that the decision examines (S **1998c**).

Defiance of the ban continued. In October 1998 Gregory Dell celebrated a holy union of two men in his Chicago church, resulting in a one-year suspension from ministry without pay. In January 1999, more than one hundred clergy co-officiated at a holy union in California. Organized by Donald Fado of St. Mark's UMC, Sacramento, the holy union celebrated the relationship of life partners Jeanne Barnett and Ellie Charlton—Barnett the California–Nevada lay leader and Charlton a member of the conference board of trustees. Complaints were filed against sixty-eight of the California–Nevada Conference clergy, dubbed the "Sacramento 68." Bishop Melvin Talbert announced that he was handling the charges in the way mandated by the *Discipline*, but called the charges an "act of injustice." He added, "I will not be silenced. I will continue . . . working to change the position of our church to be more in keeping with the teachings and compassion of Jesus." A hearing in February 2000 by the conference Committee on Investigation found insufficient cause to order a church trial (H **667nn78–79**). Almost immediately, complaints were filed against Bishop Talbert for allowing the committee to reach a conclusion that seemed to ignore the facts of the case and the laws of the denomination. The complaints against Bishop Talbert were dismissed in August 2000.

MFSA long supported same-sex unions and ordination for gays and lesbians, and was active around the church trials of Jimmy Creech, Greg Dell, and the Sacramento 68. Following the murder of Matthew Shepard in 1998, the UMC's two LGBT caucuses, Affirmation and RCP, joined the Human Rights Campaign and others in a national movement supporting hate-violence legislation to protect lesbian, gay, bisexual, and transgender Americans.

POLITICAL THEOLOGIZING

By matching liberation theologies of the left, evangelical conservatives increasingly framed concerns about abortion and homosexuality in theological and biblical terms. In Houston (1988), Durham (S **1990**), DuPage (1990), Louisville (1990), and Memphis (1992) declarations, Good News and allies interlaced social and theological concerns and successively added to the coalition. United Methodism's problems, conservatives said, went deeper than faulty communication, flagging connectionalism, and leadership indifferent to apostasy. United Methodists must confess the uniqueness of Jesus Christ as the only Savior and renew their dedication to holy living and world evangelization. Over successive strategy sessions, Good News etched bold prescriptions for Methodist reform: (1) enact membership requirements; (2) abolish guaranteed clergy appointments; (3) begin automatic four-year clergy appointments; (4) add laypeople to boards of ordained ministry; (5) give laity a voice in the executive session of the annual conference; (6) bring back local preachers; (7) enhance consultation in the process of appointing pastors; (8) make apportionments voluntary; (9) highlight preaching and worship services versus business at annual conference meetings; (10) make youth ministry a missional priority; (11) put the Ministerial Education Fund on a voucher system and funds directly in student hands, not seminary coffers; (12) remove the trust clause, which prevents splinter groups from taking church property away from the denomination; (13) split GBGM; (14) retire the quota system; and (15) make bishops lead.

In 1993, Good News board members (including Thomas Oden of Drew; Maxie Dunnam, then in Memphis, later to be president of Asbury Seminary; Bill Hinson from Houston; John Ed Mathison of Frazer Memorial, Montgomery; and Bishop William Cannon) laid plans for a Confessing Movement and invited a hundred church leaders to a Consultation on the Future of the Church. From the April 1994 Atlanta meeting came an invitation to United Methodists: either abandon the Christian faith or lead a new awakening (S **1994b**). Signers of this "Invitation" included bishops William Cannon, Earl Hunt, Richard Looney, Mack Stokes, and William Morris. Some nine hundred responded and met again in Atlanta to found the Confessing Movement. Doubtless with a nod to the November 1993 feminist Re-Imagining Conference (see last section and H **536–37, 551–53**), they declared that The UMC had abandoned classical Christianity and "lost its immune system with regard to false teaching." Pledging to contend for the ancient classical ecumenical faith and to affirm Jesus Christ as Son, Savior, and Lord, the new movement claimed that The *UMC was a confessional church* in principle, if not in practice, because of constitutional established doctrinal standards. The Confessing Movement dedicated itself to "contend for the apostolic faith" and "repudiate teachings and practices that misuse principles of inclusiveness and tolerance to distort the doctrine and discipline of the church" (H **667nn82–83**).

Progressives responded in a February 1996 open letter, "A Critical Challenge to the Confessing Movement," its signers including five seminary faculty. The Confessing Movement, it charged, aimed to make bishops, clergy, and church members "confess" a specific interpretation of Scripture and core beliefs and claim that other world religions were not means of salvation. These statements, they argued, contradicted a tradition extending back to Wesley that affirmed a variety of theologies within the denomination and respected and celebrated the diversity of world religions through which God continues to speak (H **667n84**).

Worrying that controversy over homosexuality, doctrine, and the authority of the Bible might lead to schism, GCCUIC General Secretary Bruce Robbins convened peacemaking dialogues in Nashville (1997) and Dallas (1998). Many attendees were affiliated with unofficial caucuses and renewal movements on the right and the left that had for decades castigated one another. That name-calling and stereotyping must stop, insisted several members at the outset. A breakthrough came the second day when members identified and dealt with issues that threatened the unity of the church. After its second meeting, the theological Diversity Dialogue Team reported its findings to the church. One of the most fruitful outcomes was a set of "Guidelines for Civility in The United Methodist Church." Those, along with efforts to map areas of agreement and disagreement, appear in GCCUIC's published report (S **1998d**): *In Search of Unity: A Conversation with Recommendations for the Unity of The United Methodist Church.* Naming the polarization and potential for schism, the Dialogue observed, "Compatibilists believe that both sides on the issue of the morality of homosexual behavior and the nature and status of divine revelation can be held together within the same denomination. . . . Incompatibilists do not believe that these divergent judgments can be housed indefinitely within the same denomination." The Dialogue identified ways by which compatibilists and incompatibilists could receive and create the unity that Christ wills, outlining eight action steps and recommending the reading of John Wesley's sermonic injunctions to unity: "On Schism," "A Caution Against Bigotry," and "Catholic Spirit."

CHRISTIAN UNITY

GCCUIC's unity tasks have been perhaps easier externally than internally. Acknowledging the anti-Catholic bias of the eighteenth-century Articles of Religion, the 1970 General Conference adopted a "Resolution of Intent—with a View to Unity." Reaffirmed in 2000, the statement pledged "henceforth to interpret all our Articles, Confession and other standards of doctrine in consonance with our best ecumenical insights and judgment." The revised doctrinal statement of 1988, "Our Theological Task," commits the church to "the theological, biblical and practical mandates for Christian unity." And successive General Conferences have added affirmations of Christian unity as official policy and earnest hope and commitments to its several ecumenical endeavors, in the *Discipline* and *The Book of Resolutions of The United Methodist Church* (H **667–68nn86–87**).

United Methodism and its predecessor churches had been active from the start in ecumenical projects. At the founding of the Evangelical Alliance in London in 1846, Stephen Olin, president of Wesleyan University (Connecticut), pledged The MEC's cordial cooperation. And Methodists participated in the dozen meetings in the nineteenth century of this transatlantic Protestant gathering, as also in the several meetings of its American branch, constituted in 1867. Of the dialogues and conversations between and among the several Methodist churches and the United Brethren and Evangelical churches that eventuated in the Methodist (1939), EUB (1946), and United Methodist (1968) unions, we have already taken note, as also of American Methodist participation from 1881 onward in the Ecumenical Methodist Conferences (now World Methodist Council).

In the late nineteenth- and twentieth-century missionary cooperation and in the Life and Work and Faith and Order efforts, Methodists provided key leadership. John R. Mott, a Methodist layperson, participant in the Student Volunteer Movement and staff for the YMCA, helped found (1895) and until 1930 led the World Student Christian Federation, which in turn helped launch both the International Missionary Council (1921) and the

World Council of Churches (1948). Mott, an active figure in cooperative relief in World War I and in both Faith and Order and Life and Work conferences, fittingly preached for the WCC's inaugural assembly and was elected its honorary president (since its beginning Methodists have contributed two of the five WCC chief executives, Philip Potter of the West Indies, 1972–84 and Emilio Castro of Ghana, 1985–92).

In the earlier founding of the Federal Council of Churches, Frank Mason North (MEC) and UB bishop William Bell played major roles. Among other Methodists contributing to ecumenical endeavor—leadership in the NCC, observers at the Second Vatican Council, participation in the Consultation on Church Union (COCU), multilateral, bilateral, and interreligious dialogues—were bishops Bromley Oxnam and William Cannon; theologians Albert Outler, Robert Nelson, John Deschner, and Geoffrey Wainwright; GCCUIC staff Jeanne Audrey Powers and Bruce Robbins; COCU executive Gerald Moede; and Harvard champion of interreligious studies and dialogue Diana Eck (H **668nn88–90**).

The nine US communions constituting COCU (founded in 1962), including Methodists, The EUBC, and the three Black Methodist denominations, reached sufficient agreement on ministry and sacraments to formulate in 1970 a plan for merger and the creation of a new ecclesial body. The plan for a mega-denomination failed, and COCU began exploration of nonstructural forms of unity. From 1974–88, Moede, a major interpreter of COCU's vision, served as general secretary. By 1984, under his leadership, COCU reached agreement on a Doctrinal Consensus. The 1988 UMC General Conference found the COCU consensus a "faithful expression of the apostolic faith, order, worship and witness of the church." That same year, the seventeenth COCU plenary approved a Statement of Covenanting. Its eight elements are "claiming unity in faith, commitment to seek unity with wholeness, mutual recognition of members in one baptism, mutual recognition of each other as churches, mutual recognition and reconciliation of ordained ministry, celebrating the Eucharist together, engaging together in Christ's mission and formation of covenant councils." In 1996 the General Conferences of the AME, AMEZ, and UMC adopted the COCU Covenant Proposal "Churches in Covenant Communion." Known briefly then as CICC, the multilateral soon thereafter metamorphosed into Churches Uniting in Christ (H **668nn91–92**).

Among COCU's commitments was that of combating racism. On that campaign United Methodism opened another front directly with the AME, AMEZ, and CME churches (and as of 2000, with the Union American Methodist Episcopal Church). In 1985, the four Methodisms established a Commission on Pan-Methodist Cooperation (USA), calling for full communion and joint ordinations, programming, and resourcing. Constructive talks led the commission in 1991 to request the churches to authorize a study commission to explore merger. By 1996, the General Conferences of the AME, AMEZ, and UMC churches authorized a Commission on Pan-Methodist Union to proceed to develop a plan of union. As a gesture of reconciliation, members of the 2000 UMC General Conference and leaders from the Pan-Methodist churches participated in a service of repentance and reconciliation. General Conference also authorized voting representatives from Pan-Methodist denominations on its agencies.

United Methodism continues active participation in, monetary support of, and leadership for such multilateral ecumenical endeavors, including the WCC, the NCC, and state and local councils of churches. That investment and its yield were symbolized in 1982 with British-Methodist-but-American-theologian Geoffrey Wainwright playing a major role in drafting the landmark WCC Lima text, *Baptism, Eucharist and Ministry.* The COB provided The UMC's formal response, its affirmation included in the ten volumes of *Churches Respond to BEM* (see below). In the last two decades of the twentieth century, The UMC engaged heavily in bilateral and interreligious dialogue, adopting resolutions on relations with Jews (1972), on guidelines for dialogue (1980), and on "Our Muslim Neighbors" (1992; H **668n94**).

To facilitate such explorations, the church gave GCCUIC commission status in 1980 and the COB selected a bishop as chief ecumenical officer. It held this status until 2012 when the General Conference placed it as an office lodged within the Council of Bishops.[1] Internationally, The UMC participated in dialogues through the World Methodist Council. Through the latter, Methodists formulated important theological statements with Catholics, the Orthodox, Lutherans, the Reformed, and Anglicans (detailed on H **541–42**; see **668n95**). International conversations with Anglicans and Lutherans led to sustained dialogues in the United States with the Episcopal Church and

---

1. Linda Bloom, "Church Takes Fresh Look at Christian Unity," UMNS, January 29, 2013, accessed March 22, 2022, https://www.umnews.org/en/news/church-takes-fresh-look-at-christian-unity.

the Evangelical Lutheran Church of America (ELCA). Full eucharistic unity with the ELCA and interim eucharistic unity with the Episcopalians have been approved by the respective churches, in 2008 and 2009. In 1999, The UMC gestured toward its own daughter denominations and held a consultation with churches within the Wesleyan holiness tradition. Meeting in Dallas, representatives of the Church of the Nazarene, the Church of Christ Holiness, Church of God (Anderson), Free Methodist Church, Korean Holiness Church, Wesleyan Church, and The UMC discussed history and tradition, sanctification and perfection, women's issues, racial concerns, ecumenism, and next steps.

SACRAMENTS, WORSHIP, HYMNODY

Ecumenical involvement by Methodists, EUBs, and United Methodists; participation in the interconfessional liturgical movement; and reengagement with the Wesleys led to transformation of worship understanding and practice (see chapter X). Ecumenical dialogues found common ground in early Christian texts and celebrated the Wesleys' appreciation of tradition and eucharistic devotion and hymnody. The Methodist and Roman Catholic International Dialogue, begun in 1967, focused on the Eucharist in the first two published reports, 1971 and 1976. The Methodist and Roman Catholic Dialogue in the United States, also begun in 1967, issued a shared statement on the Eucharist in 1981 detailing "converging theology" and divergent practice (H **668n98**).

The twentieth-century "ecumenical" liturgical movement also stimulated Methodist worship renewal. The Second Vatican Council brought a century's liturgical developments to focus—as it did in various dogmatic, policy, and polity matters—in its "Constitution on the Sacred Liturgy." That 1963 document revolutionized Roman Catholic worship. An English-language and much reformed mass appeared in 1969. The Episcopal Church in 1966 and the Lutheran Church in 1970 introduced new eucharistic rites. COCU, launched on the eve of the Second Vatical Council, explored Protestant unity across the several communions' sacramental practice. In 1968, COCU published a common eucharistic rite, *An Order of Worship for the Proclamation of the Word and of God and the Celebration of the Lord's Supper, with Commentary.* COCU issued revised rites in 1978, *Word, Bread and Cup*; and in

1984, *The Sacrament of the Lord's Supper: A New Text.* In 1973 COCU's Commission on Worship published *An Order for the Celebration of Holy Baptism with Commentary,* and in 1980 *An Order for an Affirmation of the Baptismal Covenant (also Called Confirmation),* resources commended to Methodist and participant churches for trial use and comment.

Transformative effect came as well from the 1982 WCC Faith and Order consensus statement, *Baptism, Eucharist and Ministry* (BEM), and ecumenical eucharistic rite, the *Lima Liturgy* (1982). The theology-changing and rite-shaping ecumenical document, seventy-five years in the making, provided authoritative warrant for reformation of sacramental theology and practice. And the *Lima Liturgy,* a Communion service, dramatized the ecclesiological convergence on the Eucharist reached in *BEM.* In its 1986 formal written response, The UMC (USA) welcomed *BEM's* appropriation of scriptural and traditional eucharistic understandings. "All this we find explicitly taught by John and Charles Wesley, who knew and respected the apostolic, patristic and reformed faith of the Church." With regard to the sacrificial aspect of the Eucharist, The UMC response argued that "as Wesleyans, we are accustomed to the language of sacrifice, and we find *BEM's* statements to be in accord with the Church's tradition and with ours." The response made similar affirmative comment on *BEM's* rich baptismal teaching (H **668nn99–100**).

Through these several international, interdenominational sacramental conversations, United Methodism came to the perception that it needed a theology of baptism, an understanding of Communion as more than memorial, and liturgical practices so informed. Reception of The UMC's authorized Communion rites, the former Methodist rite of 1966 and The EUBC rite of 1957, was mixed from the start. Anticipating the need for updating the King James Version phrasing, the 1970 special session General Conference gave a study commission four goals (a fifth added in the middle 1970s at the urging of the Women's Caucus and COSROW): (1) use modern English in place of Tudor, "thee and thou"; (2) restore the classical and ecumenical shape of Communion, uniting Word and Table with a fourfold action (taking, blessing, breaking, and giving); (3) express a contemporary theology of Eucharist with focus on Easter (resurrection) in place of the Good Friday-centered rites derived from medieval piety; (4) provide maximum pastoral flexibility; and (5) use inclusive language (H **545**).

The Commission on Worship produced *The Sacrament of the Lord's Supper: An Alternate Text* in 1971 and the next year circulated widely a trial-use leaflet version with directions for ministers. The 1972 General Conference opened with this service. Liturgical scholar James White, principal drafter, introduced the new rite in *Circuit Rider,* four months later (H **545–46**; S **1972c**). The new service, communal in nature and apostolic in form, united word and sacrament. It invited ancient sign-acts—celebrants to stand *behind* the table, facing the congregation; the wearing of ancient garb (white albs with colorful stoles); the "passing the peace," the offering of bread and wine from and by the congregation; and the breaking of the loaf. The Great Thanksgiving followed a classical Christian pattern, yet allowed variety for the great festivals of the Christian Year, weddings, and ordinations. Recovering of Wesleyan and ancient notions of *real presence* came gradually, with the 1982 phrasing of the eucharistic to invoke the Holy Spirit boldly: "Pour out your Holy Spirit on us gathered here, and on these gifts of bread and wine. Make them be for us the body and blood of Christ, that we may be for the world the body of Christ, redeemed by his blood" (H **668–69nn102–3**). "Real" wine did not fare as well as "real presence." Despite the 1966 hymnal's stipulation that only "the pure unfermented juice of the grape shall be used," liturgical reformers dropped that century-old rubric in the 1972 (and following) alternative eucharistic texts. In 1996, a motion from the floor of the General Conference passed, mandating usage of "the pure, unfermented juice of the grape."

In 1975, 1976, and 1979, the commission produced revised texts incorporating inclusive language. The 1980 General Conference commended the 1979 revised text to local churches for trial use with other new rites in *We Gather Together: Services of Public Worship.* The 1980 text, revised again beginning in 1981, was officially adopted by the 1984 General Conference and published in 1985 in *The Book of Services, Containing the General Services of the Church,* "A Service of Word and Table (Complete Text)." The *BOS* (1985) included also a "Basic Pattern for Sunday Worship," an "Outline of Sunday Worship," and a "Brief Text" and a "Minimum Text" for the Lord's Supper. These texts were not fully mainstreamed across the church until they appeared in *The United Methodist Hymnal* (1989).

*****

Development of a new baptismal rite followed a similar trajectory. Neither the Methodists nor the EUBs brought a highly developed baptismal theology into union. Indeed, both churches were conflicted about the meaning and practice of baptism (H **669nn104–5**). In 1972, the new church created a Baptism Study Commission. Its mandate was to strengthen United Methodism's "sacramental" understanding of baptism and design a unified rite for baptism of infants, children, youth, and adults, for confirmation, and for baptismal renewal. Here, too, United Methodism found itself returning to Wesleyan origins, to liturgical developments across the Christian world, to growing ecumenical consensus, and back through the life of the church to the apostolic age. Stimuli included the groundbreaking *Order for Holy Baptism* by the Church of South India in 1955 (revised 1962), and COCU's *An Order for the Celebration of Holy Baptism with Commentary* of 1973 and *An Order for an Affirmation of the Baptismal Covenant (also called Confirmation)* of 1980. Revisions by individual communions, following the ancient, ecumenical pattern, also proved influential, including Roman Catholic rites for infants in 1969 and for adults in 1972. The Lutheran Church followed in 1974, the Episcopal Church in 1977, and the Presbyterian Church in 1985. A reformed baptismal rite of the British *Methodist Service Book* of 1975 also served as a model. Dialogue between The UMC and the Lutheran Church in the United States (1977–79) helped clarify understandings of baptism in both churches (H **669n106**).

Ecumenical convergence on baptism in the 1982 *Baptism, Eucharist and Ministry* recovered tensions in Wesley, never clearly thematized theologically, between a baptismal regeneration in infants and the necessity of a subsequent spiritual rebirth. *BEM* identified norms and necessary elements that The UMC would subsequently appropriate ritually: proclamation of the Scriptures referring to baptism, a renunciation of evil, profession of faith in Christ and the holy Trinity, generous use of water, Great Thanksgiving over the water with an invocation of the Holy Spirit, and declaration that the baptized have acquired a new identity as sons and daughters of God, and as members of the church, and are called to be witnesses of the gospel. *A Celebration of Baptism* published in 1988 by the Consultation on Common Texts (CCT) proved timely. The CCT, originated in the mid-1960s as a forum for worship renewal among North American churches, had already produced a *Common Lectionary* (1983; a *Revised Common Lectionary* appeared in 1992). These several baptismal documents and rites emphasized ecclesial initiation and the paschal motif of identification with Christ's death and resurrection.

In 1976, United Methodism produced a rite so shaped, *A Service of Baptism, Confirmation, and Renewal,* for trial use. Drafter Lawrence Stookey of Wesley Seminary provided accompanying introduction and commentary. Hoyt Hickman, chair of the drafting committee, introduced the new rite that year in *Circuit Rider.* The reshaped service recovered the early church's *unified* initiation process, offering the same ritual sequence for infants and adults, both "babes in Christ." It construed confirmation as the first of many "reaffirmations" of baptism that may take place in the life of an individual or congregation, or when a person joins The United Methodist Church from another denomination.

In 1984 the new rites became official but in booklet form. Widespread use awaited a new hymnal in 1989. Five closely related services were gathered in the new hymnal under the heading "The Baptismal Covenant." Understood as sacrament and mystery, the rites dramatize baptism as primarily God's act—God's pledge. In baptism, a person enters into God's covenant, a covenanting that involves promises and responsibilities of both parties. The whole assembly makes the essential response of faith. Within this recommitment, individual candidates and their sponsors respond.

The new rite, three times longer than the older and intended to be a *major focus of worship,* took some getting used to, more so than the new hymnal (see below) or the eucharistic rites. (The latter provided alternatives—a shorter form and the older Cranmerian-Wesleyan version.) To address such concerns—including whether the new rite teaches baptismal regeneration and, if so, whether it should—the 1988 General Conference established a churchwide study commission to prepare an official theological and functional "understanding" of the new liturgies. The study committee presented a preliminary report to the 1992 General Conference, which approved it for study in local churches (1993–96). Dwight Vogel of Garrett-Evangelical Theological Seminary, prepared a study guide. Eight years of study and comment on successive drafts honed the document and the 1996 General Conference adopted *By Water and the Spirit: A United Methodist Understanding of Baptism.* Gayle Felton followed in 1997 with a study guide, *By Water and the Spirit: Making Connections for Identity and Ministry,* revised in 1998, 1999, and 2002. In the November–December 1999 *Circuit Rider,* she explained, "Baptism is the source of our Christian identity and mission," concluding, "It marks us as the people of God and impels us into ministry" (H **669nn113–17**).

*****

Recognizing the need for a hymnal to feature the new liturgies and be more generous in its recognition of the church's diversity, the 1984 General Conference established a Hymnal Revision Committee. It committed, per the *Discipline*, oversight for editorial and publishing workflow to UMPH and guidances over the contents to GBOD. The twenty-five-member committee involved a large number of readers and consultants. Proposed use of inclusive language and imagery for God and God's presence and action in the world proved controversial as also "pacifying" militaristic metaphors. The committee entertained dropping "Am I a Soldier of the Cross" and "Onward, Christian Soldiers" and modifying "The Battle Hymn of the Republic." Print, TV, and rumor media portrayed a committee committed only to gender-inclusive language. By July 1986, the committee had received more than eleven thousand pieces of mail, only forty-four of which supported controversial actions by the committee. Bowing to public outcry, the committee moderated its commitment to publish a fully sensitive hymnal (S **1996a**). It restored "Onward, Christian Soldiers," dropped "Strong Mother God," which stretched God imagery and restored masculine imagery to the Psalter. The revisers took greater liberties with texts that used masculine terms for humanity (H **550**). Black Methodist objections led to revision of sinners' bid to Jesus to wash them "whiter than snow." From "O for a Thousand Tongues to Sing," editors originally dropped a stanza proclaiming the spiritual uplifting of the "dumb" and the "lame," lest disabled persons take umbrage. They later restored the words, but suggested in a footnote that the stanza may be omitted.

The 1988 General Conference overwhelmingly approved *The United Methodist Hymnal: Book of United Methodist Worship*. Published in 1989, it met similar reception across the church, more than half of the congregations ordering the new book in the first year and is found in the racks of over 95 percent of UM congregations. While honoring traditional hymns, the hymnal shed the elitism of past hymnals, making generous space for gospel songs, verse from a wide range of ethnic groups, and contemporary hymns. The hymnal contained more than a hundred pages of worship services and resources, not counting the Psalter, and put the fourfold basic worship pattern, baptism, and Lord's Supper up front for emphasis. New liturgies for weddings and funerals, in trial use since 1972 and adopted by the 1984 General Conference, saw first general usage.

These resources and many more went into *The United Methodist Book of Worship*, designed for worship leaders, not for pews. Prepared for presentation to the 1992 General Conference, it was published the same year. Replacing that of 1964 and reflecting the harvest of United Methodism's liturgical and ecumenical engagement, it featured the Revised Common Lectionary, services for and fourteen alternative Great Thanksgivings for seasons of the Christian Year, a huge array of devotional and worship materials, and rituals for every thinkable church officer or building.

WOMEN LEAD IN CHURCH AND NATION

In the closing decades of the twentieth century, women continued to experience firsts. Leontine Kelly in 1984 became the first Black woman to be elected bishop in any mainline Protestant denomination. The next year Barbara Thompson took the reins of the General Commission on Religion and Race, the first woman general secretary of a general board or agency other than COSROW. In 1986, the Rev. Minerva Carcaño was appointed district superintendent in the Rio Grande Conference, the first Hispanic woman in that office. She would be elected bishop in 2004, another first. Bishop Sharon Zimmerman Rader assumed the prestigious position of secretary of the COB, serving from 1996 until her retirement in 2004. In 1990 the first three Black women were elected district superintendents (of fifty women DSs that year): the Rev. Charlotte Ann Nichols, Peninsula Conference; the Rev. Mary Brown Oliver, Baltimore Conference; and the Rev. J. Jeannette Cooper, West Ohio Conference. In 1985 and 1987, respectively, Hispanic and Native American women gathered for consultations. Another initiative to develop women's leadership, GBHEM's Women of Color Scholars Program, began in 1989, providing scholarships for doctoral studies and with the mission of placing faculty women of color in all thirteen UMC seminaries.

Churches confronted and sometimes differed radically on an array of stained glass ceiling or "family issues"—related to advancement, gender roles, affirmative action, human sexuality, abortion, childcare, sexual harassment, the trauma of divorce, and single-parent/income families, often impoverished. GCOM reported in 1990 that 77 percent of women clergy had experienced sexual harassment. In 1992 and 1995, COSROW developed recommendations on sexual harassment and issued a policy statement regarding abuse within ministerial relationships.

Pro-life advocates, as we noted, continued to challenge United Methodists' moderate position on abortion. Delegates to the 1988 General Conference narrowly defeated a petition to abolish COSROW. Critics charged that it had outlived its usefulness and had "expanded" its scope beyond the intent of its creators. One of the most controversial actions was its support for a study of the effects of homophobia.

That year the Women's Task Force of Good News reorganized under the name Evangelical Coalition for United Methodist Women (ECUMW), a joint effort among women from Good News, the Mission Society for United Methodists, and the Institute on Religion and Democracy. Renamed "Renew" in 1989, it dedicated itself to renewing the Women's Division. By 1991, it claimed 11,100 members or UMW member affiliates. Bolstered and resourced by the interlocking network of conservative caucus groups (Good News, IRD, Mission Society, Confessing Movement, Lifewatch, Association for Church Renewal, Foundation for Theological Education, Transforming Congregations, and, as of 2000, the Coalition for United Methodist Accountability), Renew kept up constant attack on the Women's Division. Its several "Financial Files," for instance, offered exposés of Women's Division funding of faith "subversive" programs (H **669n121**).

Renew and its collaborators took special umbrage at the November 1993 Re-Imagining Conference, something of a national coming-out party for theological feminism (women bishops, feminist leaders, some liturgical scholars, and other progressives). Sponsored by mainline denominations and by local and state ecumenical councils to mark the midpoint of the World Council of Churches' "Decade in Solidarity with Women," the Minneapolis conference celebrated the feminine attributes of God, the gift of lesbianism, and the spiritual experiences of persons who found God within themselves. Sexism, racism, and classism took center place in theological reflection. The *Christian Century* identified the Re-Imagining Conference as one of the top ten religious stories of the year (H **670n122**). The event attracted little Methodist notice until Good News charged that it had been rife with heresy— among other things, participants celebrated homosexuality, worshipped the goddess Sophia, and rejected Christ's atonement. Horror stories and charges of heresy led to hate mail, job losses, and even death threats.

To counter the charges of heresy, supporters held a news conference on March 8, 1994—International Women's Day—at the Interchurch Center (New York City). Interpreting the Re-Imagining Conference were GCCUIC staffer the Rev. Jean Audrey Powers, Bishops Susan Morrison and Forrest Stith, Drew faculty Catherine Keller and Heather Murray Elkins, and Union doctoral candidate Beryl Ingram-Ward. They released an open letter, "A Time of Hope—Time of Threat" (S **1994a**), which drew endorsements from pastors, deaconesses, laywomen, agency staff, seminary faculty members and five additional women bishops, some 830 UMC women. Heated exchanges nevertheless continued, some online, and stimulated the formation of a supportive online network of people—men and women across the church. A council was formed to organize small groups, plan gatherings, and network across denominational lines (H **670nn124–25**). The next year, Powers, associate general secretary of GCCUIC, became the highest-ranking United Methodist official to "come out" as a gay person. Powers described her action as "a political act" committed "as an act of resistance to false teachings that have contributed to heresy and homophobia within the church" (H **553, 670n126**).

The 1996 General Conference heard the first Methodist resident of the White House since William McKinley, First Lady Hillary Rodham Clinton. (A proposed rebuttal by Methodist Elizabeth Dole, wife of Senator Bob Dole, the presumed Republican presidential nominee was defeated.) In a thirty-minute speech, interrupted by no fewer than five standing ovations, Mrs. Clinton blended her familiar and vocational message of society's obligation to help its children with recollections of growing up Methodist (S **1996b**). She applauded her church's bishops for their recent call to make the welfare of children the denomination's top priority and at another point recited lyrics from the child's hymn "Jesus loves me! This I know," which tells of Christ's love for children of all colors. She said it had given her an "early lesson" in positive race relations. Citing Scripture and referring to adversity experienced by Wesley, she said, "We know acting on our faith is never easy."

CHAPTER XIII
POLITY PUSHED TO THE BREAKING POINT: 2000–2022

*The primary sources referenced in this chapter are currently housed online in cooperation with the General Commission on Archives and History. They can be found via umhistoryhub.teachable.com/.

United Methodists began the third millennium of the Christian era looking for new ways to be relevant in an increasingly secular world. What would happen over the next two decades (and counting) were expected, perhaps even planned by some, and completely unexpected by others. New forms of connection were established, new formulas used for General Conference and the denominational budget were implemented, new denominational structures were proposed yet defeated, new liturgies were written, revised theologies were wrestled with, and evolving caucus groups pushed the denomination to its breaking points. This chapter highlights the major changes from 2000 to 2022 in The UMC, and points to some future forms of (United) Methodist grace.

REALIGNMENT ATTEMPTS AND GLOBAL MEMBERSHIP SHIFT

One of the main concerns between 2000 and 2022 is how The UMC institutions and congregations interact with an increasingly digital, diversifying, globalizing, and secularizing society, while The UMC itself is facing divisions and global complexity. This complex challenge led to the creation of study groups, polity proposals, petition blocking, delegation bloc-ing, and spin cycles that mimic the national news media. Countless online blogs and social media posts seek to provide interpretations and opinions as to how certain study groups, proposals, and new ways of being in connection with one another will affect church membership, United Methodist theology, and our global stance in the world.[1] It's obvious that there's no easy way to relate to the global society post-2000. United Methodism has tied its own hands behind the back through its polity and the rigid structure of its Constitution. However, various proposals have been brought forth over two decades that pertain to the core of UMC identity and connection.

The 2000 General Conference began with a call from Bishop Robert Morgan to "embrace unity amid their diversity" with the theme "We Who Are Many . . . Are One Body." The 2000 General Conference sought to widen the Methodist circle of inclusion, particularly with Methodists of other denominations that were rooted in the 1784 MEC. The 992 delegates discussed a plan to rethink how to be in connection with one another. The Connectional Process Team was the creation of the 1996 General Conference, and its team spent the prior quadrennium developing a possible way forward for the denomination that would have "sweeping changes in both regional and international activities and organizational structure."[2] In conclusion, the process team recommended the formation of a Covenant Council to carry out the logistics and legislative means of implementing the actions of the 2000 General Conference based on its presented report. However, many pieces of this study process and report have yet to be fully implemented.

The Connectional Process Team reported on five transformational directions to the 2000 General Conference, recommending (1) a renewed centering on Christian formation, grounded in a Wesleyan sense of class meetings in the local churches and developed through Covenant Communities, "a loose affiliation of churches that fall within geographic boundaries and have other common concerns as they carry out the core task of making disciples for

---

1. In my opinion the best way to stay up to date with the latest and more popular UM blogs is to use and subscribe to UM-Insight which, amalgamates the UM blogs from across the connection, highlighting differing perspectives on major issues. They also have a decent archive and search function.

2. "Daily Wrap Up: Delegates Discuss CPT Report for First Time," May 5, 2000, gc2000.org.

the sake of the world"; (2) calling forth "spiritual leaders who are grounded in covenant relationships" from lay servant leaders through elders and deacons and into the upper administration levels of the denomination; (3) empowering the connection for ministry by building new faith communities, affirming the central conferences, aligning the work of general agencies, and improving communication (this third direction is the intellectual seed that becomes the Connectional Table in 2004); (4) redesigning General Conference as a global conference in order to de-center the US perspective (this would also mean the creation of a US central conference) with a maximum of five hundred delegates and allowing for a focus on ecumenical relationships and interreligious dialogue; (5) encouraging doctrinal and theological discourse within local churches, annual conferences, the newly created global conference, and empowering bishops as spiritual leaders in each of these areas.[3]

The report was presented to the plenary on May 5, 2000, when it was promptly referred to the General and Judicial Administrative Committee who would bring recommendations on moves forward back to the plenary prior on May 10. In a vote of 784 for and 144 against, the Connectional Process Team's report and plan to take the denomination in a "transformational direction" was rejected, and the delegation chose to maintain the current structure. The delegation did affirm a few of the "transformational directions" and referred these to the General Council on Ministries, namely (1) center on Christian formation, (2) call forth covenant leadership, (3) empower the connection for ministry, (4) strengthen global and ecumenical dialogue and relationships, and (5) encourage dialogue around church doctrine and theological understanding.[4] In effect, in a pattern of governance often repeated, the delegation chose to uphold and refer broad and abstract principles for what the denomination could uplift in future ministries without taking necessary, accompanying polity and structural changes to enable and fund implementation in an effective manner.

With this, the General Council on Ministries (GCOM) spent the next quadrennium pondering these five transformational directions. Their report presented at the 2004 General Conference was titled "Living into the Future" (**eS2004b**). A key directive studied by the GCOM was "to determine the most effective design for the work of the general agencies and to provide implement-

---

3. "Transformational Directions for The United Methodist Church for the Twenty-first Century," http://gc2000.org/studies/report/.

4. Robert Lear, "Daily Wrap Up: Archbishop Speaks to Delegates; CPT Plan Bites Dust," May 10, 2000, accessed March 14, 2022, http://gc2000.org/gc2000news/stories/gc057.htm.

ing legislation to the 2004 General Conference."[5] Originally designed to help the general agencies collaborate with one another and with other levels of the connection, the proposed Connectional Table (CT) "would be for the discernment and articulation of a vision for the church and the stewardship of the mission, ministries, and resources of The United Methodist Church as determined by the actions of General Conference and in consultation with the Council of Bishops."[6] In effect, it would be a figurative table where different connections of the denomination came together to collaborate and provide a bridge between the programmatic ministries of the denomination with the financial structure of the denomination. It would combine the GCOM with Center for Finance and Administration into one agency with a board of 127 persons—an unwieldy large and expensive board! It would be in an ideal sense an accountability center, one that held agencies accountable to the actions of and requests of General Conference and one that ensured proper distribution of funds according to those actions and requests. In theory, this body was meant to eliminate the void between the denomination's finances and the denomination's mission and programming. But the delegation did not support this super-agency. Instead, on May 5, the plenary voted to adopt the General Administration's plan over the GCOM's plan. The adopted plan had largely the same objectives and goals with a (still large) forty-seven-member board and the General Council on Finance and Administration (GCFA) as a separate entity.

As often happens with the bureaucratic format of General Conference, the delegation did not listen to the proposals and reports of their appointed quadrennial study committee, and instead opted to support a plan that would exist outside an intensive review process. The Connectional Table would be put in place by the end of 2005 and be in charge of its own staffing. It would exist with a mandate to be a go-between for the general agencies, GCFA, and the COB.[7] In this role, by 2008 and in coordination with the COB, the CT proposed *four areas of focus*, touted as a "long-term agenda to address long-term problems in both the church and the world"[8] (**eS2008a,b**). The four

5. *Advance Daily Christian Advocate*, Vol 2. (Nashville: Commission on the General Conference, 2004), 826.

6. *Advance Daily Christian Advocate, 827.*

7. "Church Creates Connectional Table to Lead General Agency Work," May 6, 2004, accessed March 14, 2022, http://gc2004.org/interior.asp?ptid=17&mid=4581.

8. "General Conference 2008 Issues," United Methodist News Service, accessed March 14, 2022, http://ee.umc.org/who-we-are/general-conference-2008-issues.

areas of focus were (1) developing principled Christian leaders for the church and the world, (2) creating new places for new people by starting new congregations and revitalizing existing ones, (3) engaging in ministry with the poor, and (4) stamping out killer diseases by improving health globally. These four areas were meant to align the connection between the COB, annual conferences, local congregations, and general agencies.

Certain agencies were tasked with taking on leadership roles within specific areas of focus. For example, the GBOD created Path One, which served as "an office of new congregational development," which would expectantly "return the denomination to its evangelistic movement of starting a new church every day" with the initial goal of 650 new congregations that could be in ministry with sixty-three thousand new members by 2012.[9] The GBHEM was tasked with finding ways to recruit younger clergy. A 2006 Study of Ministry report showed that ordained clergy under the age of thirty-five were fewer than 5 percent. The GBGM would lead the way, largely through its United Methodist Committee on Relief, to alleviate poverty and its connection to global health and disease. They worked directly with UMCOM on a Global Health Initiative called Imagine No Malaria, which sought to eradicate malaria by raising over $75 million to support doctors, provide medical supplies, and educate communities. Through this initiative, The UMC partnered with the Nothing But Nets initiative of the United Nations Foundation.[10] Within one decade, global malaria mortality rates had fallen by 60 percent, and The UMC had provided over four million bed nets, renovated sixty-one facilities, and treated over 2.7 million people for malaria.[11]

Major shifts in the demographics of delegates at General Conference in 2008 prompted significant change. First, recognizing the ongoing trend of membership loss in the US and reported growth outside the US, 278 of the 992 delegates were from outside of the US, approximately one hundred more than in 2004. The UMC also welcomed Cote d'Ivoire, the largest regional conference, into full rights and responsibilities as an annual conference in The

---

9. "General Conference 2008 Issues."

10. "Imagine No Malaria," UMCOR Advance, accessed March 14, 2022, https://advance.umcor.org/p-418-imagine-no-malaria.aspx; Christie R. House, "Still Thanking God for Imagine No Malaria," April 23, 2021, accessed March 14, 2022, https://umcmission.org/abundant-health/still-thanking-god-for-imagine-no-malaria/.

11. Imagine No Malaria Impact Overview, 2017 poster, accessed March 14, 2022, imaginenomalaria-impactreport_2017_stats_v2.ashx (umnews.org).

UMC (**eS2004a**). At future general conferences, their delegate representation will increase substantially. To acknowledge this new (and escalating) trend, a task force was asked to find new ways of dealing with an increasingly global and non-US based United Methodist membership. They proposed that the five jurisdictions in the United States become a central conference. This proposal would decolonize the denomination by providing equity at General Conference between all of the global constituencies as well as remove US-based issues from the conversation of General Conference. Thus, the US would have its own place and space to discuss US issues, in the same way that other central conferences gathered quadrennially to discuss their more regional-missional concerns. This petition was rejected in 2008 and in every General Conference since due to the lobbying of non-affirming United Methodists who fear that it was a way for US-based United Methodists to condone ordination of LGBTQ+ clergy and same-sex marriage.

It was reported in 2008 that approximately 30 percent of United Methodists lived outside the US. By 2020, the aging United Methodist membership within the US had been dropping at an average of 2 percent per year. At this continued rate, the United Methodist membership in the United States is by 2022 a minority compared to the reported growth of United Methodist members in Africa, which as of 2020 was reportedly 6.4 million members.[12] This trend was well known and prompted a wide array of potential restructuring proposals and other polity shifts. Beyond the attempts to make the five US jurisdictions into a central conference, other proposals called for a revamping of the *Book of Discipline*, largely to remove the US-centric policies and language from it. The new Global Book of Discipline would help the denomination figure out its essential policies that should be upheld and enforced on a worldwide scale. The proposed Global Book of Discipline, while first suggested at the 2008 General Conference, did not pass the legislative body until 2016. However, the 2008 delegation did decide that it was ready for a new phrase in the mission statement. United Methodists still would seek to "make disciples of Jesus Christ . . . yet now for the transformation of the world." Adding a missional directive answered the question posed by the then president of the Council of Bishops, Gregory Palmer: "To what end do we make disciples of Jesus Christ? Is making disciples an end in itself, or does God have a purpose for which He redeems us, recovers us and makes us whole?"[13]

---

12. Heather Hahn, "U.S. Dips Below Majority of Membership," United Methodist News Service, Nov. 25, 2019, accessed March 14, 2022, https://www.umnews.org/en/news/us-dips-below-majority-of-membership.

13. Christie R. House, "United Methodist Mission Statement Revised," UMNS, May 1,

BUDGET CUTS AND
THE GENERAL AGENCIES

In 2012, for the first time, a reduced expense budget was proposed by GCFA to the General Conference (**eS2012g**). As the Great Recession of 2008 gripped the world, giving had declined and donations were reducing further in The UMC, which had stimulated a Call to Action by the Council of Bishops in 2008 (**eS2010**) (**eS2012a**). The call brought together funding and staff from the Connectional Table along with senior clergy leading the one hundred largest United Methodist congregations.[14] Their 2010 proposal was coordinated with the bishops by Adam Hamilton, pastor of the twenty-five thousand-member Church of the Resurrection and Neil M. Alexander, President, Book Editor, and Publisher of UMPH (1996–2016). After three years of research and listening across the denomination regarding the factors driving or inhibiting vitality in UM congregations, the Call to Action proposal with legislation was presented to the 2012 General Conference, with recommendations aiming to fund the leading factors driving vitality in local churches. The Call to Action delineated realignment and was confronted with intense lobbying among agencies, their boards, various caucuses, seminaries, parachurch groups, and other delegates.[15] Three compromise plans were negotiated and proposed during the 2012 General Conference, and the delegates eventually by the final hours passed a modified Call to Action, but constitutional objections were maneuvered through the Judicial Council to stop the plan. At the end of an exhausting General Conference that cost $12 million to stage, it became apparent that the 1972 UMC Constitution, which delineated roles and responsibilities for legislative, judicial, and executive branches, had limited the authority of the episcopal branch to lead institutional change and realignment for the sake of congregational effectiveness, while the denomination's members, churches, institutions, and assets continued to diminish.

2008, accessed March 18, 2022, United Methodist mission statement revised | United Methodist News Service (umnews.org), emphasis added.

14.   United Methodist Communications Office of Public Information, "Call to Action Steering Team Releases Final Report," October 25, 2010, https://www.umnews.org/en/news/call-to-action-steering-team-releases-final-report, accessed April 11, 2022.

15.   For full details of research and proposals, see http://umccalltoaction.org.

The general agency structure devised by the 1972 General Conference, and expanded since, is stressed by demographic aging of The UMC. Membership in the US in all mainline denominations (and now occurring among evangelical denominations) declined steadily since the 1960s. According to Pew Research Center's 2014 Religious Landscape Study, there was a "sharp decline from 18.1 percent . . . in 2007" to 14.7 percent of US adults claiming an affiliation with a mainline Protestant tradition.[16] This percentage decline equates to approximately five million members, and this is during a time when the overall US population increased. The study showed that "mainline Protestants have declined at a faster rate than any other major Christian group, including Catholics and evangelical Protestants." Pew Research attributes this decline largely to generational replacement, though the replacements with younger members are few. Younger persons are less likely to become members of one denomination or attend worship in general. The same study showed that approximately 35 percent of millennials are "religiously unaffiliated." This lack of affiliation directly affects United Methodist membership, since the same Pew landscape study from 2007 showed in that approximately 5.7 percent of the US adult population was United Methodist. By 2014, this percentage was reduced to 3.9 percent.[17]

This generational shift in aging membership demographics (plus the fact that younger members have less income to give or do not give as consistently as older generations) means inevitable budgetary cuts in churches and consolidation of institutions.[18] The Anglicans, Presbyterians, and Lutherans have earlier closed many institutions, schools, and agencies. Younger adults under age thirty-five (who make up less than 6 percent of the membership) have less to give, due but not limited to high rates of inflation (especially for housing), no increases to the federal minimum wage, high tuition costs, student loan

---

16.   Michael Lipka, "Mainline Protestants Make Up Shrinking Number of U.S. Adults," Pew Research Center, May 18, 2015, accessed March 17, 2022, https://www.pewresearch.org/fact-tank/2015/05/18/mainline-protestants-make-up-shrinking-number-of-u-s-adults/. However, since 2014 (and in part due to the pandemic and polarizing politics), evangelical Protestant denominations are also experiencing sharp generational decline.

17.   Lipka, "Mainline Protestants Make Up Shrinking Number of U.S. Adults."

18.   A 2017 Barna Group Study found that 84 percent of millennials report "giving less than $50 to charity per annum, even though charitable giving ranks high on their priorities." John Lee, "Who Are the Most Generous? Not Who You'd Expect," *Christianity Today*, August 13, 2020, accessed March 17, 2022, https://www.christianitytoday.com/ct/2020/august-web-only/most-generous-not-who-you-expect-vertical-generosity.html.

debt, and an overall increased cost of living in the US. Younger adults of the millennial generation tend to give to idea-specific justice initiatives or goal-oriented organizations and rarely do they give regularly to one institution on a consistent basis.[19] For example, if women's reproductive rights are targeted, then many will increase giving to Planned Parenthood for a few months. If voting rights are threatened, then support shifts to the Voting Rights Alliance. If someone that they know has been diagnosed with cancer, they may begin a Facebook drive or GoFundMe campaign for that person.

If a majority of young adults don't appreciate the denomination's continued debate about same-sex marriage or LGBTQ+ ordination, they leave or designate their giving elsewhere through online and instant payments using Venmo, Cash App, PayPal, ApplePay, Zelle, and others.[20] It is interesting to note that he way people give has drastically changed. The COVID pandemic, however, accelerated the shift in congregations to electronic giving for most churches.

The generational replacement driving the decline of denominations is also linked to the flattening of funding and decision-making, which Bishop Robert Schnase observes in *Seven Levers: Missional Strategies for Conferences*.[21] For example, when sending a missionary to another country, through the hierarchical connections of twentieth-century modernism, a local church would be apportioned as a lump sum, with a portion of giving sent to the missions agency for an executive to approve, prepare, and send a missionary candidate. However, due to instant global communication, air travel, and instant financial technologies, as well as designated giving inside congregations, in the new millennium the "world is flat." Thus any congregation can and often does bypass a denominational agency and partner directly with another

---

19.   There are many articles written on this by local pastors, and published in denominational news and national news. For example, the Rev. Mark Becker, "A Giving Option a Millennial Could Embrace," Florida United Methodist Foundation, Aug. 26, 2018, accessed March 17, 2022, https://www.fumf.org/news/a-giving-option-a-millenial-could-embrace/; Joe Fischer, "How Millennials and Gen Z are Transforming the Philanthropic World," Forbes, Aug. 20, 2021, accessed March 18, 2022, https://www.forbes.com/sites/forbestechcouncil/2021/08/20/how-millennials-and-gen-z-are-revolutionizing-the-philanthropic-world/?sh=716feab2562d.

20.   Ian Urriola, "From the Young Adult Network: Involving Young People in Stewardship," Discipleship Ministries, October 26, 2017, accessed March 17, 2022, https://www.umcyoungpeople.org/lead/from-the-young-adult-network-involving-young-people-in-stewardship.

21.   Robert Schnase, *Seven Levers: Missional Strategies for Conferences* (Nashville: Abingdon Press, 2014), http://robertschnase.com/books/seven-levers/.

congregation or parachurch organization to meet a need, such as building churches, training local pastors, and digging wells in Malawi.

The budgetary cuts in 2010 of the United Methodist general agency and programming budgets would accelerate with high impact over the next decade: by 2022 standards, the budget of the 2012–2016 quadrennium of $603 million would seem providential. The proposed budget for the 2020–2024 quadrennium (which has yet to be passed due to the postponement of the 2020 General Conference) was to be $498.65 million. This decrease to the budget was established prior to the beginning of the COVID-19 pandemic, prior to the Special Session of General Conference in 2019, and was based on pre-pandemic calculations of membership decline and possible church schism. The trend will not be reversed, since most observers of American congregational life cite evidence that a significant percentage of church participants changed their habits, dropped out, and will not return to worship and Sunday school after the global pandemic becomes endemic.[22]

A half billion dollars in spending over four years for denominational operations seems surprising, but context is required to understand how United Methodist connectional budgets and ministries are structured. According to 2018 data, 85 percent of giving from members and participants remains in the local church. Approximately seven cents of every dollar collected goes to support the immediate connectional systems: the district, and annual and jurisdictional conferences. Approximately six cents of each dollar supports "second-mile giving" for disasters and relief of human suffering, coordinated by the United Methodist Committee on Relief. Two cents of every dollar collected goes to the general church budget, which funds General Conference, the bishops, eleven General Agencies (except pensions and the publishing house), the Black Church Fund, Africa University, Judicial Council, the Ministerial Education Fund, and the Interdenominational Cooperation Fund.[23]

22. Justin Nortey, "More Houses of Worship Are Returning to Normal Operations, but In-person Attendance Is Unchanged Since Fall," Pew Research Center, March 22, 2022, https://www.pewresearch.org/fact-tank/2022/03/22/more-houses-of-worship-are-returning-to-normal-operations-but-in-person-attendance-is-unchanged-since-fall/.

23. Heather Hahn, "Finance Board Moves Ahead with Budget Cuts," UMNS, November 20, 2018, accessed March 17, 2022, https://um-insight.net/in-the-church/finance-and-administration/finance-board-moves-ahead-with-budget-cuts/; David Scott, "A Primer on United Methodist Apportionments," UM Global, May 20, 2019, accessed March 17, 2022, http://www.umglobal.org/2019/05/a-primer-on-united-methodist.html.

Each of the UMC general agencies faces intense and continuing cutbacks, layoffs, forced missional recasting, and stalled programming due to budget cuts, which accelerated during the global COVID-19 pandemic as churches, conferences, and agencies locked down and reduced spending on programs, staff, curriculum, and missions. In 2021 the general church spending reduction was a 14.3 percent reduction, while it exceeded 50 percent at the self-supporting UMPH. GBCS reduced staff from twenty-one positions to seventeen and one of its core objectives for the denomination, a revised Social Principles, was delayed. GBGM budget shrank from $55 million in 2018 to $33 million in 2021, including reduction of sixty-eight positions. GBHEM reduced its staff by 25 percent, and UMPH (which is funded solely by sale of resources to congregations and bookstores) reduced its publishing and distribution staff by more than 50 percent, laying off or retiring nearly two hundred persons. A sudden shift to remote or at-home work, due to COVID-19, also caused agencies to rethink how and where they work.[24] Three agencies (including UMPH, now entirely remote) sold their buildings in Nashville, Tennessee, and two of those moved into the offices of Discipleship Ministries (formerly GBOD).[25] Churches who are dependent upon the general agencies for ministry, relief, monitoring, consulting, education, teaching, and worship resources are continuing a trend of choosing and using alternatives.

Since the elimination of the General Council on Ministries in 2004, and arguably since the 1970s when the current general agencies were created by the uniting denominations to emphasize the direct connectional nature of Methodism, direct criticisms have ramped up against their existence, programming, and funding. One of the earliest and most consistent critiques from Good News and allied caucuses is apportioned giving. Like many younger adults they prefer directed giving or (like congregational Baptists) would have the choice of which general agencies to support. Instead, GCFA allocates funds for the COB, Judicial Council, and GCAH, while the Connectional Table allocates budgets for the World Service Fund (which funds the general agencies) and (since 2008) attempts to stimulate the four transformational

---

24. Kathy L. Gilbert and Jim Patterson, "General Agencies Cutting Back," UMNews, Feb. 9, 2021, accessed March 17, 2022, https://www.umnews.org/en/news/general-agencies-cutting-back.

25. Heather Hahn, "Agencies Sell Jointly Owned Building," UMNews, July 21, 2021, accessed March 17, 2022, https://um-insight.net/in-the-church/finance-and-administration/agencies-sell-jointly-owned-building/.

areas of giving (named above). This allocation process allows for *some* theoretical equity and at least allows general agencies to avoid direct competition for monetary support from church members, though direct donor giving still comes through agency clients (e.g., The Upper Room or UMW). Instead, GCFA and CT worked as middle managers who were in charge of distributions. This alignment model failed by assuming that CT and GCFA could understand the vision, mission, and values of each of the other agencies (who have favored constituencies), and would be best informed in how to fund them. Neither congregationalism nor connectionalism seem to offer reliable systems for managing turf and funding collaborative ministry.

In addition to budget cuts, the work of The UMC's agencies is adjusted by critique from certain caucus groups.

United Methodist Women (UMW), for the first time in seventy years, became independent from GBGM in 2012 (**eS2012h**). They sought to be more autonomous and recover the calling of Methodist women to embody social holiness in their local contexts and throughout the world, empowering action and seeking radical change.[26] They became an independent organization based on individual membership and charter dues. UMW was also given oversight of deaconess and home missioner programs, which, according to Barbara Campbell, a deaconess and retired staff of the former Women's Division, "restores the break that was made in 1964 and the relationship the office of deaconess has had with women organized for mission since it was created in 1888."[27] In March 2022, UMW announced a branding name change to United Women in Faith (UWF). With a new logo and new programming, UWF "aims to welcome current members whose local churches may choose to disaffiliate from The United Methodist Church as well as women of other faith traditions who want to join."[28]

The membership association is plausible for UWF (formerly UMW), but collecting association dues seems implausible for most denominational agencies. The UMC connectional structure, beginning with the annual conference

26. Patrick Scriven, "General Conference Approves United Methodist Women Autonomy," PNW News, May 1, 2012, accessed March 18, 2022, https://www.pnwumc.org/news /general-conference-approves-united-methodist-women-autonomy/.

27. Scriven, "General Conference Approves United Methodist Women Autonomy."

28. "United Methodist Women Is Now United Women in Faith," Resource UMC, March 7, 2022, accessed March 18, 2022, https://www.resourceumc.org/en/content/united -methodist-women-is-now-united-women-in-faith.

as the basic unit of ministry, is what makes Methodist polity unique. The Methodist mindset is to avoid becoming another congregational denomination, whose collections support the local church, its mission, and its ministry . . . unless it chooses specifically as a congregation to support other causes and missions. UMC finances predominately support the local church and its ministry and mission. But there is an apportionment (in sum fifteen % of all UMC giving) that is disbursed outward to the annual and jurisdictional conferences to sponsor the regional ministries and missions that provide this first layer of connection, and then smaller percentages reach further to fund the global mission and ministries of the denomination, usually the ministries that aren't seen everyday by the typical church member.

THEOLOGICAL AND ECUMENICAL DEVELOPMENTS

Despite an emerging theological divide and an exit of congregations in process from The UMC, UMPH attempted but twice suspended a digital music and worship database, to include an online subscription and a new print hymnbook. The first suspension was triggered in 2009 by loss of UMPH investment revenue for funding the development of the worship resource, a consequence of the 2008–9 Great Recession. The second suspension of the project occurred in mid-2020 as pandemic-related market volatility with investment reserves and impending UMC schism required a pause. The 2016 General Conference had approved the creation of the fifteen-member Hymnal Revision Committee for Discipleship Ministries (DM) and UMPH to begin work together, but the 2019 special General Conference demonstrated that the singing Methodists are not presently ready to sing their theology together.

The 2012 General Conference tasked GBCS with creating new Social Principles that would "enhance its theological foundations, global relevance and meaning, along with its focus and succinctness" focusing on four sections: creation, economy, social, and political communities. The Global Social Principles have the potential to decenter US politics from denominational social stances. For example, in the US, women's reproductive health largely focuses on the legality of abortion; globally, however, the conversation expands to having access to safe, secure, and sanitary places to have basic medical care. The work was continued by the 2016 General Conference and over the next quadrennia made its way to different study groups throughout the denomination (**eS2016j/2020**). Over seventeen hundred United Methodists across the globe participated in these conversations and provided feedback over what missions and ministries are important for their contexts and where they need the guidance of the denomination. The final document was sent to the board and translated into the denomination's seven languages. It was scheduled to go before the 2020 General Conference that is postponed due to the pandemic until 2024.[29]

Alongside other theological papers, namely "By Water and the Spirit" and "This Holy Mystery" which were approved in 1996 (**eS1996**) and 2004 (**eS2004e**), respectively, in 2008 the Committee on Faith and Order (CFO) was established as "a visible expression of the commitment of The United Methodist Church to carry on informed theological reflection for the current time in dynamic continuity with the historic Christian faith, our common heritage as Christians grounded in the apostolic witness, and our distinctive Wesleyan heritage." The General Conference tasked it with "resourc[ing] the Council of Bishops as it carries out its teaching responsibilities . . . [and] to lead and coordinate studies commissioned by the General Conference in matters related to faith, doctrine, order and discipline of the Church, and to prepare and provide resources and study materials to The United Methodist Church as deemed appropriate"[30] (**eS2008f**). As a temporary committee, it worked for the next two quadrennia on a theological statement that was first presented to the 2016 General Conference as "Wonder, Love, and Praise: Sharing a Vision of the Church" (**eS2016g**). It was received by the General Conference, but was then referred to "wider church for study and feedback." During 2017, many "United Methodists from a variety of quarters, as well as representatives from ecumenical partner churches, engaged the document and submitted surveys, blog posts, papers, and detailed notes expressing their concerns and hopes related to such a statement on United Methodist ecclesiology."[31] Out of this feedback, a new document was written by the

29. Kathy L. Gilbert, "Revised Social Principles Reflect Worldwide Church," UM News, Dec. 12, 2019, https://www.umnews.org/en/news/revised-social-principles-reflect-worldwide-church.

30. *Book of Discipline of The United Methodist Church, 2016* (Nashville: United Methodist Publishing House), para 444.

31. "UMC Committee on Faith and Order Releases 'Sent in Love,'" Committee on Faith and Order, Sept. 27, 2019, accessed March 18, 2022, https://www.umc.org/en/content/umc-committee-on-faith-and-order-releases-sent-in-love.

CFO and is now called "Sent in Love: A United Methodist Understanding of the Church"[32] (**eS2017d**). Its fate is to be determined by the General Conference postponed until 2024.

The larger purpose behind these three documents is to give UM bishops[33] and merged "union" congregations (e.g., a merger of a small ELCA and UM congregation) more encouragement to relate ecumenically and liturgically: "These documents have set a precedent in relating United Methodist teaching to the growing ecumenical convergence on the topics with which they deal—respectively, Baptism and Holy Communion—and the present document provides a similar constructive synthesis."[34] The concluding remarks of the document discuss the role of United Methodists as participants "in God's redemption and renewal of all creation." Therefore, we, as United Methodists, should not be "primarily concerned with ecclesial consolidation or institutional survival but instead with the transformation of the world in accordance with the will of God." We United Methodists are "being sent in love for the transformation of the world," which "implies attention to and care for those who are not part of the church's community, and it includes stewardship of creation."[35]

A spirit of ecumenism has marked the past two decades in different ways. In the service of repentance for racism, delegates at the 2000 General Conference, in a near-unanimous vote, sent greetings to the Roman Catholic pope, John Paul II, and recognized his apology for the past harm done to Protestant denominations on behalf of the Roman Catholic Church. As a reciprocal move, The UMC also "ask[ed] forgiveness for our deeds of commission and omission."[36] And in a historic indicator of ecumenism, The UMC entered into its first full communion agreement with the Evangelical Lutheran Church of America (ELCA). Approved by The UMC's 2008

32. "UMC Committee on Faith and Order Releases 'Sent in Love.'"

33. "Ecumenical: Dialogues," Council of Bishops, https://www.unitedmethodistbishops.org/ecumenical-dialogues.

34. "Sent in Love: A United Methodist Understanding of the Church," Committee on Faith and Order, The United Methodist Church, accessed March 18, 2022, https://www.unitedmethodistbishops.org/files/websites/www/pdfs/sent+in+love-adca+report+draft+sept2019.pdf, 1.

35. "Sent in Love," 33.

36. *Daily Christian Advocate*, vol. 4, no. 5, The General Conference of The United Methodist Church, 2000), May 4, 2000.

General Conference and by the ELCA's 2009 Churchwide Assembly, "Full communion means that each church acknowledges the other as a partner in the Christian faith, recognizes the authenticity of each other's baptism and Eucharist, observes the validity of their respective ministries and is committed to working together toward greater unity"[37] (**eS2008d,e**). This agreement is different from those that The UMC currently shares with its predecessor denominations, particularly those of the Pan-Methodist Commission. This agreement took more than thirty years of conversation and will hopefully lead to other full communion partners for The UMC. One of the more unexpected complications of this agreement is that the ELCA ordains openly LGBTQ+ clergy, and by entering into this agreement in 2008, The UMC's General Conference implicitly recognized the ordination of LGBTQ+ clergy.

Currently, The UMC bishops permit an "interim Eucharist sharing agreement" with The Episcopal Church (TEC), and is working toward full communion, but this partnership was put on hold at least until the 2024 General Conference (**eS2022e,f**). However, the TEC General Convention Committee on Ecumenical and Interreligious Relations discussed a Resolution, A093, "which commends the ongoing work of The Episcopal Church—United Methodist Dialogue," but Rowan Larson "asked committee members to recommend that The Episcopal Church not move forward with any proposal until The United Methodist Church addresses its current ban on LGBTQ+ clergy and the marriage of same-sex couples." It was stated that when The UMC "finalizes a separation plan, any plan for full communion will be with those who are LGBTQ+ affirming."[38] As some Methodists embrace ecumenism with other denominations, unresolved controversy in UMC conferences about same-sex marriage and ordination for those who are LGBTQ+ (as well as theological disagreement concerning the consecration of the Eucharist in streaming worship) will complicate efforts to move forward.

---

37. Linda Bloom, "United Methodists, Lutherans Take Historic Step Forward," UMNS, August 21, 2009, accessed March 18, 2022, http://archives.gcah.org/bitstream/handle /10516/755/7299581.htm?sequence=3.

38. Melodie Woerman, "Episcopal-Methodist Full Communion Partnership on Hold as UMC Delays Vote on Split over LGBTQ+ Inclusion," Episcopal News Service, March 8, 2022, accessed March 18, 2022, https://www.episcopalnewsservice.org/2022/03/08/episcopal -methodist-full-communion-partnership-on-hold-as-umc-delays-vote-on-split-over-lgbtq -inclusion/.

THE BIBLE AND ECUMENISM

The spirit of mainline Protestant ecumenism, inspired since 1908 by the Social Creed and the Federal Council of Churches, peaked after World War II when the National Council of Churches of Christ (NCCC) formed in 1950. The International Council of Religious Education (which had copyright to the Authorized Standard Version that stabilized the KJV text and had started a revision of the KJV in 1937) became the Division of Christian Education for the NCCC. By September 1952 the NCCC released the Revised Standard Version (RSV) of the Bible, published nationwide by Thomas Nelson on a sales-embargo date (September 30, 1952) in thousands of Protestant churches. The revision of the KJV (the Bible version authorized by the Church of England and interpreted by the Wesleys) was a necessary but limited update of archaic language, applying the fruit of historical criticism and text-critical accuracy after seventy-five years of startling archaeological discoveries about biblical-era cultures and grounded on recovering thousands of ancient biblical papyri that would correct glaring textual deficiencies in the KJV. Many conservatives (especially among the National Association of Evangelicals that formed in response to creation of the NCCC and RSV) were outraged by the KJV revision, and several thousand copies of the RSV were sent to the bonfires, which was at least a more humane outcome since the days of burning Bible translators at the stake.[39]

New Bible versions are developed for particular faith communities, because translation always requires interpretation. With very rare exception, Protestant denominations do not, since the Reformation, exclusively endorse a single Bible translation, since Protestant readers (and not church authorities) are expected to read the Bible in a vernacular language and interpret the Scriptures for themselves. The RSV and subsequent 1989 NRSV (the later which shifted by intent toward more gender-inclusive language regarding human pronouns) sustained the obvious influences that prompted Calvinists to propose an English Bible translation to (Presbyterian) King James, which might unite England and end violent religious wars between Catholics, Anglicans, Presbyterians, and nonconformists.

The RSV and NRSV were led by biblical scholars from the Presbyterian seminaries (RSV was headquartered at Yale; NRSV at Princeton). MEC and

---

39.   See the preface to the RSV, also accessed at https://www.ncccusa.org/newbtu/about rsv.html.

later UMC ecumenical officers contributed funding for the RSV and NRSV translations, which took fifteen years and seventeen years, respectively, to complete. The RSV and NRSV became the norm for theological education in United Methodist seminaries, which became increasingly ecumenical in mission, in part because of the faculty hired, the alignment of biblical and theological scholars with the university academic guilds, and in part to sustain seminaries financially with a more diverse student body and clergy pool across multiple denominations.

As mainline congregations, judicatories, and institutions decline during what many historians describe as a post-denominational era, the NCCC also contracted in the early years of the new millennium to fewer than seven staff for lack of funding and diminishing ecumenical interest. A primary source of NCCC funding came from the RSV and NRSV, which by the new millennium had been replaced through the neo-Calvinist and Fundamentalist inerrancy movement by the New International Version as the Bible authority of choice in over one-third of UMC congregations.

Abingdon Press, the primary imprint at UMPH, had a long history with biblical reference, including the Strong's Exhaustive Concordance, compiled on 3 × 5 notecards by James Strong in 1896; The Interpreter's Bible 12-Volume Commentary (which sold over one million sets); the five-volume Interpreter's Dictionary of the Bible; and then the twelve-volume New Interpreter's Bible Commentary, which over sixty thousand clergy and churches purchased. Abingdon released three successful NRSV Bible editions, the first, NRSV Children's Bible (2005, with over 100,000 purchased by Sunday schools), The New Interpreter's Study Bible (2003, with over 250,000 purchased through seminaries and Disciple Bible Study), and the Wesley Study Bible (2009, with over 100,000 purchased by pastors and adult small groups).

However, as sales of the NIV escalated, rights to the NRSV translation were sold in 2008 by the NCCC, which needed funding, to HarperCollins Publishers (owned by Rupert Murdoch, who also had purchased Zondervan and Thomas Nelson, the largest Bible publishers in the world) in 2008.

After research into what Bibles were being used in United Methodist congregations and classrooms, in 2008 The UMPH board approved development of the first English translation of the Christian Bible, including the Apocrypha, to be sponsored by a Methodist publisher.

Ecumenical cooperation for the Common English Bible (CEB) was obtained from five other denominational publishers, including The Episcopal

Church (which endorsed use of the CEB in 2012, among other versions) and the Presbyterian Church USA, and Cooperative Baptists. The publishing endorsement relationships faded as TEC and PCUSA split over ordination of LGBTQ+ clergy and fundamentalist interpretation of Scripture.

The Common English Bible (CEB) project began work in January 2008, and by working through a website was completed and released as a new imprint (from UMPH) in July 2011. The effort was completed by 120 translators (including ten editors). The translators were evenly spread among scholars affiliated with UM, PCUSA, TEC, ELCA, and Cooperative Baptists, and included Catholic and Jewish scholars. More than thirty linguists were women.. Senior editors who decided key translation disagreements were United Methodists Joel B. Green (New Testament) and David deSilva (Apocrypha), and Presbyterian David Petersen from Candler School of Theology (Old Testament). Each translation was carefully scored for readability in worship and education, without harmonizing innate theological problems in Scripture. Lay reading groups in seventy-seven congregations across thirteen denominations provided online feedback directly to the editors. If the CEB tilts in an interpretative direction, it would be Wesleyan (e.g., affirming John Wesley's translation of the Beatitudes in Matthew's Gospel). More than one hundred editions of the CEB were released by 2020 for children, students, adults, seminarians, pews, pulpits, and on twenty digital platforms. Approximately 2.5 million copies of the CEB were in circulation by 2021.

In 2022, the NCCC, with assistance from the Society of Biblical Literature, an academic guild, released an NRSVue (update edition), making a limited number of syntax corrections, updating some archaic phrases, and as in the past focusing on text-critical judgments.

The near future of ecumenical English Bible translation is uncertain while US Christian institutions (academic and denominational) contract, battle, and split again over interpretation of Scripture.

ACTS OF REPENTANCE

The 2000 General Conference adopted the "Act of Repentance for Racism," which called for the adoption of a study guide (*Steps Toward Wholeness: Learning and Repentance*) "which addresses the church's role in racism, concluding with a call for repentance," urged all "local congregations in the United States to engage in study sessions" using this resource, and "requested" that all annual conferences "engage in a liturgical act of repentance in 2001" (**eS200a**).[40] The resolution recognized the systemic sin of racism present in the history of The United Methodist Church, particularly in White supremacist actions that led to the formation of the African Methodist Episcopal, the African Methodist Episcopal Zion, the Christian Methodist Episcopal denominations as well as the Central Jurisdiction within The Methodist Church. It called for education at all levels of the church when it comes to all forms of racism, but specifically named "the areas of African American race relations"[41] (**eS2000b**). By the end of 2002, it was reported that "31 annual conferences had held an Act of Repentance worship service" with another twenty-nine services to be held in spring 2003 and two in 2004. Only two conferences, by that time, had not indicated whether they would participate.[42]

The work of repenting for racism, which began in 2000, continued through the next four General Conferences. In 2004, the delegation approved the continuation of the Strengthening the Black Church for the 21st Century (SBC21) initiative (originally begun in 1996) as well as created an African American Methodist Heritage Center to ensure the preservation and promotion of African American Methodist history. According to United Methodist News Service, "The center, proposed two years ago at a national meeting of BMCR, will collect the history, memories and stories of those of African descent who have been a part of Methodism since its inception in the mid-18th century and those of African descent who have stayed throughout Methodism's history, said the approved legislation."[43] The center was and is still housed at GCAH on the campus of Drew University in Madison, New Jersey. Originally granted $100,000 to fund and sustain its ministry, the commitment to the AAMHC (and arguably to addressing and confessing its own structural racism and racist past) dwindled quickly. The AAMHC, only a few years later, was largely supported financially by GCAH and individual

---

40.   *The Book of Resolutions of The United Methodist Church*, 2000. Copyright © 2000 by The United Methodist Publishing House; ¶149, 384. Used by permission.

41.   *The Book of Resolutions*, 2000; 385.

42.   Linda Bloom, "United Methodists Continue 'Repentance' Actions," United Methodist News Service, Feb. 12, 2003, accessed March 14, 2022, http://archives.gcah.org/bitstream /handle/10516/7700/article41.aspx.htm?sequence=1.

43.   "Delegates Keep Black Church Initiative, Create Black Heritage Center," May 6, 2004, accessed March 14, 2022, http://gc2004.org/interior.asp?ptid=17&mid=4615.

(or annual conference) donations. However, as agency budgets were cut, GCAH reallocated its funds, lowering the financial support of the AAMHC to $1,000 per year during the 2016–2020 quadrennium.

In 2012, acts of repentance shifted toward Indigenous American communities. The 2012 General Conference held an "Act of Repentance toward Healing Relationships with Indigenous Peoples" on April 27, 2012, where the General Conference "pledged to work with Cheyenne and Arapaho Tribes in seeking belated justice for an 1864 massacre of 168 defenseless Native Americans in which Methodist leaders in Colorado were complicit." The resolution established an independent group to research and find full disclosure of the events, while another action provided for "widespread denominational education, repentance, and confession regarding past treatment of indigenous people" (eS2012d,e,f).[44] This resolution prompted a four-year research project that resulted in the Abingdon Press monograph, *Massacre at Sand Creek: How Methodists Were Involved in an American Tragedy*, by Gary L. Roberts. The work continued at the 2016 General Conference with the reception of the report: "We commend this report to the Church as a resource for understanding the Sand Creek Massacre and the history of the Church's role in colonization, displacement, and destruction of indigenous cultures in every land" (eS2016k,l). The Council of Bishops was tasked with "formal negotiations with official tribal representatives to produce a Memorandum of Understanding establishing an ongoing healing relationship between these tribes and The United Methodist Church." Bishop Elaine Stanovsky was appointed head of negotiations. Other connectional bodies, including GCAH and the GBCS, were tasked with education and returning of land and artifacts.[45]

With the repeated news of Black men murdered by US police officers, attention, again, returned to anti-Black racism. In 2013, the hashtag #BlackLivesMatter trended virally over Twitter. Three female Black organizers—Alicia Garza, Patrisse Cullors, and Opal Tometi—used the hashtag after George Zimmerman was acquitted in the shooting death of Trayvon Martin in 2012. Its use continued and intensified after the murder of Michael Brown

---

44. 2012 General Conference petitions #20767.

45. *The Book of Resolutions of The United Methodist Church*, 2016. Copyright © 2016 by The United Methodist Publishing House; ¶3328. Used by permission. Accessed March 14, 2022, https://www.umcjustice.org/who-we-are/social-principles-and-resolutions/united-methodist-responses-to-the-sand-creek-massacre-3328.

(Missouri) and Eric Garner (New York). By becoming a global movement acknowledging anti-Black racism around the world, and not only in the US, #BlackLivesMatter encouraged persons to *see color* and acknowledge the racism of everyday life; of the way our local, state, federal, and global systems are structured; and to tell whole histories that are from a non-White, noncolonial perspective, stories that uplift and center minority voices.

In United Methodism, the 2016 General Conference saw its first #BlackLivesMatter demonstration alongside an LGBTQ+-affirming protest. In an intersectional protest, approximately 150 persons gathered in the middle of the plenary floor holding signs that stated, "All #BlackLivesMatter: Bisexual, transgender, poor, homosexual, lesbian, gay, disabled, women, men, youth, and children." The Rev. Pamela Lightsey, one of the organizers of the protest and the first Black lesbian pastor to be ordained in The UMC, said "We are upset about the lack of voice The United Methodist Church has given against police force (toward) Black and Brown bodies across the U. S. . . . which says they do not intend to put the power of this huge denomination against this."[46]

By the summer of 2020, the Council of Bishops addressed the cry of Black United Methodists across the globe. After the murder of George Floyd, the world erupted in protest to support #BlackLivesMatter. Fueled by the casual racism of US President Donald J. Trump, the level of protest, amid the COVID-19 global pandemic, had a different taste than previous protests. On Juneteenth (June 19, 2020), the COB announced, "This time will be different," as they launched a new anti-racism campaign (**eS2020a**). Black bishop Cynthia Moore-Koikoi lamented that she was tired of statements of "sound and fury" ultimately "signifying nothing." The COB program, "Dismantling Racism: Pressing on to Freedom," was to be a multi-agency effort, which Bishop Thomas Bickerton of the New York Area described as "a journey . . . that's designed to stimulate you with frequent events—worship services, town halls, book studies, resources and honest conversations" in hopes "that we . . . can create a movement for lasting change." It was to involve all levels of the connection and culminate in a demonstration at the (postponed) 2020 General Conference.[47]

---

46. Jessica Brodie, "GC2016 Plenary Pauses for Black Lives Matter Demonstration," United Methodist News Service, May 16, 2016, accessed March 14, 2022, https://www.umnews.org/en/news/gc2016-plenary-pauses-for-black-lives-matter-demonstration.

47. Jim Patterson, "Bishops Pledge More Effective Anti-racism Campaign," UM News, June 19, 2020, accessed March 14, 2022, https://www.umnews.org/en/news/bishops-pledge

DIVISION(S) BASED ON SEXUALITY

When the new millennium began, some bishops expressed [naive] hope that the "debate on homosexuality" might not continue to divide the denomination but instead might bring "us closer together."[48] However, Good News and other conservative caucus groups such as the IRD sought to enact a punishment for clergy coming out or blessing same-sex weddings. Simultaneously and covertly in 2004 the conservative caucuses circulated among allies a blueprint for exit and dissolution of The UMC if their restrictions failed (**eS2004d**). In 2004, these caucuses convinced the delegates to enact chargeable offenses for those who publicly come out as "self-avowed, practicing homosexuals" or for those who publicly officiated at same-sex weddings.[49] This latest restriction caused, once again, rumors of division to spread among the 2004 General Conference, leading to a Statement of Unity being passed by the delegation (**eS2004c**). Once a chargeable offense was legislated, the question became "How does one define someone as 'self-avowed, practicing'?" Does this mean a public "coming out"? What does it mean to be "practicing"? Does one have to be both self-avowed and practicing (for a clergyperson) to be in violation of the *Discipline*? Many such questions were posed and taken to the Judicial Council, which largely refused to define either term and answer the overall question as to how this chargeable offense could be broken or enacted.

Over the next decade many United Methodists (leaders and members) "came out" as gay or lesbian or transgender, and many United Methodist pastors officiated at same-sex weddings. These celebrations were witnessed both as a protest of chargeable offenses in the annual conference and as a way to acknowledge that the Holy Spirit works through all of us and because *love is love.*

Two clergy trials made US national news headlines. Amy DeLong of Wisconsin admitted to her bishop that she had officiated the wedding of a lesbian couple and that she, herself, was in a lesbian partnership. For these acts, in the summer of 2011, she was tried (**eS2011**). DeLong was not

---

-more-effective-anti-racism-campaign; "United Methodists Stand Against Racism," UMC.org, accessed March 14, 2022, https://www.umc.org/en/how-we-serve/advocating-for-justice/racial-justice/united-against-racism.

48.   "Daily Wrap Up: Delegates Discuss CPT Report for First Time" May 5, 2000, accessed March 14, 2022, gc2000.org.

49.   *The Book of Discipline of The United Methodist Church*, 2004. Copyright © 2004 by The United Methodist Publishing House; ¶ 2702.1.b. This language appears in the 2004 BOD but was not effective until January 1, 2005.

the first person to be tried for conducting same-sex weddings nor was she the first openly gay or lesbian clergy to be tried for coming out or being in a same-sex, loving relationship. But she was the first person to be asked an inappropriate question, one that would never be asked of any other clergyperson, by the prosecutor (Tom Lambrecht of the Good News caucus) if she and her partner had had "genital contact." DeLong justifiably declined to answer, despite repeated attempts at the question. She was also the first pastor to not be indefinitely suspended or defrocked for conducting such a wedding. For this defiance of the *Book of Discipline*, she was suspended for twenty days. DeLong's trial sparked an uproar across the denomination as UM clergy pledged together to defy the *Book of Discipline* and perform same-sex ceremonies. Over 70 clergy signed a petition in Minnesota pledging their defiance, 134 in Northern Illinois; in sum approximately 500 active and retired UM clergy signed.[50] These pledges, expectedly, led to a conservative backlash from non-affirming caucuses and clergy. Mark Tooley (a layman and former CIA officer), director of UM Action and the IRD—a parachurch organization whose blogs and lobbying critique Protestant mainline groups over U-S-based political issues—mocked Amy DeLong as not "work[ing] for any church" and calling herself and her allies "co-belligerents." He compared The UMC to the other Protestant churches that "took the plunge" and had "abandoned their traditional teachings about marriage."[51]

In 2013 Frank Schaefer made national headlines for his officiating the 2007 wedding of his son to another man in Pennsylvania. After a two-day trial in the annual conference, Schaefer was found guilty (eS2013a) (eS2014). He was the first to be found guilty for this action since the 2012 General Conference, but his trial overlapped with four others. He was suspended for thirty days, but he refused to give up his pulpit. His refusal to adhere to the suspension resulted in revocation of his clergy credentials. Neither DeLong nor Schaefer were the first nor the last to disobey *The Book of Discipline*. Reconciling Ministries Network (RMN) maintains a list of clergy who faced charges for either identifying as LGBTQ+ or conducting a same-sex wedding. The list begins with Gene Leggett in 1971 and includes Paul Abels

---

50. Justin Horwath, "The Trial of Pastor Amy DeLong: Methodism and Same-Sex Unions," *Time*, July 1, 2011, accessed March 14, 2022, http://content.time.com/time/nation /article/0,8599,2080401,00.html.

51. Mark Tooley, "Same-Sex Marriage for Methodists?" Juicy Ecumenism, Institute for Religion and Democracy, June 27, 2011, accessed March 14, 2022, https://juicyecumenism .com/2011/06/27/same-sex-marriage-for-methodists/.

(1979), Greg Dell (1998), Jimmy Creech (1998), Mark Williams (2001), Karen Dammann (2004), Beth Stroud (2005), Drew Phoenix (2007), Amy DeLong (2011), Thomas Ogletree (2013), Cheryl A. Fear (2013), Rose Mary Denman (N/A), Rebecca Steen (2002), Steven Heiss (2013), Gordon Hutchins (2013), Frank Schaefer (2013), the Philadelphia 33 (2013), Sarah Thompson-Tweedy (2013), Bill McElvaney (2014), Ed Rowe (2014), Mike Tupper (2014), Melvin Talbert (2014), Amanda Garber (2014), John Copenhaver (2014), Larry W. Sonner (N/A), Pam Hawkins (2015), and Sid Hall III (1997, 2015, 2020).[52] Countless other individuals acknowledge that they are not in safe local churches or annual conferences to publicly identify as LGBTQ+ or to conduct same-sex weddings.

By the Fall of 2013, retired bishop Melvin Talbert began a counter-movement of "biblical obedience" (**eS2013b**). During the annual RMN convocation, Bishop Talbert called those in attendance to "mobilize United Methodists of all sexual orientations and gender identities to transform our Church and world into the full expression of Christ's inclusive love."[53] In this call, Bishop Talbert referenced Micah 6:6 and Mark 12:28-31, which he argued were at the heart of the prophetic witness and ministry of Christ. He called those gathered to love God and others above all else, claimed that the laws of God are above the laws of the church, and verbally recommitted himself to ensure that the rights of LGBTQ+ persons would be affirmed in the denomination. Bishop Mary Ann Swenson also verbally confirmed her support of LGBTQ+ persons. In a speech that reflected on her experiences of racism as a child, she called for biblical obedience as the love of God above all else. Following the convocation was a celebration of marriage equality, with over twenty-five members of the Metropolitan Memorial UMC present, alongside then-district superintendent (now Bishop) the Rev. Cynthia Moore-Koikoi, who called the denomination to "let go of the last vestiges of segregation."[54] Following Bishop Talbert's call, the proclamation of "biblical obedience" became the rallying cry of a coalition of LGBTQ+ affirming groups, ministers, and laypersons.

---

52. "Complaints Against Clergy," Reconciling Ministries Network, accessed March 14, 2022, https://rmnetwork.org/history/.

53. "A Call for Biblical Obedience," Baltimore–Washington Archives, posted September 3, 2013, accessed March 14, 2022, https://www.bwcumc.org/archives/a-call-for-biblical-obedience/.

54. "A Call for Biblical Obedience."

The 2012 General Conference, just prior to Bishop Talbert's call to biblical obedience, was dominated with legislation sponsored by the Connectional Table executives and senior clergy from the largest UM churches. Their controversial Call to Action proposal attempted restructuring of the general boards and agencies in a financially sustainable and aligned system. This agenda gave limited time to the discussion of sexuality, but two large-church senior clergy, Mike Slaughter of Ginghamsburg near Dayton and Adam Hamilton of Church of the Resurrection near Kansas City, brought a resolution that reached the floor, which put to the vote a change in *The Book of Discipline* that The UMC would "agree to disagree" concerning same-sex marriage and ordination of gay and lesbian clergy. Repeated delays from other motions and protests interfered with the contentious multilingual debate. By a vote of 53 percent to 47 percent, tipped by growing delegations from Africa and the Philippines, the delegates decided United Methodists would not "agree to disagree" and instead maintained the incompatibility clause.

In 2015 in a five to four landmark decision written by Jewish Justice Stephen Breyer, the US Supreme Court ruled in *Obergefell v. Hodges* that same-sex marriage equality is protected from discrimination under the Due Process and Equal Protection Clauses of the Fourteenth Amendment. On the team of lawyers from four states that brought the marriage-equality lawsuits were two United Methodist attorneys, Phillip Cramer and William Harbison, lay board members at Belmont UMC in Nashville, TN. In their book, *The Fight for Marriage*, the story of the landmark marriage-equality lawsuit is blended with the story at Belmont UMC concerning the suspension of Belmont clergy duties for Pam Hawkins, who, like Melvin Talbert, officiated a same-sex wedding across state lines (North Carolina) outside her Tennessee Conference. Nashville Federal Judge and active United Methodist member Aleta A. Trauger had ruled in Federal District Court:

> For the three couples Harbison and Cramer represented, marriage is not an "issue" to be resolved. Marriage is rather a sign for these couples of their faithful promise to love each other until they depart this life. Each couple married for several reasons, including their commitment to love and support one another, to demonstrate their mutual commitment to their family, friends, and colleagues, and to show others that they should be treated as a family. They also married to make a legally binding mutual commitment, to join their resources together in a legal unit, and to be treated by others as a legal family unit, rather than as legally unrelated individuals. Finally, each

couple married so that they could access the legal responsibilities of marriage to protect themselves and their families, just as heterosexual couples do.

Between 2004 and 2016 in The UMC, the several caucuses supporting or opposing marriage equality and ordination of LGBTQ+ persons grew more and more divided and hardened about their stances, each claiming faithfulness to Scripture and Wesleyan theology. In 2014, eight United Methodist bishops from the US, Germany, and Africa collaborated in an ecclesial debate with countering points of view, Finding Our Way: Love and Law in The United Methodist Church, which was mailed to conference delegates and distributed in annual conferences.[55] Also mailed by UMPH to delegates with a study edition was a dynamic translation (from Elizabethan language) of Francis Asbury's book *The Causes, Evils and Cures of Heart and Church Divisions*. Asbury distributed the book in 1792 when the Republican Methodists were sowing Calvinism, and the Methodist Book Concern reprinted and distributed the book again in 1844 on the eve of schism over slavery.

As planned by a group of eighty UM clergy in 2013, by October 2015 in preparation for the 2016 General Conference, one thousand United Methodists, including the key leadership and members of the Good News caucus and their allies (IRD, professors at Asbury Theological Seminary, several United Methodist Men's leaders, Aldersgate charismatics, several BMCR leaders, several African leaders, with support from three UM bishops), formed the Wesleyan Covenant Association (WCA)(**eS2016h**). Participants functioned as a parachurch United Methodist entity. The WCA was established as a proto-denomination, a space for non-affirming activists to join and organize if there were to be a split at the 2016 General Conference.

Just prior to the 2016 General Conference, the United Methodist Queer Clergy Caucus formed. Their first step was to write and distribute "A Love Letter to Our Church from Your LGBTQI Religious Leaders" (**eS2016a**). Dated May 9, 2016, the letter was addressed to the General Conference. It emphasized the shared covenant of baptism and the harm done to ordained persons who identify as LGBTQ+:

However, while we have sought to remain faithful to our call and covenant, you have not always remained faithful to us. While you have welcomed us as pastors, youth leaders, district superintendents, bishops, professors,

---

55. *Finding Our Way: Love and Law in The United Methodist Church*, Abingdon Press, May 14, 2014, https://www.ministrymatters.com/all/entry/5014/finding-our-way.

missionaries and other forms of religious service, you have required that we not bring our full selves to ministry, that we hide from view our sexual orientations and gender identities. As long as we did this, you gladly affirmed our gifts and graces and used us to make disciples of Jesus Christ for the transformation of the world in the varied places you sent us.[56]

This letter was an en masse "coming out" to show that LGBTQ+ United Methodists wished to remain in relationship with other United Methodists, to provide hope for LGBTQ+ young United Methodists, and to encourage those in Portland, Oregon, to "listen for God's still, small voice."[57] In a show of unity and protest, 111 United Methodist clergy and clergy candidates came out as gay in this letter. It was immediately given support by over five hundred openly LGBTQ+ clergy, future pastors, and some faith leaders of other denominations to show their support of individuals and over fifteen hundred UMC clergy who stated:

The current language prohibiting LGBTQI people from serving as ordained clergy is discriminatory, unjust, unChristlike, and inconsistent with both holy scripture and the best of our United Methodist heritage. Scores of our LGBTQI clergy colleagues have courageously declared their insistence on serving openly as ordained leaders in the United Methodist Church. We applaud this action; and, at the request of our LGBTQI colleagues, stand in solidarity with those who publicly "come out" (**eS2016c**).[58]

In a show of solidarity after the US Supreme Court decision in *Obergefall v. Hodges* legalized same-sex marriage, twenty-eight UM bishops wrote and signed a "A Pastoral Response" to the 111 clergy and candidates, acknowledging them as equals in Christ (**eS2016b**).[59] Thus the politicking ahead of the

---

56. "A Love Letter to Our Church from Your LGBTQI Religious Leaders," UM Queer Clergy Caucus, May 9, 2016, accessed March 14, 2022, https://www.umqcc.org/a-love-letter -to-our-church-from-your-lgbtqi-religious-leaders.

57. "A Love Letter to Our Church from Your LGBTQI Religious Leaders."

58. Heather Hahn and Kathy L. Gilbert, "500 Clergy Support Gay United Methodist Clergy Who Came Out," United Methodist News Service, May 9, 2016, accessed March 14, 2022, https://www.umnews.org/en/news/111-clergy-clergy-candidates-come-out-as-gay; Jeremy Smith, "1500+ Clergy Allies Stand with LGBTQ Clergy in the #UMC," Hacking Christianity, accessed March 14, 2022, https://hackingchristianity.net/2016/05/1500-clergy -allies-stand-with-lgbtq-clergy-in-the-umc.html (emphasis original).

59. "A Pastoral Response to *A Love Letter to Our Church* from LGBTQI Religious Leaders," accessed March 14, 2022, https://westernjurisdictionumc.org/a-pastoral-response -to-a-love-letter-to-our-church-from-lgbtqi-religious-leaders/?mc_cid=3f0920b9f3&mc _eid=0315cb2b5d.

2016 General Conference acknowledged growing support (in the US) for marriage equality and potentially ordination for LGBTQ+ clergy and candidates. With discrimination regarding same-sex marriage illegal in the US and given the complex partnership between church and state governing marriage laws, the prohibition of homosexual behavior in the *Book of Discipline* made it more likely (but not mandatory) that clergy could be asked to legally officiate at a same-sex wedding.

Clearly human sexuality would dominate the 2016 General Conference. The session began with a three-day debate concerning Rule 44, a rule that would establish a consensus-building process for holy conferencing and spiritual discernment.[60] With Robert's Rules of Order for parliamentary procedures proving harmful and unworkable when nearly one thousand delegates are negotiating and voting about church-dividing issues, a better process for discernment was requested in 2012 of the General Commission on General Conference—after delegates could not "agree to disagree" about restrictive language in the *Discipline*.[61] The Commission on General Conference had previously suggested that this rule could be used to discuss legislation regarding sexuality, but it had many other benefits to proposed legislation that would have deeply enriched conversation about how to be connectional in an increasingly diverse and global denomination. Thus the session began with a three-day debate regarding how UMC delegates talk to and with one another about one of the more contested aspects of our connection. Keith Boyette, a lawyer and clergy member in the Northern Illinois

---

60.   The architects selected for the consensus-building discernment process were United Methodists Terence Corkin (former presiding moderator of Australia's Uniting Church conference) and Julia Kuhm Wallace, a former consultant from Discipleship Ministries (GBOD). Their process is represented in the book *The Church Guide for Making Decisions Together* (Nashville: Abingdon Press, 2017).

61.   According to Heather Hahn, the official process would be: "Under General Conference's usual procedure, delegates first meet in legislative committees that consider petitions. The committees typically decide what goes before the whole body for a vote. Under the commission's plan, all 864 delegates would review the same group of petitions in small groups with no more than 15 members. The commission sees the small groups as a way for everyone to have a voice. Each small group's recommendations would then go to a six-member 'facilitation group' elected by General Conference and responsible for crafting a petition or group of petitions based on the small-group recommendations. The results of the facilitation group's work would then go to the full plenary, and General Conference would resume its usual procedures including Robert's Rules of Order." Heather Hahn, "GC2016: The Debate About How to Debate Sexuality," United Methodist News Service, April 15, 2016, accessed March 14, 2022, https://www.umnews.org/en/news/gc2016-the-debate-about-how-to-debate-sexuality.

Conference, and by 2017 president of the WCA, argued regarding Rule 44, "I find this Group Discernment Process especially troublesome. I was going to use the word 'pernicious.' It is fraught with potholes, fraught with places where problems can arise and where people can walk away from it saying I wasn't really heard." Others expressed concerns as well. Dorothee Benz, delegate from New York Conference, worried that if in a discernment group a delegate "came out" as part of the discussion that there was nothing in the process to protect that person from trial. Benz said, "What's important for LGBTQI people at General Conference is that the church live up to its Wesleyan mandate to 'do no harm,' and that means preventing a repeat of the abuse and hate speech that has been directed at us at past General Conferences. Whether that is using the Rule 44 process or the existing rules, it's the church's job to keep us from ending up as spiritual roadkill yet again." Yet some delegates did see Rule 44 as a new way to do Christian Conferencing, referencing the lofty but elusive John Wesley principle for discerning when to agree on essentials and hold in tension conflicting opinions. Andy Bryan, a clergy reserve delegate from Missouri, believed that new processes such as Rule 44 might remind us that, as Christians, we are called to "higher standards than Roberts Rules of Order." We are called "to be witnesses and models of love and grace and Christ-like relationships."[62]

The 2016 General Conference did not seem any more hopeful on affirming LGBTQ+ persons than any prior conference. The Connectional Table of The UMC had brought forward a plan to get the denomination beyond its impasse, but the plan failed quickly as it was not allowed to be considered and bundled as a group of petitions, and was thus spread among varied legislative committees. The delegations sensed that conferencing on sexuality would be no different than it had been in the past. After three days of debating the rules, largely out of fear about consensus through Rule 44, one delegate appealed for leadership from the bishops, a risk for Methodists who devalue the episcopacy.

Amid social media–based rumors about schism or behind-the-scenes meetings between bishops and key caucus groups, on May 17, 2016, Bishop Bruce Ough, president of the Council of Bishops, gave an address on unity of the denomination. His apparent intent was to quell schism rumors and affirm a united denomination; however, in his statement some listeners did not apprehend sufficient concern for the pain of LGBTQ+ delegates, clergy members, and observers. Later that morning, Tom Berlin, clergy delegate

---

62.   Hahn, "GC2016: The Debate about How to Debate Sexuality."

from Virginia, made a request from the plenary floor. He began by referencing Bishop Ough's call to unity: "This morning, Bishop Ough said that at General Conference, the role of the bishop was to preside." But then, he challenged the bishops (or rather the delegates) by saying, "Quite frankly, bishop, we think it's your role to lead. We are asking for your leadership." For the first time in recent memory of the forty-eight-year-old UMC, from the floor of the plenary, bishops were asked to take a direct role in General Conference. In a follow-up motion, the COB were asked to depart the stage and bring back a recommendation on a way forward to the plenary the following day. This motion passed by a vote of 428 to 364, and the bishops went into closed session at four p.m. that day.[63]

On May 18, 2016, Bishop Ough again spoke on behalf of the COB. In the statement, "An offering for a way forward," the bishops committed themselves to "lead the church toward new behaviors, a new way of being, and new forms and structures which allow a unity of our mission." They asked the General Conference to "affirm your own commitment to maintaining and strengthening the unity of the church." They suggested a "pause for prayer" in order to "step back from attempts at legislative solutions and to intentionally seek God's will for the future." In this statement, the bishops did not put forth a scripted process for moving forward, but they did suggest that a "called General Conference in 2018 or 2019" would be an option. The main impetus of the statement was the formation of a special commission:

> We recommend that the General Conference defer all votes on human sexuality and refer this entire subject to a special Commission, named by the Council of Bishops, to develop a complete examination and possible revision of every paragraph in our *Book of Discipline* regarding human sexuality. We continue to hear from many people on the debate over sexuality that our current *Discipline* contains language which is contradictory, unnecessarily hurtful, and inadequate for the variety of local, regional and global contexts. We will name such a Commission to include persons from every region of our UMC, and will include representation from differing perspectives on the debate. We commit to maintain an on-going dialogue with this Commission as they do their work, including clear objectives and

---

63. Kathy L. Gilbert and Sam Hodges, "Conference Pleads with Bishops for Leadership," United Methodist News Service," May 17, 2016, accessed March 14, 2022, https://www.um news.org/en/news/conference-pleads-with-bishops-for-leadership.

outcomes. Should they complete their work in time for a called General Conference, then we will call a two- to three-day gathering before the 2020 General Conference.[64]

The recommendation was accepted by a vote of 428 to 405, and the bishops were then tasked with forming the commission.[65] In July 2016 the COB identified the mission, vision, and scope of the work and selected three moderators for the Commission on a Way Forward (CWF). They then nominated and selected thirty-two members to serve on the commission, trying to emphasize the global church as well as the competing factions, including the WCA. Those serving represented nine countries, diverse theological positions, and equal representation of laity, clergy, and bishops. Over the following seventeen months, the CWF met nine times, and provided the Council of Bishops with an interim report in November 2017 and a final report in 2018 (**eS2019b**). Their interim report began to sketch the three plans that would be finalized by 2018 in legislative form.

Some moments of General Conference 2016 were not contentious. In a surprising vote, delegates voted to pass five constitutional amendments, two of which dealt positively with women's place in the denomination. The first would add a new paragraph 6 to the *Discipline* which would read, "men and women are of equal value in the eyes of God," and continues on to a commitment to "seek to eliminate discrimination against women and girls, whether in organizations or in individuals, in every facet of life and in society at large." This amendment was approved overwhelmingly by General Conference with a vote of 746 to 56. Another amendment sought to add "gender, ability, age, and marital status" to the list of characteristics that do not bar a person from membership. Women's organizations, especially COSROW, have been trying to add "gender" to this clause since the early 1990s. Amended paragraph 4 would thus read that no member could be "denied access to an equal place in the life, worship and governance of the Church because of race, color, gender,

---

64. "An Offering for a Way Forward," Council of Bishops, accessed March 14, 2022, https://s3.amazonaws.com/Website_Properties/general-conference/2016/documents/council-bishops-statement-offering-way-forward-may-18-gc2016.pdf.

65. Heather Hahn and Sam Hodges, "GC2016 Puts Hold on Sexuality Debate," United Methodist News Service, May 18, 2016, accessed March 14, 2022, https://www.umnews.org/en/news/bishops-ask-for-hold-on-sexuality-debate.

national origin, ability, age, marital status or economic condition." Again, this passed with a healthy majority at General Conference, 509 to 242.[66]

The UMC government was established in 1972 and is somewhat similar to the branches of government laid out in the US Constitution. Similar to the US Congress, in order for a constitutional amendment to pass, two-thirds of t+The UMC membership (clergy and lay delegates) of an annual conference must approve. It was initially reported that the first amendment, to create a new paragraph 6 that sought to focus on gender justice, barely failed, receiving 66.5 percent of a needed 66.6 percent of the vote![67] However, upon this announcement, it was realized that the wrong wording was sent around for ratification to the annual conference delegates. At the 2016 General Conference, amendments were made to the original petition to remove the sentence "The United Methodist Church recognizes it is contrary to Scripture and to logic to say that God is male or female, as maleness and femaleness are characteristics of human bodies and cultures, not characteristics of the divine." This sentence remained in the amendment sent to annual conferences for discussion, despite General Conference removal of it. Another round of voting ensued by annual conference delegations. After the correct petition circled back to the annual conferences, in November 2019 the first women's equality amendment passed (**eS2019a**)[68] The second amendment, which attempted to add "gender, ability, age, and marital status" to the list of protected classes failed ratification, receiving 61.3 percent of annual conference votes.[69]

During the summer after the 2016 General Conference, a new form of protest, Acts of Non-Conformity, emerged to challenge the continued prohibitions regarding same-sex weddings and LGBTQ+ ordination in the *Discipline*. New England, Desert Southwest, California–Pacific, California Nevada, and Pacific Northwest conferences passed "Acts of Non-Conformity"

---

66.   Heather Hahn, "5 Constitutional Amendments Head to Vote," United Methodist News Service, Feb. 8, 2017, accessed March 18, 2022, https://www.umnews.org/en/news/5-constitutional-amendments-head-to-vote.

67.   "Bishops Announce Results of Five Constitutional Amendments; Two Fail to Get Two-thirds Majority," COB, May 7, 2017, accessed March 18, 2022, https://www.umc.org/en/content/bishops-announce-results-of-five-constitutional-amendments-two-fail-to-get.

68.   Heather Hahn, "Church Ratifies Women's Equality Amendment," UM News, Nov. 6, 2019, accessed March 18, 2022, https://www.umnews.org/en/news/church-ratifies-womens-equality-amendment.

69.   "Bishops Announce Results of Five Constitutional Amendments."

stating they no longer would comply with the *Discipline* when it comes to the enforcement of anti-LGBTQ+ inclusion in the church. Other annual conferences used this protest as a way to criticize The UMC's withdrawal from the Religious Coalition for Reproductive Choice, an ecumenical women's reproductive rights organization that it founded in the 1970s to give a positive religious influence to ongoing discussions of women's rights (**eS2016m**).

In July 2016, the Western Jurisdiction rocked other jurisdictions by electing Karen Oliveto, senior pastor at Glide Memorial UMC in San Francisco, California, as the first *openly* LGBTQ+ Methodist bishop (**eS2017a,b**). For many delegates who voted for her, the close election "wasn't a vote focused on sexual orientation," but was done because "we felt God pulling, pushing, and nudging us to elect the best person on the ballot as our next bishop."[70] Bishop Oliveto was married to Robin Ridenour, a United Methodist deaconess, in 2014. Within minutes of her election, delegates from the South Central Jurisdiction, led by Dixie Brewster of Oklahoma, passed a motion attempting to nullify her election, a move that questioned the power and highlighted the boundaries of jurisdictions in the US. The case was argued by Keith Boyette, president of the WCA, representing Brewster, and by Richard Marsh, representing Oliveto. In a complex ruling, the Judicial Council stated, "It is not lawful for the college of bishops of any jurisdictional or central conference to consecrate a self-avowed practicing homosexual bishop." However, self-avowal does not, in and of itself, nullify the consecration; a trial for misconduct is the process for nullification. And only the jurisdictional or central conference that the person is a member of can bring about those charges and lead that trial.[71] Without trial, Bishop Oliveto was a bishop in good standing and thus could not be tried or have her consecration nullified (**eS2017c**). In response to the challenge, Bishop Oliveto stated, "I am not the first gay bishop, and I won't be the last."[72]

70.   Kent Ingram and Emily Allen, "Karen Oliveto's Election as Bishop Was a Movement of the Holy Spirit," UM-Insight, March 14, 2017, accessed March 14, 2022, https://um-insight.net/karen-oliveto%E2%80%99s-election-as-bishop-was-a-movement-of-the-hol/.

71.   Linda Bloom, "UMC Judicial Council Decision on Consecration of Bishop Oliveto," Central Texas Conference Archives, accessed March 14, 2022, https://www.ctcumc.org/JudicialCouncilDecision_Oliveto

72.   Rachel Zoll, "Methodist Court Takes Up Challenge to Election of Gay Bishop," AP News, April 25, 2017, accessed March 14, 2022, https://apnews.com/article/4445243478ac44e9bc3cbf1af3285972.

THE COMMISSION ON
A WAY FORWARD (CWF)

Amid these maneuvers, the Council of Bishops was appointing members for the Commission on a Way Forward and convening their first meeting. Their subsequent two years of work led to three plans for a way forward (**eS2019b**). The first concept presented by the CWF was the One Church Plan (OCP), and it was eventually the plan supported by over two-thirds of the active bishops. According to the summary report, the One Church Plan, provides a generous unity that gives conferences, churches, and pastors the flexibility to uniquely reach their missional context without disbanding the connectional nature of The United Methodist Church. In the One Church Plan, no annual conferences, bishops, congregations, or pastors are compelled to act contrary to their convictions. The plan maintains the leadership structure of The United Methodist Church, including the Council of Bishops, the General Conference, and the annual conferences as one body and one church. It offers greater freedom to many who desire change but do not want to violate *The Book of Discipline*.[73]

No church or conference would be required to vote, and this plan offered what seemed to most bishops and the CWF the best option forward while maintaining the unity of the denomination and sustaining the connectional structure that guided Methodist churches for over two centuries. It offered space "for traditionalists to continue to offer ministry as they have in the past; space for progressives to exercise freely a more complete ministry with LGBTQ+ persons; and space for all United Methodists to continue to coexist without disrupting their ministries."[74] It offered the most flexibility to account for regional difference and cultural difference while adding language that intentionally sought to protect those who refused to conduct same-gender marriage rituals or ordain LGBTQ+ candidates. It also ended all church trials for those who identified as LGBTQ+ or clergy officiated at same-sex weddings.

The second option from the CWF was called the Connectional Conference Plan. It reminded progressive critics of the discrimination baked into the

---

73. "Commission on a Way Forward's Report to the General Conference," accessed March 14, 2022, https://s3.amazonaws.com/Website_Properties/council-of-bishops/news _and_statements/documents/Way_Forward_Report_-_Final_-_ENGLISH.pdf .

74. "Commission on a Way Forward's Report to the General Conference," 11.

racially segregated Central Jurisdiction. Through this plan there would be three "values-based connectional conferences that have distinctive definitions of accountability, contextualization and justice." The largest change under this plan would take place in the United States where the five regionally based jurisdictions would be replaced with three connectional conferences, each covering the entire US. Clergy, churches, annual conferences, and jurisdictional conferences would have the choice to join a connectional conference based on their understanding of LGBTQ+ ministry, given the options to join the "progressive," "unity," or "traditional" connectional conference. Each connectional conference would create its own *Book of Discipline*, maintaining a "General Book of Discipline" that was consistent across the board, the Articles of Religion, Confessions of Faith, and General Rules. Outside the US annual conferences, some critics thought colonialism was still lurking. The central conferences outside the US had the option of joining a US Connectional Conference or forming their own based on similar "values" or their own values. Each connectional conference would develop its own standards for same-sex weddings and LGBTQ+ ordination, for ministerial credentials, and for seminaries. No one would be forced to minister or worship in a connection with whom they disagreed, and no UMC delegate or member would be forced to vote on which connection to join if they did not wish to. Many progressives in the institutional structures of the church considered offensive the confused if naive nature of this plan, its parallel with the segregated Central Jurisdiction (of 1939–68), and its colonial structure—while many traditionalists still could not be in communion with a denomination that was affirming of LGBTQ+ persons in any form of connection. Its fate was also unlikely as it required many constitutional amendments and would restructure the work of the denomination though the overhaul of annual conferences and elimination of general agencies. However, the CCP did receive a January push, just prior to General Conference, to remind delegates that it existed and was a "valid" option. Primarily conceived and supported by southern bishops Gary Mueller and Scott Jones, the support for this option presented as the true "one church plan" or the only viable option for unity forward.

The third option, eventually called the Traditionalist Plan, was presented by dissenting members of the CWF as part of the interim report sent to the Council of Bishops in November 2017, but at the time, the COB felt it was prudent to focus on and continue to develop the other two plans. The inclusion of this third plan was an attempt to see if the denomination preferred to maintain, and even strengthen, its non-affirming stance toward LGBTQ+

persons. It was received by the CWF on May 14, 2018. This plan did not receive the same "conciliar process" that the other two plans received by the CWF. The other two plans "received intensive and comprehensive participation from the Commission and the Council of Bishops over an extended period of time."[75] Instead, the Traditionalist Plan was developed between May 4 and May 18, 2018.

Other plans came forward as well, written and proposed by those outside of the CWF. The Simple Plan would eliminate all restrictive language found within the *Book of Discipline* regarding any rights of LGBTQ+ persons. This approach quickly became a favorite among affirming caucus groups as it avoided perceived, unnecessary complexities of the CWF plans while still allowing for freedom. They argued that (as it was currently legislated) the *Book of Discipline* granted Boards of Ordained Ministry within each annual conference the full authority to set their own ministerial standards as well as authorizing clergy to decide who is and is not ready or fit for marriage. Thus, as long as the restrictive language was removed, the tenor of the other plans— allowing for freedom according to context—could still be met.[76]

In April 2017 the COB officially called for a special three-day session of the General Conference to be held February 23–26, 2019, in St. Louis, Missouri (**eS2017e**). The purpose of the sessions was "limited to receiving and acting on a report from the Council of Bishops based on the recommendations of the Commission on a Way Forward," although the Judicial Council would later open up the session to other petitions pertaining to related paragraphs and matters of the above three plans.[77]

The lead-up to the 2019 General Conference furthered the division that surfaced in 1972 with the formation of The United Methodist Church. Caucuses were consulted and given voice within the CWF, but local churches, some of whom were previously unaware of the debates concerning LGBTQ+ persons in many Protestant denominations, became painfully aware of the conflict due to viral media news coverage about the impending conference. Many local churches and clergy feared that they would be asked to vote on

---

75.   "Commission on a Way Forward's Report to the General Conference,"55.

76.   "The Simple Plan," UM-Forward, accessed March 14, 2022, https://um-forward.org /simpleplan.

77.   PNW Conference, "UMC Bishops Call Special Session of General Conference for 2019," April 24, 2017, accessed March 14, 2022, https://www.pnwumc.org/news/umc -bishops-call-special-session-of-general-conference-for-2019/.

whether or not to affirm same-sex weddings or LGBTQ+ clergy. In an effort to avoid potential conflict in congregations where conflict had not previously existed, the One Church Plan was presented as the most conflict-free plan before the denomination. Many in the COB and other caucuses worked tirelessly to garner denominational support for the OCP. But most conservative caucuses, aligned with Good News and the WCA, sought to expand the agenda of the special session to include other proposals outside the plans set forth via the COB and its CWF. Conservatives sought to ensure that if the Traditional Plan did not pass with help from conference delegates in Africa that they would have the option to cancel the trust clause in church property deeds and leave the denomination with church property and pension obligations at a cost lower than prescribed in the *Book of Discipline*. The Constitution of The UMC lays out clearly that the bishops can limit the scope of a special session and then once gathered, the delegation can expand that scope if two-thirds of the delegation decides that the agenda should be expanded.

In fact, it is apparent that as the 2019 special session began in February, a majority of bishops, even a majority of caucus leaders and prominent laypersons, believed that the OCP was almost a done deal, needing only the legislative process and stamp of General Conference. Perhaps polity lessons were neglected from denominational splitting over LGBTQ+ ordination and marriage during the dramatic General Convention of The Episcopal Church in 2007 or the General Assembly of the Presbyterian Church (USA) in 2012.

One of the questions in the lead-up to General Conference was how to logistically present, discuss, and vote on the three different plans before the plenary (the entire *Daily Christian Advocate* from the 2019 Special Session is available as eS2019c). One of the first actions of the 2019 session was to decide the presentation order to plans to consider for a vote, under the presumption that all the plans would be voted upon and perfected by the plenary before a final vote of preference. With a denomination and delegation led by United Methodists nearing or in retirement, top of the list for a plenary vote was a Wespath plan regarding funding of clergy, conference, and general agency pensions, regardless of changes to church discipline and structure.

Next in line was the Traditional Plan (TP), which, to the shock of centrists in the US, received fifty-six more votes of "priority consideration" than the OCP. The breakdown of priority according to United Methodist News Service was:

Legislation recommended by Wespath Benefits and Investments, the denomination's pension agency, topped the final tally with 518 high-priority votes . . .

The Traditional Plan received 459 votes.

The next highest vote getters were two different plans for how exiting congregations could leave with their property, with 412 and 406 votes respectively.

The One Church Plan received 403 high-priority votes.

The Simple Plan, which would eliminate all restrictive Disciplinary language related to homosexuality, received 153 high-priority votes.

The Connectional Conference Plan, which would restructure the church around theological lines, drew 102 votes.[78]

Aging delegates (especially from the US) found it most important to secure pensions should the denomination split. Second most important—with crucial support among the central conferences in Europe, Africa, and the Philippines—was consideration of the Traditional Plan, a plan that most bishops did not support, and which did not experience the same discernment process as the other plans. Then followed two petitions on how to separate the denomination. And, finally, the plan requested by General Conference from the bishops, the One Church Plan. Through lobbying and informational breakfasts hosted by the various conservative caucuses present, to the shock and dismay of many centrists in the US the Traditional Plan passed by a vote of 438 to 384.[79]

The question then became, how do churches leave if they still desire to form a new or different denomination. Other plans, again mostly proposed by and supported by conservative caucus groups, came to the floor and passed, allowing local churches to leave an annual conference after paying two years of apportionments and liability for future clergy pensions. However, in connection with this vote came a claim of improper voting. Substantial proof had been found and brought to the floor of General Conference. This was referred to the Committee on Ethics, who did not have the time to investigate

78. United Methodist News Service, "GC2019 Daily Update: Feb. 24," accessed March 14, 2022, https://www.umnews.org/en/news/gc2019-daily-feb-24.

79. Joe Iovino, "What Happened and What Didn't at General Conference 2019," UMC. org feature, accessed March 14, 2022, https://www.umc.org/en/content/what-happened-and -what-didnt-at-general-conference-2019.

the matter. In August 2019, six months later, the Commission on General Conference confirmed that four persons who were not eligible to vote cast votes using the credentials of delegates not present.[80]

During the special session, it became clear that conservatives had largely won the day. They had succeeded in securing The UMC as a denomination that would exclude LGBTQ+ members and clergy and had made the stance more (re)strict(ive). So progressive delegates from the floor of General Conference began to "troll" the process. Jeffrey Kuan (California–Nevada clergy delegate) asked to amend the Traditional Plan's petition regarding the authority of bishops. Originally, the TP was meant to prevent LGBTQ+ persons from being consecrated as bishops and allow Colleges of Bishops to hold one another accountable across jurisdictions. Kuan (a biblical studies scholar) believed that if identifying as LGBTQ+ was going to be disqualifier, other "violations of scripture" should be as well. He proposed that after the phrase "bishops who are self-avowed homosexual" to add the phrase in the *Discipline* "polygamous, divorced, and/or remarried" throughout. His rationale, tinged with irony and sarcasm, being:

I continue to be frustrated with our confused ethical standards based on the Bible. We continue to single out homosexuality as incompatible with Christian practices. We say nothing about divorce as incompatible not only with biblical teaching and practices, but accept divorce and remarriage as compatible with Christian practices and teaching. As my brother, Mark Holland, has mentioned the passage from the Gospel, [in which] Jesus spoke much against divorce and remarriage. Moreover, polygamy is compatible with the Bible. Persons with whom we hail as heroes, heroes of faith, Abraham, David, Solomon, all had multiple wives! What ethical standards are we using to determine what is compatible and incompatible with biblical teaching and Christian practices? If we want to single out one form of human sexuality, we need to capture all of the others. I have said this before and I will say it again, when are we going to stop our hypocrisy? Thank you.[81]

His amendment for the *Discipline*, of course failed, but it foreshadowed a strategy by progressives and centrists or any who were opposed to the passage

---

80. Heather Hahn, "Improper Voting at GC2019 Voids Key Vote," UM News, Aug. 10, 2019, accessed March 14, 2022, https://www.umnews.org/en/news/improper-voting-at-gc2019-voids-key-vote.

81. *Daily Christian Advocate*, vol. 2, no. 5, The General Conference of The United Methodist Church, 2019), 508.

of the TP. The TP had seven unconstitutional petitions as part of its plan, and those needed to be perfected (and legislation existed ready to perfect them by traditionalist leaders), but progressives and centrists decided to filibuster the floor of the plenary with amendments, points of order, and other clarifications in order to block traditionalists, and ensure that the bulk of the TP could not be enacted, and thus inch the plenary closer and closer to its 6:30 p.m. deadline (when monster trucks were famously entering the St. Louis arena). The chaos that ensued on the floor of General Conference 2019 was atypical but had happened before. It's normative for delegates to use the floor of General Conference to grind out denominational polity, to either pass or delay amendments or petitions. Delegates sometimes take advantage of the microphone to make lengthy speeches that speak more to their personal faith than to the missional purposes of Methodism. However, as happened at General Conferences during prior schisms over Scripture, theology, episcopal authority, and White supremacy, General Conference 2019 proved that the discernment process can be broken by power struggle, becoming ineffective and vulnerable to subversive self-interests, which can and do disrupt God's mission of making disciples and transforming the world.

After the special session ended and the Traditional Plan passed, the basic statements regarding homosexuality in the *Book of Discipline* had not changed; in this way, the special session repeated every General Conference since 1972. The changes that did occur were more strict measures put into place for those who "violate" the *Discipline* by either coming out as homosexual or officiating a same-sex wedding. Another major piece of legislation was passed, a disaffiliation plan, which provided guidelines for congregations who wanted to leave The UMC. As with most petitions that pass General Conference, the changes then went before Judicial Council. If any of these items are ruled unconstitutional, then they would be amended or addressed in some way at the scheduled 2020 General Conference. Judicial Council met in April 2019 to rule on the "constitutionality, meaning, application, and effect" of the TP. In Decision 1378, the Judicial Council examined each petition that made up the TP, instead of considering it as a whole. It ruled (as it had previously in Decision 1366 and 1377 just prior to the Special Session)[82]

---

82. Linda Bloom, "Court to GC2019: Legislation Needs More Work," United Methodist News Service, Feb. 26 2019, accessed March 14 2022, https://www.umnews.org/en/news/court-to-gc2019-legislation-needs-more-work.

that seven of the TP's petitions were unconstitutional and therefore "null and void." The rationale was stated as follows:

> Under the principle of legality, the General Conference can prescribe or proscribe a particular conduct but cannot contradict itself by prescribing prohibited conduct or prohibiting prescribed conduct. It can require bishops, annual conferences, nominees, and members of boards of ordained ministry to certify or declare that they will uphold The Discipline in its entirety and impose sanctions in case of non-compliance. But it may not choose standards related to ordination, marriage, and human sexuality over other provisions of The Discipline for enhanced application and certification. The General Conference has the authority to require that the board of ordained ministry conduct a careful and thorough examination to ascertain if an individual meets all disciplinary requirements and certify that such an examination has occurred. But it cannot reduce the scope of the board examination to one aspect only and unfairly single out one particular group of candidates (self-avowed practicing homosexuals) for disqualification. Marriage and sexuality are but two among numerous standards candidates must meet to be commissioned or ordained; other criteria include, for example, being committed to social justice, racial and gender equality, and personal and financial integrity, that all should be part of a careful and thorough examination.[83]

Though single-issue examination of clergy candidates did not pass constitutional testing, other key aspects of the TP did, including expanding the definition of "self-avowed practicing homosexual" to include persons "living in a same-sex marriage, domestic partnership or civil union, or is a person who publicly states she or he is a practicing homosexual." For decades, persons had managed to publicly identify as LGBTQ+ and still be ordained because the phrase "self-avowed practicing homosexual" had not been clearly defined. Penalties were also put in place that would suspend clergy for one year if they performed a same-sex marriage and would terminate conference membership and clergy credentials upon a second offense.[84] This penalty went into effect on January 1, 2020, in the US and January 1, 2021, outside the US.

---

83. Judicial Council Decision 1366.

84. "What Did the Judicial Council Decide about the Traditional Plan?" UMC.org, accessed March 14, 2022, https://www.umc.org/en/content/ask-the-umc-what-did-the-judicial-council-decide-about-the-traditional-plan.

The controversy is not over for the continuing UMC or for any breakaway denomination. With a then-scheduled General Conference only fifteen months away, many leaders began writing petitions and various other plans to undo the Traditional Plan or to prevent fully implementing it (to fix the unconstitutional aspects). Centrist bishop John Yambasu of Sierra Leone (who died tragically in an auto accident in August 2020) invited five persons from each of the ideological groups alongside two other bishops (Bishop Mande Muyombo and Bishop Christian Alstead) to Chicago for a meeting in the summer of 2019. This meeting was fully led by the central conferences. Representing the "traditionalist" camp was Keith Boyette (WCA), Maxie Dunnam (Confessing Movement), Patricia Miller (Confessing Movement), Rob Renfroe (Good News), and Mark Tooley (IRD/UM Action). Representing the "centrist" caucus were Thomas Berlin (UMNext), Junius Dotson (UMNext), Adam Hamilton (UMNext), Mark Holland (Mainstream UMC), and Jasmine R. Smothers (UMNext). For the progressives, Ginger Gaines-Cirelli (UMNext), Janet Lawrence (RMN), Randall Miller (RMN), Karen Prudente (MIND), and Kimberly Scott (United Methodist Queer Clergy Caucus) were present. Those gathered then identified two persons from each group and two central conference bishops to continue discussions on their behalf. Before they left, an agreement regarding a moratorium on clergy trials and complaints was established.

Those eight persons developed and wrote what was called "the Protocol of Reconciliation and Grace through Separation and Restructuring," or "the Protocol" (**eS2019d,e**). This smaller group was later expanded and included an "outer circle" of advisors and participants. They met with help from a mediator three times for two days each. By February 6, 2020, the legislation that made up the protocol was made public. According to its own website, the protocol "was a mediated agreement for separation in The United Methodist Church that allows those who want to separate and form new denominations to do so, and those who remain to reform The United Methodist Church." It continued the moratorium on trials and complaints for clergy through the next General Conference, then scheduled for May 2020. If passed by the 2020 General Conference, the protocol would:

- require those who wanted to form a new denomination to register intent with the Council of Bishops by May 15, 2021;

- allow central conferences to align with a new Methodist denomination by a 66.6 percent vote (vote to be taken by December 31, 2021);

- allow annual conferences to affiliate with a new Methodist denomination if 57 percent of those voting approve (vote to be taken by July 1, 2021);

- allow local churches to affiliate with a new Methodist denomination with the church council determining the voting threshold (either simple majority or 66.6 percent majority) (vote to be taken by December 31, 2024);

- allow local churches to disaffiliate from the denomination with their property (suspending the trust clause);

- protect clergy and general church pensions regardless of Methodist denominational affiliation;

- provide a new traditionalist denomination with $25 million over the course of the 2021–2024 quadrennium;

- provide $2 million, to be split, to any other denomination formed from the protocol, again to be paid over the 2021–2024 quadrennium; and

- provide $39 million to support communities historically marginalized by the social sin of racism.[85]

There are other main points and small but significant details in the protocol, but the above bulleted items outline the main agreements set forth. The protocol became the rallying cry of most major leaders weary of pending schism, and it became the new way forward, one with a hefty price tag and a puzzling if not vague sourcing for the funds to manage schism.

85. "Protocol of Reconciliation and Grace through Separation FAQ," Jan. 3, 2020, UM News, accessed March 14 2022, https://www.umnews.org/en/news/protocol-of-reconciliation -and-grace-through-separation-faq; "A Proposal to Restructure The United Methodist Church by Separation as the Best Means to Resolve Our Differences," accessed March 14, 2022, https://www.gracethroughseparation.com/.

The protocol was not the only post–2019 General Conference plan to try to "fix" or undo the Traditional Plan. There were also the Indianapolis Plan for Amicable Separation, the Christmas Covenant (**eS2019f**), the Next Generation UMC plan, but the Protocol sustained the most "high-level" support and seemed to be the plan for separation as of February 2020 because it was unanimously endorsed by individuals and caucuses representing Mainstream UMC; Uniting Methodists; UMC Next; Reconciling Ministries Network; Methodist Federation for Social Action; Affirmation, Wesleyan Covenant Association; Institute on Religion and Democracy; Good News; Confessing Movement; and bishops from the US, Africa, Europe, and the Philippines.[86]

But a deadly global pandemic disrupted church life and postponed plans for General Conference 2020 while office workers and congregations around the world shifted to working and worshipping from home.

A VIRTUAL CONNECTION

January 1, 1983, may be considered the "birthday" of digital communication when the use of personal computers from Apple, Tandy, IBM, and Commodore began spreading quickly. By the mid-1990s email, websites, digital publishing, and digital commerce drove rapid proliferation of social changes that would eliminate barriers of distance to communication while remaking and energizing the globalized financial economy. The communication changes transformed and disrupted the publishing and distribution revenues for UMPH as well as communication and training practices among all UMC agencies, colleges, and seminaries.

As broadband cable modems at home or church, and mobile smart phones became ubiquitous and normative for UMC leaders after the first century of the new millennium, virtual and unmoderated or unfiltered communication made its way into everyday (US) lives. For the aging UMC leadership, which was slower to adopt technology in some places, social shifts accelerated during the 2010s. In the late 1990s annual conferences, agencies, UMC publishers, and most congregations began communicating and doing business, including online shopping, through websites. Pastors routinely shared sermons over the internet during the first years of the new millennium.

---

86. Mark R. Holland, "The Protocol Is Only the First Step," Mainstream UMC, Jan. 21, 2020, accessed March 14, 2022, https://mainstreamumc.com/blog/the-protocol-is-only-the-first-step/.

But until the 2010s it would have been uncommon to find livestreaming of worship services and social media accounts for churches. UMPH began in the 1990s routinely surveying its customer segments about *digital* book and Bible resources, worship and Communion practices, music sourcing, textbook adoptions, church supplies, and online church purchasing. Typically through social media, such as the UM Clergy Forum on Facebook, pastors began discussing lurking questions regarding the digitally connected future for UM congregations. A recurring hot topic is whether Holy Communion can be consecrated during streaming worship over the internet. Andy Langford, an executive at GBOD who sponsored and managed the *UM Book of Worship* that published in 1992, became co-pastor of Concord UMC in North Carolina. He launched an online worship service in 2013 that attracted a congregation of young adults, and then brought a position paper regarding online consecration of Communion to the COB, but the COB and many liturgy professors decided against virtual Communion, reasoning that Holy Communion and real divine presence in Wesleyan theology is a means of grace and more than a symbolic or virtual memory.

In 2013 Gregory S. Neal asked, "Is Virtual Church possible? Can Christian community be established via dial-up? Is it possible to offer the Sacrament of Holy Communion over the Internet?" In 2020 and following, some COVID-19, quarantined, masked, virtually worshipping, socially distanced observers among congregations with dramatically reduced attendance might find this sacramental and theological dispute difficult to understand. In a 2013 commentary, Neal argued that virtual, online communion could work, for "there are times and places in which it may be impossible, or at least very difficult, for someone to attend public worship, hear the preached Word, and receive the blessed Sacrament," and thus "offering the Means of Grace over the Internet serves a useful purpose."[87] After the beginning of COVID-19, the question of online Communion became more hotly debated and brought UM liturgy professors, Discipleship Ministries staff, UMPH, and bishops again into a conversation.[88]

87. Gregory S. Neal, "Theological Reflections on the Internet as a Means of Grace," United Methodist Insight, Sept. 30, 2013, https://um-insight.net/perspectives/online-communion-theology/.

88. See practical and theological guidance for what UM leaders can and cannot so in worship, as well as video-streaming resources for worship and education in "Christian Worship and Devotion During Social Distancing: A Resource for United Methodists," Ministry

Though broadband and cell phone technology provide church leaders with ways to interact as a global denomination in real and immediate time, it is not universally available in parts of the world that are not hard-wired down to the last mile. COVID-19 reminded cultures of many inequities in our world, including internet access. The conversation about equity of internet access has largely been one of the Global North vs. Global South, but even in the United States, COVID-19 and at-home schooling revealed that approximately one in four homes does not have reliable internet access.[89] Many rely on cell-phone data for internet access, which brings up other financial barriers and obstacles for those who cannot afford high-speed internet.

And while the internet provides The UMC with new forms of connecting, it also arguably distances people from making connection. The protective layer of a screen can lead many to say, post, or comment negatively ("trolling") in ways and words they would avoid using in person. Jeremy Smith, UM clergy, blogger, critic of UMC agencies and bishops, and founder of the UM Clergy Forum on Facebook, in 2014 wrote "Engaging the Powers in Online Religious Discussion," which depicts some of the ways that the internet has drastically changed many facets of our everyday lives. This particular blog, however, argues that social media shifts how or at least which Christians speak to one another. Smith states, "Christian discourse is changing—and it is changing *dramatically.*"[90] Smith begins by arguing that until about twenty years ago, most religious discussion would only happen "in the academic halls where rhetoric could be evaluated, fallacies pointed out, and people played by the rules of debate." If conversation happened in a congregational setting, it was most likely "cultural niceties" of "face-to-face communities" with "common arenas for discourse." Then social media entered, and conversations began taking place, not in the pew or narthex, face-to-face, but from the comfort of our couches and in the midst of our late-night binge-watching of Netflix. Suddenly, "Doctrines were critiqued online, answers to religious

Matters, https://www.ministrymatters.com/pandemic/165/christian-worship-and-devotion-during-social-distancing-a-resource-for-united-methodists.

89.   Colleen McClain, Emily Vogels, Andrew Perrin, Stella Sechopoulous, and Lee Rainie, "The Internet and the Pandemic," Pew Research Center, Sept. 1, 2021, accessed March 18, 2022, https://www.pewresearch.org/internet/2021/09/01/the-internet-and-the-pandemic/.

90.   Jeremy Smith, "Engaging the Powers of Online Religious Discussion," *Hacking Christianity*, Oct. 16, 2014, accessed March 17, 2022, https://um-insight.net/perspectives/jeremy-smith/engaging-the-powers-online/.

questions were found online, and safe places to question authority were anonymously engaged in—and this is key—by *both* majority and minority voices in the same arenas."[91] Many would agree that "we are in the middle of the most radical shift since Gutenberg's Press moved reading the Bible from the pews to the homes in the people's language."[92]

The internet power of convergence potentially changes how *everything* is done. New evolving and unrigid rules, new nonhierarchical roles, and new vocabulary (from LOL and FOMO to emojis) create alternatives for how we interact and worship together. Taurai Emmanuel Maforo, communicator and webmaster for the Zimbabwe Episcopal Area, based his doctoral research on "Rethink Church! An analysis of the impact of social media and virtual communities on the physical church" and found that "the church of God now thrives on the internet-based platforms." His research focused on a UM-COM advertising campaign, beginning in 2012, to #RethinkChurch, which included the rhetorical and missional question, "What if church wasn't just a place to go, but something we do?"[93] Maforo believes that this campaign has taken on a new flavor with COVID-19. Rethinking church during a pandemic triggered the urgent shift to hybrid streaming and in-person worship, which "opened the gates for realizing the biblical mandate 'Go into all the world' creating what I now call the 'Generation 28:19'—a generation that is not limited to geographical boundaries."[94]

As a worldwide denomination, however, and given known communication inequities even with the US, how do we use the digital space to create new connections that "all" have access to? David Scott, Mission Theologian at GBGM, observes how the internet affects the global UMC:

> "Facebook is king—especially in Africa": many European conferences might have a Twitter page, but most often, in Africa, episcopal areas' main form of communication and presence is via Facebook.

---

91.   Smith, "Engaging the Powers of Online Religious Discussion."

92.   Smith, "Engaging the Powers of Online Religious Discussion."

93.   "Rethink Church," Facebook, accessed March 18, 2022, https://www.facebook.com/umcrethinkchurch/.

94.   Taurai Emmanual Maforo, "Virtual Church Is the New Ministry Paradigm," UM Insight, Sept. 27, 2021, accessed March 18, 2022, https://um-insight.net/perspectives/virtual-church-is-the-new-ministry-paradigm/.

"Different communications channels carry different types of news": Most annual conferences outside the US utilize either websites, Facebook, or Twitter, or all of these, to communicate in different ways. The information found on Facebook might be different from that found on the website.

"Size does not determine theological sophistication": The flashiness of the website or social media account is not accountable to size but to membership makeup. In order words, does that annual conference have a tech wizard who can support multiple forms of digital communication?

"There is difference between and within regions": Non-US regions cannot be universalized. Some parts of Africa may have barren Facebook pages, while others don't. The same goes for Europe and the Philippines. It is most likely a regional preference for communication.

"Some places in Africa have no official web presence": reiterating the above, not all places have equitable access to internet, and even if they do, they might not have the preference to communicate via the internet.

"Personal networks still matter": The above annual conferences may not maintain an official annual conference website or Facebook page, but a lot of communication happens via individual, personal websites, emails, or social media accounts. Important issues are still discussed online, but through these personal accounts and not necessarily institutionally affiliated accounts.[95]

While forms of church communication moved online since the early years of the new millennium, few were ready for the urgent shift to livestreaming worship that occurred during the lockdown waves of COVID-19. Within a week of a declared global health pandemic, UM bloggers, worship consultants, large-church media ministries, annual conference teams, and church agencies (such as UMCOM or UMPH sites, MinistryMatters.com[96] and AmplifyMedia.com) pushed web content and streaming video webinars that offered guidance to church staff on how to produce streaming worship—

---

95.   David W. Scott, "What I've Learned about the Global UMC Internet Presence," United Methodist Insight, May 12, 2020, accessed March 17, 2022, https://um-insight.net/in-the-church/umc-global-nature/what-i-ve-learned-about-the-global-umc-internet-presence/.

96.   See the worship resources and guidance offered through https://www.ministry matters.com/pandemic.

from home desktop equipment. The number of sources and saturation of advice for this instant pandemic guidance is also an indicator of how expertise and coaching for ministry skills was disintermediated and has shifted over thirty years—well beyond the influence of denominational publishers and church agencies.

TOGETHER/APART: COVID-19

As of January 2020, a novel and deadly coronavirus began to make headlines across the world, and between the end of February and mid-March the world came to a standstill as government leaders acknowledged the impact of COVID-19. On March 11, 2020, the World Health Organization officially declared COVID-19 a global pandemic. Soon after, businesses, congregations, schools, universities, and all non-essential aspects of society began to socially distance and quarantine. Some government leaders were in denial about the virus's seriousness and predicted a shutdown lasting only for two weeks.

Within a week, the Executive Committee of the General Commission on the General Conference (GCGC) had been informed by the Minneapolis Convention Center that events for fifty or more persons, which meant the scheduled 2020 General Conference, were restricted, and thus the 2020 General Conference was postponed.[97] The new date for the postponed 2020 General Conference was August 29 through September 7, 2021. However, as of February 2021, the world was still not yet ready to have a global gathering because "the number of COVID cases continues to rise . . . vaccine is not expected to be widely available . . . new variants . . . and [difficulties of testing for] international travelers."[98] The Technology Study Team of the GCGC "analyzed a variety of options, including an entirely electronic General Conference with participation from individual locations; an entirely electronic General Conference with delegates gathering at regional satellite hubs; and two sessions, with the first part streaming online and the second part in-person when it is safe to convene" but "none of these options were

---

97. "UMC General Conference 2020 Postponed," Council of Bishops, March 18, 2020, accessed March 14, 2022, https://www.unitedmethodistbishops.org/newsdetail/umc-general-conference-2020-postponed-13533796.

98. "General Conference Postponed to 2022," Commission on the General Conference, Resource UMC, February 25, 2021, accessed March 14, 2022, https://www.resourceumc.org/en/content/General-Conference-Postponed-to-2022.

determined . . . to be viable."[99] Paper ballots were considered instead of an electronic-base, but even with paper ballots only, there was concern for a "lack of infrastructure in some areas . . . complexity of the legislative committee process . . . security of voting" and other major concerns that made paper ballots not a viable option. Thus the 2020 General Conference was, again, postponed until August 29 through September 6, 2022 (**eS2020a**) (**eS2021a**). In response to the further postponement of General Conference and knowing that certain actions of the denomination could not take place without "setting the bar" of General Conference (for example, Jurisdictional Conferences and Central Conferences could not easily meet to retire bishops or consecrate new bishops), the COB called a (one-day only) Special Session of the General Conference to meet online on May 8, 2021. Its purpose was limited to "gaining a quorum in order to suspend the rules for the sole purpose of allowing the use of paper ballots to act upon 12 pieces of legislation that would enable the church to effectively continue its work until the postponed 2020 General Conference is held in 2022."[100] The twelve pieces of legislation would largely allow for the General Conference to gather electronically (or in some other creative form) in the midst of a global pandemic, allow for the retirement of bishops, and continue an established budget from the prior General Conference in case of postponement. It would also allow the annual conference to act on certain issues, including the election of an annual conference treasurer and board of ordained ministry.[101] Bishop Cynthia Fierro Harvey, president of the COB, remarked, "Our current *Book of Discipline* was never written with a worldwide pandemic in mind. When we became aware of the need for a further postponement, we knew that some action needed to be taken in order to free the church to operate and continue to fulfill its current mission until we could gather in person."[102] In the spirit of equity, it was understood that following this called Special Session of the General Conference, special sessions of the

---

99. "General Conference Postponed to 2022."

100. "Bishops Call Special Session of General Conference, Issue Timeline Forward," Bishop News, Feb. 24, 2021, accessed March 14, 2022, https://www.unitedmethodistbishops .org/newsdetail/15074669.

101. Council of Bishops, "12 Items to Be Decided by the 2021 Special Session," news release, accessed March 14, 2022, https://www.unitedmethodistbishops.org/files/websites /www/pdfs/12+legislations+to+be+decided+by+the+2021+special+session+of+genera l+conference.pdf.

102. "Bishops Call Special Session of General Conference, Issue Timeline Forward."

Jurisdictional Conferences could also be called in July 2021, also expected to be held virtually, and mostly for the purpose of allowing bishops to retire, announcing new episcopal areas, and determining the number of bishops needed in a jurisdiction. However, under much criticism and, contrary to Bishop Harvey's statement, backlash emerged largely because the Special Session called by the COB dealt with bishops' retirement, bishops' episcopal assignments, and the budget. By not prioritizing, during a special session, matters of local congregational ministry, pandemic relief, and clergy care, the spectral fears of the ancestral Republican Methodists, Methodist Protestants, Wesleyan Methodists, Free Methodists, and all those partisans who fear episcopal overreach were triggered, as they were in 2012 and 2016. The bishops admitted publicly that, even during a global pandemic, their public agenda reflected a primarily fiscal concern: establishing a temporary budget that safeguarded the retirement of bishops while ignoring the mission and ministry of the annual conferences and local churches. Other partisans lamented that the Protocol would not be considered during the Special Session. Even more raised concerns that, consistent with accessibility concerns that prohibited a full electronic session of General Conference, lack of access to reliable internet services disproportionately diminished delegate participation from non-US areas or rural areas of the US. Jerry P. Kulah, coordinator for African Initiative, stated, "This is absolutely true for us here in Africa. How can we have this Special Called Session without delegates from Africa being disenfranchised?"[103] By March 22, 2021, due to criticism about the equity of a one-day, virtual, limited-agenda General Conference, the Council of Bishops canceled the scheduled Special Session that was to be held on May 8, 2021.[104]

COVID-19 abruptly changed how United Methodists worshipped. Local churches that had access to technology and media staff who knew how to take the most advantage of technology, quickly moved Sunday morning worship services online. Facebook Live or YouTube became ways to "go to church." UMPH, Discipleship Ministries, GBHEM, and UMCOM began

103. Heather Hahn, "Bishops Cancel May 8 General Conference," UM News, March 22, 2021, accessed March 14, 2022, https://www.umnews.org/en/news/bishops-cancel-may-8-general-conference.

104. "United Methodist Bishops Reconsider May 8 Special Session of General Conference," Bishop News, March 22, 2021, accessed March 14, 2022, https://www.unitedmethodistbishops.org/newsdetail/bishops-cancel-may-8-special-session-of-general-conference-15174326.

to provide guidelines and tips for how to navigate streaming worship, how to keep congregations engaged when they cannot safely enter a church, and how to assist in public health initiatives, including social distancing, mask wearing, and vaccine equity.[105]

This shift to digital comes with challenges about discipleship in a shared Christian life as participants experience the means of grace together. How do we participate and measure "engagement" by *observers* in streaming worship? Can the local and physical body of Christ experience the *real presence* of Jesus if consecration of the bread and the cup is dispersed over wires and Wi-Fi? After tongue-in-cheek memes of babies being baptized using water pistols were shared on social media, ordained clergy and liturgists pondered (for a moment) whether "baptism" is valid (real) without the water and touch of the ordained pastor's hands (**eS2021b**). "Christian conferencing" in Wesleyan practice and jargon pertains precisely to weekly physical assembly (sabbath) as a means of grace. Can Methodists *sustain* a *community* that may never step in the same physical space together?

The switch to a hybrid streaming and physical church life was expected to be short-lived when it began, and thus some small congregations simply closed down for the time being. However, as COVID-19 numbers continued to rise and wave after wave continued to sweep across the globe, it became clearer that streaming worship would be sustained for some in the future. Congregational and annual conference planning meetings and adult Christian education, however, were not constrained by core liturgical and Wesleyan theological perspectives. Churches quickly found ways to do Christian education online, with streaming small group studies, youth engagement, and outdoor gatherings for children.

One of the controversies was whether Holy Communion could and should be celebrated virtually. Can a clergyperson consecrate bread and juice on camera while observers at home ate the bread and drank from prepackaged communion cups or by using whatever bread and juice at hand? The Council of Bishops was split on the legitimacy of this as orthodox. Theologians and scholars were split. Ordained clergy and local pastors were split. Five bishops in the Western Jurisdiction issued a letter just prior to Holy Week 2020 saying that online Communion (or other creative expressions of this means

---

105. "Helping Your Church Respond to the Coronavirus," Resource UMC, accessed March 14, 2022, https://www.resourceumc.org/en/topics/helping-your-church-respond-to -the-coronavirus.

of grace) would be permitted as long as restrictions preventing in-person worship were in place: "We stand with our clergy who through reflection and prayer have come to the place of believing that their congregation would be strengthened in this hour through the sharing of Holy Communion. We trust the wisdom and the faithfulness of our Clergy to discern such pastoral matters in their own context" (**eS2021c**).[106] After deliberation and Christian conferencing among the COB, a majority of the US began to permit some form of online Communion, with Bishop Park of Susquehanna citing the fact that John Wesley also "offered the means of grace outside the normal practice of the Church of England in his time."[107] However, not all agreed. Ryan Danker, then an associate professor of church history and Methodist studies at Wesley Theological Seminary, argued that online Communion was "sacramentally impossible" for United Methodists who "believe that the real presence of Christ is available by means of bread and wine within the gathered community, administered by ordained or licensed clergy."[108]

Many churches were prevented from hosting indoor (and some even outdoor) gatherings due to state restrictions. This forced many congregations outside or online. Yet new avenues of worship were begun as well. The ability to worship online and the mass move to live streaming services meant that anyone could worship anywhere and at any time. In a way, it had analogy to the connectional nature of The UMC if persons in Portland, Oregon, could log on and worship virtually alongside those in Washington D.C. Central Conference members could log on to one another's worship services, experience one another's traditions, and worship in one another's languages. Sunday morning suddenly became a matrix space where, if the technology was available to you, you could feasibly join in to any United Methodist congregation around the world.

---

106. "Western Jurisdiction Bishops Offer Guidance for the Observance of Holy Communion," Greater NW Communications, March 24, 2020, accessed March 14, 2022, https://greaternw.org/western-jurisdiction-bishops-offer-guidance-for-the-observance-of-holy-communion/.

107. Sam Hodges, "Both Green Light, Red Light for Online Communion," UM News, April 30, 2020, accessed March 14, 2022, https://www.umnews.org/en/news/both-green-light-red-light-for-online-communion-2.

108. "Bishops Call Special Session of General Conference, Issue Timeline Forward," Council of Bishops, Feb. 25, 2021, https://www.umc.org/en/content/bishops-call-special-session-of-general-conference-create-timeline-for-moving-forward.

As the doors to churches slowly began to open, mask mandates began to divide congregations that were trying to find a new sense of "normal." Across the globe, mask mandates went into effect as the world slowly opened back up. However, not everyone believed in the effectiveness of masks or the science of the Centers for Disease Control (CDC) that proved their effectiveness. These debates played out across national news media, social media, families, schools, and into the local church. New variants, vaccine inequity, and vaccine hesitancy prevented the new normal from being realized. As churches began to open back up, most continued streaming worship.

After two years of worshipping from home, most clergy (80 percent serve churches with fewer than fifty worshippers) find it unsustainable in their ministry context, while other leaders argue that streaming worship viewed on home screens is here to stay. Some members appreciate that they can worship from their couch, in their pajamas! (As a mother of two small children, it has made Sunday morning feel like much more of a Sabbath!) UMNews interviewed select clergy from across the worldwide connection who agreed that a hybrid streaming and in-person worship experience is the new norm. Streaming worship offers persons who moved away from a beloved congregation to reconnect from home online. It offers students at college an option to join their parents and their original church family in worship. Forest Chapel UMC in Cincinnati, Ohio, gained 750 new members on May 30, 2021—mostly from India, but also from Bhutan, Nepal, and Indonesia.[109] Methodist leaders are discovering an alternative meaning for *circuit* riding in a global parish.

On March 3, 2022, due to another wave of a new COVID-19 variant, limited COVID vaccination in UMC central conferences in Africa and Asia, global travel quarantines, and passport approval delays (due to government remote work), the GCGC announced the further postponement of the 2020 General Conference until 2024 (**eS2022g**). Why not state that the 2020 conference is canceled and move ahead to the already scheduled 2024 General Conference? However, this quandary is based in The UMC Constitution (Section II, Article II) that stipulates General Conference "shall meet once in four years." Thus General Conference cannot be canceled, only postponed. This also has implications for elected delegations—those delegations selected for 2020 apparently have a right to be seated at the General Conference for

---

109. Heather Hahn and the Rev. Gustavo Vasquez, "Social Media Takes Disciple-Making Global," UMNews, July 1, 2021, accessed March 18, 2022, https://um-insight.net/in-the-church/local-church/social-media-takes-disciple-making-global/.

which they were elected—even if that General Conference is postponed four years.

The continued postponement brought up numerous questions, inconsistencies, and problems with United Methodist polity. In an ever-changing world that is both getting more flat and more and more inequitable, how do we feasibly continue to meet in person every four years? Is every four years enough? Is it too often? Are delegations too large? Do we need General Conference to meet to tip the first domino that would allow for the mission and ministry of the church to continue (or not, in schism)? What is the purpose of General Conference and general (US church) agencies in a world that prioritizes regional context, local content, and adaptable ministry?

Immediately after the March 2022 postponement, which triggered protest from conservatives and a few progressives counting on the Protocol for Reconciliation to lower the cost of their exit, the Wesleyan Covenant Association announced that their new denomination, the Global Methodist Church (GMC), would formally launch on May 1, 2022 (eS2022c,d).[110]

The GMC is not waiting on the clock for General Conference 2024 approval of a settlement negotiated by a self-designated set of protagonists. Keith Boyette of the WCA said,

> Many United Methodists have grown impatient with a denomination clearly struggling to function effectively at the general church level. Theologically conservative local churches and annual conferences want to be free of divisive and destructive debates, and to have the freedom to move forward together. We are confident many existing congregations will join the new Global Methodist Church in waves over the next few years, and new church plants will sprout up as faithful members exit the UM Church and coalesce into new congregations.[111]

Since 2014 the WCA has been organizing and actively recruiting churches and entire annual conferences (such as Texas, North Texas, and South Georgia) to exit The UMC (see Judicial Council Decisions 1444, 1445. Available as **eS2024b, eS2024d,e**). So splintering began gathering momentum when some megachurches, such as Asbury UMC in Tulsa, Oklahoma, and Frazer

---

110. https://globalmethodist.org.

111. "Global Methodist Church Sets Official Launch Date," Global Methodist Church, March 3, 2022, accessed March 14, 2022, https://globalmethodist.org/global-methodist-church-sets-official-launch-date/.

Memorial UMC in Montgomery, Alabama, voted in the first quarter of 2022 to exit, pay off their financial liabilities, and jump into independence or to other branches on the Methodist tree, such as the Free Methodist Church or the Wesleyan Church. Some of these exits used the newly inserted paragraph 2553 of the 2019 General Conference, which drastically reduced the cost to disaffiliate. However, others sought to misuse long-standing paragraphs in the *Book of Discipline* to try to circumvent the trust clause and effectively untie the connectional system of (United) Methodism. Paragraph 2548.2 of the 2016 *Book of Discipline* became quite the point of contentious conversation, multiple blog posts, podcasts, and even a request for a Declaratory Decision from the Council of Bishops to the Judicial Council (**eS2024f,g**).[112] Furthermore, the official launching of the Global Methodist Church on May 1, 2022, triggered a response from many of the original supporters of the Protocol who began to circulate a petition that read,

> Out of a spirit of transparency, trust, and accountability, members of the mediation team have reached out to the organizations that initially supported the Protocol Agreement, General Conference delegates, and others within our broad constituencies. The overwhelming consensus among those with whom we spoke is that the once-promising Protocol Agreement no longer offers a viable path forward, particularly given the long delays, the changing circumstances within the United Methodist Church, and the formal launch of the Global Methodist Church in May of this year. (**eS2024a**)[113]

Proclaiming themselves a new denomination (despite not holding a founding General Conference) and attempting to circumvent the trust clause through the implementation of paragraph 2548.2, the Global Methodist Church (GMC) and its partners advanced targeted disinformation campaigns throughout the summer of 2022. Despite their best efforts to, in late August 2022, Judicial Council rendered Decision 1449 which ruled that paragraph 2548.2 could not be used for disaffiliation and, significantly, confirmed that the authority to determine what ecclesial bodies qualify as "another

112. "Bishops Seek Ruling on Application and Meaning of Paragraph 2548.2," Bishop News, May 12, 2022, https://www.unitedmethodistbishops.org/newsdetail/bishops-seek-ruling-on-application-and-meaning-on-paragraph-2548-2-16497213.

113. "A Statement About the Protocol of Reconciliation and Grace Through Separation," Protocolresponse.com.

evangelical denomination" rested in the hands of the Council of Bishops, subject to General Conference approval and ratification (**eS2024h**). These issues having been clarified, by early September, several Bishops began to stridently call out, correct, and condemn the ongoing disinformation efforts of the Wesleyan Covenant Association, Good News Movement, and the Institute for Religion and Democracy. Bishop Tom Bickerton, President of the Council of Bishops, publicly denounced such efforts in his presidential address to the Council of Bishops in August, and president elect Bishop Tracey Malone directly named the Wesleyan Covenant Association for sewing discord, division, and spreading disinformation. In an unexpected blow to the GMC's "global" aspirations, on September 8th, 2022, the Africa College of Bishops published a letter denouncing the Africa Initiative and the Wesleyan Covenant Association for "wrongly influencing God's people in our areas." Declaring, in line with Judicial Council Decision No. 1449, that the GMC was not a legitimately recognized denomination, the thirteen signatories affirmed:

> Therefore, we, the Bishops of The United Methodist Church in Africa, declare the following:
>
> • We will dissociate from any activities of the Africa Initiative and will not allow any activities of the Africa Initiative in our areas.
>
> • We will not allow or entertain any activities of the Wesleyan Covenant Association who are wrongly influencing God's people in our areas.
>
> • We will not tolerate anyone giving false information about The United Methodist Church in our areas.
>
> • We will continue to be shepherds of all of God's people throughout our beloved continent. (**eS2024i**)

The launching of the GMC cemented a fracture that had been forming since 1972—the future is set in stone and new forms of Methodism are emerging.

CLIFFHANGER

Thousands of pages or gigabytes will be devoted to the connectional changes, internet convergences, and public health disruptions for Methodism in America during the first twenty-two years of the third millennium in the Christian era. It seems that the fifty-year-old United Methodist expression of Christian life and ministry was pushed to the breaking point by aging leaders at the 2019 General Conference. The center did not hold for the denomination's half-century debate and disagreement about divine grace, human love, human sexuality, and scriptural interpretation. The unwieldy United Methodist General Conference of nearly nine hundred delegates once again did not trust episcopal leadership to negotiate and resolve a difference of scriptural interpretation and theological opinion. The trauma in 2019 for several thousand UM leaders spawned intense fury as new forms of grace were churning, looking for ways to organize new forms of Methodism. But God's creation disrupted plans and ecclesial power when a virus pushed The UMC back from internal divisions and a focus on human connections, while mission teams found new and urgent ways of collaboration to relieve human suffering and plead with the Creator.

Thus new forms of Methodism are set to begin, and new schisms will be added to the Methodist historic timeline. This schism will *not* solve the divisions from neo-Calvinist and holiness flavors of Wesleyan thought within The UMC, because some in Good News, the Confessing Movement, and the Wesleyan Covenant Association plan to stay with The UMC and continue to fight for a more "orthodox" understanding of Scripture.[114] Some co-dependent clergy eyeing the exit would prefer to remain as delegates to the next General Conference, admittedly to prevent The UMC from "lurching" further to the left on cultural and social issues.[115]

But the spawning denomination provides some space for non-affirming congregations, clergy, and bishops to go and rewrite Methodist polity. Questions (and legal challenges) remain unresolved regarding church property, the trust clause, certain paragraphs in the *Book of Discipline* (2548.2), and how the General Conference might rethink and (without doubt) lower the expense for our entire connectional structure.

John Wesley took the gospel outside the four walls of the church. He took the Word of God to the people where they were—in the coal mine, the street, the hospital, the prison, and the orphanage. He broke the Anglican

---

114. "Global Methodist Church Sets Official Launch Date."

115. See the prolific and influential commentary of conservative UM pastor Chris Ritter, member of the Illinois–Great Rivers Conference at https://peopleneedjesus.net. Specific quote from "On Postludes and Preludes: A Collaborative Approach to General Conference 2024" *People Need Jesus* (June 22, 2022)

rules of worship, preaching, and ordination to heed the call of the Spirit who desires to dwell among all.

New forms of Methodist grace are blooming. They're prompting questions about how the Spirit can travel through circuit boards, the keys of a keyboard, the pixels of a webpage, and the waves of broadband. While there are many ways that The UMC has changed over the first fifty years, future forms of grace are still in the works. Some bishops stated that the "continuing UMC" will be "a church" that is

> confident in what God has done in Christ Jesus for all humankind;
>
> committed to personal and social salvation/transformation; and
>
> courageous in dismantling the powers of racism, tribalism, and colonialism. (eS2022b)[116]

Their proposed vision is directly aligned with Wesleyan roots. If Methodism in the Americas, Asia, Africa, and Europe can authentically live into this mission with integrity, then Methodism hasn't gone over the cliff, yet. If Methodists continue repeating the habitual sins of their past and not living up to expectations, theological proclamations, and God's mission to transform the world, then have we failed Methodism or has Methodism failed us?

116. "Bishops Agree on Narrative for the Continuing United Methodist Church," Bishop News, Nov. 8, 2021, accessed March 14, 2022, https://www.unitedmethodistbishops.org/newsdetail/bishops-agree-on-narrative-for-continuing-umc-15749733.

ABBREVIATIONS

DENOMINATION-RELATED AGENCIES AND GROUPS

AALM   Asian American Language Ministry

BOM   Board of Missions

BMCR   Black Methodists for Church Renewal

COB   Council of Bishops

COCU   Consultation on Church Union

COSMOS   Commission on the Structure of Methodism Overseas

COSROW   General Commission on the Status and Role of Women

CSR/LCA   Christian Social Relations and Local Church Activities

ECUMW   Evangelical Coalition for United Methodist Women

EMLC   Ethnic Minority Local Church

GBCS   General Board of Church and Society

GBGM   General Board of Global Ministries

GBOD   General Board of Discipleship, now Discipleship Ministries

GBHEM	General Board of Higher Education and Ministry
GBPHB	General Board of Pensions and Health Benefits, now Wespath
GCAH	General Commission on Archives and History
GCCUIC	General Commission on Christian Unity and Interreligious Concerns
GCFA	General Council on Finance and Administration
GCOM	General Council on Ministries
GCORR	General Commission on Religion and Race
GCOSROW	General Commission on the Status and Role of Women
KAM	Korean American Missions
KMC	Korean Methodist Church
LPCU	Ladies' and Pastors' Christian Union
MARCHA	Methodists Associated Representing the Cause of Hispanic Americans
MCOR	Methodist Committee for Overseas Relief
MFSA	Methodist Federation for Social Action
MFSS	Methodist Federation for Social Service
MoSAIC	Methodist Students for an All-Inclusive Church
MSF	Methodist Sacramental Fellowship
MSM	Methodist Student Movement
MYF	Methodist Youth Fellowship
NAKAUMC	National Association of Korean American United Methodist Churches
NFAAUM	National Federation of Asian American United Methodists

OIMC	Oklahoma Indian Missionary Conference
RCP	Reconciling Congregation Program
SSU	Sunday School Union (MEC)
SVM	Student Volunteer Movement
TCP	Transforming Congregation Program
UMCOR	United Methodist Committee on Relief
UMCYM	United Methodist Council on Youth Ministries
UMPH	United Methodist Publishing House
UMW	United Methodist Women, now United Women in Faith
WFMS	Woman's Foreign Missionary Society
WHMS	Woman's Home Missionary Society
WMC	World Methodist Council
WMUSS	Wesleyan Methodist Union for Social Service
WSCS	Woman's Society of Christian Service (Central Jurisdiction)
WSG	Wesleyan Service Guild

OTHER AGENCIES AND GROUPS

ASWPL	Association of Southern Women for the Prevention of Lynching
CIC	Commission on Interracial Cooperation
CORE	Congress of Racial Equality
CORNET	Covenant Relationship Network
FCC	Federal Council of Churches
HUAC	House Un-American Activities Committee

IAWP	International Association of Women Preachers
IRD	Institute on Religion and Democracy
LAMAG	Latin American Action Group
NAIC	Native American International Caucus
NCC	National Council of Churches
NCKAM	National Committee on Korean-American Ministries
OSL	Order of Saint Luke
RCAR	Religious Coalition for Abortion Rights
RCP	Reconciling Church Program
RCRC	Religious Coalition for Reproductive Choice
RMN	Reconciling Ministry Network
SCLC	Southern Christian Leadership Conference
USSC	United States Sanitary Commission
WCC	World Council of Churches
WCRA	Woman's Central Relief Association
WCTU	Woman's Christian Temperance Union
YMCA	Young Men's Christian Association
YWCA	Young Women's Christian Association

An index is available online at umhistoryhub.teachable.com.

CPSIA information can be obtained
at www.ICGtesting.com
Printed in the USA
LVHW091339231122
733742LV00005B/6